RSMeans Residential Repair & Remodeling Costs

2011 CONTRACTOR'S PRICING GUIDE

Senior Editor
Bob Mewis, CCC

Contributing Editors
Christopher Babbitt
Ted Baker
Barbara Balboni
John H. Chiang, PE
Gary W. Christensen
David G. Drain, PE
Cheryl Elsmore
Robert J. Kuchta
Robert C. McNichols
Melville J. Mossman, PE
Jeannene D. Murphy
Stephen C. Plotner
Eugene R. Spencer
Phillip R. Waier, PE

Cover Design
Paul Robertson
Wayne Engebretson

President & CEO
Iain Melville

**Vice President,
Product & Development**
Richard Remington

**Vice President of
Finance & Operations**
David C. Walsh

**Vice President, Data
Aquisition & Fulfillment**
Jane Rafeedie

Chief Customer Officer
Lisa Fiondella

Director, RSMeans
Daimon Bridge

**Vice President, Marketing
& Business**
Steven Ritchie

Engineering Manager
Bob Mewis, CCC

Product Manager
Andrea Sillah

Production Manager
Michael Kokernak

Production Coordinator
Jill Goodman

Production
Paula Reale-Camelio
Sheryl A. Rose
Jonathan Forgit
Debbie Panarelli
Mary Lou Geary
Caroline Sullivan

Technical Support
Chris Anderson
Tom Dion
Gary L. Hoitt
Genevieve Medeiros
Kathryn S. Rodriguez
Sharon Proulx

PRINTED WITH SOY INK

RSMeans
Residential
Repair &
Remodeling Costs

2011
CONTRACTOR'S PRICING GUIDE

Quick costs to help you estimate

Easy-to-use format . . . organized the way you build

Hundreds of work items with material, labor, and equipment

Built for the small residential contractor/insurance repair specialist

$39.95 per copy (in United States)
Price subject to change without prior notice.

RS**Means**

Copyright © 2010
A division of Reed Construction Data
Construction Publishers & Consultants
700 Longwater Drive
Norwell, MA 02061
www.reedconstructiondata/rsmeans.com

Printed in the United States of America

ISSN 1074-0481

ISBN 978-1-936335-21-3

This book is printed on recycled paper, using soy-based printing ink. This book is recyclable.

Foreword

Our Mission

Since 1942, RSMeans has been actively engaged in construction cost publishing and consulting throughout North America.

Today, more than 65 years after RSMeans began, our primary objective remains the same: to provide you, the construction and facilities professional, with the most current and comprehensive construction cost data possible.

Whether you are a contractor, owner, architect, engineer, facilities manager, or anyone else who needs a reliable construction cost estimate, you'll find this publication to be a highly useful and necessary tool.

With the constant flow of new construction methods and materials today, it's difficult to find the time to look at and evaluate all the different construction cost possibilities. In addition, because labor and material costs keep changing, last year's cost information is not a reliable basis for today's estimate or budget.

That's why so many construction professionals turn to RSMeans. We keep track of the costs for you, along with a wide range of other key information, from city cost indexes . . . to productivity rates . . . to crew composition . . . to contractors' overhead and profit rates.

RSMeans performs these functions by collecting data from all facets of the industry and organizing it in a format that is instantly accessible to you. From the preliminary budget to the detailed unit price estimate, you'll find the data in this book useful for all phases of construction cost determination.

The Staff, the Organization, and Our Services

When you purchase one of RSMeans' publications, you are, in effect, hiring the services of a full-time staff of construction and engineering professionals.

Our thoroughly experienced and highly qualified staff works daily at collecting, analyzing, and disseminating comprehensive cost information for your needs. These staff members have years of practical construction

experience and engineering training prior to joining the firm. As a result, you can count on them not only for accurate cost figures, but also for additional background reference information that will help you create a realistic estimate.

The RSMeans organization is always prepared to help you solve construction problems through its variety of data solutions, including online, CD, and print book formats, as well as cost estimating expertise available via our business solutions, training, and seminars.

Besides a full array of construction cost estimating books, RSMeans also publishes a number of other reference works for the construction industry. Subjects include construction estimating and project and business management, special topics such as green building and job order contracting, and a library of facility management references.

In addition, you can access all of our construction cost data electronically using *Means CostWorks*® CD or on the Web using **MeansCostWorks.com**.

What's more, you can increase your knowledge and improve your construction estimating and management performance with an RSMeans construction seminar or in-house training program. These two-day seminar programs offer unparalleled opportunities for everyone in your organization to become updated on a wide variety of construction-related issues.

RSMeans is also a worldwide provider of construction cost management and analysis services for commercial and government owners.

In short, RSMeans can provide you with the tools and expertise for constructing accurate and dependable construction estimates and budgets in a variety of ways.

Robert Snow Means Established a Tradition of Quality That Continues Today

Robert Snow Means spent years building RSMeans, making certain he always delivered a quality product.

Today, at RSMeans, we do more than talk about the quality of our data and the usefulness of our books. We stand behind all of our data, from historical cost indexes to construction materials and techniques to current costs.

If you have any questions about our products or services, please call us toll-free at 1-800-334-3509. Our customer service representatives will be happy to assist you. You can also visit our Web site at **www.rsmeans.com**.

Table of Contents

How the Book is Built: An Overview

A Powerful Construction Tool

You have in your hands one of the most powerful construction tools available today. A successful project is built on the foundation of an accurate and dependable estimate. This book will enable you to construct just such an estimate.

For the casual user the book is designed to be:

- quickly and easily understood so you can get right to your estimate.
- filled with valuable information so you can understand the necessary factors that go into the cost estimate.

For the regular user, the book is designed to be:

- a handy desk reference that can be quickly referred to for key costs.
- a comprehensive, fully reliable source of current construction costs, so you'll be prepared to estimate any project.
- a source book for project cost, product selections, and alternate materials and methods.

To meet all of these requirements we have organized the book into the following clearly defined sections.

Unit Price Section

The cost data has been divided into 23 sections representing the order of construction. Within each section is a listing of components and variations to those components applicable to that section. Costs are shown for the various actions that must be done to that component.

Reference Section

This section includes information on Location Factors and a listing of Abbreviations.

Location Factors: You can adjust total project costs to over 900 locations throughout the U.S. and Canada by using the data in this section.

Abbreviations: A listing of the abbreviations used throughout this book, along with the terms they represent, is included.

Index

A comprehensive listing of all terms and subjects in this book will help you quickly find what you need when you are not sure where it falls in the order of construction.

The Scope of This Book

This book is designed to be as comprehensive and as easy to use as possible. To that end we have made certain assumptions and limited its scope in two key ways:

1. We have established material prices based on a national average.
2. We have computed labor costs based on a seven major-region average of open shop wage rates.

Project Size

This book is intended for use by those involved primarily in residential repair and remodeling construction costing between $10,000–$100,000.

With reasonable exercise of judgment, the figures can be used for any building work. For other types of projects, such as new home construction or commercial buildings, consult the appropriate RSMeans publication for more information.

How to Use the Book: The Details

What's Behind the Numbers? The Development of Cost Data

The staff at RSMeans continuously monitors developments in the construction industry in order to ensure reliable, thorough, and up-to-date cost information.

While *overall* construction costs may vary relative to general economic conditions, price fluctuations within the industry are dependent upon many factors. Individual price variations may, in fact, be opposite to overall economic trends. Therefore, costs are continually monitored and complete updates are published yearly. Also, new items are frequently added in response to changes in materials and methods.

Costs—$ (U.S.)

All costs represent U.S. national averages and are given in U.S. dollars. The RSMeans Location Factors can be used to adjust costs to a particular location. The Location Factors for Canada can be used to adjust U.S. national averages to local costs in Canadian dollars. No exchange rate conversion is necessary.

Material Costs

The RSMeans staff contacts manufacturers, dealers, distributors, and contractors all across the U.S. and Canada to determine national average material costs. If you have access to current material costs for your specific location, you may wish to make adjustments to reflect differences from the national average.

Included within material costs are fasteners for a normal installation. RSMeans engineers use manufacturers' recommendations, written specifications, and/or standard construction practice for size and spacing of fasteners. Adjustments to material costs may be required for your specific application or location. Material costs do not include sales tax.

Labor Costs

Labor costs are based on the average of residential wages from across the U.S. for the current year. Rates, along with overhead and profit markups, are listed on the inside back cover of this book.

- If wage rates in your area vary from those used in this book, or if rate increases are expected within a given year, labor costs should be adjusted accordingly.

Labor costs reflect productivity based on actual working conditions. These figures include time spent during a normal workday on tasks other than actual installation, such as material receiving and handling, mobilization at site, site movement, breaks, and cleanup.

Productivity data is developed over an extended period so as not to be influenced by abnormal variations and reflects a typical average.

Equipment Costs

Equipment costs include not only rental costs, but also operating costs for equipment under normal use. Equipment and rental rates are obtained from industry sources throughout North America—contractors, suppliers, dealers, manufacturers, and distributors.

Factors Affecting Costs

Costs can vary depending upon a number of variables. Here's how we have handled the main factors affecting costs.

Quality—The prices for materials and the workmanship upon which productivity is based represent sound construction work. They are also in line with U.S. government specifications.

Overtime—We have made no allowance for overtime. If you anticipate premium time or work beyond normal working hours, be sure to make an appropriate adjustment to your labor costs.

Productivity—The labor costs for each line item are based on working an eight-hour day in daylight hours in moderate temperatures. For work that extends beyond normal work hours or is performed under adverse conditions, productivity may decrease.

Size of Project—The size, scope of work, and type of construction project will have a significant impact on cost. Economies of scale can reduce costs for large projects. Unit costs can often run higher for small projects. Costs in this book are intended for the size and type of project as previously described in "How the Book Is Built: An Overview." Costs for projects of a significantly different size or type should be adjusted accordingly.

Location—Material prices in this book are for metropolitan areas. However, in dense urban areas, traffic and site storage limitations may increase costs. Beyond a 20-mile radius of large cities, extra trucking or transportation charges may also increase the material costs slightly. On the other hand, lower wage rates may be in effect. Be sure to consider both of these factors when preparing an estimate, particularly if the job site is located in a central city or remote rural location.

In addition, highly specialized subcontract items may require travel and per diem expenses for mechanics.

Other Factors—

- season of year
- contractor management
- weather conditions
- building code requirements
- availability of:
  - adequate energy
  - skilled labor
  - building materials
- owner's special requirements/ restrictions
- safety requirements
- environmental considerations

Overhead & Profit—The extreme right-hand column of each chart gives the "Totals." These figures contain the installing contractor's O&P. Therefore, it is necessary for a general contractor to add a percentage of all subcontracted items. For a detailed breakdown of O&P see the inside back cover of this book.

Unpredictable Factors—General business conditions influence "in-place" costs of all items. Substitute materials and construction methods may have to be employed. These may affect the installed cost and/or life cycle costs. Such factors may be difficult to evaluate and cannot necessarily be predicted on the basis of the job's location in a particular section of the country. Thus, where these factors apply, you may find significant but unavoidable cost variations for which you will have to apply a measure of judgment to your estimate.

Final Checklist

Estimating can be a straightforward process provided you remember the basics. Here's a checklist of some of the steps you should remember to complete before finalizing your estimate.

Did you remember to . . .

* factor in the Location Factor for your locale?
* take into consideration which items have been marked up and by how much?
* mark up the entire estimate sufficiently for your purposes?
* include all components of your project in the final estimate?
* double check your figures to be sure of your accuracy?
* call RSMeans if you have any questions about your estimate or the data you've found in our publications?

Remember, RSMeans stands behind its publications. If you have any questions about your estimate . . . about the costs you've used from our books . . . or even about the technical aspects of the job that may affect your estimate, feel free to call the RSMeans editors at 1-800-334-3509.

Unit Price Section

Table of Contents

Table of Contents (cont.)

How to Use the Unit Price Pages

The prices in this publication include all overhead and profit mark-ups for the installing contractor. If a general contractor is involved, an additional 10% should be added to the cost shown in the "Total" column.

The costs for material, labor and any equipment are shown here. Material costs include delivery and a 10% mark-up. No sales taxes are included. Labor costs include all mark-ups as shown on the inside back cover of this book. Equipment costs also include a 10% mark-up.

The cost in the total column should be multiplied by the quantity of each item to determine the total cost for that item. The sum of all item's total costs becomes the project's total cost.

The book is arranged into 23 categories that follow the order of construction for residential projects. The category is shown as white letters on a black background at the top of each page.

A brief specification of the cost item is shown here.

Graphics representing some of the cost items are found at the beginning of each category.

The cost data is arranged in a tree structure format. Major cost sections are left justified and are shown as bold headings within a grey background. Cost items and sub-cost items are found under the bold headings. The complete description should read as "bold heading, cost item, sub-cost item."
For example, the identified item's description is "Beam/Girder, Solid Wood Beam, 2″ x 8″."

Each action performed to the cost item is conveniently listed to the right of the description. See the explanation below for the scope of work included as part of the action.

The unit of measure upon which all the costs are based is shown here. An abbreviations list is included within the reference section found at the back of this book.

Rough Frame / Structure

Rough Framing

Beam / Girder	Unit	Material	Labor	Equip.	Total	Specification
Solid Wood Beam						
2″ x 8″						
Demolish	L.F.		.78		.78	Cost includes material and labor to
Install	L.F.	.62	1.21		1.83	install 2″ x 8″ beam.
Demolish and Install	L.F.	.62	1.99		2.61	
Clean	L.F.	.12	.26		.38	
Paint	L.F.	.13	1.82		1.95	
Minimum Charge	Job		196		196	
2″ x 10″						
Demolish	L.F.		.97		.97	Cost includes material and labor to
Install	L.F.	.79	1.31		2.10	install 2″ x 10″ beam.
Demolish and Install	L.F.	.79	2.28		3.07	
Clean	L.F.	.14	.31		.45	
Paint	L.F.	.18	1.12		1.30	
Minimum Charge	Job		196		196	
2″ x 12″						
Demolish	L.F.		1.17		1.17	Cost includes material and labor to
Install	L.F.	1.17	1.42		2.59	install 2″ x 12″ beam.
Demolish and Install	L.F.	1.17	2.59		3.76	
Clean	L.F.	.17	.36		.53	
Paint	L.F.	.20	2.69		2.89	
Minimum Charge	Job		196		196	
4″ x 8″						
Demolish	L.F.		2.41		2.41	Cost includes material and labor to
Install	L.F.	3.17	1.77	.72	5.66	install 4″ x 8″ beam.
Demolish and Install	L.F.	3.17	4.18	.72	8.07	
Clean	L.F.	.14	.31		.45	
Paint	L.F.	.18	1.12		1.30	
Minimum Charge	Job		196		196	
4″ x 10″						
Demolish	L.F.		3.01		3.01	Cost includes material and labor to
Install	L.F.	4	1.86	.76	6.62	install 4″ x 10″ beam.
Demolish and Install	L.F.	4	4.87	.76	9.63	
Clean	L.F.	.17	.36		.53	
Paint	L.F.	.20	1.31		1.51	
Minimum Charge	Job		196		196	
4″ x 12″						
Demolish	L.F.		3.62		3.62	Cost includes material and labor to
Install	L.F.	6.70	1.96	.80	9.46	install 4″ x 12″ beam.
Demolish and Install	L.F.	6.70	5.58	.80	13.08	
Clean	L.F.	.19	.41		.60	
Paint	L.F.	.20	2.69		2.89	
Minimum Charge	Job		196		196	

Action	Scope
Demolish	Includes removal of the item and hauling the debris to a truck, dumpster, or storage area.
Install	Includes the installation of the item with normal placement and spacing of fasteners.
Demolish and Install	Includes the demolish action and the install action.
Reinstall	Includes the reinstallation of a removed item.
Clean	Includes cleaning of the item.
Paint	Includes up to two coats of finish on the item (unless otherwise indicated).
Minimum Charge	Includes the minimum labor or the minimum labor and equipment cost. Use this charge for small quantities of material.

Scaffolding	Temporary Electrical Service	Air Compressor

Construction Fees		Unit	Material	Labor	Equip.	Total	Specification
Asbestos Test	Minimum Charge	Job		232		232	Minimum charge for testing.
Architectural	Minimum Charge	Day	1975			1975	Minimum labor charge for architect.
Engineering	Minimum Charge	Day	1850			1850	Minimum labor charge for field engineer.

Construction Permits		Unit	Material	Labor	Equip.	Total	Specification
Job (less than 5K)	Minimum Charge	Job	110			110	Permit fees, job less than 5K.
Job (5K to 10K)	Minimum Charge	Job	220			220	Permit fees, job more than 5K, but less than 10K.
Job (10K to 25K)	Minimum Charge	Job	550			550	Permit fees, job more than 10K, but less than 25K.
Job (25K to 50K)	Minimum Charge	Job	1100			1100	Permit fees, job more than 25K, but less than 50K.
Job (50K to 100K)	Minimum Charge	Job	2200			2200	Permit fees, job more than 50K, but less than 100K.
Job (100K to 250K)	Minimum Charge	Job	5500			5500	Permit fees, job more than 100K, but less than 250K.
Job (250K to 500K)	Minimum Charge	Job	11000			11000	Permit fees, job more than 250K, but less than 500K.
Job (500K to 1M)	Minimum Charge	Job	22000			22000	Permit fees, job more than 500K, but less than 1 million.

Job Costs

Trade Labor		Unit	Material	Labor	Equip.	Total	Specification
Carpenter							
Daily (8 hours)							
	Install	Day		405		405	Daily labor rate for one carpenter.
	Minimum Charge	Job		202		202	
Weekly (40 hours)							
	Install	Week		2025		2025	Weekly labor rate for one carpenter.
	Minimum Charge	Job		202		202	
Drywaller							
Daily (8 hours)							
	Install	Day		405		405	Daily labor rate for one carpenter.
	Minimum Charge	Job		202		202	
Weekly (40 hours)							
	Install	Week		2025		2025	Weekly labor rate for one carpenter.
	Minimum Charge	Job		202		202	
Roofer							
Daily (8 hours)							
	Install	Day		365		365	Daily labor rate for one skilled roofer.
	Minimum Charge	Job		182		182	
Weekly (40 hours)							
	Install	Week		1825		1825	Weekly labor rate for one skilled
	Minimum Charge	Job		182		182	roofer.
Painter							
Daily (8 hours)							
	Install	Day		345		345	Daily labor rate for one painter.
	Minimum Charge	Job		173		173	
Weekly (40 hours)							
	Install	Week		1725		1725	Weekly labor rate for one painter.
	Minimum Charge	Job		173		173	
Mason							
Daily (8 hours)							
	Install	Day		395		395	Daily labor rate for one skilled mason.
	Minimum Charge	Job		198		198	
Weekly (40 hours)							
	Install	Week		1975		1975	Weekly labor rate for one skilled
	Minimum Charge	Job		198		198	mason.
Electrician							
Daily (8 hours)							
	Install	Day		435		435	Daily labor rate for an electrician.
	Minimum Charge	Job		219		219	
Weekly (40 hours)							
	Install	Week		2175		2175	Weekly labor rate for an electrician.
	Minimum Charge	Job		219		219	
Plumber							
Daily (8 hours)							
	Install	Day		460		460	Daily labor rate for a plumber.
	Minimum Charge	Job		231		231	
Weekly (40 hours)							
	Install	Week		2300		2300	Weekly labor rate for a plumber.
	Minimum Charge	Job		231		231	
Common Laborer							
Daily (8 hours)							
	Install	Day		299		299	Daily labor rate for a common
	Minimum Charge	Job		150		150	laborer.

Job Costs

Trade Labor

Trade Labor		Unit	Material	Labor	Equip.	Total	Specification
Weekly (40 hours)							
	Install	Week		1500		1500	Weekly labor rate for a common
	Minimum Charge	Job		150		150	laborer.

Temporary Utilities

Temporary Utilities		Unit	Material	Labor	Equip.	Total	Specification
Power Pole							
Job Site Electricity							
	Install	Month	55			55	Includes average cost of electricity per
	Minimum Charge	Job		219		219	month.
Water Service							
Job Site Water							
	Install	Month	68			68	Includes average costs for water for
	Minimum Charge	Month	68			68	one month.
Telephone							
	Install	Month	89			89	Includes average cost for local and
	Minimum Charge	Month	89			89	long distance telephone service for
							one month.
Chemical Toilet							
	Install	Month			280	280	Monthly rental of portable toilet.
	Minimum Charge	Day			14	14	
Office Trailer							
Place and Remove							
	Install	Job	370			370	Includes cost to a contractor to deliver,
	Minimum Charge	Job		162		162	place and level an office trailer and
							remove at end of job.
Storage Container							
	Install	Job	209			209	Includes cost to a contractor to deliver
	Minimum Charge	Job		162		162	and place a storage container and
							remove at end of job.
Fencing							
	Install	L.F.	3.62			3.62	Includes material costs for temporary
	Minimum Charge	L.F.	275			275	fencing.
Railing							
	Install	L.F.	14.40	11.45	.68	26.53	Includes material and labor to install
	Minimum Charge	L.F.	275			275	primed steel pipe.

Equipment Rental

Equipment Rental		Unit	Material	Labor	Equip.	Total	Specification
Flatbed Truck							
Daily Rental							
	Install	Day			189	189	Daily rental of flatbed truck.
	Minimum Charge	Job			189	189	
Weekly Rental							
	Install	Week			945	945	Weekly rental of flatbed truck.
	Minimum Charge	Job			189	189	
Monthly Rental							
	Install	Month			3775	3775	Monthly rental of flatbed truck.
	Minimum Charge	Job			189	189	

Job Costs

Equipment Rental

Equipment Rental		Unit	Material	Labor	Equip.	Total	Specification
Dump Truck							
Daily Rental							
	Install	Day			345	345	Daily rental of dump truck.
	Minimum Charge	Day			345	345	
Weekly Rental							
	Install	Week			1725	1725	Weekly rental of dump truck.
	Minimum Charge	Day			345	345	
Monthly Rental							
	Install	Month			6950	6950	Monthly rental of dump truck.
	Minimum Charge	Day			345	345	
Forklift							
Daily Rental							
	Install	Day			305	305	Daily rental of forklift.
	Minimum Charge	Day			305	305	
Weekly Rental							
	Install	Week			1525	1525	Weekly rental of forklift.
	Minimum Charge	Day			305	305	
Monthly Rental							
	Install	Month			6150	6150	Monthly rental of forklift.
	Minimum Charge	Day			305	305	
Bobcat							
Daily Rental							
	Install	Day			167	167	Daily rental of wheeled, skid steer loader.
	Minimum Charge	Day			167	167	
Weekly Rental							
	Install	Week			835	835	Weekly rental of wheeled, skid steer loader.
	Minimum Charge	Day			167	167	
Monthly Rental							
	Install	Month			3350	3350	Monthly rental of wheeled, skid steer loader.
	Minimum Charge	Day			167	167	
Air Compressor							
Daily Rental							
	Install	Day			121	121	Daily rental of air compressor.
	Minimum Charge	Day			121	121	
Weekly Rental							
	Install	Week			605	605	Weekly rental of air compressor.
	Minimum Charge	Day			121	121	
Monthly Rental							
	Install	Month			2425	2425	Monthly rental of air compressor.
	Minimum Charge	Day			121	121	
Jackhammer							
Daily Rental							
	Install	Day			10.80	10.80	Daily rental of air tool, jackhammer.
	Minimum Charge	Day			10.80	10.80	
Weekly Rental							
	Install	Week			54	54	Weekly rental of air tool, jackhammer.
	Minimum Charge	Day			10.80	10.80	
Monthly Rental							
	Install	Month			216	216	Monthly rental of air tool, jackhammer.
	Minimum Charge	Day			10.80	10.80	
Concrete Mixer							
Daily Rental							
	Install	Day			136	136	Daily rental of concrete mixer.
	Minimum Charge	Day			136	136	

Equipment Rental		Unit	Material	Labor	Equip.	Total	Specification
Weekly Rental							
	Install	Week			680	680	Weekly rental of concrete mixer.
	Minimum Charge	Day			136	136	
Monthly Rental							
	Install	Month			2725	2725	Monthly rental of concrete mixer.
	Minimum Charge	Day			136	136	
Concrete Bucket							
Daily Rental							
	Install	Day			22	22	Daily rental of concrete bucket.
	Minimum Charge	Day			22	22	
Weekly Rental							
	Install	Week			109	109	Weekly rental of concrete bucket.
	Minimum Charge	Day			22	22	
Monthly Rental							
	Install	Month			435	435	Monthly rental of concrete bucket.
	Minimum Charge	Day			22	22	
Concrete Pump							
Daily Rental							
	Install	Day			815	815	Daily rental of concrete pump.
	Minimum Charge	Day			815	815	
Weekly Rental							
	Install	Week			4075	4075	Weekly rental of concrete pump.
	Minimum Charge	Day			815	815	
Monthly Rental							
	Install	Month			16300	16300	Monthly rental of concrete pump.
	Minimum Charge	Day			815	815	
Generator							
Daily Rental							
	Install	Day			32	32	Daily rental of generator.
	Minimum Charge	Day			32	32	
Weekly Rental							
	Install	Week			161	161	Weekly rental of generator.
	Minimum Charge	Day			32	32	
Monthly Rental							
	Install	Month			645	645	Monthly rental of generator.
	Minimum Charge	Day			32	32	
Welder							
Daily Rental							
	Install	Day			26.50	26.50	Daily rental of welder.
	Minimum Charge	Day			26.50	26.50	
Weekly Rental							
	Install	Week			132	132	Weekly rental of welder.
	Minimum Charge	Day			26.50	26.50	
Monthly Rental							
	Install	Month			530	530	Monthly rental of welder.
	Minimum Charge	Day			26.50	26.50	
Sandblaster							
Daily Rental							
	Install	Day			22.50	22.50	Daily rental of sandblaster.
	Minimum Charge	Day			22.50	22.50	
Weekly Rental							
	Install	Week			113	113	Weekly rental of sandblaster.
	Minimum Charge	Day			22.50	22.50	

Job Costs

Equipment Rental

		Unit	Material	Labor	Equip.	Total	Specification
Monthly Rental							
	Install	Month			455	455	Monthly rental of sandblaster.
	Minimum Charge	Day			22.50	22.50	
Space Heater							
Daily Rental							
	Install	Day			21.50	21.50	Daily rental of space heater.
	Minimum Charge	Day			11.30	11.30	
Weekly Rental							
	Install	Day			107	107	Weekly rental of space heater.
	Minimum Charge	Day			11.30	11.30	
Monthly Rental							
	Install	Day			430	430	Monthly rental of space heater.
	Minimum Charge	Day			11.30	11.30	

Move / Reset Contents

		Unit	Material	Labor	Equip.	Total	Specification
Small Room							
	Install	Room		36		36	Includes cost to remove and reset the
	Minimum Charge	Job		150		150	contents of a small room.
Average Room							
	Install	Room		44		44	Includes cost to remove and reset the
	Minimum Charge	Job		150		150	contents of an average room.
Large Room							
	Install	Room		60.50		60.50	Includes cost to remove and reset the
	Minimum Charge	Job		150		150	contents of a large room.
Extra Large Room							
	Install	Room		96		96	Includes cost to remove and reset the
	Minimum Charge	Job		150		150	contents of a extra large room.
Store Contents							
Weekly							
	Install	Week	171			171	Storage fee, per week.
Monthly							
	Install	Month	510			510	Storage fee, per month.

Cover and Protect

		Unit	Material	Labor	Equip.	Total	Specification
Cover / Protect Walls							
	Install	SF Wall		.12		.12	Includes labor costs to cover and
	Minimum Charge	Job		150		150	protect walls.
Cover / Protect Floors							
	Install	SF Flr.		.12		.12	Includes labor costs to cover and
	Minimum Charge	Job		150		150	protect floors.

Temporary Bracing

		Unit	Material	Labor	Equip.	Total	Specification
Shim Support Piers							
	Install	Ea.	3.70	117		120.70	Includes labor and material to install
	Minimum Charge	Job		350		350	shims support for piers.

Job Costs

Jack and Relevel

		Unit	Material	Labor	Equip.	Total	Specification
Single Story							
	Install	S.F.	1.76	1.41		3.17	Includes labor and equipment to jack
	Minimum Charge	Job		350		350	and relevel single-story building.
Two-story							
	Install	S.F.	1.76	2.34		4.10	Includes labor and equipment to jack
	Minimum Charge	Job		350		350	and relevel two-story building.

Dumpster Rental

		Unit	Material	Labor	Equip.	Total	Specification
Small Load							
	Install	Week			665	665	Dumpster, weekly rental, 2 dumps, 5
	Minimum Charge	Week			665	665	yard container.
Medium Load							
	Install	Week			785	785	Dumpster, weekly rental, 2 dumps, 10
	Minimum Charge	Week			785	785	yard container.
Large Load							
	Install	Week			1250	1250	Dumpster, weekly rental, 2 dumps, 30
	Minimum Charge	Week			1250	1250	yard container.

Debris Hauling

		Unit	Material	Labor	Equip.	Total	Specification
Per Ton							
	Install	Ton		92.50	41	133.50	Includes hauling of debris by trailer or
	Minimum Charge	Ton		695	310	1005	dump truck.
Per Cubic Yard							
	Install	C.Y.		31	13.75	44.75	Includes hauling of debris by trailer or
	Minimum Charge	Job		695	310	1005	dump truck.
Per Pick-up Truck Load							
	Install	Ea.		166		166	Includes hauling of debris by pick-up
	Minimum Charge	Ea.		166		166	truck.

Dump Fees

		Unit	Material	Labor	Equip.	Total	Specification
Per Cubic Yard							
	Install	C.Y.	20.50			20.50	Dump charges, building materials.
	Minimum Charge	C.Y.	20.50			20.50	
Per Ton							
	Install	Ton	127			127	Dump charges, building materials.
	Minimum Charge	Ton	127			127	

Scaffolding

		Unit	Material	Labor	Equip.	Total	Specification
4' to 6' High							
	Install	Month	67			67	Includes monthly rental of scaffolding,
	Minimum Charge	Month	67			67	steel tubular, 30" wide, 7' long, 5' high.
7' to 11' High							
	Install	Month	80.50			80.50	Includes monthly rental of scaffolding,
	Minimum Charge	Month	80.50			80.50	steel tubular, 30" wide, 7' long, 10' high.

Job Costs

Scaffolding

Scaffolding		Unit	Material	Labor	Equip.	Total	Specification
12' to 16' High							
	Install	Month	93.50			93.50	Includes monthly rental of scaffolding,
	Minimum Charge	Month	93.50			93.50	steel tubular, 30" wide, 7' long, 15' high.
17' to 21' High							
	Install	Month	122			122	Includes monthly rental of scaffolding,
	Minimum Charge	Month	122			122	steel tubular, 30" wide, 7' long, 20' high.
22' to 26' High							
	Install	Month	135			135	Includes monthly rental of scaffolding,
	Minimum Charge	Month	135			135	steel tubular, 30" wide, 7' long, 25' high.
27' to 30' High							
	Install	Month	149			149	Includes monthly rental of scaffolding,
	Minimum Charge	Month	149			149	steel tubular, 30" wide, 7' long, 30' high.

Construction Clean-up

Construction Clean-up		Unit	Material	Labor	Equip.	Total	Specification
Initial							
	Clean	S.F.		.37		.37	Includes labor for general clean-up.
	Minimum Charge	Job		150		150	
Progressive							
	Clean	S.F.		.19		.19	Includes labor for progressive site/job
	Minimum Charge	Job		150		150	clean-up on a weekly basis.

Building Demolition		Unit	Material	Labor	Equip.	Total	Specification
Wood-framed Building							
1 Story Demolition							
	Demolish	S.F.		1.39	1.56	2.95	Includes demolition of 1 floor only
	Minimum Charge	Job		2200	2475	4675	light wood-framed building, including hauling of debris. Dump fees not included.
2nd Story Demolition							
	Demolish	S.F.		1.42	1.59	3.01	Includes demolition of 2nd floor only
	Minimum Charge	Job		2200	2475	4675	light wood-framed building, including hauling of debris. Dump fees not included.
3rd Story Demolition							
	Demolish	S.F.		1.84	2.07	3.91	Includes demolition of 3rd floor only
	Minimum Charge	Job		2200	2475	4675	light wood-framed building, including hauling of debris. Dump fees not included.
Masonry Building							
	Demolish	S.F.		1.98	2.22	4.20	Includes demolition of one story
	Minimum Charge	Job		2200	2475	4675	masonry building, including hauling of debris. Dump fees not included.
Concrete Building							
Unreinforced							
	Demolish	S.F.		4.08	1.01	5.09	Includes demolition of a one story
	Minimum Charge	Job		2200	2475	4675	non-reinforced concrete building, including hauling of debris. Dump fees not included.
Reinforced							
	Demolish	S.F.		4.68	1.16	5.84	Includes demolition of a one story
	Minimum Charge	Job		2200	2475	4675	reinforced concrete building, including hauling of debris. Dump fees not included.
Steel Building							
	Demolish	S.F.		2.64	2.96	5.60	Includes demolition of a metal
	Minimum Charge	Job		2200	2475	4675	building, including hauling of debris. Dump fees not included. No salvage value assumed for scrap metal.

Job Preparation

General Clean-up

General Clean-up		Unit	Material	Labor	Equip.	Total	Specification
Remove Debris							
	Clean	S.F.		.91	.19	1.10	Includes removal of debris caused by
	Minimum Charge	Job		455	94.50	549.50	the loss including contents items and
							loose debris.
Muck-out							
	Clean	S.F.		.58		.58	Includes labor to remove 2″ of muck
	Minimum Charge	Job		150		150	and mud after a flood loss.
Deodorize / Disinfect							
	Clean	SF Flr.		.20		.20	Includes deodorizing building with
	Minimum Charge	Job		150		150	application of mildicide and
							disinfectant to floors and walls - will
							vary depending on the extent of
							deodorization required.
Clean Walls							
Heavy							
	Clean	S.F.		.14		.14	Includes labor and material for heavy
	Minimum Charge	Job		150		150	cleaning (multiple applications) with
							detergent and solvent.
Clean Ceiling							
Light							
	Clean	S.F.		.23		.23	Includes labor and material to clean
	Minimum Charge	Job		150		150	light to moderate smoke and soot.
Heavy							
	Clean	S.F.		.35		.35	Includes labor and material to clean
	Minimum Charge	Job		150		150	heavy smoke and soot.

Flood Clean-up

Flood Clean-up		Unit	Material	Labor	Equip.	Total	Specification
Emergency Service Call							
After Hours / Weekend							
	Minimum Charge	Job		199		199	Includes minimum charges for
							deflooding clean-up after hours or on
							weekends.
Grey Water / Sewage							
	Minimum Charge	Job		150		150	Includes minimum charges for
							deflooding clean-up.
Water Extraction							
Clean (non-grey)							
	Clean	SF Flr.	.06	.60		.66	Includes labor to remove clean
	Minimum Charge	Job		150		150	uncontaminated water from the loss.
Grey (non-solids)							
	Clean	SF Flr.	.06	1.20		1.26	Includes labor to remove non-solid
	Minimum Charge	Job		150		150	grey water from the loss.
Sewage / Solids							
	Clean	SF Flr.	.09	1.50		1.59	Includes labor to remove water from
	Minimum Charge	Job		150		150	the loss that may contain sewage or
							solids.

Job Preparation

Flood Clean-up

Flood Clean-up		Unit	Material	Labor	Equip.	Total	Specification
Mildicide Walls							
Topographical							
	Clean	SF Wall		.27		.27	Clean-up of deflooding including
	Minimum Charge	Job		150		150	topographical mildicide application.
Injection Treatments							
	Clean	SF Flr.	29.50	4.60		34.10	Clean-up of deflooding including
	Minimum Charge	Job		150		150	mildicide injection.
Carpet Cleaning							
Uncontaminated							
	Clean	SF Flr.		.19		.19	Includes labor to clean carpet.
	Minimum Charge	Job		150		150	
Contaminated							
	Clean	SF Flr.		.30		.30	Includes labor to clean contaminated
	Minimum Charge	Job		150		150	carpet.
Stairway							
	Clean	Ea.	.10	3.52		3.62	Includes labor to clean contaminated
	Minimum Charge	Job		150		150	carpet on a stairway.
Carpet Treatment							
Disinfect / Deodorize							
	Clean	SF Flr.		.19		.19	Includes disinfecting and deodorizing
	Minimum Charge	Job		150		150	of carpet.
Disinfect For Sewage							
	Clean	SF Flr.		.48		.48	Includes labor to disinfect and
	Minimum Charge	Job		150		150	deodorize carpet exposed to sewage.
Mildicide							
	Clean	SF Flr.	.01	.19		.20	Includes labor and materials to apply
	Minimum Charge	Job		150		150	mildicide to carpet.
Thermal Fog Area							
	Clean	SF Flr.	.03	.46		.49	Includes labor and materials to
	Minimum Charge	Job		150		150	perform thermal fogging during
							deflooding clean-up.
Wet Fog / ULV Area							
	Clean	SF Flr.	.02	.26		.28	Includes labor and materials to
	Minimum Charge	Job		150		150	perform wet fogging / ULV during
							deflooding clean-up.
Steam Clean Fixtures							
	Clean	Ea.	.01	30		30.01	Includes labor and materials to steam
	Minimum Charge	Job		150		150	clean fixtures during deflooding
							clean-up.
Pressure Wash Sewage							
	Clean	SF Flr.		2.72		2.72	Includes labor to pressure wash
	Minimum Charge	Job		150		150	sewage contamination.
Air Mover							
	Minimum Charge	Day			22.50	22.50	Daily rental of air mover.

11

Job Preparation

Flood Clean-up		Unit	Material	Labor	Equip.	Total	Specification
Dehumidifier							
Medium Size							
	Minimum Charge	Day			48	48	Daily rental of dehumidifier, medium.
Large Size							
	Minimum Charge	Day			97	97	Daily rental of dehumidifier, large.
Air Purifier							
HEPA Filter-Bacteria							
	Minimum Charge	Ea.	335			335	HEPA filter for air purifier.

Asbestos Removal		Unit	Material	Labor	Equip.	Total	Specification
Asbestos Analysis							
	Minimum Charge	Job		232		232	Minimum charge for testing.
Asbestos Pipe Insulation							
1/2" to 3/4" Diameter							
	Demolish	L.F.	.34	6		6.34	Minimum charge to remove asbestos. Includes full Tyvek suits for workers changed four times per eight-hour shift with respirators, air monitoring and supervision by qualified professionals.
	Minimum Charge	Job		3725		3725	
1" to 3" Diameter							
	Demolish	L.F.	1.07	18.60		19.67	Minimum charge to remove asbestos. Includes full Tyvek suits for workers changed four times per eight-hour shift with respirators, air monitoring and supervision by qualified professionals.
	Minimum Charge	Job		3725		3725	
Asbestos-based Siding							
	Demolish	S.F.	2.38	41.50		43.88	Minimum charge to remove asbestos. Includes full Tyvek suits for workers changed four times per eight-hour shift with respirators, air monitoring and supervision by qualified professionals.
	Minimum Charge	Job		3725		3725	
Asbestos-based Plaster							
	Demolish	S.F.	1.83	32		33.83	Minimum charge to remove asbestos. Includes full Tyvek suits for workers changed four times per eight-hour shift with respirators, air monitoring and supervision by qualified professionals.
	Minimum Charge	Job		3725		3725	
Encapsulate Asbestos Ceiling							
	Install	S.F.	.30	.18		.48	Includes encapsulation with penetrating sealant sprayed onto ceiling and walls with airless sprayer.
	Minimum Charge	Job		3725		3725	
Scrape Acoustical Ceiling							
	Demolish	S.F.	.07	1.05		1.12	Minimum charge to remove asbestos. Includes full Tyvek suits for workers changed four times per eight-hour shift with respirators, air monitoring and supervision by qualified professionals.
	Minimum Charge	Job		3725		3725	

Job Preparation

Asbestos Removal

Asbestos Removal		Unit	Material	Labor	Equip.	Total	Specification
Seal Ceiling Asbestos	Install	S.F.	2.26	3.50		5.76	Includes attaching plastic cover to ceiling area and sealing where asbestos exists, taping all seams, caulk or foam insulation in cracks and negative air system.
	Minimum Charge	Job		3725		3725	
Seal Wall Asbestos	Install	S.F.	2.26	3.11		5.37	Includes attaching plastic cover to wall area and sealing where asbestos exists, taping all seams, caulk or foam insulation in cracks and negative air system.
	Minimum Charge	Job		3725		3725	
Seal Floor Asbestos	Install	S.F.	3.61	6.20		9.81	Includes attaching plastic cover to floor area and sealing where asbestos exists, taping all seams, caulk or foam insulation in cracks and negative air system.
	Minimum Charge	Job		3725		3725	
Negative Air Vent System	Install	Day			44	44	Daily rental of negative air vent system.
	Minimum Charge	Week			220	220	
HEPA Vacuum Cleaner	Install	Day			15.05	15.05	Daily rental of HEPA vacuum, 16 gallon.
	Minimum Charge	Week			75	75	
Airless Sprayer	Install	Day			59	59	Daily rental of airless sprayer.
	Minimum Charge	Week			296	296	
Decontamination Unit	Install	Day			140	140	Daily rental of decontamination unit.
	Minimum Charge	Week			700	700	
Light Stand	Install	Day			11.60	11.60	Daily rental of floodlight w/tripod.
	Minimum Charge	Week			58	58	

Room Demolition

Room Demolition		Unit	Material	Labor	Equip.	Total	Specification
Strip Typical Room	Demolish	S.F.		2.99		2.99	Includes 4 labor hours for general demolition.
	Minimum Charge	Job		166		166	
Strip Typical Bathroom	Demolish	S.F.		3.99		3.99	Includes 4 labor hours for general demolition.
	Minimum Charge	Job		166		166	
Strip Typical Kitchen	Demolish	S.F.		3.84		3.84	Includes 4 labor hours for general demolition.
	Minimum Charge	Job		166		166	
Strip Typical Laundry	Demolish	S.F.		3.42		3.42	Includes 4 labor hours for general demolition.
	Minimum Charge	Job		166		166	

Selective Demolition		Unit	Material	Labor	Equip.	Total	Specification
Concrete Slab							
4" Unreinforced							
	Demolish	S.F.		1.99	.28	2.27	Includes labor and equipment to remove unreinforced concrete slab and haul debris to truck or dumpster.
	Minimum Charge	Job		845	119	964	
6" Unreinforced							
	Demolish	S.F.		2.82	.40	3.22	Includes labor and equipment to remove unreinforced concrete slab and haul debris to truck or dumpster.
	Minimum Charge	Job		845	119	964	
8" Unreinforced							
	Demolish	S.F.		4.64	.65	5.29	Includes labor and equipment to remove unreinforced concrete slab and haul debris to truck or dumpster.
	Minimum Charge	Job		845	119	964	
4" Reinforced							
	Demolish	S.F.		2.51	.35	2.86	Includes labor and equipment to remove reinforced concrete slab and haul debris to truck or dumpster.
	Minimum Charge	Job		845	119	964	
6" Reinforced							
	Demolish	S.F.		3.76	.53	4.29	Includes labor and equipment to remove reinforced concrete slab and haul debris to truck or dumpster.
	Minimum Charge	Job		845	119	964	
8" Reinforced							
	Demolish	S.F.		6.15	.87	7.02	Includes labor and equipment to remove reinforced concrete slab and haul debris to truck or dumpster.
	Minimum Charge	Job		845	119	964	
Brick Wall							
4" Thick							
	Demolish	S.F.		2.77	.39	3.16	Includes labor and equipment to remove brick wall and haul debris to a central location for disposal.
	Minimum Charge	Job		845	119	964	
8" Thick							
	Demolish	S.F.		3.81	.54	4.35	Includes labor and equipment to remove brick wall and haul debris to a central location for disposal.
	Minimum Charge	Job		845	119	964	
12" Thick							
	Demolish	S.F.		5.10	.71	5.81	Includes labor and equipment to remove brick wall and haul debris to a central location for disposal.
	Minimum Charge	Job		845	119	964	
Concrete Masonry Wall							
4" Thick							
	Demolish	S.F.		3.08	.43	3.51	Includes minimum labor and equipment to remove 4" block wall and haul debris to a central location for disposal.
	Minimum Charge	Job		845	119	964	
6" Thick							
	Demolish	S.F.		3.81	.54	4.35	Includes minimum labor and equipment to remove 6" block wall and haul debris to a central location for disposal.
	Minimum Charge	Job		845	119	964	

Job Preparation

Selective Demolition		Unit	Material	Labor	Equip.	Total	Specification
8″ Thick							
	Demolish	S.F.		4.69	.66	5.35	Includes minimum labor and
	Minimum Charge	Job		845	119	964	equipment to remove 8″ block wall and haul debris to a central location for disposal.
12″ Thick							
	Demolish	S.F.		6.75	.95	7.70	Includes minimum labor and
	Minimum Charge	Job		845	119	964	equipment to remove 12″ block wall and haul debris to a central location for disposal.
Tree Removal							
Small, 4″ - 8″							
	Demolish	Ea.		107	80	187	Minimum charge, tree removal.
	Minimum Charge	Job		150		150	
Medium, 9″ - 12″							
	Demolish	Ea.		161	120	281	Minimum charge, tree removal.
	Minimum Charge	Job		150		150	
Large, 13″ - 18″							
	Demolish	Ea.		193	144	337	Minimum charge, tree removal.
	Minimum Charge	Job		495	181	676	
Very Large, 19″ - 24″							
	Demolish	Ea.		242	180	422	Minimum charge, tree removal.
	Minimum Charge	Job		495	181	676	
Stump Removal							
	Demolish	Ea.		66	135	201	Includes minimum charges for a site
	Minimum Charge	Job		276	98	374	demolition crew and backhoe / loader.

Backhoe/Loader - Wheel Type Tractor Loader - Wheel Type Backhoe - Crawler Type

Excavation		Unit	Material	Labor	Equip.	Total	Specification
Footings							
Hand Trenching							
	Install	L.F.		1.87		1.87	Includes hand excavation for footing
	Minimum Charge	Job		75		75	or trench up to 10″ deep and 12″ wide.
Machine Trenching							
	Install	L.F.		.71	.35	1.06	Includes machine excavation for
	Minimum Charge	Job		355	176	531	footing or trench up to 10″ deep and 12″ wide.
Trenching w / Backfill							
Hand							
	Install	L.F.		2.99		2.99	Includes hand excavation, backfill and
	Minimum Charge	Job		75		75	compaction.
Machine							
	Install	L.F.		3.54	13.80	17.34	Includes machine excavation, backfill
	Minimum Charge	Job		150	31.50	181.50	and compaction.

Backfill		Unit	Material	Labor	Equip.	Total	Specification
Hand (no compaction)							
	Install	L.C.Y.		25		25	Includes backfill by hand in average
	Minimum Charge	Job		150		150	soil without compaction.
Hand (w / compaction)							
	Install	E.C.Y.		35		35	Includes backfill by hand in average
	Minimum Charge	Job		150		150	soil with compaction.
Machine (no compaction)							
	Install	L.C.Y.		3.54	1.76	5.30	Includes backfill, by 55 HP wheel
	Minimum Charge	Job		355	176	531	loader, of trenches from loose material piled adjacent without compaction.
Machine (w / compaction)							
	Install	L.C.Y.		9.45	4.70	14.15	Includes backfill, by 55 HP wheel
	Minimum Charge	Job		355	176	531	loader, of trenches from loose material piled adjacent with compaction by vibrating tampers.

Concrete Footing and Formwork

Wood Pile

Piles	Unit	Material	Labor	Equip.	Total	Specification
Treated Wood, 12″ Butt						
To 30′						
Demolish	L.F.		4.79	1.70	6.49	Includes material, labor and
Install	V.L.F.	12	4.47	3.25	19.72	equipment to install up to 30′ long
Demolish and Install	V.L.F.	12	9.26	4.95	26.21	treated wood piling.
Paint	L.F.	.41	1.98		2.39	
Minimum Charge	Job		2800	2025	4825	
30′ to 40′						
Demolish	L.F.		4.79	1.70	6.49	Includes material, labor and
Install	V.L.F.	11.70	4	2.90	18.60	equipment to install 30′ to 40′ long
Demolish and Install	V.L.F.	11.70	8.79	4.60	25.09	treated wood piling.
Paint	L.F.	.41	1.98		2.39	
Minimum Charge	Job		2800	2025	4825	
40′ to 50′						
Demolish	L.F.		4.79	1.70	6.49	Includes material, labor and
Install	V.L.F.	12.55	3.88	2.82	19.25	equipment to install 40′ to 50′ long
Demolish and Install	V.L.F.	12.55	8.67	4.52	25.74	treated wood piling.
Paint	L.F.	.41	1.98		2.39	
Minimum Charge	Job		2800	2025	4825	
50′ to 60′						
Demolish	L.F.		4.79	1.70	6.49	Includes material, labor and
Install	V.L.F.	13.85	3.50	2.54	19.89	equipment to install 50′ to 60′ long
Demolish and Install	V.L.F.	13.85	8.29	4.24	26.38	treated wood piling.
Paint	L.F.	.41	1.98		2.39	
Minimum Charge	Job		2800	2025	4825	
60′ to 80′						
Demolish	L.F.		4.79	1.70	6.49	Includes material, labor and
Install	V.L.F.	23.50	3.91	2.95	30.36	equipment to install 60′ to 80′ long
Demolish and Install	V.L.F.	23.50	8.70	4.65	36.85	treated wood piling.
Paint	L.F.	.41	1.98		2.39	
Minimum Charge	Job		2800	2025	4825	
Untreated Wood, 12″ Butt						
To 30′						
Demolish	L.F.		4.79	1.70	6.49	Includes material, labor and
Install	V.L.F.	8.80	4.47	3.25	16.52	equipment to install up to 30′ long
Demolish and Install	V.L.F.	8.80	9.26	4.95	23.01	untreated wood piling.
Paint	L.F.	.41	1.98		2.39	
Minimum Charge	Job		2800	2025	4825	

Foundation

Piles		Unit	Material	Labor	Equip.	Total	Specification
30' to 40'							
	Demolish	L.F.		4.79	1.70	6.49	Includes material, labor and
	Install	V.L.F.	8.80	4	2.90	15.70	equipment to install 30' to 40' long
	Demolish and Install	V.L.F.	8.80	8.79	4.60	22.19	untreated wood piling.
	Paint	L.F.	.41	1.98		2.39	
	Minimum Charge	Job		2800	2025	4825	
40' to 50'							
	Demolish	L.F.		4.79	1.70	6.49	Includes material, labor and
	Install	V.L.F.	8.80	3.88	2.82	15.50	equipment to install 40' to 50' long
	Demolish and Install	V.L.F.	8.80	8.67	4.52	21.99	untreated wood piling.
	Paint	L.F.	.41	1.98		2.39	
	Minimum Charge	Job		2800	2025	4825	
50' to 60'							
	Demolish	L.F.		4.79	1.70	6.49	Includes material, labor and
	Install	V.L.F.	8.80	3.50	2.54	14.84	equipment to install 50' to 60' long
	Demolish and Install	V.L.F.	8.80	8.29	4.24	21.33	untreated wood piling.
	Paint	L.F.	.41	1.98		2.39	
	Minimum Charge	Job		2800	2025	4825	
60' to 80'							
	Demolish	L.F.		4.79	1.70	6.49	Includes material, labor and
	Install	V.L.F.	11	3.33	2.42	16.75	equipment to install 60' to 80' long
	Demolish and Install	V.L.F.	11	8.12	4.12	23.24	untreated wood piling.
	Paint	L.F.	.41	1.98		2.39	
	Minimum Charge	Job		2800	2025	4825	
Precast Concrete							
10" Square							
	Demolish	L.F.		4.90	1.74	6.64	Includes material, labor and
	Install	V.L.F.	18	4	2.90	24.90	equipment to install a precast,
	Demolish and Install	V.L.F.	18	8.90	4.64	31.54	prestressed, 40' long, 10" square
	Paint	L.F.	.41	1.98		2.39	concrete pile.
	Minimum Charge	Job		2800	2025	4825	
12" Square							
	Demolish	L.F.		5.25	1.87	7.12	Includes material, labor and
	Install	V.L.F.	22.50	4.11	2.99	29.60	equipment to install a precast,
	Demolish and Install	V.L.F.	22.50	9.36	4.86	36.72	prestressed, 40' long, 12" square
	Paint	L.F.	.41	1.98		2.39	concrete pile.
	Minimum Charge	Job		2800	2025	4825	
14" Square							
	Demolish	L.F.		5.40	1.91	7.31	Includes material, labor and
	Install	V.L.F.	26.50	4.66	3.39	34.55	equipment to install a precast,
	Demolish and Install	V.L.F.	26.50	10.06	5.30	41.86	prestressed, 40' long, 14" square
	Paint	L.F.	.41	1.98		2.39	concrete pile.
	Minimum Charge	Job		2800	2025	4825	
16" Square							
	Demolish	L.F.		5.65	2.01	7.66	Includes material, labor and
	Install	V.L.F.	42	4.99	3.63	50.62	equipment to install a precast,
	Demolish and Install	V.L.F.	42	10.64	5.64	58.28	prestressed, 40' long, 16" square
	Paint	L.F.	.41	1.98		2.39	concrete pile.
	Minimum Charge	Job		2800	2025	4825	
18" Square							
	Demolish	L.F.		6.10	2.18	8.28	Includes material, labor and
	Install	V.L.F.	50.50	6.30	4.76	61.56	equipment to install a precast,
	Demolish and Install	V.L.F.	50.50	12.40	6.94	69.84	prestressed, 40' long, 18" square
	Paint	L.F.	.41	1.98		2.39	concrete pile.
	Minimum Charge	Job		2800	2025	4825	

Foundation

Piles

	Unit	Material	Labor	Equip.	Total	Specification
Cross Bracing						
Treated 2″ x 6″						
Demolish	L.F.		.98		.98	Cost includes material and labor to
Install	L.F.	.68	5.65		6.33	install 2″ x 6″ lumber for cross-bracing
Demolish and Install	L.F.	.68	6.63		7.31	of foundation piling or posts.
Reinstall	L.F.		4.54		4.54	
Clean	S.F.		.37		.37	
Paint	L.F.	.37	1.33		1.70	
Minimum Charge	Job		705		705	
Treated 2″ x 8″						
Demolish	L.F.		.98		.98	Cost includes material and labor to
Install	L.F.	1.05	5.85		6.90	install 2″ x 8″ lumber for cross-bracing
Demolish and Install	L.F.	1.05	6.83		7.88	of foundation piling or posts.
Reinstall	L.F.		4.69		4.69	
Clean	S.F.		.37		.37	
Paint	L.F.	.50	1.39		1.89	
Minimum Charge	Job		705		705	
Treated 2″ x 10″						
Demolish	L.F.		1.01		1.01	Cost includes material and labor to
Install	L.F.	1.42	6.05		7.47	install 2″ x 10″ lumber for
Demolish and Install	L.F.	1.42	7.06		8.48	cross-bracing of foundation piling or
Reinstall	L.F.		4.85		4.85	posts.
Clean	S.F.		.37		.37	
Paint	L.F.	.61	1.41		2.02	
Minimum Charge	Job		705		705	
Treated 2″ x 12″						
Demolish	L.F.		1.21		1.21	Cost includes material and labor to
Install	L.F.	1.87	6.30		8.17	install 2″ x 12″ lumber for
Demolish and Install	L.F.	1.87	7.51		9.38	cross-bracing of foundation piling or
Reinstall	L.F.		5.02		5.02	posts.
Clean	S.F.		.37		.37	
Paint	L.F.	.72	1.44		2.16	
Minimum Charge	Job		705		705	
Metal Pipe						
6″ Concrete Filled						
Demolish	L.F.		6.80	2.42	9.22	Includes material, labor and
Install	V.L.F.	25.50	5.85	4.23	35.58	equipment to install concrete filled
Demolish and Install	V.L.F.	25.50	12.65	6.65	44.80	steel pipe pile.
Paint	L.F.	.31	1.98		2.29	
Minimum Charge	Job		2800	2025	4825	
6″ Unfilled						
Demolish	L.F.		6.80	2.42	9.22	Includes material, labor and
Install	V.L.F.	21	5.35	3.87	30.22	equipment to install unfilled steel pipe
Demolish and Install	V.L.F.	21	12.15	6.29	39.44	pile.
Paint	L.F.	.31	1.98		2.29	
Minimum Charge	Job		2800	2025	4825	
8″ Concrete Filled						
Demolish	L.F.		6.80	2.42	9.22	Includes material, labor and
Install	V.L.F.	22.50	6.10	4.42	33.02	equipment to install concrete filled
Demolish and Install	V.L.F.	22.50	12.90	6.84	42.24	steel pipe pile.
Paint	L.F.	.31	1.98		2.29	
Minimum Charge	Job		2800	2025	4825	
8″ Unfilled						
Demolish	L.F.		6.80	2.42	9.22	Includes material, labor and
Install	V.L.F.	21.50	5.60	4.06	31.16	equipment to install unfilled steel pipe
Demolish and Install	V.L.F.	21.50	12.40	6.48	40.38	pile.
Paint	L.F.	.31	1.98		2.29	
Minimum Charge	Job		2800	2025	4825	

Foundation

Piles	Unit	Material	Labor	Equip.	Total	Specification
10″ Concrete Filled						
Demolish	L.F.		7	2.50	9.50	Includes material, labor and
Install	V.L.F.	29	6.20	4.52	39.72	equipment to install concrete filled
Demolish and Install	V.L.F.	29	13.20	7.02	49.22	steel pipe pile.
Paint	L.F.	.31	1.98		2.29	
Minimum Charge	Job		2800	2025	4825	
10″ Unfilled						
Demolish	L.F.		7	2.50	9.50	Includes material, labor and
Install	V.L.F.	27	5.60	4.06	36.66	equipment to install unfilled steel pipe
Demolish and Install	V.L.F.	27	12.60	6.56	46.16	pile.
Paint	L.F.	.31	1.98		2.29	
Minimum Charge	Job		2800	2025	4825	
12″ Concrete Filled						
Demolish	L.F.		7	2.50	9.50	Includes material, labor and
Install	V.L.F.	33.50	6.75	4.90	45.15	equipment to install concrete filled
Demolish and Install	V.L.F.	33.50	13.75	7.40	54.65	steel pipe pile.
Paint	L.F.	.31	1.98		2.29	
Minimum Charge	Job		2800	2025	4825	
12″ Unfilled						
Demolish	L.F.		7	2.50	9.50	Includes material, labor and
Install	V.L.F.	32.50	5.90	4.28	42.68	equipment to install unfilled steel pipe
Demolish and Install	V.L.F.	32.50	12.90	6.78	52.18	pile.
Paint	L.F.	.31	1.98		2.29	
Minimum Charge	Job		2800	2025	4825	
Steel H Section						
H Section 8 x 8 x 36#						
Demolish	L.F.		4.75	1.69	6.44	Includes material, labor and
Install	V.L.F.	19.65	4.37	3.18	27.20	equipment to install steel H section
Demolish and Install	V.L.F.	19.65	9.12	4.87	33.64	pile.
Paint	L.F.	.31	1.98		2.29	
Minimum Charge	Job		2800	2025	4825	
H Section 10 x 10 x 57#						
Demolish	L.F.		5.20	1.85	7.05	Includes material, labor and
Install	V.L.F.	31	4.58	3.33	38.91	equipment to install steel H section
Demolish and Install	V.L.F.	31	9.78	5.18	45.96	pile.
Paint	L.F.	.31	1.98		2.29	
Minimum Charge	Job		2800	2025	4825	
H Section 12 x 12 x 74#						
Demolish	L.F.		5.40	1.91	7.31	Includes material, labor and
Install	V.L.F.	41.50	5.55	4.20	51.25	equipment to install steel H section
Demolish and Install	V.L.F.	41.50	10.95	6.11	58.56	pile.
Paint	L.F.	.31	1.98		2.29	
Minimum Charge	Job		2800	2025	4825	
H Section 14 x 14 x 89#						
Demolish	L.F.		5.65	2.01	7.66	Includes material, labor and equipment to install steel H section
Install	V.L.F.	50	6.10	4.58	60.68	pile.
Demolish and Install	V.L.F.	50	11.75	6.59	68.34	
Paint	L.F.	.31	1.98		2.29	
Minimum Charge	Job		2800	2025	4825	

Foundation Post		Unit	Material	Labor	Equip.	Total	Specification
Wood Foundation Post							
4" x 4"							
	Demolish	L.F.		.77	.27	1.04	Cost includes material and labor to
	Install	L.F.	1.13	4.99		6.12	install 4" x 4" treated wood post by
	Demolish and Install	L.F.	1.13	5.76	.27	7.16	hand in normal soil conditions.
	Reinstall	L.F.		3.99		3.99	
	Minimum Charge	Job		705		705	
4" x 6"							
	Demolish	L.F.		.77	.27	1.04	Cost includes material and labor to
	Install	L.F.	1.68	4.99		6.67	install 4" x 6" treated wood post by
	Demolish and Install	L.F.	1.68	5.76	.27	7.71	hand in normal soil conditions.
	Reinstall	L.F.		3.99		3.99	
	Minimum Charge	Job		705		705	
6" x 6"							
	Demolish	L.F.		.77	.27	1.04	Cost includes material and labor to
	Install	L.F.	2.50	4.99		7.49	install 6" x 6" treated wood post by
	Demolish and Install	L.F.	2.50	5.76	.27	8.53	hand in normal soil conditions.
	Reinstall	L.F.		3.99		3.99	
	Minimum Charge	Job		705		705	
Water Jet							
	Demolish	Ea.		88.50		88.50	Includes material, labor and
	Install	Ea.	66	685		751	equipment to water jet a 6" x 6" wood
	Demolish and Install	Ea.	66	773.50		839.50	post under an existing building. Cost
	Reinstall	Ea.		683.89		683.89	may vary depending upon location
	Minimum Charge	Job		600		600	and access.
Shim							
	Install	Ea.	3.67	70.50		74.17	Includes labor and material to trim or
	Minimum Charge	Job		705		705	readjust existing foundation posts
							under an existing building. Access of
							2 - 4 foot assumed.
Cross-bracing							
Treated 2" x 6"							
	Demolish *	L.F.		.98		.98	Cost includes material and labor to
	Install	L.F.	.68	5.65		6.33	install 2" x 6" lumber for cross-bracing
	Demolish and Install	L.F.	.68	6.63		7.31	of foundation piling or posts.
	Reinstall	L.F.		4.54		4.54	
	Clean	S.F.		.37		.37	
	Paint	L.F.	.37	1.33		1.70	
	Minimum Charge	Job		705		705	
Treated 2" x 8"							
	Demolish	L.F.		.98		.98	Cost includes material and labor to
	Install	L.F.	1.05	5.85		6.90	install 2" x 8" lumber for cross-bracing
	Demolish and Install	L.F.	1.05	6.83		7.88	of foundation piling or posts.
	Reinstall	L.F.		4.69		4.69	
	Clean	S.F.		.37		.37	
	Paint	L.F.	.50	1.39		1.89	
	Minimum Charge	Job		705		705	
Treated 2" x 10"							
	Demolish	L.F.		1.01		1.01	Cost includes material and labor to
	Install	L.F.	1.42	6.05		7.47	install 2" x 10" lumber for
	Demolish and Install	L.F.	1.42	7.06		8.48	cross-bracing of foundation piling or
	Reinstall	L.F.		4.85		4.85	posts.
	Clean	S.F.		.37		.37	
	Paint	L.F.	.61	1.41		2.02	
	Minimum Charge	Job		705		705	

Foundation

Foundation Post

	Unit	Material	Labor	Equip.	Total	Specification
Treated 2" x 12"						
Demolish	L.F.		1.21		1.21	Cost includes material and labor to
Install	L.F.	1.87	6.30		8.17	install 2" x 12" lumber for
Demolish and Install	L.F.	1.87	7.51		9.38	cross-bracing of foundation piling or
Reinstall	L.F.		5.02		5.02	posts.
Clean	S.F.		.37		.37	
Paint	L.F.	.72	1.44		2.16	
Minimum Charge	Job		705		705	

Concrete Footing

	Unit	Material	Labor	Equip.	Total	Specification
Continuous						
12" w x 6" d						
Demolish	L.F.		1.45	1.18	2.63	Includes material and labor to install
Install	L.F.	4.04	3.32	.02	7.38	continuous reinforced concrete footing
Demolish and Install	L.F.	4.04	4.77	1.20	10.01	poured by chute cast against earth
Minimum Charge	Job		805		805	including reinforcing, forming and
						finishing.
12" w x 12" d						
Demolish	L.F.		2.79	2.26	5.05	Includes material and labor to install
Install	L.F.	8.65	6.65	.03	15.33	continuous reinforced concrete footing
Demolish and Install	L.F.	8.65	9.44	2.29	20.38	poured by chute cast against earth
Minimum Charge	Job		805		805	including reinforcing, forming and
						finishing.
18" w x 10" d						
Demolish	L.F.		3.63	2.94	6.57	Includes material and labor to install
Install	L.F.	8.10	8.20	.04	16.34	continuous reinforced concrete footing
Demolish and Install	L.F.	8.10	11.83	2.98	22.91	poured by chute cast against earth
Minimum Charge	Job		805		805	including reinforcing, forming and
						finishing.
24" w x 24" d						
Demolish	L.F.		6.05	4.90	10.95	Includes material and labor to install
Install	L.F.	24	26.50	.13	50.63	continuous reinforced concrete footing
Demolish and Install	L.F.	24	32.55	5.03	61.58	poured by chute cast against earth
Minimum Charge	Job		805		805	including reinforcing, forming and
						finishing.
Stem Wall						
Single Story						
Demolish	L.F.		13.45	10.90	24.35	Includes material and labor to install
Install	L.F.	20	71	57.50	148.50	stem wall 24" above and 18" below
Demolish and Install	L.F.	20	84.45	68.40	172.85	grade for a single story structure.
Minimum Charge	Job		805		805	Includes 12" wide and 8" deep
						footing.
Two Story						
Demolish	L.F.		13.45	10.90	24.35	Includes material and labor to install
Install	L.F.	25	102	82.50	209.50	stem wall 24" above and 18" below
Demolish and Install	L.F.	25	115.45	93.40	233.85	grade typical for a two story structure,
Minimum Charge	Job		805		805	includes 18" wide and 10" deep
						footing.

Foundation

Concrete Slab

	Unit	Material	Labor	Equip.	Total	Specification
Reinforced						
4″						
Demolish	S.F.		2.51	.35	2.86	Cost includes material and labor to
Install	S.F.	2.11	.38		2.49	install 4″ reinforced concrete
Demolish and Install	S.F.	2.11	2.89	.35	5.35	slab-on-grade poured by chute
Clean	S.F.	.09	.33		.42	including forms, vapor barrier, wire
Paint	S.F.	.13	.75		.88	mesh, 3000 PSI concrete, float finish,
Minimum Charge	Job		183		183	and curing.
6″						
Demolish	S.F.		3.76	.53	4.29	Cost includes material and labor to
Install	S.F.	2.89	.57		3.46	install 6″ reinforced concrete
Demolish and Install	S.F.	2.89	4.33	.53	7.75	slab-on-grade poured by chute
Clean	S.F.	.09	.33		.42	including forms, vapor barrier, wire
Paint	S.F.	.13	.75		.88	mesh, 3000 PSI concrete, float finish,
Minimum Charge	Job		183		183	and curing.
8″						
Demolish	S.F.		6.15	.87	7.02	Cost includes material and labor to
Install	S.F.	3.75	.74	.01	4.50	install 8″ reinforced concrete
Demolish and Install	S.F.	3.75	6.89	.88	11.52	slab-on-grade poured by chute
Clean	S.F.	.09	.33		.42	including forms, vapor barrier, wire
Paint	S.F.	.13	.75		.88	mesh, 3000 PSI concrete, float finish,
Minimum Charge	Job		183		183	and curing.
Unreinforced						
4″						
Demolish	S.F.		1.99	.28	2.27	Cost includes material and labor to
Install	S.F.	1.42	.91	.01	2.34	install 4″ concrete slab-on-grade
Demolish and Install	S.F.	1.42	2.90	.29	4.61	poured by chute, including forms,
Clean	S.F.	.09	.33		.42	vapor barrier, 3000 PSI concrete, float
Paint	S.F.	.13	.75		.88	finish, and curing.
Minimum Charge	Job		183		183	
6″						
Demolish	S.F.		2.82	.40	3.22	Cost includes material and labor to
Install	S.F.	2.08	.93	.01	3.02	install 6″ concrete slab-on-grade
Demolish and Install	S.F.	2.08	3.75	.41	6.24	poured by chute, including forms,
Clean	S.F.	.09	.33		.42	vapor barrier, 3000 PSI concrete, float
Paint	S.F.	.13	.75		.88	finish, and curing.
Minimum Charge	Job		183		183	
8″						
Demolish	S.F.		4.64	.65	5.29	Cost includes material and labor to
Install	S.F.	2.85	.98	.01	3.84	install 8″ concrete slab-on-grade
Demolish and Install	S.F.	2.85	5.62	.66	9.13	poured by chute, including forms,
Clean	S.F.	.09	.33		.42	vapor barrier, 3000 PSI concrete, float
Paint	S.F.	.13	.75		.88	finish, and curing.
Minimum Charge	Job		183		183	
Lightweight						
Demolish	S.F.		.89	.21	1.10	Includes material and labor to install
Install	S.F.	1.80	2.75		4.55	lightweight concrete, 3″ - 4″ thick.
Demolish and Install	S.F.	1.80	3.64	.21	5.65	
Clean	S.F.	.09	.33		.42	
Paint	S.F.	.13	.75		.88	
Minimum Charge	Job		183		183	

Concrete Slab

Concrete Slab	Unit	Material	Labor	Equip.	Total	Specification
Gunite						Includes material and labor to install
Demolish	S.F.		1.10	.39	1.49	gunite on flat plane per inch of
Install	S.F.	.36	1.18	.11	1.65	thickness using 1″ as base price. No
Demolish and Install	S.F.	.36	2.28	.50	3.14	forms or reinforcing are included.
Clean	S.F.	.09	.33		.42	
Paint	S.F.	.13	.75		.88	
Minimum Charge	Job		1025		1025	
Epoxy Inject						Includes labor and material to inject
Install	L.F.	7	3.65		10.65	epoxy into cracks.
Minimum Charge	Job		183		183	
Pressure Grout						Includes labor, material and
Install	S.F.	3.17	2.71		5.88	equipment to install pressure grout
Minimum Charge	Job		183		183	under an existing building.
Scrape and Paint						Includes labor and materials to scrape
Paint	S.F.	.23	.87		1.10	and paint a concrete floor.
Minimum Charge	Job		173		173	
Vapor Barrier						Cost includes material and labor to
Install	S.F.	.03	.11		.14	install 4 mil polyethylene vapor barrier
Minimum Charge	Job		202		202	10′ wide sheets with 6″ overlaps.

Rough Framing

Beam / Girder		Unit	Material	Labor	Equip.	Total	Specification
Solid Wood Beam							
2" x 8"							
	Demolish	L.F.		.81		.81	Cost includes material and labor to
	Install	L.F.	.80	1.24		2.04	install 2" x 8" beam.
	Demolish and Install	L.F.	.80	2.05		2.85	
	Clean	L.F.	.18	.27		.45	
	Paint	L.F.	.12	1.87		1.99	
	Minimum Charge	Job		202		202	
2" x 10"							
	Demolish	L.F.		1		1	Cost includes material and labor to
	Install	L.F.	1.22	1.35		2.57	install 2" x 10" beam.
	Demolish and Install	L.F.	1.22	2.35		3.57	
	Clean	L.F.	.21	.32		.53	
	Paint	L.F.	.18	1.15		1.33	
	Minimum Charge	Job		202		202	
2" x 12"							
	Demolish	L.F.		1.21		1.21	Cost includes material and labor to
	Install	L.F.	1.50	1.47		2.97	install 2" x 12" beam.
	Demolish and Install	L.F.	1.50	2.68		4.18	
	Clean	L.F.	.23	.37		.60	
	Paint	L.F.	.19	2.77		2.96	
	Minimum Charge	Job		202		202	
4" x 8"							
	Demolish	L.F.		2.49		2.49	Cost includes material and labor to
	Install	L.F.	3.28	1.83	.72	5.83	install 4" x 8" beam.
	Demolish and Install	L.F.	3.28	4.32	.72	8.32	
	Clean	L.F.	.21	.32		.53	
	Paint	L.F.	.18	1.15		1.33	
	Minimum Charge	Job		202		202	
4" x 10"							
	Demolish	L.F.		3.11		3.11	Cost includes material and labor to
	Install	L.F.	4.17	1.92	.76	6.85	install 4" x 10" beam.
	Demolish and Install	L.F.	4.17	5.03	.76	9.96	
	Clean	L.F.	.23	.37		.60	
	Paint	L.F.	.20	1.35		1.55	
	Minimum Charge	Job		202		202	
4" x 12"							
	Demolish	L.F.		3.74		3.74	Cost includes material and labor to
	Install	L.F.	6.05	2.03	.80	8.88	install 4" x 12" beam.
	Demolish and Install	L.F.	6.05	5.77	.80	12.62	
	Clean	L.F.	.28	.43		.71	
	Paint	L.F.	.19	2.77		2.96	
	Minimum Charge	Job		202		202	

Rough Frame / Structure

Beam / Girder		Unit	Material	Labor	Equip.	Total	Specification
6" x 8"							
	Demolish	L.F.		3.74		3.74	Cost includes material and labor to
	Install	L.F.	5.30	3.48	1.37	10.15	install 6" x 8" beam.
	Demolish and Install	L.F.	5.30	7.22	1.37	13.89	
	Clean	L.F.	.23	.37		.60	
	Paint	L.F.	.20	1.35		1.55	
	Minimum Charge	Job		202		202	
6" x 10"							
	Demolish	L.F.		4.67		4.67	Cost includes material and labor to
	Install	L.F.	3.67	1.61		5.28	install 6" x 10" triple beam.
	Demolish and Install	L.F.	3.67	6.28		9.95	
	Clean	L.F.	.28	.43		.71	
	Paint	L.F.	.23	1.54		1.77	
	Minimum Charge	Job		202		202	
6" x 12"							
	Demolish	L.F.		5.55		5.55	Cost includes material and labor to
	Install	L.F.	4.49	1.70		6.19	install 6" x 12" triple beam.
	Demolish and Install	L.F.	4.49	7.25		11.74	
	Clean	L.F.	.31	.48		.79	
	Paint	L.F.	.25	1.73		1.98	
	Minimum Charge	Job		202		202	
Steel I-type							
W8 x 31							
	Demolish	L.F.		8.65	3.66	12.31	Includes material and labor to install
	Install	L.F.	42.50	2.71	1.65	46.86	W shaped steel beam / girder.
	Demolish and Install	L.F.	42.50	11.36	5.31	59.17	
	Minimum Charge	Job		495		495	
W8 x 48							
	Demolish	L.F.		8.65	3.66	12.31	Includes material and labor to install
	Install	L.F.	65.50	2.84	1.73	70.07	W shaped steel beam / girder.
	Demolish and Install	L.F.	65.50	11.49	5.39	82.38	
	Minimum Charge	Job		495		495	
W8 x 67							
	Demolish	L.F.		8.65	3.66	12.31	Includes material and labor to install
	Install	L.F.	91.50	2.98	1.81	96.29	W shaped steel beam / girder.
	Demolish and Install	L.F.	91.50	11.63	5.47	108.60	
	Minimum Charge	Job		495		495	
W10 x 45							
	Demolish	L.F.		8.65	3.66	12.31	Includes material and labor to install
	Install	L.F.	61	2.84	1.73	65.57	W shaped steel beam / girder.
	Demolish and Install	L.F.	61	11.49	5.39	77.88	
	Minimum Charge	Job		495		495	
W10 x 68							
	Demolish	L.F.		8.65	3.66	12.31	Includes material and labor to install
	Install	L.F.	92.50	2.98	1.81	97.29	W shaped steel beam / girder.
	Demolish and Install	L.F.	92.50	11.63	5.47	109.60	
	Minimum Charge	Job		495		495	
W12 x 50							
	Demolish	L.F.		8.65	3.66	12.31	Includes material and labor to install
	Install	L.F.	68	2.84	1.73	72.57	W shaped steel beam / girder.
	Demolish and Install	L.F.	68	11.49	5.39	84.88	
	Minimum Charge	Job		495		495	
W12 x 87							
	Demolish	L.F.		12.70	5.40	18.10	Includes material and labor to install
	Install	L.F.	119	2.98	1.81	123.79	W shaped steel beam / girder.
	Demolish and Install	L.F.	119	15.68	7.21	141.89	
	Minimum Charge	Job		495		495	

Rough Frame / Structure

Beam / Girder

Beam / Girder		Unit	Material	Labor	Equip.	Total	Specification
W12 x 120							
	Demolish	L.F.		12.70	5.40	18.10	Includes material and labor to install
	Install	L.F.	164	3.05	1.86	168.91	W shaped steel beam / girder.
	Demolish and Install	L.F.	164	15.75	7.26	187.01	
	Minimum Charge	Job		495		495	
W14 x 74							
	Demolish	L.F.		12.70	5.40	18.10	Includes material and labor to install
	Install	L.F.	101	2.98	1.81	105.79	W shaped steel beam / girder.
	Demolish and Install	L.F.	101	15.68	7.21	123.89	
	Minimum Charge	Job		495		495	
W14 x 120							
	Demolish	L.F.		12.70	5.40	18.10	Includes material and labor to install
	Install	L.F.	164	3.05	1.86	168.91	W shaped steel beam / girder.
	Demolish and Install	L.F.	164	15.75	7.26	187.01	
	Minimum Charge	Job		495		495	

Column

Column		Unit	Material	Labor	Equip.	Total	Specification
Concrete							
Small Diameter							
	Demolish	L.F.		14.10	1.99	16.09	Includes material and labor to install
	Install	L.F.	71	12.90	2.48	86.38	small diameter concrete column.
	Demolish and Install	L.F.	71	27	4.47	102.47	
	Minimum Charge	Job		645	124	769	
Large Diameter							
	Demolish	L.F.		42.50	5.95	48.45	Includes material and labor to install
	Install	L.F.	274	15.20	2.92	292.12	large diameter concrete column.
	Demolish and Install	L.F.	274	57.70	8.87	340.57	
	Minimum Charge	Job		645	124	769	

Floor Framing System

Floor Framing System		Unit	Material	Labor	Equip.	Total	Specification
12″ O.C.							
2″ x 6″ Joists							
	Demolish	S.F.		.69		.69	Cost includes material and labor to
	Install	S.F.	.68	.64		1.32	install 2″ x 6″ joists, 12″ O.C.
	Demolish and Install	S.F.	.68	1.33		2.01	including box or band joist. Blocking
	Reinstall	S.F.		.52		.52	or bridging not included.
	Minimum Charge	Job		202		202	
2″ x 8″ Joists							
	Demolish	S.F.		.71		.71	Cost includes material and labor to
	Install	S.F.	.94	.74		1.68	install 2″ x 8″ joists, 12″ O.C.
	Demolish and Install	S.F.	.94	1.45		2.39	including box or band joist. Blocking
	Reinstall	S.F.		.59		.59	or bridging not included.
	Minimum Charge	Job		202		202	
2″ x 10″ Joists							
	Demolish	S.F.		.73		.73	Cost includes material and labor to
	Install	S.F.	1.43	.90		2.33	install 2″ x 10″ joists, 12″ O.C.
	Demolish and Install	S.F.	1.43	1.63		3.06	including box or band joist. Blocking
	Reinstall	S.F.		.72		.72	or bridging not included.
	Minimum Charge	Job		202		202	

Rough Frame / Structure

Floor Framing System

		Unit	Material	Labor	Equip.	Total	Specification
2" x 12" Joists							
	Demolish	S.F.		.75		.75	Cost includes material and labor to
	Install	S.F.	1.75	.92		2.67	install 2" x 12" joists, 12" O.C.
	Demolish and Install	S.F.	1.75	1.67		3.42	including box or band joist. Blocking
	Reinstall	S.F.		.74		.74	or bridging not included.
	Minimum Charge	Job		202		202	
Block / Bridge							
	Demolish	Ea.		1.04		1.04	Includes material and labor to install
	Install	Ea.	1.64	2.27		3.91	set of cross bridging or per block of
	Demolish and Install	Ea.	1.64	3.31		4.95	solid bridging for 2" x 10" joists cut to
	Minimum Charge	Job		202		202	size on site.
16" O.C.							
2" x 6" Joists							
	Demolish	S.F.		.51		.51	Cost includes material and labor to
	Install	S.F.	.52	.48		1	install 2" x 6" joists including box or
	Demolish and Install	S.F.	.52	.99		1.51	band joist installed 16" O.C. Does not
	Reinstall	S.F.		.39		.39	include beams, blocking or bridging.
	Minimum Charge	Job		202		202	
2" x 8" Joists							
	Demolish	S.F.		.53		.53	Cost includes material and labor to
	Install	S.F.	.72	.55		1.27	install 2" x 8" joists including box or
	Demolish and Install	S.F.	.72	1.08		1.80	band joist installed 16" O.C. Does not
	Reinstall	S.F.		.44		.44	include beams, blocking or bridging.
	Minimum Charge	Job		202		202	
2" x 10" Joists							
	Demolish	S.F.		.55		.55	Cost includes material and labor to
	Install	S.F.	1.10	.67		1.77	install 2" x 10" joists including box or
	Demolish and Install	S.F.	1.10	1.22		2.32	band joist 16" O.C. Does not include
	Reinstall	S.F.		.54		.54	beams, blocking or bridging.
	Minimum Charge	Job		202		202	
2" x 12" Joists							
	Demolish	S.F.		.57		.57	Cost includes material and labor to
	Install	S.F.	1.34	.69		2.03	install 2" x 12" joists including box or
	Demolish and Install	S.F.	1.34	1.26		2.60	band joist installed 16" O.C. Does not
	Reinstall	S.F.		.55		.55	include beams, blocking or bridging.
	Minimum Charge	Job		202		202	
Block / Bridge							
	Demolish	Ea.		1.04		1.04	Includes material and labor to install
	Install	Ea.	1.64	2.27		3.91	set of cross bridging or per block of
	Demolish and Install	Ea.	1.64	3.31		4.95	solid bridging for 2" x 10" joists cut to
	Minimum Charge	Job		202		202	size on site.
24" O.C.							
2" x 6" Joists							
	Demolish	S.F.		.34		.34	Cost includes material and labor to
	Install	S.F.	.37	.32		.69	install 2" x 6" joists including box or
	Demolish and Install	S.F.	.37	.66		1.03	band joist installed 24" O.C. Does not
	Reinstall	S.F.		.26		.26	include beams, blocking or bridging.
	Minimum Charge	Job		202		202	
2" x 8" Joists							
	Demolish	S.F.		.35		.35	Cost includes material and labor to
	Install	S.F.	.51	.37		.88	install 2" x 8" joists including box or
	Demolish and Install	S.F.	.51	.72		1.23	band joist installed 24" O.C. Does not
	Reinstall	S.F.		.29		.29	include beams, blocking or bridging.
	Minimum Charge	Job		202		202	

Floor Framing System		Unit	Material	Labor	Equip.	Total	Specification
2″ x 10″ Joists							Cost includes material and labor to
	Demolish	S.F.		.37		.37	install 2″ x 10″ joists including box or
	Install	S.F.	.78	.45		1.23	band joist installed 24″ O.C. Does not
	Demolish and Install	S.F.	.78	.82		1.60	include beams, blocking or bridging.
	Reinstall	S.F.		.36		.36	
	Minimum Charge	Job		202		202	
2″ x 12″ Joists							Cost includes material and labor to
	Demolish	S.F.		.38		.38	install 2″ x 12″ joists including box or
	Install	S.F.	.96	.46		1.42	band joist installed 24″ O.C. Does not
	Demolish and Install	S.F.	.96	.84		1.80	include beams, blocking or bridging.
	Reinstall	S.F.		.37		.37	
	Minimum Charge	Job		202		202	
Block / Bridge							Includes material and labor to install
	Demolish	Ea.		1.04		1.04	set of cross bridging or per block of
	Install	Ea.	1.64	2.27		3.91	solid bridging for 2″ x 10″ joists cut to
	Demolish and Install	Ea.	1.64	3.31		4.95	size on site.
	Minimum Charge	Job		202		202	
Engineered Lumber, Joist							
9-1/2″							Includes material and labor to install
	Demolish	S.F.		.55		.55	engineered lumber truss / joists per
	Install	S.F.	1.53	.40		1.93	S.F. of floor area based on joists 16″
	Demolish and Install	S.F.	1.53	.95		2.48	O.C. Beams, supports and bridging
	Reinstall	S.F.		.32		.32	are not included.
	Minimum Charge	Job		202		202	
11-7/8″							Includes material and labor to install
	Demolish	S.F.		.57		.57	engineered lumber truss / joists per
	Install	S.F.	1.72	.41		2.13	S.F. of floor area based on joists 16″
	Demolish and Install	S.F.	1.72	.98		2.70	O.C. Beams, supports and bridging
	Reinstall	S.F.		.33		.33	are not included.
	Minimum Charge	Job		202		202	
14″							Includes material and labor to install
	Demolish	S.F.		.59		.59	engineered lumber truss / joists per
	Install	S.F.	2.38	.44		2.82	S.F. of floor area based on joists 16″
	Demolish and Install	S.F.	2.38	1.03		3.41	O.C. Beams, supports and bridging
	Reinstall	S.F.		.35		.35	are not included.
	Minimum Charge	Job		202		202	
16″							Includes material and labor to install
	Demolish	S.F.		.61		.61	engineered lumber truss / joists per
	Install	S.F.	2.94	.47		3.41	S.F. of floor area based on joists 16″
	Demolish and Install	S.F.	2.94	1.08		4.02	O.C. Beams, supports and bridging
	Reinstall	S.F.		.37		.37	are not included.
	Minimum Charge	Job		202		202	
Block / Bridge							Includes material and labor to install
	Demolish	Pr.		1.04		1.04	set of steel, one-nail type cross
	Install	Pr.	2.04	2.99		5.03	bridging for trusses placed 16″ O.C.
	Demolish and Install	Pr.	2.04	4.03		6.07	
	Minimum Charge	Job		202		202	
Block / Bridge							
2″ x 6″							Includes material and labor to install
	Demolish	Ea.		1.04		1.04	set of cross bridging or per block of
	Install	Ea.	.78	1.82		2.60	solid bridging for 2″ x 6″ joists cut to
	Demolish and Install	Ea.	.78	2.86		3.64	size on site.
	Minimum Charge	Job		202		202	

Floor Framing System		Unit	Material	Labor	Equip.	Total	Specification
2″ x 8″							
	Demolish	Ea.		1.04		1.04	Includes material and labor to install
	Install	Ea.	1.07	2.02		3.09	set of cross bridging or per block of
	Demolish and Install	Ea.	1.07	3.06		4.13	solid bridging for 2″ x 8″ joists cut to
	Minimum Charge	Job		202		202	size on site.
2″ x 10″							
	Demolish	Ea.		1.04		1.04	Includes material and labor to install
	Install	Ea.	1.64	2.27		3.91	set of cross bridging or per block of
	Demolish and Install	Ea.	1.64	3.31		4.95	solid bridging for 2″ x 10″ joists cut to
	Minimum Charge	Job		202		202	size on site.
2″ x 12″							
	Demolish	Ea.		1.04		1.04	Includes material and labor to install
	Install	Ea.	2	2.67		4.67	set of cross bridging or per block of
	Demolish and Install	Ea.	2	3.71		5.71	solid bridging for 2″ x 12″ joists cut to
	Minimum Charge	Job		202		202	size on site.
Ledger Strips							
1″ x 2″							
	Demolish	L.F.		.28		.28	Cost includes material and labor to
	Install	L.F.	.28	1.17		1.45	install 1″ x 2″ ledger strip nailed to the
	Demolish and Install	L.F.	.28	1.45		1.73	face of studs, beams or joist.
	Minimum Charge	Job		202		202	
1″ x 3″							
	Demolish	L.F.		.28		.28	Includes material and labor to install
	Install	L.F.	.58	1.35		1.93	up to 1″ x 4″ ledger strip nailed to the
	Demolish and Install	L.F.	.58	1.63		2.21	face of studs, beams or joist.
	Minimum Charge	Job		202		202	
1″ x 4″							
	Demolish	L.F.		.28		.28	Includes material and labor to install
	Install	L.F.	.58	1.35		1.93	up to 1″ x 4″ ledger strip nailed to the
	Demolish and Install	L.F.	.58	1.63		2.21	face of studs, beams or joist.
	Minimum Charge	Job		202		202	
2″ x 2″							
	Demolish	L.F.		.30		.30	Cost includes material and labor to
	Install	L.F.	.36	1.22		1.58	install 2″ x 2″ ledger strip nailed to the
	Demolish and Install	L.F.	.36	1.52		1.88	face of studs, beams or joist.
	Minimum Charge	Job		202		202	
2″ x 4″							
	Demolish	L.F.		.33		.33	Cost includes material and labor to
	Install	L.F.	.36	1.61		1.97	install 2″ x 4″ ledger strip nailed to the
	Demolish and Install	L.F.	.36	1.94		2.30	face of studs, beams or joist.
	Reinstall	L.F.		1.29		1.29	
	Minimum Charge	Job		202		202	
Ledger Boards							
2″ x 6″							
	Demolish	L.F.		.33		.33	Cost includes material and labor to
	Install	L.F.	4.57	2.52		7.09	install 2″ x 6″ ledger board fastened to
	Demolish and Install	L.F.	4.57	2.85		7.42	a wall, joists or studs.
	Reinstall	L.F.		2.02		2.02	
	Minimum Charge	Job		202		202	
4″ x 6″							
	Demolish	L.F.		.55		.55	Cost includes material and labor to
	Install	L.F.	7.80	2.52		10.32	install 4″ x 6″ ledger board fastened to
	Demolish and Install	L.F.	7.80	3.07		10.87	a wall, joists or studs.
	Reinstall	L.F.		2.02		2.02	
	Minimum Charge	Job		202		202	

Rough Frame / Structure

Floor Framing System

	Unit	Material	Labor	Equip.	Total	Specification
4″ x 8″						
Demolish	L.F.		.74		.74	Cost includes material and labor to
Install	L.F.	8.55	2.52		11.07	install 4″ x 8″ ledger board fastened to
Demolish and Install	L.F.	8.55	3.26		11.81	a wall, joists or studs.
Reinstall	L.F.		2.02		2.02	
Minimum Charge	Job		202		202	
Sill Plate Per L.F.						
2″ x 4″						
Demolish	L.F.		.28		.28	Cost includes material and labor to
Install	L.F.	.40	1.47		1.87	install 2″ x 4″ pressure treated lumber,
Demolish and Install	L.F.	.40	1.75		2.15	drilled and installed on foundation
Reinstall	L.F.		1.17		1.17	bolts 48″ O.C. Bolts, nuts and washers
Minimum Charge	Job		202		202	are not included.
2″ x 6″						
Demolish	L.F.		.43		.43	Cost includes material and labor to
Install	L.F.	.68	1.61		2.29	install 2″ x 6″ pressure treated lumber,
Demolish and Install	L.F.	.68	2.04		2.72	drilled and installed on foundation
Reinstall	L.F.		1.29		1.29	bolts 48″ O.C. Bolts, nuts and washers
Minimum Charge	Job		202		202	not included.
2″ x 8″						
Demolish	L.F.		.57		.57	Cost includes material and labor to
Install	L.F.	1.05	1.79		2.84	install 2″ x 8″ pressure treated lumber,
Demolish and Install	L.F.	1.05	2.36		3.41	drilled and installed on foundation
Reinstall	L.F.		1.44		1.44	bolts 48″ O.C. Bolts, nuts and washers
Minimum Charge	Job		202		202	not included.
Earthquake Strapping						
Install	Ea.	2.99	2.52		5.51	Includes labor and material to replace
Minimum Charge	Job		202		202	an earthquake strap.

Subflooring

	Unit	Material	Labor	Equip.	Total	Specification
Plywood						
1/2″						
Demolish	S.F.		.87		.87	Cost includes material and labor to
Install	SF Flr.	.48	.43		.91	install 1/2″ plywood subfloor, CD
Demolish and Install	SF Flr.	.48	1.30		1.78	standard interior grade, plugged and
Minimum Charge	Job		202		202	touch sanded.
5/8″						
Demolish	S.F.		.87		.87	Cost includes material and labor to
Install	SF Flr.	.59	.48		1.07	install 5/8″ plywood subfloor, CD
Demolish and Install	SF Flr.	.59	1.35		1.94	standard interior grade, plugged and
Reinstall	SF Flr.		.39		.39	touch sanded.
Minimum Charge	Job		202		202	
3/4″						
Demolish	S.F.		.89		.89	Cost includes material and labor to
Install	SF Flr.	.69	.52		1.21	install 3/4″ plywood subfloor, CD
Demolish and Install	SF Flr.	.69	1.41		2.10	standard interior grade, plugged and
Reinstall	SF Flr.		.42		.42	touch sanded.
Minimum Charge	Job		202		202	

Rough Frame / Structure

Subflooring		Unit	Material	Labor	Equip.	Total	Specification
Particle Board							
1/2″							
	Demolish	S.F.		.43		.43	Cost includes material and labor to
	Install	SF Flr.	.40	.54		.94	install 1/2″ particle board subfloor.
	Demolish and Install	SF Flr.	.40	.97		1.37	
	Minimum Charge	Job		202		202	
5/8″							
	Demolish	S.F.		.44		.44	Cost includes material and labor to
	Install	SF Flr.	.51	.59		1.10	install 5/8″ particle board subfloor.
	Demolish and Install	SF Flr.	.51	1.03		1.54	
	Minimum Charge	Job		202		202	
3/4″							
	Demolish	S.F.		.44		.44	Cost includes material and labor to
	Install	SF Flr.	.72	.65		1.37	install 3/4″ particle board subfloor.
	Demolish and Install	SF Flr.	.72	1.09		1.81	
	Minimum Charge	Job		202		202	
Plank Board							
	Demolish	S.F.		1.38		1.38	Cost includes material and labor to
	Install	SF Flr.	1.62	.90		2.52	install 1″ x 6″ standard grade plank
	Demolish and Install	SF Flr.	1.62	2.28		3.90	flooring.
	Reinstall	SF Flr.		.90		.90	
	Minimum Charge	Job		202		202	
Felt Underlay							
	Demolish	S.F.		.08		.08	Includes material and labor to install
	Install	S.F.	.07	.11		.18	#15 felt building paper.
	Demolish and Install	S.F.	.07	.19		.26	
	Minimum Charge	Job		202		202	
Prep (for flooring)							
	Install	S.F.		.34		.34	Preparation of subflooring for
	Minimum Charge	Job		181		181	installation of new finished flooring. Cost reflects average time to prep area.

Wall Framing System		Unit	Material	Labor	Equip.	Total	Specification
2″ x 4″							
8′ High							
	Demolish	L.F.		4.43		4.43	Cost includes material and labor to
	Install	L.F.	3.67	4.75		8.42	install 2″ x 4″ x 8′ high wall system,
	Demolish and Install	L.F.	3.67	9.18		12.85	including studs, treated bottom plate,
	Reinstall	L.F.		3.80		3.80	double top plate and one row of fire
	Minimum Charge	Job		202		202	blocking.
9′ High							
	Demolish	L.F.		4.96		4.96	Cost includes material and labor to
	Install	L.F.	3.94	4.75		8.69	install 2″ x 4″ x 9′ wall system
	Demolish and Install	L.F.	3.94	9.71		13.65	including studs, treated bottom plate,
	Reinstall	L.F.		3.80		3.80	double top plate and one row of fire
	Minimum Charge	Job		202		202	blocking.
10′ High							
	Demolish	L.F.		5.55		5.55	Cost includes material and labor to
	Install	L.F.	4.21	4.75		8.96	install 2″ x 4″ x 10′ wall system
	Demolish and Install	L.F.	4.21	10.30		14.51	including studs, treated bottom plate,
	Reinstall	L.F.		3.80		3.80	double top plate and one row of fire
	Minimum Charge	Job		202		202	blocking.

Rough Frame / Structure

Wall Framing System	Unit	Material	Labor	Equip.	Total	Specification
12' High						
Demolish	L.F.		6.65		6.65	Cost includes material and labor to
Install	L.F.	4.76	5.75		10.51	install 2" x 4" x 12' wall system
Demolish and Install	L.F.	4.76	12.40		17.16	including studs, treated bottom plate,
Reinstall	L.F.		4.61		4.61	double top plate and one row of fire
Minimum Charge	Job		202		202	blocking.
2" x 6"						
8' High						
Demolish	L.F.		4.16		4.16	Cost includes material and labor to
Install	L.F.	5.90	8.80		14.70	install 2" x 6" x 8' wall system
Demolish and Install	L.F.	5.90	12.96		18.86	including studs, treated bottom plate,
Reinstall	L.F.		7.03		7.03	double top plate and one row of fire
Minimum Charge	Job		202		202	blocking.
9' High						
Demolish	L.F.		4.68		4.68	Cost includes material and labor to
Install	L.F.	6.35	8.80		15.15	install 2" x 6" x 9' wall system
Demolish and Install	L.F.	6.35	13.48		19.83	including studs, treated bottom plate,
Reinstall	L.F.		7.03		7.03	double top plate and one row of fire
Minimum Charge	Job		202		202	blocking.
10' High						
Demolish	L.F.		5.10		5.10	Cost includes material and labor to
Install	L.F.	6.75	8.80		15.55	install 2" x 6" x 10' wall system
Demolish and Install	L.F.	6.75	13.90		20.65	including studs, treated bottom plate,
Reinstall	L.F.		7.03		7.03	double top plate and one row of fire
Minimum Charge	Job		202		202	blocking.
12' High						
Demolish	L.F.		6.05		6.05	Cost includes material and labor to
Install	L.F.	7.65	10.80		18.45	install 2" x 6" x 12' wall system
Demolish and Install	L.F.	7.65	16.85		24.50	including studs, treated bottom plate,
Reinstall	L.F.		8.65		8.65	double top plate and one row of fire
Minimum Charge	Job		202		202	blocking.
Fireblock						
2" x 4", 16" O.C. System						
Demolish	L.F.		.55		.55	Cost includes material and labor to
Install	L.F.	.36	1.35		1.71	install 2" x 4" fireblocks in wood frame
Demolish and Install	L.F.	.36	1.90		2.26	walls per L.F. of wall to be blocked.
Reinstall	L.F.		1.08		1.08	
Minimum Charge	Job		202		202	
2" x 4", 24" O.C. System						
Demolish	L.F.		.55		.55	Cost includes material and labor to
Install	L.F.	.36	1.35		1.71	install 2" x 4" fireblocks in wood frame
Demolish and Install	L.F.	.36	1.90		2.26	walls per L.F. of wall to be blocked.
Reinstall	L.F.		1.08		1.08	
Minimum Charge	Job		202		202	
2" x 6", 16" O.C. System						
Demolish	L.F.		.83		.83	Cost includes material and labor to
Install	L.F.	.58	1.35		1.93	install 2" x 6" fireblocks in wood frame
Demolish and Install	L.F.	.58	2.18		2.76	walls per L.F. of wall to be blocked.
Reinstall	L.F.		1.08		1.08	
Minimum Charge	Job		202		202	
2" x 6", 24" O.C. System						
Demolish	L.F.		.83		.83	Cost includes material and labor to
Install	L.F.	.58	1.35		1.93	install 2" x 6" fireblocks in wood frame
Demolish and Install	L.F.	.58	2.18		2.76	walls per L.F. of wall to be blocked.
Reinstall	L.F.		1.08		1.08	
Minimum Charge	Job		202		202	

Rough Frame / Structure

Wall Framing System	Unit	Material	Labor	Equip.	Total	Specification
Bracing						
1" x 3"						
Demolish	L.F.		.32		.32	Cost includes material and labor to
Install	L.F.	.37	2.52		2.89	install 1" x 3" let-in bracing.
Demolish and Install	L.F.	.37	2.84		3.21	
Minimum Charge	Job		202		202	
1" x 4"						
Demolish	L.F.		.32		.32	Cost includes material and labor to
Install	L.F.	.58	2.52		3.10	install 1" x 4" let-in bracing.
Demolish and Install	L.F.	.58	2.84		3.42	
Minimum Charge	Job		202		202	
1" x 6"						
Demolish	L.F.		.32		.32	Cost includes material and labor to
Install	L.F.	.74	2.69		3.43	install 1" x 6" let-in bracing.
Demolish and Install	L.F.	.74	3.01		3.75	
Minimum Charge	Job		202		202	
2" x 3"						
Demolish	L.F.		.42		.42	Cost includes material and labor to
Install	L.F.	.36	2.69		3.05	install 2" x 3" let-in bracing.
Demolish and Install	L.F.	.36	3.11		3.47	
Reinstall	L.F.		2.15		2.15	
Minimum Charge	Job		202		202	
2" x 4"						
Demolish	L.F.		.42		.42	Cost includes material and labor to
Install	L.F.	.36	2.69		3.05	install 2" x 4" let-in bracing.
Demolish and Install	L.F.	.36	3.11		3.47	
Reinstall	L.F.		2.15		2.15	
Minimum Charge	Job		202		202	
2" x 6"						
Demolish	L.F.		.42		.42	Cost includes material and labor to
Install	L.F.	.58	2.88		3.46	install 2" x 6" let-in bracing.
Demolish and Install	L.F.	.58	3.30		3.88	
Reinstall	L.F.		2.31		2.31	
Minimum Charge	Job		202		202	
2" x 8"						
Demolish	L.F.		.42		.42	Cost includes material and labor to
Install	L.F.	.80	2.88		3.68	install 2" x 8" let-in bracing.
Demolish and Install	L.F.	.80	3.30		4.10	
Reinstall	L.F.		2.31		2.31	
Minimum Charge	Job		202		202	
Earthquake Strapping						
Install	Ea.	2.99	2.52		5.51	Includes labor and material to replace
Minimum Charge	Job		202		202	an earthquake strap.
Hurricane Clips						
Install	Ea.	1.12	2.78		3.90	Includes labor and material to install a
Minimum Charge	Job		202		202	hurricane clip.
Stud						
2" x 4"						
Demolish	L.F.		.33		.33	Cost includes material and labor to
Install	L.F.	.36	.73		1.09	install 2" x 4" wall stud per L.F. of stud.
Demolish and Install	L.F.	.36	1.06		1.42	
Reinstall	L.F.		.59		.59	
Minimum Charge	Job		202		202	

Rough Frame / Structure

Wall Framing System		Unit	Material	Labor	Equip.	Total	Specification
2″ x 6″							
	Demolish	L.F.		.42		.42	Cost includes material and labor to
	Install	L.F.	.58	.81		1.39	install 2″ x 6″ stud per L.F. of stud.
	Demolish and Install	L.F.	.58	1.23		1.81	
	Reinstall	L.F.		.65		.65	
	Minimum Charge	Job		202		202	
Plates							
2″ x 4″							
	Demolish	L.F.		.30		.30	Cost includes material and labor to
	Install	L.F.	.36	1.01		1.37	install 2″ x 4″ plate per L.F. of plate.
	Demolish and Install	L.F.	.36	1.31		1.67	
	Reinstall	L.F.		.81		.81	
	Minimum Charge	Job		202		202	
2″ x 6″							
	Demolish	L.F.		.32		.32	Cost includes material and labor to
	Install	L.F.	.58	1.08		1.66	install 2″ x 6″ plate per L.F. of plate.
	Demolish and Install	L.F.	.58	1.40		1.98	
	Reinstall	L.F.		.86		.86	
	Minimum Charge	Job		202		202	
Headers							
2″ x 6″							
	Demolish	L.F.		.30		.30	Includes material and labor to install
	Install	L.F.	.58	2.24		2.82	header over wall openings and
	Demolish and Install	L.F.	.58	2.54		3.12	around floor, ceiling and roof
	Clean	L.F.	.02	.38		.40	openings or flush beam.
	Paint	L.F.	.09	1.39		1.48	
	Minimum Charge	Job		202		202	
2″ x 8″							
	Demolish	L.F.		.32		.32	Includes material and labor to install
	Install	L.F.	.80	2.37		3.17	header over wall openings and
	Demolish and Install	L.F.	.80	2.69		3.49	around floor, ceiling and roof
	Clean	L.F.	.03	.38		.41	openings or flush beam.
	Paint	L.F.	.12	1.87		1.99	
	Minimum Charge	Job		202		202	
2″ x 10″							
	Demolish	L.F.		.32		.32	Includes material and labor to install
	Install	L.F.	1.22	2.52		3.74	header over wall openings and
	Demolish and Install	L.F.	1.22	2.84		4.06	around floor, ceiling and roof
	Clean	L.F.	.04	.38		.42	openings or flush beam.
	Paint	L.F.	.15	2.31		2.46	
	Minimum Charge	Job		202		202	
2″ x 12″							
	Demolish	L.F.		.33		.33	Includes material and labor to install
	Install	L.F.	1.50	2.69		4.19	header over wall openings and
	Demolish and Install	L.F.	1.50	3.02		4.52	around floor, ceiling and roof
	Clean	L.F.	.06	.38		.44	openings or flush beam.
	Paint	L.F.	.19	2.77		2.96	
	Minimum Charge	Job		202		202	
4″ x 8″							
	Demolish	L.F.		.59		.59	Includes material and labor to install
	Install	L.F.	3.28	3.10		6.38	header over wall openings and
	Demolish and Install	L.F.	3.28	3.69		6.97	around floor, ceiling and roof
	Clean	L.F.	.03	.38		.41	openings or flush beam.
	Paint	L.F.	.12	1.87		1.99	
	Minimum Charge	Job		202		202	

Rough Frame / Structure

Wall Framing System	Unit	Material	Labor	Equip.	Total	Specification
4" x 10"						
Demolish	L.F.		.63		.63	Includes material and labor to install
Install	L.F.	4.17	3.36		7.53	header over wall openings and
Demolish and Install	L.F.	4.17	3.99		8.16	around floor, ceiling and roof
Clean	L.F.	.04	.38		.42	openings or flush beam.
Paint	L.F.	.15	2.31		2.46	
Minimum Charge	Job		202		202	
4" x 12"						
Demolish	L.F.		.66		.66	Includes material and labor to install
Install	L.F.	6.05	4.25		10.30	header over wall openings and
Demolish and Install	L.F.	6.05	4.91		10.96	around floor, ceiling and roof
Clean	L.F.	.06	.38		.44	openings or flush beam.
Paint	L.F.	.19	2.77		2.96	
Minimum Charge	Job		202		202	
6" x 8"						
Demolish	L.F.		.59		.59	Includes material and labor to install
Install	L.F.	5.30	2.24		7.54	header over wall openings and
Demolish and Install	L.F.	5.30	2.83		8.13	around floor, ceiling and roof
Clean	L.F.	.03	.38		.41	openings or flush beam.
Paint	L.F.	.12	1.87		1.99	
Minimum Charge	Job		202		202	
6" x 10"						
Demolish	L.F.		.63		.63	Includes material and labor to install
Install	L.F.	7.15	4.89		12.04	header over wall openings and
Demolish and Install	L.F.	7.15	5.52		12.67	around floor, ceiling and roof
Clean	L.F.	.04	.38		.42	openings or flush beam.
Paint	L.F.	.15	2.31		2.46	
Minimum Charge	Job		202		202	
6" x 12"						
Demolish	L.F.		.66		.66	Includes material and labor to install
Install	L.F.	11.15	5.75		16.90	header over wall openings and
Demolish and Install	L.F.	11.15	6.41		17.56	around floor, ceiling and roof
Clean	L.F.	.06	.38		.44	openings or flush beam.
Paint	L.F.	.19	.96		1.15	
Minimum Charge	Job		202		202	

Rough-in Opening	Unit	Material	Labor	Equip.	Total	Specification
Door w / 2" x 4" Lumber						
3' Wide						
Demolish	Ea.		10.40		10.40	Includes material and labor to install
Install	Ea.	15.40	12.60		28	header, double studs each side,
Demolish and Install	Ea.	15.40	23		38.40	cripples, blocking and nails, up to 3'
Reinstall	Ea.		10.09		10.09	opening in 2" x 4" stud wall 8' high.
Minimum Charge	Job		202		202	
4' Wide						
Demolish	Ea.		10.40		10.40	Includes material and labor to install
Install	Ea.	16.55	12.60		29.15	header, double studs each side,
Demolish and Install	Ea.	16.55	23		39.55	cripples, blocking and nails, up to 4'
Reinstall	Ea.		10.09		10.09	opening in 2" x 4" stud wall 8' high.
Minimum Charge	Job		202		202	
5' Wide						
Demolish	Ea.		10.40		10.40	Includes material and labor to install
Install	Ea.	20	12.60		32.60	header, double studs each side,
Demolish and Install	Ea.	20	23		43	cripples, blocking and nails, up to 5'
Reinstall	Ea.		10.09		10.09	opening in 2" x 4" stud wall 8' high.
Minimum Charge	Job		202		202	

Rough Frame / Structure

Rough-in Opening		Unit	Material	Labor	Equip.	Total	Specification
6' Wide							
	Demolish	Ea.		10.40		10.40	Includes material and labor to install
	Install	Ea.	21.50	12.60		34.10	header, double studs each side,
	Demolish and Install	Ea.	21.50	23		44.50	cripples, blocking and nails, up to 6'
	Reinstall	Ea.		10.09		10.09	opening in 2" x 4" stud wall 8' high.
	Minimum Charge	Job		202		202	
8' Wide							
	Demolish	Ea.		11.10		11.10	Includes material and labor to install
	Install	Ea.	32	13.45		45.45	header, double studs each side,
	Demolish and Install	Ea.	32	24.55		56.55	cripples, blocking and nails, up to 8'
	Reinstall	Ea.		10.76		10.76	opening in 2" x 4" stud wall 8' high.
	Minimum Charge	Job		202		202	
10' Wide							
	Demolish	Ea.		11.10		11.10	Includes material and labor to install
	Install	Ea.	42.50	13.45		55.95	header, double studs each side,
	Demolish and Install	Ea.	42.50	24.55		67.05	cripples, blocking and nails, up to 10'
	Reinstall	Ea.		10.76		10.76	opening in 2" x 4" stud wall 8' high.
	Minimum Charge	Job		202		202	
12' Wide							
	Demolish	Ea.		11.10		11.10	Includes material and labor to install
	Install	Ea.	57	13.45		70.45	header, double studs each side,
	Demolish and Install	Ea.	57	24.55		81.55	cripples, blocking and nails, up to 12'
	Reinstall	Ea.		10.76		10.76	opening in 2" x 4" stud wall 8' high.
	Minimum Charge	Job		202		202	
Door w / 2" x 6" Lumber							
3' Wide							
	Demolish	Ea.		10.40		10.40	Includes material and labor to install
	Install	Ea.	22.50	12.60		35.10	header, double studs each side,
	Demolish and Install	Ea.	22.50	23		45.50	cripples, blocking and nails, up to 3'
	Reinstall	Ea.		10.09		10.09	opening in 2" x 6" stud wall 8' high.
	Minimum Charge	Job		202		202	
4' Wide							
	Demolish	Ea.		10.40		10.40	Includes material and labor to install
	Install	Ea.	23.50	12.60		36.10	header, double studs each side,
	Demolish and Install	Ea.	23.50	23		46.50	cripples, blocking and nails, up to 4'
	Reinstall	Ea.		10.09		10.09	opening in 2" x 6" stud wall 8' high.
	Minimum Charge	Job		202		202	
5' Wide							
	Demolish	Ea.		10.40		10.40	Includes material and labor to install
	Install	Ea.	27	12.60		39.60	header, double studs each side,
	Demolish and Install	Ea.	27	23		50	cripples, blocking and nails up to 5'
	Reinstall	Ea.		10.09		10.09	opening in 2" x 6" stud wall 8' high.
	Minimum Charge	Job		202		202	
6' Wide							
	Demolish	Ea.		10.40		10.40	Includes material and labor to install
	Install	Ea.	28.50	12.60		41.10	header, double studs each side,
	Demolish and Install	Ea.	28.50	23		51.50	cripples, blocking and nails up to 6'
	Reinstall	Ea.		10.09		10.09	opening in 2" x 6" stud wall 8' high.
	Minimum Charge	Job		202		202	
8' Wide							
	Demolish	Ea.		11.10		11.10	Includes material and labor to install
	Install	Ea.	38.50	13.45		51.95	header, double studs each side,
	Demolish and Install	Ea.	38.50	24.55		63.05	cripples, blocking and nails up to 8'
	Reinstall	Ea.		10.76		10.76	opening in 2" x 6" stud wall 8' high.
	Minimum Charge	Job		202		202	
10' Wide							
	Demolish	Ea.		11.10		11.10	Includes material and labor to install
	Install	Ea.	49	13.45		62.45	header, double studs each side,
	Demolish and Install	Ea.	49	24.55		73.55	cripples, blocking and nails up to 10'
	Reinstall	Ea.		10.76		10.76	opening in 2" x 6" stud wall 8' high.
	Minimum Charge	Job		202		202	

Rough Frame / Structure

Rough-in Opening

Rough-in Opening	Unit	Material	Labor	Equip.	Total	Specification
12' Wide						
Demolish	Ea.		11.10		11.10	Includes material and labor to install
Install	Ea.	64.50	13.45		77.95	header, double studs each side,
Demolish and Install	Ea.	64.50	24.55		89.05	cripples, blocking and nails, up to 12'
Reinstall	Ea.		10.76		10.76	opening in 2" x 6" stud wall 8' high.
Minimum Charge	Job		202		202	

Rough-in Opening

Rough-in Opening	Unit	Material	Labor	Equip.	Total	Specification
Window w / 2" x 4" Lumber						
2' Wide						
Demolish	Ea.		13.85		13.85	Includes material and labor to install
Install	Ea.	16.15	16.80		32.95	header, double studs each side of
Demolish and Install	Ea.	16.15	30.65		46.80	opening, cripples, blocking, nails and
Reinstall	Ea.		13.45		13.45	sub-sills for opening up to 2' in a 2" x
Minimum Charge	Job		202		202	4" stud wall 8' high.
3' Wide						
Demolish	Ea.		13.85		13.85	Includes material and labor to install
Install	Ea.	19.05	16.80		35.85	header, double studs each side of
Demolish and Install	Ea.	19.05	30.65		49.70	opening, cripples, blocking, nails and
Reinstall	Ea.		13.45		13.45	sub-sills for opening up to 3' in a 2" x
Minimum Charge	Job		202		202	4" stud wall 8' high.
4' Wide						
Demolish	Ea.		13.85		13.85	Includes material and labor to install
Install	Ea.	21	16.80		37.80	header, double studs each side of
Demolish and Install	Ea.	21	30.65		51.65	opening, cripples, blocking, nails and
Reinstall	Ea.		13.45		13.45	sub-sills for opening up to 4' in a 2" x
Minimum Charge	Job		202		202	4" stud wall 8' high.
5' Wide						
Demolish	Ea.		13.85		13.85	Includes material and labor to install
Install	Ea.	24	16.80		40.80	header, double studs each side of
Demolish and Install	Ea.	24	30.65		54.65	opening, cripples, blocking, nails and
Reinstall	Ea.		13.45		13.45	sub-sills for opening up to 5' in a 2" x
Minimum Charge	Job		202		202	4" stud wall 8' high.
6' Wide						
Demolish	Ea.		13.85		13.85	Includes material and labor to install
Install	Ea.	27	16.80		43.80	header, double studs each side of
Demolish and Install	Ea.	27	30.65		57.65	opening, cripples, blocking, nails and
Reinstall	Ea.		13.45		13.45	sub-sills for opening up to 6' in a 2" x
Minimum Charge	Job		202		202	4" stud wall 8' high.
7' Wide						
Demolish	Ea.		13.85		13.85	Includes material and labor to install
Install	Ea.	36	16.80		52.80	header, double studs each side of
Demolish and Install	Ea.	36	30.65		66.65	opening, cripples, blocking, nails and
Reinstall	Ea.		13.45		13.45	sub-sills for opening up to 7' in a 2" x
Minimum Charge	Job		202		202	4" stud wall 8' high.
8' Wide						
Demolish	Ea.		15.10		15.10	Includes material and labor to install
Install	Ea.	39.50	18.35		57.85	header, double studs each side of
Demolish and Install	Ea.	39.50	33.45		72.95	opening, cripples, blocking, nails and
Reinstall	Ea.		14.68		14.68	sub-sills for opening up to 8' in a 2" x
Minimum Charge	Job		202		202	4" stud wall 8' high.

Rough Frame / Structure

Rough-in Opening		Unit	Material	Labor	Equip.	Total	Specification
10' Wide							
	Demolish	Ea.		15.10		15.10	Includes material and labor to install
	Install	Ea.	51	18.35		69.35	header, double studs each side of
	Demolish and Install	Ea.	51	33.45		84.45	opening, cripples, blocking, nails and
	Reinstall	Ea.		14.68		14.68	sub-sills for opening up to 10' in a 2"
	Minimum Charge	Job		202		202	x 4" stud wall 8' high.
12' Wide							
	Demolish	Ea.		15.10		15.10	Includes material and labor to install
	Install	Ea.	68	18.35		86.35	header, double studs each side of
	Demolish and Install	Ea.	68	33.45		101.45	opening, cripples, blocking, nails and
	Reinstall	Ea.		14.68		14.68	sub-sills for opening up to 12' in a 2"
	Minimum Charge	Job		202		202	x 4" stud wall 8' high.
Window w / 2" x 6" Lumber							
2' Wide							
	Demolish	Ea.		13.85		13.85	Includes material and labor to install
	Install	Ea.	25	16.80		41.80	header, double studs each side of
	Demolish and Install	Ea.	25	30.65		55.65	opening, cripples, blocking, nails and
	Reinstall	Ea.		13.45		13.45	sub-sills for opening up to 2' in a 2" x
	Minimum Charge	Job		202		202	6" stud wall 8' high.
3' Wide							
	Demolish	Ea.		13.85		13.85	Includes material and labor to install
	Install	Ea.	28	16.80		44.80	header, double studs each side of
	Demolish and Install	Ea.	28	30.65		58.65	opening, cripples, blocking, nails and
	Reinstall	Ea.		13.45		13.45	sub-sills for opening up to 3' in a 2" x
	Minimum Charge	Job		202		202	6" stud wall 8' high.
4' Wide							
	Demolish	Ea.		13.85		13.85	Includes material and labor to install
	Install	Ea.	30.50	16.80		47.30	header, double studs each side of
	Demolish and Install	Ea.	30.50	30.65		61.15	opening, cripples, blocking, nails and
	Reinstall	Ea.		13.45		13.45	sub-sills for opening up to 4' in a 2" x
	Minimum Charge	Job		202		202	6" stud wall 8' high.
5' Wide							
	Demolish	Ea.		13.85		13.85	Includes material and labor to install
	Install	Ea.	34	16.80		50.80	header, double studs each side of
	Demolish and Install	Ea.	34	30.65		64.65	opening, cripples, blocking, nails and
	Reinstall	Ea.		13.45		13.45	sub-sills for opening up to 5' in a 2" x
	Minimum Charge	Job		202		202	6" stud wall 8' high.
6' Wide							
	Demolish	Ea.		13.85		13.85	Includes material and labor to install
	Install	Ea.	37.50	16.80		54.30	header, double studs each side of
	Demolish and Install	Ea.	37.50	30.65		68.15	opening, cripples, blocking, nails and
	Reinstall	Ea.		13.45		13.45	sub-sills for opening up to 6' in a 2" x
	Minimum Charge	Job		202		202	6" stud wall 8' high.
7' Wide							
	Demolish	Ea.		13.85		13.85	Includes material and labor to install
	Install	Ea.	47	16.80		63.80	header, double studs each side of
	Demolish and Install	Ea.	47	30.65		77.65	opening, cripples, blocking, nails and
	Reinstall	Ea.		13.45		13.45	sub-sills for opening up to 7' in a 2" x
	Minimum Charge	Job		202		202	6" stud wall 8' high.

Rough Frame / Structure

Rough-in Opening

Rough-in Opening	Unit	Material	Labor	Equip.	Total	Specification
8' Wide						
Demolish	Ea.		15.10		15.10	Includes material and labor to install
Install	Ea.	51	18.35		69.35	header, double studs each side of
Demolish and Install	Ea.	51	33.45		84.45	opening, cripples, blocking, nails and
Reinstall	Ea.		14.68		14.68	sub-sills for opening up to 8' in a 2" x
Minimum Charge	Job		202		202	6" stud wall 8' high.
10' Wide						
Demolish	Ea.		15.10		15.10	Includes material and labor to install
Install	Ea.	63.50	18.35		81.85	header, double studs each side of
Demolish and Install	Ea.	63.50	33.45		96.95	opening, cripples, blocking, nails and
Reinstall	Ea.		14.68		14.68	sub-sills for opening up to 10' in a 2"
Minimum Charge	Job		202		202	x 6" stud wall 8' high.
12' Wide						
Demolish	Ea.		15.10		15.10	Includes material and labor to install
Install	Ea.	81.50	18.35		99.85	header, double studs each side of
Demolish and Install	Ea.	81.50	33.45		114.95	opening, cripples, blocking, nails and
Reinstall	Ea.		14.68		14.68	sub-sills for opening up to 12' in a 2"
Minimum Charge	Job		202		202	x 6" stud wall 8' high.

Glue-Laminated Beams

Glue-Laminated Beams	Unit	Material	Labor	Equip.	Total	Specification
3-1/2" x 6"						
Demolish	L.F.		2.49		2.49	Includes material and labor to install
Install	L.F.	5.65	3.04	1.20	9.89	glue-laminated wood beam.
Demolish and Install	L.F.	5.65	5.53	1.20	12.38	
Reinstall	L.F.		2.43	.96	3.39	
Clean	L.F.	.18	.37		.55	
Paint	L.F.	.35	1.02		1.37	
Minimum Charge	Job		202		202	
3-1/2" x 9"						
Demolish	L.F.		2.49		2.49	Includes material and labor to install
Install	L.F.	7.60	3.04	1.20	11.84	glue-laminated wood beam.
Demolish and Install	L.F.	7.60	5.53	1.20	14.33	
Reinstall	L.F.		2.43	.96	3.39	
Clean	L.F.	.23	.39		.62	
Paint	L.F.	.46	1.32		1.78	
Minimum Charge	Job		202		202	
3-1/2" x 12"						
Demolish	L.F.		3.74		3.74	Includes material and labor to install
Install	L.F.	10.10	3.04	1.20	14.34	glue-laminated wood beam.
Demolish and Install	L.F.	10.10	6.78	1.20	18.08	
Reinstall	L.F.		2.43	.96	3.39	
Clean	L.F.	.28	.40		.68	
Paint	L.F.	.57	1.65		2.22	
Minimum Charge	Job		202		202	
3-1/2" x 15"						
Demolish	L.F.		3.74		3.74	Includes material and labor to install
Install	L.F.	12.65	3.15	1.24	17.04	glue-laminated wood beam.
Demolish and Install	L.F.	12.65	6.89	1.24	20.78	
Reinstall	L.F.		2.52	.99	3.51	
Clean	L.F.	.33	.41		.74	
Paint	L.F.	.67	1.92		2.59	
Minimum Charge	Job		202		202	

Rough Frame / Structure

Glue-Laminated Beams		Unit	Material	Labor	Equip.	Total	Specification
3-1/2" x 18"							
	Demolish	L.F.		4.67		4.67	Includes material and labor to install
	Install	L.F.	17.05	3.15	1.24	21.44	glue-laminated wood beam.
	Demolish and Install	L.F.	17.05	7.82	1.24	26.11	
	Reinstall	L.F.		2.52	.99	3.51	
	Clean	L.F.	.39	.43		.82	
	Paint	L.F.	.79	2.23		3.02	
	Minimum Charge	Job		202		202	
5-1/8" x 6"							
	Demolish	L.F.		3.74		3.74	Includes material and labor to install
	Install	L.F.	8.30	3.04	1.20	12.54	glue-laminated wood beam.
	Demolish and Install	L.F.	8.30	6.78	1.20	16.28	
	Reinstall	L.F.		2.43	.96	3.39	
	Clean	L.F.	.19	.37		.56	
	Paint	L.F.	.39	1.12		1.51	
	Minimum Charge	Job		202		202	
5-1/8" x 9"							
	Demolish	L.F.		4.67		4.67	Includes material and labor to install
	Install	L.F.	12.50	3.04	1.20	16.74	glue-laminated wood beam.
	Demolish and Install	L.F.	12.50	7.71	1.20	21.41	
	Reinstall	L.F.		2.43	.96	3.39	
	Clean	L.F.	.24	.39		.63	
	Paint	L.F.	.50	1.43		1.93	
	Minimum Charge	Job		202		202	
5-1/8" x 12"							
	Demolish	L.F.		5.55		5.55	Includes material and labor to install
	Install	L.F.	16.60	3.04	1.20	20.84	glue-laminated wood beam.
	Demolish and Install	L.F.	16.60	8.59	1.20	26.39	
	Reinstall	L.F.		2.43	.96	3.39	
	Clean	L.F.	.30	.40		.70	
	Paint	L.F.	.61	1.73		2.34	
	Minimum Charge	Job		202		202	
5-1/8" x 18"							
	Demolish	L.F.		9.35		9.35	Includes material and labor to install
	Install	L.F.	25	3.15	1.24	29.39	glue-laminated wood beam.
	Demolish and Install	L.F.	25	12.50	1.24	38.74	
	Reinstall	L.F.		2.52	.99	3.51	
	Clean	L.F.	.40	.43		.83	
	Paint	L.F.	.70	2.34		3.04	
	Minimum Charge	Job		202		202	
6-3/4" x 12"							
	Demolish	L.F.		5.55		5.55	Includes material and labor to install
	Install	L.F.	22	3.15	1.24	26.39	glue-laminated wood beam.
	Demolish and Install	L.F.	22	8.70	1.24	31.94	
	Reinstall	L.F.		2.52	.99	3.51	
	Clean	L.F.	.33	.41		.74	
	Paint	L.F.	.67	1.92		2.59	
	Minimum Charge	Job		202		202	
6-3/4" x 15"							
	Demolish	L.F.		9.35		9.35	Includes material and labor to install
	Install	L.F.	27.50	3.15	1.24	31.89	glue-laminated wood beam.
	Demolish and Install	L.F.	27.50	12.50	1.24	41.24	
	Reinstall	L.F.		2.52	.99	3.51	
	Clean	L.F.	.39	.43		.82	
	Paint	L.F.	.79	2.23		3.02	
	Minimum Charge	Job		202		202	

Rough Frame / Structure

Glue-Laminated Beams

	Unit	Material	Labor	Equip.	Total	Specification
6-3/4″ x 18″						
Demolish	L.F.		9.35		9.35	Includes material and labor to install
Install	L.F.	33	3.26	1.29	37.55	glue-laminated wood beam.
Demolish and Install	L.F.	33	12.61	1.29	46.90	
Reinstall	L.F.		2.61	1.03	3.64	
Clean	L.F.	.43	.44		.87	
Paint	L.F.	.89	2.55		3.44	
Minimum Charge	Job		202		202	
Hardware						
5-1/4″ Glue-Lam Seat						
Install	Ea.	211	2.24		213.24	Includes labor and material to install
Minimum Charge	Job		202		202	beam hangers.
6-3/4″ Glue-Lam Seat						
Install	Ea.	217	2.24		219.24	Includes labor and material to install
Minimum Charge	Job		202		202	beam hangers.
Earthquake Strapping						
Install	Ea.	2.99	2.52		5.51	Includes labor and material to replace
Minimum Charge	Job		202		202	an earthquake strap.
Hurricane Clips						
Install	Ea.	1.12	2.78		3.90	Includes labor and material to install a
Minimum Charge	Job		202		202	hurricane clip.

Metal Stud Framing

	Unit	Material	Labor	Equip.	Total	Specification
16″ O.C. System						
4″, 16 Ga.						
Demolish	S.F.		1.22		1.22	Includes material and labor to install
Install	S.F.	1.13	1.24		2.37	load bearing cold rolled metal stud
Demolish and Install	S.F.	1.13	2.46		3.59	walls, to 10′ high, including studs, top
Reinstall	S.F.		.99		.99	and bottom track and screws.
Minimum Charge	Job		202		202	
6″, 16 Ga.						
Demolish	S.F.		1.22		1.22	Includes material and labor to install
Install	S.F.	1.41	1.26		2.67	load bearing cold rolled metal stud
Demolish and Install	S.F.	1.41	2.48		3.89	walls, to 10′ high, including studs, top
Reinstall	S.F.		1.01		1.01	and bottom track and screws.
Minimum Charge	Job		202		202	
4″, 25 Ga.						
Demolish	S.F.		.85		.85	Includes material and labor to install
Install	S.F.	.39	.85		1.24	cold rolled metal stud walls, to 10′
Demolish and Install	S.F.	.39	1.70		2.09	high, including studs, top and bottom
Reinstall	S.F.		.68		.68	track and screws.
Minimum Charge	Job		202		202	
6″, 25 Ga.						
Demolish	S.F.		.85		.85	Includes material and labor to install
Install	S.F.	.48	.86		1.34	cold rolled metal stud walls, to 10′
Demolish and Install	S.F.	.48	1.71		2.19	high, including studs, top and bottom
Reinstall	S.F.		.69		.69	track and screws.
Minimum Charge	Job		202		202	
24″ O.C. System						
4″, 25 Ga.						
Demolish	S.F.		.72		.72	Includes material and labor to install
Install	S.F.	.28	.55		.83	cold rolled metal stud walls, to 10′
Demolish and Install	S.F.	.28	1.27		1.55	high, including studs, top and bottom
Reinstall	S.F.		.44		.44	track and screws.
Minimum Charge	Job		202		202	

Rough Frame / Structure

Metal Stud Framing

	Unit	Material	Labor	Equip.	Total	Specification
6", 25 Ga.						
Demolish	S.F.		.72		.72	Includes material and labor to install
Install	S.F.	.35	.56		.91	cold rolled metal stud walls, to 10'
Demolish and Install	S.F.	.35	1.28		1.63	high, including studs, top and bottom
Reinstall	S.F.		.45		.45	track and screws.
Minimum Charge	Job		202		202	
4", 16 Ga.						
Demolish	L.F.		8.20		8.20	Includes material and labor to install
Install	S.F.	.83	.90		1.73	load bearing cold rolled metal stud
Demolish and Install	S.F.	.83	9.10		9.93	walls, to 10' high, including studs, top
Reinstall	S.F.		.72		.72	and bottom track and screws.
Minimum Charge	Job		202		202	
6", 16 Ga.						
Demolish	L.F.		8.20		8.20	Includes material and labor to install
Install	S.F.	1.03	.92		1.95	load bearing cold rolled metal stud
Demolish and Install	S.F.	1.03	9.12		10.15	walls, to 10' high, including studs, top
Reinstall	S.F.		.73		.73	and bottom track and screws.
Minimum Charge	Job		202		202	

Metal Joist

	Unit	Material	Labor	Equip.	Total	Specification
Bar Joist						
18K9						
Demolish	L.F.		.98	.42	1.40	Includes material, labor and
Install	L.F.	7.15	2.21	1.01	10.37	equipment to install open web joist.
Demolish and Install	L.F.	7.15	3.19	1.43	11.77	
Reinstall	L.F.		1.77	.81	2.58	
Minimum Charge	Job		1825	720	2545	
16K6						
Demolish	L.F.		.98	.42	1.40	Includes material, labor and
Install	L.F.	4.36	1.49	.09	5.94	equipment to install open web joist.
Demolish and Install	L.F.	4.36	2.47	.51	7.34	
Reinstall	L.F.		1.19	.07	1.26	
Minimum Charge	Job		1825	720	2545	

Exterior Sheathing

	Unit	Material	Labor	Equip.	Total	Specification
CDX Plywood						
5/16"						
Demolish	S.F.		.57		.57	Cost includes material and labor to
Install	S.F.	.61	.50		1.11	install 5/16" CDX plywood sheathing.
Demolish and Install	S.F.	.61	1.07		1.68	
Minimum Charge	Job		202		202	
3/8"						
Demolish	S.F.		.58		.58	Cost includes material and labor to
Install	S.F.	.52	.67		1.19	install 3/8" CDX plywood sheathing.
Demolish and Install	S.F.	.52	1.25		1.77	
Minimum Charge	Job		202		202	
1/2"						
Demolish	S.F.		.59		.59	Cost includes material and labor to
Install	S.F.	.64	.72		1.36	install 1/2" CDX plywood sheathing.
Demolish and Install	S.F.	.64	1.31		1.95	
Minimum Charge	Job		202		202	

Rough Frame / Structure

Exterior Sheathing

	Unit	Material	Labor	Equip.	Total	Specification
5/8"						
Demolish	S.F.		.60		.60	Cost includes material and labor to
Install	S.F.	.77	.77		1.54	install 5/8" CDX plywood sheathing.
Demolish and Install	S.F.	.77	1.37		2.14	
Minimum Charge	Job		202		202	
3/4"						
Demolish	S.F.		.62		.62	Cost includes material and labor to
Install	S.F.	.90	.83		1.73	install 3/4" CDX plywood sheathing.
Demolish and Install	S.F.	.90	1.45		2.35	
Minimum Charge	Job		202		202	
OSB						
1/2"						
Demolish	S.F.		.59		.59	Cost includes material and labor to
Install	S.F.	.36	.61		.97	install 4' x 8' x 1/2" OSB sheathing.
Demolish and Install	S.F.	.36	1.20		1.56	
Minimum Charge	Job		202		202	
5/8"						
Demolish	S.F.		.60		.60	Cost includes material and labor to
Install	S.F.	.36	.49		.85	install 4' x 8' x 5/8" OSB sheathing.
Demolish and Install	S.F.	.36	1.09		1.45	
Minimum Charge	Job		202		202	
Vapor Barrier						
Black Paper						
Install	S.F.	.07	.11		.18	Includes material and labor to install
Minimum Charge	Job		202		202	#15 felt building paper.

Plywood Sheathing

	Unit	Material	Labor	Equip.	Total	Specification
Finish Plywood						
5/16"						
Demolish	S.F.		.57		.57	Includes material and labor to install
Install	S.F.	.85	.25		1.10	exterior 5/16" AC plywood on walls.
Demolish and Install	S.F.	.85	.82		1.67	
Minimum Charge	Job		202		202	
3/8"						
Demolish	S.F.		.58		.58	Includes material and labor to install
Install	S.F.	.85	.34		1.19	exterior 3/8" AC plywood on walls.
Demolish and Install	S.F.	.85	.92		1.77	
Minimum Charge	Job		202		202	
1/2"						
Demolish	S.F.		.59		.59	Includes material and labor to install
Install	S.F.	.88	.36		1.24	exterior 1/2" AC plywood on walls.
Demolish and Install	S.F.	.88	.95		1.83	
Minimum Charge	Job		202		202	
5/8"						
Demolish	S.F.		.60		.60	Includes material and labor to install
Install	S.F.	1.11	.36		1.47	exterior 5/8" AC plywood on walls.
Demolish and Install	S.F.	1.11	.96		2.07	
Reinstall	S.F.		.36		.36	
Minimum Charge	Job		202		202	
3/4"						
Demolish	S.F.		.62		.62	Includes material and labor to install
Install	S.F.	1.35	.36		1.71	exterior 3/4" AC plywood on walls.
Demolish and Install	S.F.	1.35	.98		2.33	
Reinstall	S.F.		.36		.36	
Minimum Charge	Job		202		202	

Rough Frame / Structure

Stairs

Stairs	Unit	Material	Labor	Equip.	Total	Specification
Job-built						
Treads and Risers						
Demolish	Ea.		41.50		41.50	Includes material and labor to install
Install	Ea.	565	405		970	three 2″ x 12″ stringers, treads and
Demolish and Install	Ea.	565	446.50		1011.50	risers of 3/4″ CDX plywood, installed
Clean	Flight	5.20	25.50		30.70	in a straight or "L" shaped run
Paint	Ea.	.09	69.50		69.59	including carpet.
Minimum Charge	Job		202		202	
Landing						
Demolish	S.F.		.33		.33	Includes material and labor to install
Install	S.F.	66.50	2.80		69.30	landing framing, 3/4″ CDX plywood
Demolish and Install	S.F.	66.50	3.13		69.63	surface and carpet.
Clean	S.F.		.37		.37	
Paint	S.F.	.39	.86		1.25	
Minimum Charge	Job		202		202	

Ceiling Framing

Ceiling Framing	Unit	Material	Labor	Equip.	Total	Specification
16″ O.C. System						
2″ x 6″ Joists						
Demolish	S.F.		.51		.51	Cost includes material and labor to
Install	S.F.	.44	.66		1.10	install 2″ x 6″ joists including end and
Demolish and Install	S.F.	.44	1.17		1.61	header joist installed 16″ O.C. Does
Reinstall	S.F.		.53		.53	not include beams, ledger strips,
Minimum Charge	Job		202		202	blocking or bridging.
2″ x 8″ Joists						
Demolish	S.F.		.53		.53	Cost includes material and labor to
Install	S.F.	.61	.82		1.43	install 2″ x 8″ joists including end and
Demolish and Install	S.F.	.61	1.35		1.96	header joist installed 16″ O.C. Does
Reinstall	S.F.		.65		.65	not include beams, ledger strips,
Minimum Charge	Job		202		202	blocking or bridging.
2″ x 10″ Joists						
Demolish	S.F.		.55		.55	Cost includes material and labor to
Install	S.F.	.94	.97		1.91	install 2″ x 10″ joists including end
Demolish and Install	S.F.	.94	1.52		2.46	and header joist installed 16″ O.C.
Reinstall	S.F.		.77		.77	Does not include beams, ledger strips,
Minimum Charge	Job		202		202	blocking or bridging.
2″ x 12″ Joists						
Demolish	S.F.		.57		.57	Cost includes material and labor to
Install	S.F.	1.13	1.18		2.31	install 2″ x 12″ joists including end
Demolish and Install	S.F.	1.13	1.75		2.88	and header joist installed 16″ O.C.
Reinstall	S.F.		.94		.94	Does not include beams, ledger strips,
Minimum Charge	Job		202		202	blocking or bridging.
Block / Bridge						
Demolish	Ea.		1.04		1.04	Includes material and labor to install
Install	Ea.	1.64	2.27		3.91	set of cross bridging or per block of
Demolish and Install	Ea.	1.64	3.31		4.95	solid bridging for 2″ x 10″ joists cut to
Minimum Charge	Job		202		202	size on site.

Rough Frame / Structure

Ceiling Framing		Unit	Material	Labor	Equip.	Total	Specification
24″ O.C. System							
2″ x 6″ Joists							
	Demolish	S.F.		.34		.34	Cost includes material and labor to
	Install	S.F.	.30	.44		.74	install 2″ x 6″ joists including end and
	Demolish and Install	S.F.	.30	.78		1.08	header joist installed 24″ O.C. Does
	Reinstall	S.F.		.35		.35	not include beams, ledger strips,
	Minimum Charge	Job		202		202	blocking or bridging.
2″ x 8″ Joists							
	Demolish	S.F.		.35		.35	Cost includes material and labor to
	Install	S.F.	.41	.54		.95	install 2″ x 8″ joists including end and
	Demolish and Install	S.F.	.41	.89		1.30	header joist installed 24″ O.C. Does
	Reinstall	S.F.		.44		.44	not include beams, ledger strips,
	Minimum Charge	Job		202		202	blocking or bridging.
2″ x 10″ Joists							
	Demolish	S.F.		.37		.37	Cost includes material and labor to
	Install	S.F.	.63	.64		1.27	install 2″ x 10″ joists including end
	Demolish and Install	S.F.	.63	1.01		1.64	and header joist installed 24″ O.C.
	Reinstall	S.F.		.51		.51	Does not include beams, ledger strips,
	Minimum Charge	Job		202		202	blocking or bridging.
2″ x 12″ Joists							
	Demolish	S.F.		.38		.38	Cost includes material and labor to
	Install	S.F.	.76	.79		1.55	install 2″ x 12″ joists including end
	Demolish and Install	S.F.	.76	1.17		1.93	and header joist installed 24″ O.C.
	Reinstall	S.F.		.63		.63	Does not include beams, ledger strips,
	Minimum Charge	Job		202		202	blocking or bridging.
Block / Bridge							
	Demolish	Ea.		1.04		1.04	Includes material and labor to install
	Install	Ea.	1.64	2.27		3.91	set of cross bridging or per block of
	Demolish and Install	Ea.	1.64	3.31		4.95	solid bridging for 2″ x 10″ joists cut to
	Minimum Charge	Job		202		202	size on site.
Ledger Strips							
1″ x 2″							
	Demolish	L.F.		.28		.28	Cost includes material and labor to
	Install	L.F.	.28	1.17		1.45	install 1″ x 2″ ledger strip nailed to the
	Demolish and Install	L.F.	.28	1.45		1.73	face of studs, beams or joist.
	Minimum Charge	Job		202		202	
1″ x 3″							
	Demolish	L.F.		.28		.28	Includes material and labor to install
	Install	L.F.	.58	1.35		1.93	up to 1″ x 4″ ledger strip nailed to the
	Demolish and Install	L.F.	.58	1.63		2.21	face of studs, beams or joist.
	Minimum Charge	Job		202		202	
1″ x 4″							
	Demolish	L.F.		.28		.28	Includes material and labor to install
	Install	L.F.	.58	1.35		1.93	up to 1″ x 4″ ledger strip nailed to the
	Demolish and Install	L.F.	.58	1.63		2.21	face of studs, beams or joist.
	Minimum Charge	Job		202		202	
2″ x 2″							
	Demolish	L.F.		.30		.30	Cost includes material and labor to
	Install	L.F.	.36	1.22		1.58	install 2″ x 2″ ledger strip nailed to the
	Demolish and Install	L.F.	.36	1.52		1.88	face of studs, beams or joist.
	Minimum Charge	Job		202		202	
2″ x 4″							
	Demolish	L.F.		.33		.33	Cost includes material and labor to
	Install	L.F.	.36	1.61		1.97	install 2″ x 4″ ledger strip nailed to the
	Demolish and Install	L.F.	.36	1.94		2.30	face of studs, beams or joist.
	Reinstall	L.F.		1.29		1.29	
	Minimum Charge	Job		202		202	

Rough Frame / Structure

Ceiling Framing

Ceiling Framing	Unit	Material	Labor	Equip.	Total	Specification
Ledger Boards						
2″ x 4″						
Demolish	L.F.		.33		.33	Cost includes material and labor to
Install	L.F.	4.53	2.24		6.77	install 2″ x 4″ ledger board fastened to
Demolish and Install	L.F.	4.53	2.57		7.10	a wall, joists or studs.
Reinstall	L.F.		1.79		1.79	
Minimum Charge	Job		202		202	
4″ x 6″						
Demolish	L.F.		.55		.55	Cost includes material and labor to
Install	L.F.	7.80	2.52		10.32	install 4″ x 6″ ledger board fastened to
Demolish and Install	L.F.	7.80	3.07		10.87	a wall, joists or studs.
Reinstall	L.F.		2.02		2.02	
Minimum Charge	Job		202		202	
4″ x 8″						
Demolish	L.F.		.74		.74	Cost includes material and labor to
Install	L.F.	8.55	2.52		11.07	install 4″ x 8″ ledger board fastened to
Demolish and Install	L.F.	8.55	3.26		11.81	a wall, joists or studs.
Reinstall	L.F.		2.02		2.02	
Minimum Charge	Job		202		202	
Earthquake Strapping						
Install	Ea.	2.99	2.52		5.51	Includes labor and material to replace
Minimum Charge	Job		202		202	an earthquake strap.
Hurricane Clips						
Install	Ea.	1.12	2.78		3.90	Includes labor and material to install a
Minimum Charge	Job		202		202	hurricane clip.

Roof Framing

Roof Framing	Unit	Material	Labor	Equip.	Total	Specification
16″ O.C. System						
2″ x 4″ Rafters						
Demolish	S.F.		.76		.76	Cost includes material and labor to
Install	S.F.	.28	.72		1	install 2″ x 4″, 16″ O.C. rafter framing
Demolish and Install	S.F.	.28	1.48		1.76	for flat, shed or gable roofs, 25′ span,
Reinstall	S.F.		.58		.58	up to 5/12 slope, per S.F. of roof.
Minimum Charge	Job		202		202	
2″ x 6″ Rafters						
Demolish	S.F.		.79		.79	Cost includes material and labor to
Install	S.F.	.44	.76		1.20	install 2″ x 6″, 16″ O.C. rafter framing
Demolish and Install	S.F.	.44	1.55		1.99	for flat, shed or gable roofs, 25′ span,
Reinstall	S.F.		.61		.61	up to 5/12 slope, per S.F. of roof.
Minimum Charge	Job		202		202	
2″ x 8″ Rafters						
Demolish	S.F.		.81		.81	Cost includes material and labor to
Install	S.F.	.59	.81		1.40	install 2″ x 8″, 16″ O.C. rafter framing
Demolish and Install	S.F.	.59	1.62		2.21	for flat, shed or gable roofs, 25′ span,
Reinstall	S.F.		.65		.65	up to 5/12 slope, per S.F. of roof.
Minimum Charge	Job		202		202	
2″ x 10″ Rafters						
Demolish	S.F.		.81		.81	Cost includes material and labor to
Install	S.F.	.92	1.22		2.14	install 2″ x 10″, 16″ O.C. rafter
Demolish and Install	S.F.	.92	2.03		2.95	framing for flat, shed or gable roofs,
Reinstall	S.F.		.98		.98	25′ span, up to 5/12 slope, per S.F.
Minimum Charge	Job		202		202	of roof.

Rough Frame / Structure

Roof Framing

	Unit	Material	Labor	Equip.	Total	Specification
2" x 12" Rafters						
Demolish	S.F.		.82		.82	Cost includes material and labor to
Install	S.F.	1.12	1.33		2.45	install 2" x 12", 16" O.C. rafter
Demolish and Install	S.F.	1.12	2.15		3.27	framing for flat, shed or gable roofs,
Reinstall	S.F.		1.06		1.06	25' span, up to 5/12 slope, per S.F.
Minimum Charge	Job		202		202	of roof.
24" O.C. System						
2" x 4" Rafters						
Demolish	S.F.		.57		.57	Cost includes material and labor to
Install	S.F.	.19	.54		.73	install 2" x 4", 24" O.C. rafter framing
Demolish and Install	S.F.	.19	1.11		1.30	for flat, shed or gable roofs, 25' span,
Reinstall	S.F.		.43		.43	up to 5/12 slope, per S.F. of roof.
Minimum Charge	Job		202		202	
2" x 6" Rafters						
Demolish	S.F.		.60		.60	Cost includes material and labor to
Install	S.F.	.29	.57		.86	install 2" x 6", 24" O.C. rafter framing
Demolish and Install	S.F.	.29	1.17		1.46	for flat, shed or gable roofs, 25' span,
Reinstall	S.F.		.46		.46	up to 5/12 slope, per S.F. of roof.
Minimum Charge	Job		202		202	
2" x 8" Rafters						
Demolish	S.F.		.61		.61	Cost includes material and labor to
Install	S.F.	.40	.61		1.01	install 2" x 8", 24" O.C. rafter framing
Demolish and Install	S.F.	.40	1.22		1.62	for flat, shed or gable roofs, 25' span,
Reinstall	S.F.		.49		.49	up to 5/12 slope, per S.F. of roof.
Minimum Charge	Job		202		202	
2" x 10" Rafters						
Demolish	S.F.		.61		.61	Cost includes material and labor to
Install	S.F.	.62	.92		1.54	install 2" x 10", 24" O.C. rafter
Demolish and Install	S.F.	.62	1.53		2.15	framing for flat, shed or gable roofs,
Reinstall	S.F.		.74		.74	25' span, up to 5/12 slope, per S.F.
Minimum Charge	Job		202		202	of roof.
2" x 12" Rafters						
Demolish	S.F.		.62		.62	Cost includes material and labor to
Install	S.F.	.75	1		1.75	install 2" x 12", 24" O.C. rafter
Demolish and Install	S.F.	.75	1.62		2.37	framing for flat, shed or gable roofs,
Reinstall	S.F.		.80		.80	25' span, up to 5/12 slope, per S.F.
Minimum Charge	Job		202		202	of roof.
Rafter						
2" x 4"						
Demolish	L.F.		.77		.77	Cost includes material and labor to
Install	L.F.	.36	1.01		1.37	install 2" x 4" rafters for flat, shed or
Demolish and Install	L.F.	.36	1.78		2.14	gable roofs, up to 5/12 slope, 25'
Reinstall	L.F.		.81		.81	span, per L.F.
Minimum Charge	Job		202		202	
2" x 6"						
Demolish	L.F.		.78		.78	Cost includes material and labor to
Install	L.F.	.58	1.01		1.59	install 2" x 6" rafters for flat, shed or
Demolish and Install	L.F.	.58	1.79		2.37	gable roofs, up to 5/12 slope, 25'
Reinstall	L.F.		.81		.81	span, per L.F.
Minimum Charge	Job		202		202	
2" x 8"						
Demolish	L.F.		.79		.79	Cost includes material and labor to
Install	L.F.	.80	1.08		1.88	install 2" x 8" rafters for flat, shed or
Demolish and Install	L.F.	.80	1.87		2.67	gable roofs, up to 5/12 slope, 25'
Reinstall	L.F.		.86		.86	span, per L.F.
Minimum Charge	Job		202		202	

Rough Frame / Structure

Roof Framing

	Unit	Material	Labor	Equip.	Total	Specification
2″ x 10″						
Demolish	L.F.		.81		.81	Cost includes material and labor to
Install	L.F.	1.22	1.63		2.85	install 2″ x 10″ rafters for flat, shed or
Demolish and Install	L.F.	1.22	2.44		3.66	gable roofs, up to 5/12 slope, 25′
Reinstall	L.F.		1.30		1.30	span, per L.F.
Minimum Charge	Job		202		202	
2″ x 12″						
Demolish	L.F.		.82		.82	Cost includes material and labor to
Install	L.F.	1.50	1.77		3.27	install 2″ x 12″ rafters for flat, shed or
Demolish and Install	L.F.	1.50	2.59		4.09	gable roofs, up to 5/12 slope, 25′
Reinstall	L.F.		1.42		1.42	span, per L.F.
Minimum Charge	Job		202		202	
2″ x 4″ Valley / Jack						
Demolish	L.F.		.77		.77	Includes material and labor to install
Install	L.F.	.58	1.70		2.28	up to 2″ x 6″ valley/jack rafters for
Demolish and Install	L.F.	.58	2.47		3.05	flat, shed or gable roofs, up to 5/12
Reinstall	L.F.		1.36		1.36	slope, 25′ span, per L.F.
Minimum Charge	Job		202		202	
2″ x 6″ Valley / Jack						
Demolish	L.F.		.78		.78	Includes material and labor to install
Install	L.F.	.58	1.70		2.28	up to 2″ x 6″ valley/jack rafters for
Demolish and Install	L.F.	.58	2.48		3.06	flat, shed or gable roofs, up to 5/12
Reinstall	L.F.		1.36		1.36	slope, 25′ span, per L.F.
Minimum Charge	Job		202		202	

Ridgeboard

	Unit	Material	Labor	Equip.	Total	Specification
2″ x 4″						
Demolish	L.F.		.74		.74	Cost includes material and labor to
Install	L.F.	.36	1.47		1.83	install 2″ x 4″ ridgeboard for flat, shed
Demolish and Install	L.F.	.36	2.21		2.57	or gable roofs, up to 5/12 slope, 25′
Reinstall	L.F.		1.17		1.17	span, per L.F.
Minimum Charge	Job		202		202	
2″ x 6″						
Demolish	L.F.		.76		.76	Cost includes material and labor to
Install	L.F.	.58	1.61		2.19	install 2″ x 6″ ridgeboard for flat, shed
Demolish and Install	L.F.	.58	2.37		2.95	or gable roofs, up to 5/12 slope, 25′
Reinstall	L.F.		1.29		1.29	span, per L.F.
Minimum Charge	Job		202		202	
2″ x 8″						
Demolish	L.F.		.78		.78	Cost includes material and labor to
Install	L.F.	.80	1.79		2.59	install 2″ x 8″ ridgeboard for flat, shed
Demolish and Install	L.F.	.80	2.57		3.37	or gable roofs, up to 5/12 slope, 25′
Reinstall	L.F.		1.44		1.44	span, per L.F.
Minimum Charge	Job		202		202	
2″ x 10″						
Demolish	L.F.		.81		.81	Cost includes material and labor to
Install	L.F.	1.22	2.02		3.24	install 2″ x 10″ ridgeboard for flat,
Demolish and Install	L.F.	1.22	2.83		4.05	shed or gable roofs, up to 5/12
Reinstall	L.F.		1.61		1.61	slope, 25′ span, per L.F.
Minimum Charge	Job		202		202	
2″ x 12″						
Demolish	L.F.		.83		.83	Cost includes material and labor to
Install	L.F.	1.50	1.15		2.65	install 2″ x 12″ ridgeboard for flat,
Demolish and Install	L.F.	1.50	1.98		3.48	shed or gable roofs, up to 5/12
Reinstall	L.F.		.92		.92	slope, 25′ span, per L.F.
Minimum Charge	Job		202		202	

Rough Frame / Structure

Roof Framing

	Unit	Material	Labor	Equip.	Total	Specification
Collar Beam						
1" x 6"						
Demolish	L.F.		.59		.59	Cost includes material and labor to
Install	L.F.	.74	.50		1.24	install 1" x 6" collar beam or tie for
Demolish and Install	L.F.	.74	1.09		1.83	roof framing.
Reinstall	L.F.		.40		.40	
Minimum Charge	Job		202		202	
2" x 6"						
Demolish	L.F.		.69		.69	Cost includes material and labor to
Install	L.F.	.58	.50		1.08	install 2" x 6" collar beam or tie for
Demolish and Install	L.F.	.58	1.19		1.77	roof framing.
Reinstall	L.F.		.40		.40	
Minimum Charge	Job		202		202	
Purlins						
2" x 6"						
Demolish	L.F.		.66		.66	Cost includes material and labor to
Install	L.F.	.58	.45		1.03	install 2" x 6" purlins below roof
Demolish and Install	L.F.	.58	1.11		1.69	rafters.
Reinstall	L.F.		.36		.36	
Minimum Charge	Job		202		202	
2" x 8"						
Demolish	L.F.		.67		.67	Cost includes material and labor to
Install	L.F.	.80	.45		1.25	install 2" x 8" purlins below roof
Demolish and Install	L.F.	.80	1.12		1.92	rafters.
Reinstall	L.F.		.36		.36	
Minimum Charge	Job		202		202	
2" x 10"						
Demolish	L.F.		.68		.68	Cost includes material and labor to
Install	L.F.	1.22	.46		1.68	install 2" x 10" purlins below roof
Demolish and Install	L.F.	1.22	1.14		2.36	rafters.
Reinstall	L.F.		.37		.37	
Minimum Charge	Job		202		202	
2" x 12"						
Demolish	L.F.		.69		.69	Cost includes material and labor to
Install	L.F.	1.50	.46		1.96	install 2" x 12" purlins below roof
Demolish and Install	L.F.	1.50	1.15		2.65	rafters.
Reinstall	L.F.		.37		.37	
Minimum Charge	Job		202		202	
4" x 6"						
Demolish	L.F.		.69		.69	Cost includes material and labor to
Install	L.F.	2.59	.46		3.05	install 4" x 6" purlins below roof
Demolish and Install	L.F.	2.59	1.15		3.74	rafters.
Reinstall	L.F.		.37		.37	
Minimum Charge	Job		202		202	
4" x 8"						
Demolish	L.F.		.69		.69	Cost includes material and labor to
Install	L.F.	3.28	.47		3.75	install 4" x 8" purlins below roof
Demolish and Install	L.F.	3.28	1.16		4.44	rafters.
Reinstall	L.F.		.38		.38	
Minimum Charge	Job		202		202	
Ledger Board						
2" x 6"						
Demolish	L.F.		.33		.33	Cost includes material and labor to
Install	L.F.	.58	1.82		2.40	install 2" x 6" ledger board nailed to
Demolish and Install	L.F.	.58	2.15		2.73	the face of a rafter.
Reinstall	L.F.		1.45		1.45	
Minimum Charge	Job		202		202	

Rough Frame / Structure

Roof Framing		Unit	Material	Labor	Equip.	Total	Specification
4" x 6"							
	Demolish	L.F.		.55		.55	Cost includes material and labor to
	Install	L.F.	2.59	2.67		5.26	install 4" x 6" ledger board nailed to
	Demolish and Install	L.F.	2.59	3.22		5.81	the face of a rafter.
	Reinstall	L.F.		2.14		2.14	
	Minimum Charge	Job		202		202	
4" x 8"							
	Demolish	L.F.		.74		.74	Cost includes material and labor to
	Install	L.F.	3.28	3.08		6.36	install 4" x 8" ledger board nailed to
	Demolish and Install	L.F.	3.28	3.82		7.10	the face of a rafter.
	Reinstall	L.F.		2.46		2.46	
	Minimum Charge	Job		202		202	
Outriggers							
2" x 4"							
	Demolish	L.F.		.23		.23	Cost includes material and labor to
	Install	L.F.	.36	1.61		1.97	install 2" x 4" outrigger rafters for flat,
	Demolish and Install	L.F.	.36	1.84		2.20	shed or gabled roofs, up to 5/12
	Reinstall	L.F.		1.29		1.29	slope, per L.F.
	Minimum Charge	Job		202		202	
2" x 6"							
	Demolish	L.F.		.34		.34	Cost includes material and labor to
	Install	L.F.	.58	1.61		2.19	install 2" x 6" outrigger rafters for flat,
	Demolish and Install	L.F.	.58	1.95		2.53	shed or gabled roofs, up to 5/12
	Reinstall	L.F.		1.29		1.29	slope, per L.F.
	Minimum Charge	Job		202		202	
Lookout Rafter							
2" x 4"							
	Demolish	L.F.		.77		.77	Cost includes material and labor to
	Install	L.F.	.36	.67		1.03	install 2" x 4" lookout rafters for flat,
	Demolish and Install	L.F.	.36	1.44		1.80	shed or gabled roofs, up to 5/12
	Reinstall	L.F.		.54		.54	slope, per L.F.
	Minimum Charge	Job		202		202	
2" x 6"							
	Demolish	L.F.		.78		.78	Cost includes material and labor to
	Install	L.F.	.58	.68		1.26	install 2" x 6" lookout rafters for flat,
	Demolish and Install	L.F.	.58	1.46		2.04	shed or gabled roofs, up to 5/12
	Reinstall	L.F.		.55		.55	slope, per L.F.
	Minimum Charge	Job		202		202	
Fly Rafter							
2" x 4"							
	Demolish	L.F.		.77		.77	Cost includes material and labor to
	Install	L.F.	.36	.67		1.03	install 2" x 4" fly rafters for flat, shed
	Demolish and Install	L.F.	.36	1.44		1.80	or gabled roofs, up to 5/12 slope,
	Reinstall	L.F.		.54		.54	per L.F.
	Minimum Charge	Job		202		202	
2" x 6"							
	Demolish	L.F.		.78		.78	Cost includes material and labor to
	Install	L.F.	.58	.68		1.26	install 2" x 6" fly rafters for flat, shed
	Demolish and Install	L.F.	.58	1.46		2.04	or gabled roofs, up to 5/12 slope,
	Reinstall	L.F.		.55		.55	per L.F.
	Minimum Charge	Job		202		202	

Rough Frame / Structure

Residential Trusses

	Unit	Material	Labor	Equip.	Total	Specification
W or Fink Truss						
24' Span						
Demolish	Ea.		30.50	12.15	42.65	Includes material, labor and
Install	Ea.	84.50	30.50	12	127	equipment to install wood gang-nailed
Demolish and Install	Ea.	84.50	61	24.15	169.65	residential truss, up to 24' span.
Reinstall	Ea.		30.42	12.02	42.44	
Minimum Charge	Job		202		202	
28' Span						
Demolish	Ea.		32.50	12.90	45.40	Includes material, labor and
Install	Ea.	102	34.50	13.60	150.10	equipment to install wood gang-nailed
Demolish and Install	Ea.	102	67	26.50	195.50	residential truss, up to 28' span.
Reinstall	Ea.		34.44	13.61	48.05	
Minimum Charge	Job		202		202	
32' Span						
Demolish	Ea.		36	14.30	50.30	Includes material, labor and
Install	Ea.	120	36.50	14.40	170.90	equipment to install wood gang-nailed
Demolish and Install	Ea.	120	72.50	28.70	221.20	residential truss, up to 32' span.
Reinstall	Ea.		36.50	14.42	50.92	
Minimum Charge	Job		202		202	
36' Span						
Demolish	Ea.		39	15.40	54.40	Includes material, labor and
Install	Ea.	146	39.50	15.70	201.20	equipment to install wood gang-nailed
Demolish and Install	Ea.	146	78.50	31.10	255.60	residential truss, up to 36' span.
Reinstall	Ea.		39.68	15.68	55.36	
Minimum Charge	Job		202		202	
Gable End						
24' Span						
Demolish	Ea.		30.50	12.15	42.65	Includes material, labor and
Install	Ea.	118	32.50	12.90	163.40	equipment to install wood gang-nailed
Demolish and Install	Ea.	118	63	25.05	206.05	residential gable end truss, up to 24'
Reinstall	Ea.		32.59	12.88	45.47	span.
Clean	Ea.	2.17	40		42.17	
Paint	Ea.	4.46	46		50.46	
Minimum Charge	Job		202		202	
28' Span						
Demolish	Ea.		32.50	12.90	45.40	Includes material, labor and
Install	Ea.	145	39	15.35	199.35	equipment to install wood gang-nailed
Demolish and Install	Ea.	145	71.50	28.25	244.75	residential gable end truss, up to 30'
Reinstall	Ea.		38.83	15.34	54.17	span.
Clean	Ea.	2.27	54.50		56.77	
Paint	Ea.	4.65	63		67.65	
Minimum Charge	Job		202		202	
32' Span						
Demolish	Ea.		36	14.30	50.30	Includes material, labor and
Install	Ea.	160	39.50	15.70	215.20	equipment to install wood gang-nailed
Demolish and Install	Ea.	160	75.50	30	265.50	residential gable end truss, up to 32'
Reinstall	Ea.		39.68	15.68	55.36	span.
Clean	Ea.	2.37	71		73.37	
Paint	Ea.	4.86	82.50		87.36	
Minimum Charge	Job		202		202	
36' Span						
Demolish	Ea.		39	15.40	54.40	Includes material, labor and
Install	Ea.	206	45.50	18.05	269.55	equipment to install wood gang-nailed
Demolish and Install	Ea.	206	84.50	33.45	323.95	residential gable end truss, up to 36'
Reinstall	Ea.		45.63	18.03	63.66	span.
Clean	Ea.	2.48	90		92.48	
Paint	Ea.	5.10	104		109.10	
Minimum Charge	Job		202		202	

Rough Frame / Structure

Residential Trusses

	Unit	Material	Labor	Equip.	Total	Specification
Truss Hardware						
5-1/4" Glue-Lam Seat						
Install	Ea.	211	2.24		213.24	Includes labor and material to install
Minimum Charge	Job		202		202	beam hangers.
6-3/4" Glue-Lam Seat						
Install	Ea.	217	2.24		219.24	Includes labor and material to install
Minimum Charge	Job		202		202	beam hangers.
2" x 4" Joist Hanger						
Install	Ea.	.74	2.31		3.05	Includes labor and material to install
Minimum Charge	Job		202		202	joist and beam hangers.
2" x 12" Joist Hanger						
Install	Ea.	1.41	2.45		3.86	Cost includes labor and material to
Minimum Charge	Job		202		202	install 2" x 12" joist hanger.

Commercial Trusses

	Unit	Material	Labor	Equip.	Total	Specification
Engineered Lumber, Truss / Joist						
9-1/2"						
Demolish	S.F.		.55		.55	Includes material and labor to install
Install	S.F.	1.53	.40		1.93	engineered lumber truss / joists per
Demolish and Install	S.F.	1.53	.95		2.48	S.F. of floor area based on joists 16"
Reinstall	S.F.		.32		.32	O.C. Beams, supports and bridging
Minimum Charge	Job		202		202	are not included.
11-7/8"						
Demolish	S.F.		.57		.57	Includes material and labor to install
Install	S.F.	1.72	.41		2.13	engineered lumber truss / joists per
Demolish and Install	S.F.	1.72	.98		2.70	S.F. of floor area based on joists 16"
Reinstall	S.F.		.33		.33	O.C. Beams, supports and bridging
Minimum Charge	Job		202		202	are not included.
14"						
Demolish	S.F.		.59		.59	Includes material and labor to install
Install	S.F.	2.38	.44		2.82	engineered lumber truss / joists per
Demolish and Install	S.F.	2.38	1.03		3.41	S.F. of floor area based on joists 16"
Reinstall	S.F.		.35		.35	O.C. Beams, supports and bridging
Minimum Charge	Job		202		202	are not included.
16"						
Demolish	S.F.		.61		.61	Includes material and labor to install
Install	S.F.	2.94	.47		3.41	engineered lumber truss / joists per
Demolish and Install	S.F.	2.94	1.08		4.02	S.F. of floor area based on joists 16"
Reinstall	S.F.		.37		.37	O.C. Beams, supports and bridging
Minimum Charge	Job		202		202	are not included.
Bowstring Truss						
100' Clear Span						
Demolish	SF Flr.		.56	.52	1.08	Includes material, labor and
Install	SF Flr.	7.50	.46	.33	8.29	equipment to install bow string truss
Demolish and Install	SF Flr.	7.50	1.02	.85	9.37	system up to 100' clear span per S.F.
Minimum Charge	Job		202		202	of floor area.
120' Clear Span						
Demolish	SF Flr.		.62	.57	1.19	Includes material, labor and
Install	SF Flr.	8	.51	.37	8.88	equipment to install bow string truss
Demolish and Install	SF Flr.	8	1.13	.94	10.07	system up to 120' clear span per S.F.
Minimum Charge	Job		202		202	of floor area.

Rough Frame / Structure

Roof Sheathing	Unit	Material	Labor	Equip.	Total	Specification
Plywood						
3/8"						
Demolish	S.F.		.43		.43	Cost includes material and labor to
Install	S.F.	.52	.53		1.05	install 3/8" CDX plywood roof
Demolish and Install	S.F.	.52	.96		1.48	sheathing.
Reinstall	S.F.		.53		.53	
Minimum Charge	Job		202		202	
1/2"						
Demolish	S.F.		.43		.43	Cost includes material and labor to
Install	S.F.	.64	.58		1.22	install 1/2" CDX plywood roof
Demolish and Install	S.F.	.64	1.01		1.65	sheathing.
Minimum Charge	Job		202		202	
5/8"						
Demolish	S.F.		.43		.43	Cost includes material and labor to
Install	S.F.	.77	.62		1.39	install 5/8" CDX plywood roof
Demolish and Install	S.F.	.77	1.05		1.82	sheathing.
Minimum Charge	Job		202		202	
3/4"						
Demolish	S.F.		.43		.43	Cost includes material and labor to
Install	S.F.	.90	.67		1.57	install 3/4" CDX plywood roof
Demolish and Install	S.F.	.90	1.10		2	sheathing.
Minimum Charge	Job		202		202	
OSB						
1/2"						
Demolish	S.F.		.43		.43	Cost includes material and labor to
Install	S.F.	.36	.61		.97	install 4' x 8' x 1/2" OSB sheathing.
Demolish and Install	S.F.	.36	1.04		1.40	
Minimum Charge	Job		202		202	
5/8"						
Demolish	S.F.		.43		.43	Cost includes material and labor to
Install	S.F.	.36	.49		.85	install 4' x 8' x 5/8" OSB sheathing.
Demolish and Install	S.F.	.36	.92		1.28	
Minimum Charge	Job		202		202	
Plank						
Demolish	S.F.		.43		.43	Cost includes material and labor to
Install	S.F.	1.71	1.11		2.82	install 1" x 6" or 1" x 8" utility T&G
Demolish and Install	S.F.	1.71	1.54		3.25	board sheathing laid diagonal.
Reinstall	S.F.		1.11		1.11	
Minimum Charge	Job		202		202	
Skip-type						
1" x 4"						
Demolish	S.F.		.66		.66	Includes material and labor to install
Install	S.F.	.73	.34		1.07	sheathing board material 1" x 4", 7"
Demolish and Install	S.F.	.73	1		1.73	O.C.
Minimum Charge	Job		202		202	
1" x 6"						
Demolish	S.F.		.66		.66	Includes material and labor to install
Install	S.F.	.74	.28		1.02	sheathing board material 1" x 6", 7"
Demolish and Install	S.F.	.74	.94		1.68	or 9" O.C.
Minimum Charge	Job		202		202	

Rough Frame / Structure

Wood Deck	Unit	Material	Labor	Equip.	Total	Specification
Treated						
Demolish	S.F.		1.39		1.39	Includes material and labor to install
Install	S.F.	3.88	10.10		13.98	unfinished deck using 2" x 4" treated
Demolish and Install	S.F.	3.88	11.49		15.37	decking, with 2" x 6" double beams
Reinstall	S.F.		8.07		8.07	24" O.C., 4" x 4" posts 5' O.C. set in
Clean	S.F.	.10	.31		.41	concrete.
Paint	S.F.	.13	.27		.40	
Minimum Charge	Job		202		202	
Redwood						
Demolish	S.F.		1.39		1.39	Includes material and labor to install
Install	S.F.	10.75	10.10		20.85	unfinished deck using 2" x 4" select
Demolish and Install	S.F.	10.75	11.49		22.24	redwood decking, with 2" x 6" double
Reinstall	S.F.		8.07		8.07	beams 24" O.C., 4" x 4" posts 5'
Clean	S.F.	.10	.31		.41	O.C. set in concrete.
Paint	S.F.	.13	.27		.40	
Minimum Charge	Job		202		202	
Cedar						
Demolish	S.F.		1.39		1.39	Includes material and labor to install
Install	S.F.	8.80	10.10		18.90	unfinished deck using 2" x 4" select
Demolish and Install	S.F.	8.80	11.49		20.29	cedar decking, with 2" x 6" double
Reinstall	S.F.		8.07		8.07	beams 24" O.C., 4" x 4" posts 5'
Clean	S.F.	.10	.31		.41	O.C. set in concrete.
Paint	S.F.	.13	.27		.40	
Minimum Charge	Job		202		202	
Stairs						
Demolish	Ea.		390		390	Includes material and labor to install
Install	Ea.	140	705		845	wood steps. 5 - 7 risers included.
Demolish and Install	Ea.	140	1095		1235	
Reinstall	Ea.		562.43		562.43	
Clean	Flight	5.20	25.50		30.70	
Paint	Flight	18.30	46		64.30	
Minimum Charge	Job		202		202	
Railing						
Demolish	L.F.		5.10		5.10	Includes material and labor to install
Install	L.F.	25	18.35		43.35	porch rail with balusters.
Demolish and Install	L.F.	25	23.45		48.45	
Clean	L.F.	1.05	1.87		2.92	
Paint	L.F.	.76	2.89		3.65	
Minimum Charge	Job		202		202	
Bench Seating						
Demolish	L.F.		5.55		5.55	Includes material and labor to install
Install	L.F.	1.75	20		21.75	pressure treated bench seating.
Demolish and Install	L.F.	1.75	25.55		27.30	
Reinstall	L.F.		16.14		16.14	
Clean	L.F.	.21	1.50		1.71	
Paint	L.F.	.64	2.77		3.41	
Minimum Charge	Job		202		202	
Privacy Wall						
Demolish	SF Flr.		1.33		1.33	Includes material, labor and
Install	SF Flr.	1.21	.69	.15	2.05	equipment to install privacy wall.
Demolish and Install	SF Flr.	1.21	2.02	.15	3.38	
Reinstall	SF Flr.		.55	.12	.67	
Clean	SF Flr.	.10	.31		.41	
Paint	S.F.	.13	.27		.40	
Minimum Charge	Job		202		202	

Porch

Porch	Unit	Material	Labor	Equip.	Total	Specification
Treated						
Demolish	S.F.		2.77		2.77	Includes material and labor to install
Install	S.F.	4.81	20		24.81	floor and roof frame and decking
Demolish and Install	S.F.	4.81	22.77		27.58	using 2" x 4" treated decking, with 2"
Reinstall	S.F.		16.14		16.14	x 6" double beams 24" O.C., 4" x 4"
Clean	S.F.	.21	.62		.83	posts 5' O.C. set in concrete.
Paint	S.F.	.21	.69		.90	
Minimum Charge	Job		202		202	
Redwood						
Demolish	S.F.		2.77		2.77	Includes material and labor to install
Install	S.F.	11.90	20		31.90	floor and roof frame and decking
Demolish and Install	S.F.	11.90	22.77		34.67	using 2" x 4" redwood decking, with
Reinstall	S.F.		16.14		16.14	2" x 6" double beams 24" O.C., 4" x
Clean	S.F.	.21	.62		.83	4" posts 5' O.C. set in concrete.
Paint	S.F.	.21	.69		.90	
Minimum Charge	Job		202		202	
Cedar						
Demolish	S.F.		2.77		2.77	Includes material and labor to install
Install	S.F.	9.95	20		29.95	floor and roof frame and cedar
Demolish and Install	S.F.	9.95	22.77		32.72	decking using 2" x 4" select cedar,
Reinstall	S.F.		16.14		16.14	with 2" x 6" double beams 24" O.C.,
Clean	S.F.	.21	.62		.83	4" x 4" posts 5' O.C. set in concrete.
Paint	S.F.	.21	.69		.90	
Minimum Charge	Job		202		202	
Stairs						
Demolish	Ea.		390		390	Includes material and labor to install
Install	Ea.	140	705		845	wood steps. 5 - 7 risers included.
Demolish and Install	Ea.	140	1095		1235	
Reinstall	Ea.		562.43		562.43	
Clean	Flight	5.20	25.50		30.70	
Paint	Flight	18.30	46		64.30	
Minimum Charge	Job		202		202	
Railing						
Demolish	L.F.		5.10		5.10	Includes material and labor to install
Install	L.F.	25	18.35		43.35	porch rail with balusters.
Demolish and Install	L.F.	25	23.45		48.45	
Clean	L.F.	1.05	2.34		3.39	
Paint	L.F.	.76	2.89		3.65	
Minimum Charge	Job		202		202	
Bench Seating						
Demolish	L.F.		5.55		5.55	Includes material and labor to install
Install	L.F.	1.75	20		21.75	pressure treated bench seating.
Demolish and Install	L.F.	1.75	25.55		27.30	
Reinstall	L.F.		16.14		16.14	
Clean	L.F.	.21	1.50		1.71	
Paint	L.F.	.64	2.77		3.41	
Minimum Charge	Job		202		202	
Privacy Wall						
Demolish	SF Flr.		1.33		1.33	Includes material, labor and
Install	SF Flr.	1.21	.69	.15	2.05	equipment to install privacy wall.
Demolish and Install	SF Flr.	1.21	2.02	.15	3.38	
Reinstall	SF Flr.		.55	.12	.67	
Clean	SF Flr.	.10	.31		.41	
Paint	S.F.	.13	.27		.40	
Minimum Charge	Job		202		202	

Rough Frame / Structure

Porch		Unit	Material	Labor	Equip.	Total	Specification
Wood Board Ceiling							
	Demolish	S.F.		.55		.55	Includes material and labor to install
	Install	S.F.	3.15	1.79		4.94	wood board on ceiling.
	Demolish and Install	S.F.	3.15	2.34		5.49	
	Clean	S.F.	.04	.17		.21	
	Paint	S.F.	.17	.43		.60	
	Minimum Charge	Job		202		202	
Re-screen							
	Install	S.F.	1.67	1.61		3.28	Includes labor and material to
	Minimum Charge	Job		202		202	re-screen wood frame.

Exterior Trim

Exterior Trim		Unit	Material	Labor	Equip.	Total	Specification
Stock Lumber							
1″ x 2″							
	Demolish	L.F.		.28		.28	Cost includes material and labor to
	Install	L.F.	.28	1.22		1.50	install 1″ x 2″ pine trim.
	Demolish and Install	L.F.	.28	1.50		1.78	
	Clean	L.F.	.01	.20		.21	
	Paint	L.F.	.02	.54		.56	
	Minimum Charge	Job		202		202	
1″ x 3″							
	Demolish	L.F.		.28		.28	Cost includes material and labor to
	Install	L.F.	.28	1.39		1.67	install 1″ x 3″ pine trim.
	Demolish and Install	L.F.	.28	1.67		1.95	
	Clean	L.F.	.01	.20		.21	
	Paint	L.F.	.02	.54		.56	
	Minimum Charge	Job		202		202	
1″ x 4″							
	Demolish	L.F.		.28		.28	Cost includes material and labor to
	Install	L.F.	.58	1.61		2.19	install 1″ x 4″ pine trim.
	Demolish and Install	L.F.	.58	1.89		2.47	
	Clean	L.F.	.02	.20		.22	
	Paint	L.F.	.02	.54		.56	
	Minimum Charge	Job		202		202	
1″ x 6″							
	Demolish	L.F.		.28		.28	Cost includes material and labor to
	Install	L.F.	.74	1.61		2.35	install 1″ x 6″ pine trim.
	Demolish and Install	L.F.	.74	1.89		2.63	
	Clean	L.F.	.02	.20		.22	
	Paint	L.F.	.07	.54		.61	
	Minimum Charge	Job		202		202	
1″ x 8″							
	Demolish	L.F.		.30		.30	Cost includes material and labor to
	Install	L.F.	1.07	2.02		3.09	install 1″ x 8″ pine trim.
	Demolish and Install	L.F.	1.07	2.32		3.39	
	Reinstall	L.F.		1.61		1.61	
	Clean	L.F.	.04	.21		.25	
	Paint	L.F.	.07	.54		.61	
	Minimum Charge	Job		202		202	

Exterior Trim

Exterior Trim		Unit	Material	Labor	Equip.	Total	Specification
1″ x 10″							
	Demolish	L.F.		.46		.46	Cost includes material and labor to
	Install	L.F.	1.33	2.24		3.57	install 1″ x 10″ pine trim.
	Demolish and Install	L.F.	1.33	2.70		4.03	
	Minimum Charge	Job		202		202	
1″ x 12″							
	Demolish	L.F.		.46		.46	Cost includes material and labor to
	Install	L.F.	1.61	2.24		3.85	install 1″ x 12″ pine trim.
	Demolish and Install	L.F.	1.61	2.70		4.31	
	Minimum Charge	Job		202		202	

Fascia		Unit	Material	Labor	Equip.	Total	Specification
Aluminum							
	Demolish	L.F.		.58		.58	Includes material and labor to install
	Install	S.F.	2.16	1.92		4.08	aluminum fascia.
	Demolish and Install	S.F.	2.16	2.50		4.66	
	Reinstall	S.F.		1.54		1.54	
	Clean	L.F.		.37		.37	
	Minimum Charge	Job		202		202	
Vinyl							
	Demolish	L.F.		.58		.58	Cost includes material and labor to
	Install	L.F.	4.79	2.31		7.10	install 6″ vinyl fascia with 12″ vinyl
	Demolish and Install	L.F.	4.79	2.89		7.68	soffit and J-channel.
	Reinstall	L.F.		1.85		1.85	
	Clean	L.F.		.37		.37	
	Minimum Charge	Job		202		202	
Plywood							
	Demolish	L.F.		.57		.57	Cost includes material and labor to
	Install	L.F.	1.35	.90		2.25	install 12″ wide plywood fascia.
	Demolish and Install	L.F.	1.35	1.47		2.82	
	Reinstall	L.F.		.72		.72	
	Clean	L.F.	.06	.25		.31	
	Paint	L.F.	.15	.87		1.02	
	Minimum Charge	Job		202		202	
Cedar							
	Demolish	L.F.		.57		.57	Cost includes material and labor to
	Install	L.F.	2.74	.90		3.64	install 12″ wide cedar fascia.
	Demolish and Install	L.F.	2.74	1.47		4.21	
	Reinstall	L.F.		.72		.72	
	Clean	L.F.	.06	.25		.31	
	Paint	L.F.	.15	.87		1.02	
	Minimum Charge	Job		202		202	
Redwood							
1″ x 6″							
	Demolish	L.F.		.45		.45	Cost includes material and labor to
	Install	L.F.	1.91	1.61		3.52	install 1″ x 6″ redwood fascia board.
	Demolish and Install	L.F.	1.91	2.06		3.97	
	Reinstall	L.F.		1.29		1.29	
	Minimum Charge	Job		202		202	
1″ x 8″							
	Demolish	L.F.		.50		.50	Cost includes material and labor to
	Install	L.F.	2.54	1.75		4.29	install 1″ x 8″ redwood fascia board.
	Demolish and Install	L.F.	2.54	2.25		4.79	
	Reinstall	L.F.		1.40		1.40	
	Minimum Charge	Job		202		202	

Exterior Trim

Fascia		Unit	Material	Labor	Equip.	Total	Specification
2″ x 6″							
	Demolish	L.F.		.45		.45	Cost includes material and labor to
	Install	L.F.	.58	3.23		3.81	install 2″ x 6″ hem-fir exterior trim
	Demolish and Install	L.F.	.58	3.68		4.26	board.
	Reinstall	L.F.		2.58		2.58	
	Minimum Charge	Job		202		202	
2″ x 8″							
	Demolish	L.F.		.50		.50	Cost includes material and labor to
	Install	L.F.	.80	3.59		4.39	install 2″ x 8″ hem-fir exterior trim
	Demolish and Install	L.F.	.80	4.09		4.89	board.
	Reinstall	L.F.		2.87		2.87	
	Minimum Charge	Job		202		202	
Hem-fir Std & Better							
2″ x 6″							
	Demolish	L.F.		.45		.45	Cost includes material and labor to
	Install	L.F.	.58	3.23		3.81	install 2″ x 6″ hem-fir exterior trim
	Demolish and Install	L.F.	.58	3.68		4.26	board.
	Reinstall	L.F.		2.58		2.58	
	Clean	L.F.	.02	.25		.27	
	Paint	L.F.	.15	.87		1.02	
	Minimum Charge	Job		202		202	
2″ x 8″							
	Demolish	L.F.		.50		.50	Cost includes material and labor to
	Install	L.F.	.80	3.59		4.39	install 2″ x 8″ hem-fir exterior trim
	Demolish and Install	L.F.	.80	4.09		4.89	board.
	Reinstall	L.F.		2.87		2.87	
	Clean	L.F.	.04	.25		.29	
	Paint	L.F.	.15	.87		1.02	
	Minimum Charge	Job		202		202	
2″ x 10″							
	Demolish	L.F.		.57		.57	Cost includes material and labor to
	Install	L.F.	1.22	4.48		5.70	install 2″ x 10″ hem-fir exterior trim
	Demolish and Install	L.F.	1.22	5.05		6.27	board.
	Reinstall	L.F.		3.59		3.59	
	Clean	L.F.	.06	.27		.33	
	Paint	L.F.	.15	.87		1.02	
	Minimum Charge	Job		202		202	
Barge Rafter							
2″ x 6″							
	Demolish	L.F.		.89		.89	Cost includes material and labor to
	Install	L.F.	.58	.45		1.03	install 2″ x 6″ barge rafters.
	Demolish and Install	L.F.	.58	1.34		1.92	
	Reinstall	L.F.		.36		.36	
	Clean	L.F.	.02	.25		.27	
	Paint	L.F.	.15	.87		1.02	
	Minimum Charge	Job		202		202	
2″ x 8″							
	Demolish	L.F.		.90		.90	Cost includes material and labor to
	Install	L.F.	.80	.47		1.27	install 2″ x 8″ barge rafters.
	Demolish and Install	L.F.	.80	1.37		2.17	
	Reinstall	L.F.		.38		.38	
	Clean	L.F.	.04	.25		.29	
	Paint	L.F.	.15	.87		1.02	
	Minimum Charge	Job		202		202	

Exterior Trim

Fascia

	Unit	Material	Labor	Equip.	Total	Specification
2″ x 10″						
Demolish	L.F.		.92		.92	Cost includes material and labor to
Install	L.F.	1.22	.49		1.71	install 2″ x 10″ barge rafters.
Demolish and Install	L.F.	1.22	1.41		2.63	
Reinstall	L.F.		.39		.39	
Clean	L.F.	.06	.27		.33	
Paint	L.F.	.15	.87		1.02	
Minimum Charge	Job		202		202	

Soffit

	Unit	Material	Labor	Equip.	Total	Specification
Aluminum						
12″ w / Fascia						
Demolish	L.F.		.58		.58	Cost includes material and labor to
Install	L.F.	4.79	2.31		7.10	install 12″ aluminum soffit with 6″
Demolish and Install	L.F.	4.79	2.89		7.68	fascia and J-channel.
Reinstall	L.F.		1.85		1.85	
Clean	L.F.		.37		.37	
Paint	L.F.	.19	.87		1.06	
Minimum Charge	Job		202		202	
18″ w / Fascia						
Demolish	L.F.		.58		.58	Cost includes material and labor to
Install	L.F.	5.90	2.69		8.59	install 18″ aluminum soffit with 6″
Demolish and Install	L.F.	5.90	3.27		9.17	fascia and J-channel.
Reinstall	L.F.		2.15		2.15	
Clean	L.F.		.37		.37	
Paint	L.F.	.19	.87		1.06	
Minimum Charge	Job		202		202	
24″ w / Fascia						
Demolish	L.F.		.58		.58	Cost includes material and labor to
Install	L.F.	6.95	2.99		9.94	install 24″ aluminum soffit with 6″
Demolish and Install	L.F.	6.95	3.57		10.52	fascia and J-channel.
Reinstall	L.F.		2.39		2.39	
Clean	L.F.		.54		.54	
Paint	L.F.	.19	.87		1.06	
Minimum Charge	Job		202		202	
Vinyl						
Demolish	L.F.		.58		.58	Cost includes material and labor to
Install	L.F.	4.79	2.31		7.10	install 6″ vinyl fascia with 12″ vinyl
Demolish and Install	L.F.	4.79	2.89		7.68	soffit and J-channel.
Reinstall	L.F.		1.85		1.85	
Clean	L.F.		.37		.37	
Paint	L.F.	.19	.87		1.06	
Minimum Charge	Job		202		202	
Plywood						
Demolish	L.F.		.64		.64	Cost includes material and labor to
Install	L.F.	1.35	1.15		2.50	install 12″ wide plywood soffit.
Demolish and Install	L.F.	1.35	1.79		3.14	
Reinstall	L.F.		.92		.92	
Clean	L.F.	.06	.25		.31	
Paint	L.F.	.15	.87		1.02	
Minimum Charge	Job		202		202	

Soffit

Soffit	Unit	Material	Labor	Equip.	Total	Specification
Redwood						
Demolish	L.F.		.64		.64	Cost includes material and labor to
Install	L.F.	5.15	1.15		6.30	install 12" wide redwood soffit.
Demolish and Install	L.F.	5.15	1.79		6.94	
Reinstall	L.F.		.92		.92	
Clean	L.F.	.06	.25		.31	
Paint	L.F.	.15	.87		1.02	
Minimum Charge	Job		202		202	
Cedar						
Demolish	L.F.		.64		.64	Cost includes material and labor to
Install	L.F.	2.74	1.15		3.89	install 12" wide cedar soffit.
Demolish and Install	L.F.	2.74	1.79		4.53	
Reinstall	L.F.		.92		.92	
Clean	L.F.	.06	.25		.31	
Paint	L.F.	.15	.87		1.02	
Minimum Charge	Job		202		202	
Douglas Fir						
Demolish	L.F.		.64		.64	Cost includes material and labor to
Install	L.F.	1.61	1.15		2.76	install 12" wide Douglas fir soffit.
Demolish and Install	L.F.	1.61	1.79		3.40	
Reinstall	L.F.		.92		.92	
Clean	L.F.	.06	.25		.31	
Paint	L.F.	.15	.87		1.02	
Minimum Charge	Job		202		202	

Roofing and Flashing

Tile Roofing

Metal Flashing		Unit	Material	Labor	Equip.	Total	Specification
Galvanized							
6"							
	Demolish	L.F.		.22		.22	Includes material and labor to install
	Install	L.F.	.86	.91		1.77	flat galvanized steel flashing, 6" wide.
	Demolish and Install	L.F.	.86	1.13		1.99	
	Paint	L.F.	.10	.43		.53	
	Minimum Charge	Job		182		182	
14"							
	Demolish	L.F.		.22		.22	Includes material and labor to install
	Install	L.F.	2	.91		2.91	flat galvanized steel flashing, 14"
	Demolish and Install	L.F.	2	1.13		3.13	wide.
	Paint	L.F.	.10	.43		.53	
	Minimum Charge	Job		182		182	
20"							
	Demolish	L.F.		.22		.22	Includes material and labor to install
	Install	L.F.	2.88	.91		3.79	flat galvanized steel flashing, 20"
	Demolish and Install	L.F.	2.88	1.13		4.01	wide.
	Paint	L.F.	.10	.43		.53	
	Minimum Charge	Job		182		182	
Aluminum							
6"							
	Demolish	L.F.		.22		.22	Includes material and labor to install
	Install	L.F.	.40	.91		1.31	flat aluminum flashing, 6" wide.
	Demolish and Install	L.F.	.40	1.13		1.53	
	Paint	L.F.	.10	.43		.53	
	Minimum Charge	Job		182		182	
14"							
	Demolish	L.F.		.22		.22	Includes material and labor to install
	Install	L.F.	.67	.91		1.58	flat aluminum flashing, 14" wide.
	Demolish and Install	L.F.	.67	1.13		1.80	
	Paint	L.F.	.10	.43		.53	
	Minimum Charge	Job		182		182	
20"							
	Demolish	L.F.		.22		.22	Includes material and labor to install
	Install	L.F.	.98	.91		1.89	flat aluminum flashing, 20" wide.
	Demolish and Install	L.F.	.98	1.13		2.11	
	Paint	L.F.	.10	.43		.53	
	Minimum Charge	Job		182		182	

Metal Flashing	Unit	Material	Labor	Equip.	Total	Specification
Copper						
6"						
Demolish	L.F.		.22		.22	Includes material and labor to install
Install	L.F.	3.25	1.21		4.46	flat copper flashing, 6" wide.
Demolish and Install	L.F.	3.25	1.43		4.68	
Minimum Charge	Job		225		225	
14"						
Demolish	L.F.		.22		.22	Includes material and labor to install
Install	L.F.	7.60	1.21		8.81	flat copper flashing, 14" wide.
Demolish and Install	L.F.	7.60	1.43		9.03	
Minimum Charge	Job		225		225	
18"						
Demolish	L.F.		.22		.22	Includes material and labor to install
Install	L.F.	10.85	1.21		12.06	flat copper flashing, 18" wide.
Demolish and Install	L.F.	10.85	1.43		12.28	
Minimum Charge	Job		225		225	
Aluminum Valley						
Demolish	L.F.		.22		.22	Includes material and labor to install
Install	L.F.	3.19	2.37		5.56	aluminum valley flashing, .024" thick.
Demolish and Install	L.F.	3.19	2.59		5.78	
Paint	L.F.	.10	.43		.53	
Minimum Charge	Job		202		202	
Gravel Stop						
Demolish	L.F.		.20		.20	Includes material and labor to install
Install	L.F.	6.70	3.11		9.81	aluminum gravel stop, .050" thick, 4"
Demolish and Install	L.F.	6.70	3.31		10.01	high, mill finish.
Reinstall	L.F.		2.49		2.49	
Paint	L.F.	.17	.43		.60	
Minimum Charge	Job		202		202	
Drip Edge						
Demolish	L.F.		.20		.20	Includes material and labor to install
Install	L.F.	.42	1.01		1.43	aluminum drip edge, .016" thick, 5"
Demolish and Install	L.F.	.42	1.21		1.63	wide, mill finish.
Reinstall	L.F.		.81		.81	
Paint	L.F.	.17	.43		.60	
Minimum Charge	Job		202		202	
End Wall						
Demolish	L.F.		1.02		1.02	Includes material and labor to install
Install	L.F.	1.96	2.37		4.33	aluminum end wall flashing, .024"
Demolish and Install	L.F.	1.96	3.39		5.35	thick.
Minimum Charge	Job		202		202	
Side Wall						
Demolish	L.F.		.20		.20	Includes material and labor to install
Install	L.F.	1.96	2.37		4.33	aluminum side wall flashing, .024"
Demolish and Install	L.F.	1.96	2.57		4.53	thick.
Minimum Charge	Job		202		202	
Coping and Wall Cap						
Demolish	L.F.		1.39		1.39	Includes material and labor to install
Install	L.F.	2.35	2.51		4.86	aluminum flashing, mill finish, 0.40
Demolish and Install	L.F.	2.35	3.90		6.25	thick, 12" wide.
Clean	L.F.	.13	.94		1.07	
Minimum Charge	Job		182		182	

Roofing

Roof Shingles

Roof Shingles	Unit	Material	Labor	Equip.	Total	Specification
Underlayment						
15#						
Demolish	Sq.		11.10		11.10	Includes material and labor to install
Install	Sq.	6.20	5.70		11.90	#15 felt underlayment.
Demolish and Install	Sq.	6.20	16.80		23	
Minimum Charge	Job		182		182	
30#						
Demolish	Sq.		11.10		11.10	Includes material and labor to install
Install	Sq.	10.40	6.30		16.70	#30 felt underlayment.
Demolish and Install	Sq.	10.40	17.40		27.80	
Minimum Charge	Job		182		182	
Self Adhering						
Demolish	Sq.		27.50		27.50	Includes material and labor to install
Install	Sq.	77	16.55		93.55	self adhering ice barrier roofing
Demolish and Install	Sq.	77	44.05		121.05	underlayment.
Minimum Charge	Job		182		182	

Rolled Roofing

Rolled Roofing	Unit	Material	Labor	Equip.	Total	Specification
90 lb						
Demolish	Sq.		27.50		27.50	Cost includes material and labor to
Install	Sq.	38	30.50		68.50	install 90 lb mineral surface rolled
Demolish and Install	Sq.	38	58		96	roofing.
Minimum Charge	Job		182		182	

Composition Shingles

Composition Shingles	Unit	Material	Labor	Equip.	Total	Specification
Fiberglass (3-tab)						
225 lb, 20 Year						
Demolish	Sq.		30		30	Cost includes material and labor to
Install	Sq.	71.50	71		142.50	install 225 lb, 20 year fiberglass
Demolish and Install	Sq.	71.50	101		172.50	shingles.
Minimum Charge	Job		182		182	
300 lb, 25 Year						
Demolish	Sq.		30		30	Cost includes material and labor to
Install	Sq.	74.50	71		145.50	install 300 lb, 25 year fiberglass
Demolish and Install	Sq.	74.50	101		175.50	shingles.
Minimum Charge	Job		182		182	
Emergency Repairs						
Install	Ea.	132	182		314	Includes labor and material for
Minimum Charge	Job		182		182	emergency repairs.
Architectural						
Laminated, 25 Year						
Demolish	Sq.		30		30	Cost includes material and labor to
Install	Sq.	91.50	71		162.50	install 25 year fiberglass roof shingles.
Demolish and Install	Sq.	91.50	101		192.50	
Minimum Charge	Job		182		182	
Laminated, 30 Year						
Demolish	Sq.		30		30	Cost includes material and labor to
Install	Sq.	98.50	71		169.50	install 30 year fiberglass roof shingles.
Demolish and Install	Sq.	98.50	101		199.50	
Minimum Charge	Job		182		182	

Roofing

Composition Shingles	Unit	Material	Labor	Equip.	Total	Specification
Laminated, 40 Year						
Demolish	Sq.		30		30	Cost includes material and labor to
Install	Sq.	112	71		183	install 40 year fiberglass roof shingles.
Demolish and Install	Sq.	112	101		213	
Minimum Charge	Job		182		182	
Laminated Shake, 40 Year						
Demolish	Sq.		30		30	Cost includes material and labor to
Install	Sq.	123	94.50		217.50	install 40 year fiberglass roof shakes.
Demolish and Install	Sq.	123	124.50		247.50	
Minimum Charge	Job		182		182	
Emergency Repairs						
Install	Ea.	132	182		314	Includes labor and material for
Minimum Charge	Job		182		182	emergency repairs.
Roof Jack						
Demolish	Ea.		6.05		6.05	Includes material and labor to install
Install	Ea.	23.50	41		64.50	residential roof jack, w/bird screen,
Demolish and Install	Ea.	23.50	47.05		70.55	backdraft damper, 3" & 4" dia. round
Paint	Ea.	.06	4.33		4.39	duct.
Minimum Charge	Job		219		219	
Ridge Vent						
Demolish	L.F.		1.07		1.07	Includes material and labor to install a
Install	L.F.	3	2.91		5.91	mill finish aluminum ridge vent strip.
Demolish and Install	L.F.	3	3.98		6.98	
Minimum Charge	Job		202		202	
Shingle Molding						
1" x 2"						
Demolish	L.F.		.21		.21	Cost includes material and labor to
Install	L.F.	.28	1.22		1.50	install 1" x 2" pine trim.
Demolish and Install	L.F.	.28	1.43		1.71	
Paint	L.F.	.02	.54		.56	
Minimum Charge	Job		202		202	
1" x 3"						
Demolish	L.F.		.21		.21	Cost includes material and labor to
Install	L.F.	.28	1.39		1.67	install 1" x 3" pine trim.
Demolish and Install	L.F.	.28	1.60		1.88	
Paint	L.F.	.02	.54		.56	
Minimum Charge	Job		202		202	
1" x 4"						
Demolish	L.F.		.21		.21	Cost includes material and labor to
Install	L.F.	.58	1.61		2.19	install 1" x 4" pine trim.
Demolish and Install	L.F.	.58	1.82		2.40	
Paint	L.F.	.02	.54		.56	
Minimum Charge	Job		202		202	
Add for Steep Pitch						
Install	Sq.		23		23	Includes labor and material added for
Add for Additional Story						2nd story or steep roofs.
Install	Sq.		23		23	Includes labor and material added for
						2nd story or steep roofs.

Wood Shingles	Unit	Material	Labor	Equip.	Total	Specification
Cedar Wood Shingles						
16″ Red Label (#2)						
Demolish	Sq.		74		74	Includes material and labor to install
Install	Sq.	164	161		325	wood shingles/shakes.
Demolish and Install	Sq.	164	235		399	
Minimum Charge	Job		202		202	
16″ Blue Label (#1)						
Demolish	Sq.		74		74	Includes material and labor to install
Install	Sq.	237	124		361	wood shingles/shakes.
Demolish and Install	Sq.	237	198		435	
Minimum Charge	Job		202		202	
18″ Red Label (#2)						
Demolish	Sq.		74		74	Includes material and labor to install
Install	Sq.	262	103		365	wood shingles/shakes.
Demolish and Install	Sq.	262	177		439	
Minimum Charge	Job		202		202	
18″ Blue Label (#1)						
Demolish	Sq.		74		74	Includes material and labor to install
Install	Sq.	242	113		355	wood shingles/shakes.
Demolish and Install	Sq.	242	187		429	
Minimum Charge	Job		202		202	
Replace Shingle						
Install	Ea.	37.50	10.10		47.60	Includes labor and material to replace
Minimum Charge	Job		202		202	individual wood shingle/shake. Cost is per shingle.
Cedar Shake						
18″ Medium Handsplit						
Demolish	Sq.		74		74	Includes material and labor to install
Install	Sq.	175	155		330	wood shingles/shakes.
Demolish and Install	Sq.	175	229		404	
Minimum Charge	Job		202		202	
18″ Heavy Handsplit						
Demolish	Sq.		74		74	Includes material and labor to install
Install	Sq.	175	172		347	wood shingles/shakes.
Demolish and Install	Sq.	175	246		421	
Minimum Charge	Job		202		202	
24″ Heavy Handsplit						
Demolish	Sq.		74		74	Includes material and labor to install
Install	Sq.	256	138		394	wood shingles/shakes.
Demolish and Install	Sq.	256	212		468	
Minimum Charge	Job		202		202	
24″ Medium Handsplit						
Demolish	Sq.		74		74	Includes material and labor to install
Install	Sq.	256	124		380	wood shingles/shakes.
Demolish and Install	Sq.	256	198		454	
Minimum Charge	Job		202		202	
24″ Straight Split						
Demolish	Sq.		74		74	Includes material and labor to install
Install	Sq.	264	183		447	wood shingles/shakes.
Demolish and Install	Sq.	264	257		521	
Minimum Charge	Job		202		202	
24″ Tapersplit						
Demolish	Sq.		74		74	Includes material and labor to install
Install	Sq.	320	183		503	wood shingles/shakes.
Demolish and Install	Sq.	320	257		577	
Minimum Charge	Job		202		202	

Roofing

Wood Shingles

Wood Shingles		Unit	Material	Labor	Equip.	Total	Specification
18" Straight Split							
	Demolish	Sq.		74		74	Includes material and labor to install
	Install	Sq.	256	183		439	wood shingles/shakes.
	Demolish and Install	Sq.	256	257		513	
	Minimum Charge	Job		202		202	
Replace Shingle							
	Install	Ea.	37.50	10.10		47.60	Includes labor and material to replace
	Minimum Charge	Job		202		202	individual wood shingle/shake. Cost is per shingle.

Slate Tile Roofing

Slate Tile Roofing		Unit	Material	Labor	Equip.	Total	Specification
Unfading Green							
	Demolish	Sq.		66.50		66.50	Includes material and labor to install
	Install	Sq.	530	209		739	clear Vermont slate tile.
	Demolish and Install	Sq.	530	275.50		805.50	
	Reinstall	Sq.		167.31		167.31	
	Minimum Charge	Job		183		183	
Unfading Purple							
	Demolish	Sq.		66.50		66.50	Includes material and labor to install
	Install	Sq.	470	209		679	clear Vermont slate tile.
	Demolish and Install	Sq.	470	275.50		745.50	
	Reinstall	Sq.		167.31		167.31	
	Minimum Charge	Job		183		183	
Replace Slate Tiles							
	Install	Ea.	6.50	19.25		25.75	Includes labor and material to replace
	Minimum Charge	Job		183		183	individual slate tiles. Cost is per tile.
Variegated Purple							
	Demolish	Sq.		66.50		66.50	Includes material and labor to install
	Install	Sq.	455	209		664	clear Vermont slate tile.
	Demolish and Install	Sq.	455	275.50		730.50	
	Reinstall	Sq.		167.31		167.31	
	Minimum Charge	Job		183		183	
Unfading Grey / Black							
	Demolish	Sq.		66.50		66.50	Includes material and labor to install
	Install	Sq.	505	209		714	clear Vermont slate tile.
	Demolish and Install	Sq.	505	275.50		780.50	
	Reinstall	Sq.		167.31		167.31	
	Minimum Charge	Job		183		183	
Unfading Red							
	Demolish	Sq.		66.50		66.50	Includes material and labor to install
	Install	Sq.	1300	209		1509	clear Vermont slate tile.
	Demolish and Install	Sq.	1300	275.50		1575.50	
	Reinstall	Sq.		167.31		167.31	
	Minimum Charge	Job		183		183	
Weathering Black							
	Demolish	Sq.		66.50		66.50	Includes material and labor to install
	Install	Sq.	540	209		749	clear Pennsylvania slate tile.
	Demolish and Install	Sq.	540	275.50		815.50	
	Reinstall	Sq.		167.31		167.31	
	Minimum Charge	Job		183		183	

Roofing

Slate Tile Roofing

Slate Tile Roofing		Unit	Material	Labor	Equip.	Total	Specification
Weathering Green							
	Demolish	Sq.		66.50		66.50	Includes material and labor to install
	Install	Sq.	385	209		594	clear Vermont slate tile.
	Demolish and Install	Sq.	385	275.50		660.50	
	Reinstall	Sq.		167.31		167.31	
	Minimum Charge	Job		183		183	

Flat Clay Tile Roofing

Flat Clay Tile Roofing		Unit	Material	Labor	Equip.	Total	Specification
Glazed							
	Demolish	Sq.		74		74	Includes material and labor to install
	Install	Sq.	360	146		506	tile roofing. Cost based on terra cotta
	Demolish and Install	Sq.	360	220		580	red flat clay tile and includes ridge
	Reinstall	Sq.		117.12		117.12	and rake tiles.
	Minimum Charge	Job		183		183	
Terra Cotta Red							
	Demolish	Sq.		74		74	Includes material and labor to install
	Install	Sq.	360	146		506	tile roofing. Cost based on terra cotta
	Demolish and Install	Sq.	360	220		580	red flat clay tile and includes ridge
	Reinstall	Sq.		117.12		117.12	and rake tiles.
	Minimum Charge	Job		183		183	

Mission Tile Roofing

Mission Tile Roofing		Unit	Material	Labor	Equip.	Total	Specification
Glazed Red							
	Demolish	Sq.		74		74	Includes material and labor to install
	Install	Sq.	835	244		1079	tile roofing. Cost based on glazed red
	Demolish and Install	Sq.	835	318		1153	tile and includes birdstop, ridge and
	Reinstall	Sq.		195.20		195.20	rake tiles.
	Minimum Charge	Job		183		183	
Unglazed Red							
	Demolish	Sq.		74		74	Includes material and labor to install
	Install	Sq.	835	244		1079	tile roofing. Cost based on unglazed
	Demolish and Install	Sq.	835	318		1153	red tile and includes birdstop, ridge
	Reinstall	Sq.		195.20		195.20	and rake tiles.
	Minimum Charge	Job		183		183	
Glazed Blue							
	Demolish	Sq.		74		74	Includes material and labor to install
	Install	Sq.	835	244		1079	tile roofing. Cost based on glazed
	Demolish and Install	Sq.	835	318		1153	blue tile and includes birdstop, ridge
	Reinstall	Sq.		195.20		195.20	and rake tiles.
	Minimum Charge	Job		183		183	
Glazed White							
	Demolish	Sq.		74		74	Includes material and labor to install
	Install	Sq.	835	244		1079	tile roofing. Cost based on glazed
	Demolish and Install	Sq.	835	318		1153	white tile and includes birdstop, ridge
	Reinstall	Sq.		195.20		195.20	and rake tiles.
	Minimum Charge	Job		183		183	
Unglazed White							
	Demolish	Sq.		74		74	Includes material and labor to install
	Install	Sq.	835	244		1079	tile roofing. Cost based on unglazed
	Demolish and Install	Sq.	835	318		1153	white tile and includes birdstop, ridge
	Reinstall	Sq.		195.20		195.20	and rake tiles.
	Minimum Charge	Job		183		183	

Roofing

Mission Tile Roofing

Mission Tile Roofing		Unit	Material	Labor	Equip.	Total	Specification
Color Blend							Includes material and labor to install tile roofing. Cost based on color blend tile and includes birdstop, ridge and rake tiles.
	Demolish	Sq.		74		74	
	Install	Sq.	835	244		1079	
	Demolish and Install	Sq.	835	318		1153	
	Reinstall	Sq.		195.20		195.20	
	Minimum Charge	Job		183		183	
Accessories / Extras							
Add for Cap Furring Strips							Includes labor and material to install vertically placed wood furring strips under cap tiles.
	Install	Sq.	98	229		327	
Add for Tile Adhesive							Includes material and labor for adhesive material placed between tiles.
	Install	Sq.	23	13.35		36.35	
Add for Wire Attachment							Includes labor and material to install single wire anchors for attaching tile.
	Install	Sq.	15.15	159		174.15	
Add for Braided Runners							Includes labor and material to install braided wire runners for secure attachment in high wind areas.
	Install	Sq.	38	153		191	
Add for Stainless Steel Nails							Includes material only for stainless steel nails.
	Install	Sq.	25.50			25.50	
Add for Brass Nails							Includes material only for brass nails.
	Install	Sq.	44			44	
Add for Hurricane Clips							Includes material and labor for Hurricane or wind clips for high wind areas.
	Install	Sq.	22.50	215		237.50	
Add for Copper Nails							Includes material only for copper nails.
	Install	Sq.	44			44	
Add for Vertical Furring Strips							Includes labor and material to install vertically placed wood furring strips under tiles.
	Install	Sq.	19.30	42.50		61.80	
Add for Horizontal Furring Strips							Includes labor and material to install horizontally placed wood furring strips under tiles.
	Install	Sq.	12.45	19.05		31.50	

Spanish Tile Roofing

Spanish Tile Roofing		Unit	Material	Labor	Equip.	Total	Specification
Glazed Red							Includes material and labor to install tile roofing. Cost based on glazed red tile and includes birdstop, ridge and rake tiles.
	Demolish	Sq.		74		74	
	Install	Sq.	695	153		848	
	Demolish and Install	Sq.	695	227		922	
	Reinstall	Sq.		122		122	
	Minimum Charge	Job		183		183	
Glazed White							Includes material and labor to install tile roofing. Cost based on glazed white tile and includes birdstop, ridge and rake tiles.
	Demolish	Sq.		74		74	
	Install	Sq.	695	203		898	
	Demolish and Install	Sq.	695	277		972	
	Reinstall	Sq.		162.67		162.67	
	Minimum Charge	Job		183		183	

Roofing

Spanish Tile Roofing		Unit	Material	Labor	Equip.	Total	Specification
Glazed Blue							
	Demolish	Sq.		74		74	Includes material and labor to install
	Install	Sq.	695	153		848	tile roofing. Cost based on glazed
	Demolish and Install	Sq.	695	227		922	blue tile and includes birdstop, ridge
	Reinstall	Sq.		122		122	and rake tiles.
	Minimum Charge	Job		183		183	
Unglazed Red							
	Demolish	Sq.		74		74	Includes material and labor to install
	Install	Sq.	540	153		693	tile roofing. Cost based on unglazed
	Demolish and Install	Sq.	540	227		767	red tile and includes birdstop, ridge
	Reinstall	Sq.		122		122	and rake tiles.
	Minimum Charge	Job		183		183	
Unglazed White							
	Demolish	Sq.		74		74	Includes material and labor to install
	Install	Sq.	605	153		758	tile roofing. Cost based on unglazed
	Demolish and Install	Sq.	605	227		832	white tile and includes birdstop, ridge
	Reinstall	Sq.		122		122	and rake tiles.
	Minimum Charge	Job		183		183	
Color Blend							
	Demolish	Sq.		74		74	Includes material and labor to install
	Install	Sq.	605	153		758	tile roofing. Cost based on color blend
	Demolish and Install	Sq.	605	227		832	tile and includes birdstop, ridge and
	Reinstall	Sq.		122		122	rake tiles.
	Minimum Charge	Job		183		183	
Accessories / Extras							
Add for Vertical Furring Strips							
	Install	Sq.	19.30	42.50		61.80	Includes labor and material to install vertically placed wood furring strips under tiles.
Add for Wire Attachment							
	Install	Sq.	7.75	122		129.75	Includes labor and material to install single wire ties.
Add for Braided Runners							
	Install	Sq.	29	105		134	Includes labor and material to install braided wire runners for secure attachment in high wind areas.
Add for Stainless Steel Nails							
	Install	Sq.	19			19	Includes material only for stainless steel nails.
Add for Copper Nails							
	Install	Sq.	33			33	Includes material only for copper nails.
Add for Brass Nails							
	Install	Sq.	32.50			32.50	Includes material only for brass nails.
Add for Hurricane Clips							
	Install	Sq.	11.60	126		137.60	Includes material and labor to install hurricane or wind clips for high wind areas.
Add for Mortar Set Tiles							
	Install	Sq.	48	183		231	Includes material and labor to install setting tiles by using mortar material placed between tiles.
Add for Tile Adhesive							
	Install	Sq.	11.75	11.90		23.65	Includes material and labor for adhesive placed between tiles.

Roofing

Spanish Tile Roofing

Spanish Tile Roofing		Unit	Material	Labor	Equip.	Total	Specification
Add for Cap Furring Strips	Install	Sq.	98	229		327	Includes labor and material to install vertically placed wood furring strips under cap tiles.
Add for Horizontal Furring Strips	Install	Sq.	12.45	19.05		31.50	Includes labor and material to install horizontally placed wood furring strips under tiles.

Concrete Tile Roofing

Concrete Tile Roofing		Unit	Material	Labor	Equip.	Total	Specification
Corrugated Red / Brown							
	Demolish	Sq.		74		74	Includes material and labor to install tile roofing. Cost includes birdstop, booster, ridge and rake tiles.
	Install	Sq.	107	271		378	
	Demolish and Install	Sq.	107	345		452	
	Reinstall	Sq.		216.89		216.89	
	Minimum Charge	Job		183		183	
Corrugated Gray							
	Demolish	Sq.		74		74	Includes material and labor to install tile roofing. Cost includes birdstop, booster, ridge and rake tiles.
	Install	Sq.	111	271		382	
	Demolish and Install	Sq.	111	345		456	
	Reinstall	Sq.		216.89		216.89	
	Minimum Charge	Job		183		183	
Corrugated Bright Red							
	Demolish	Sq.		74		74	Includes material and labor to install tile roofing. Cost includes birdstop, booster, ridge and rake tiles.
	Install	Sq.	111	271		382	
	Demolish and Install	Sq.	111	345		456	
	Reinstall	Sq.		216.89		216.89	
	Minimum Charge	Job		183		183	
Corrugated Black							
	Demolish	Sq.		74		74	Includes material and labor to install tile roofing. Cost includes birdstop, booster, ridge and rake tiles.
	Install	Sq.	111	271		382	
	Demolish and Install	Sq.	111	345		456	
	Reinstall	Sq.		216.89		216.89	
	Minimum Charge	Job		183		183	
Corrugated Green							
	Demolish	Sq.		74		74	Includes material and labor to install tile roofing. Cost includes birdstop, booster, ridge and rake tiles.
	Install	Sq.	111	271		382	
	Demolish and Install	Sq.	111	345		456	
	Reinstall	Sq.		216.89		216.89	
	Minimum Charge	Job		183		183	
Corrugated Blue							
	Demolish	Sq.		74		74	Includes material and labor to install tile roofing. Cost includes birdstop, booster, ridge and rake tiles.
	Install	Sq.	111	271		382	
	Demolish and Install	Sq.	111	345		456	
	Reinstall	Sq.		216.89		216.89	
	Minimum Charge	Job		183		183	
Flat Natural Gray							
	Demolish	Sq.		74		74	Includes material and labor to install tile roofing. Cost includes birdstop, booster, ridge and rake tiles.
	Install	Sq.	237	271		508	
	Demolish and Install	Sq.	237	345		582	
	Reinstall	Sq.		216.89		216.89	
	Minimum Charge	Job		183		183	

Roofing

Concrete Tile Roofing

	Unit	Material	Labor	Equip.	Total	Specification
Flat Red / Brown						
Demolish	Sq.		74		74	Includes material and labor to install
Install	Sq.	237	271		508	tile roofing. Cost includes birdstop,
Demolish and Install	Sq.	237	345		582	booster, ridge and rake tiles.
Reinstall	Sq.		216.89		216.89	
Minimum Charge	Job		183		183	
Flat Bright Red						
Demolish	Sq.		74		74	Includes material and labor to install
Install	Sq.	237	271		508	tile roofing. Cost includes birdstop,
Demolish and Install	Sq.	237	345		582	booster, ridge and rake tiles.
Reinstall	Sq.		216.89		216.89	
Minimum Charge	Job		183		183	
Flat Green						
Demolish	Sq.		74		74	Includes material and labor to install
Install	Sq.	237	271		508	tile roofing. Cost includes birdstop,
Demolish and Install	Sq.	237	345		582	booster, ridge and rake tiles.
Minimum Charge	Job		183		183	
Flat Blue						
Demolish	Sq.		74		74	Includes material and labor to install
Install	Sq.	237	271		508	tile roofing. Cost includes birdstop,
Demolish and Install	Sq.	237	345		582	booster, ridge and rake tiles.
Reinstall	Sq.		216.89		216.89	
Minimum Charge	Job		183		183	
Flat Black						
Demolish	Sq.		74		74	Includes material and labor to install
Install	Sq.	237	271		508	tile roofing. Cost includes birdstop,
Demolish and Install	Sq.	237	345		582	booster, ridge and rake tiles.
Reinstall	Sq.		216.89		216.89	
Minimum Charge	Job		183		183	

Aluminum Sheet

	Unit	Material	Labor	Equip.	Total	Specification
Corrugated						
.019″ Thick Natural						
Demolish	S.F.		.79		.79	Includes material and labor to install
Install	S.F.	1.40	1.88		3.28	aluminum sheet metal roofing.
Demolish and Install	S.F.	1.40	2.67		4.07	
Reinstall	S.F.		1.50		1.50	
Minimum Charge	Job		450		450	
.016″ Thick Natural						
Demolish	S.F.		.79		.79	Includes material and labor to install
Install	S.F.	1.06	1.88		2.94	aluminum sheet metal roofing.
Demolish and Install	S.F.	1.06	2.67		3.73	
Reinstall	S.F.		1.50		1.50	
Minimum Charge	Job		450		450	
.016″ Colored Finish						
Demolish	S.F.		.79		.79	Includes material and labor to install
Install	S.F.	1.54	1.88		3.42	aluminum sheet metal roofing.
Demolish and Install	S.F.	1.54	2.67		4.21	
Reinstall	S.F.		1.50		1.50	
Minimum Charge	Job		450		450	
.019″ Colored Finish						
Demolish	S.F.		.79		.79	Includes material and labor to install
Install	S.F.	1.71	1.88		3.59	aluminum sheet metal roofing.
Demolish and Install	S.F.	1.71	2.67		4.38	
Reinstall	S.F.		1.50		1.50	
Minimum Charge	Job		450		450	

Aluminum Sheet	Unit	Material	Labor	Equip.	Total	Specification
Ribbed						
.019″ Thick Natural						
Demolish	S.F.		.79		.79	Includes material and labor to install
Install	S.F.	1.40	1.88		3.28	aluminum sheet metal roofing.
Demolish and Install	S.F.	1.40	2.67		4.07	
Reinstall	S.F.		1.50		1.50	
Minimum Charge	Job		450		450	
.016″ Thick Natural						
Demolish	S.F.		.79		.79	Includes material and labor to install
Install	S.F.	1.06	1.88		2.94	aluminum sheet metal roofing.
Demolish and Install	S.F.	1.06	2.67		3.73	
Reinstall	S.F.		1.50		1.50	
Minimum Charge	Job		450		450	
.050″ Colored Finish						
Demolish	S.F.		.79		.79	Includes material and labor to install
Install	S.F.	4.76	1.88		6.64	aluminum sheet metal roofing.
Demolish and Install	S.F.	4.76	2.67		7.43	
Reinstall	S.F.		1.50		1.50	
Minimum Charge	Job		450		450	
.032″ Thick Natural						
Demolish	S.F.		.79		.79	Includes material and labor to install
Install	S.F.	2.70	1.88		4.58	aluminum sheet metal roofing.
Demolish and Install	S.F.	2.70	2.67		5.37	
Reinstall	S.F.		1.50		1.50	
Minimum Charge	Job		450		450	
.040″ Thick Natural						
Demolish	S.F.		.79		.79	Includes material and labor to install
Install	S.F.	3.29	1.88		5.17	aluminum sheet metal roofing.
Demolish and Install	S.F.	3.29	2.67		5.96	
Reinstall	S.F.		1.50		1.50	
Minimum Charge	Job		450		450	
.050″ Thick Natural						
Demolish	S.F.		.79		.79	Includes material and labor to install
Install	S.F.	3.94	1.88		5.82	aluminum sheet metal roofing.
Demolish and Install	S.F.	3.94	2.67		6.61	
Reinstall	S.F.		1.50		1.50	
Minimum Charge	Job		450		450	
.016″ Colored Finish						
Demolish	S.F.		.79		.79	Includes material and labor to install
Install	S.F.	1.54	1.88		3.42	aluminum sheet metal roofing.
Demolish and Install	S.F.	1.54	2.67		4.21	
Reinstall	S.F.		1.50		1.50	
Minimum Charge	Job		450		450	
.019″ Colored Finish						
Demolish	S.F.		.79		.79	Includes material and labor to install
Install	S.F.	1.71	1.88		3.59	aluminum sheet metal roofing.
Demolish and Install	S.F.	1.71	2.67		4.38	
Reinstall	S.F.		1.50		1.50	
Minimum Charge	Job		450		450	
.032″ Colored Finish						
Demolish	S.F.		.79		.79	Includes material and labor to install
Install	S.F.	3.31	1.88		5.19	aluminum sheet metal roofing.
Demolish and Install	S.F.	3.31	2.67		5.98	
Reinstall	S.F.		1.50		1.50	
Minimum Charge	Job		450		450	

Roofing

Aluminum Sheet

Aluminum Sheet	Unit	Material	Labor	Equip.	Total	Specification
.040″ Colored Finish						
Demolish	S.F.		.79		.79	Includes material and labor to install
Install	S.F.	3.95	1.88		5.83	aluminum sheet metal roofing.
Demolish and Install	S.F.	3.95	2.67		6.62	
Reinstall	S.F.		1.50		1.50	
Minimum Charge	Job		450		450	

Fiberglass Sheet

Fiberglass Sheet	Unit	Material	Labor	Equip.	Total	Specification
12 Ounce Corrugated						
Demolish	S.F.		1.41		1.41	Cost includes material and labor to
Install	S.F.	3.78	1.50		5.28	install 12 ounce corrugated fiberglass
Demolish and Install	S.F.	3.78	2.91		6.69	sheet roofing.
Reinstall	S.F.		1.20		1.20	
Minimum Charge	Job		182		182	
8 Ounce Corrugated						
Demolish	S.F.		1.41		1.41	Cost includes material and labor to
Install	S.F.	1.91	1.50		3.41	install 8 ounce corrugated fiberglass
Demolish and Install	S.F.	1.91	2.91		4.82	roofing.
Reinstall	S.F.		1.20		1.20	
Minimum Charge	Job		182		182	

Galvanized Steel

Galvanized Steel	Unit	Material	Labor	Equip.	Total	Specification
Corrugated						
24 Gauge						
Demolish	S.F.		.79		.79	Includes material and labor to install
Install	S.F.	3.20	1.58		4.78	galvanized steel sheet metal roofing.
Demolish and Install	S.F.	3.20	2.37		5.57	Cost based on 24 gauge corrugated
Reinstall	S.F.		1.26		1.26	or ribbed steel roofing.
Minimum Charge	Job		182		182	
26 Gauge						
Demolish	S.F.		.79		.79	Includes material and labor to install
Install	S.F.	2.04	1.50		3.54	galvanized steel sheet metal roofing.
Demolish and Install	S.F.	2.04	2.29		4.33	Cost based on 26 gauge corrugated
Reinstall	S.F.		1.20		1.20	or ribbed steel roofing.
Minimum Charge	Job		182		182	
28 Gauge						
Demolish	S.F.		.79		.79	Includes material and labor to install
Install	S.F.	1.97	1.43		3.40	galvanized steel sheet metal roofing.
Demolish and Install	S.F.	1.97	2.22		4.19	Cost based on 28 gauge corrugated
Reinstall	S.F.		1.14		1.14	or ribbed steel roofing.
Minimum Charge	Job		182		182	
30 Gauge						
Demolish	S.F.		.79		.79	Includes material and labor to install
Install	S.F.	1.85	1.36		3.21	galvanized steel sheet metal roofing.
Demolish and Install	S.F.	1.85	2.15		4	Cost based on 30 gauge corrugated
Reinstall	S.F.		1.09		1.09	or ribbed steel roofing.
Minimum Charge	Job		182		182	

Roofing

Galvanized Steel

Galvanized Steel	Unit	Material	Labor	Equip.	Total	Specification
Ribbed						
24 Gauge						
Demolish	S.F.		.79		.79	Includes material and labor to install
Install	S.F.	3.20	1.58		4.78	galvanized steel sheet metal roofing.
Demolish and Install	S.F.	3.20	2.37		5.57	Cost based on 24 gauge corrugated
Reinstall	S.F.		1.26		1.26	or ribbed steel roofing.
Minimum Charge	Job		182		182	
26 Gauge						
Demolish	S.F.		.79		.79	Includes material and labor to install
Install	S.F.	2.04	1.50		3.54	galvanized steel sheet metal roofing.
Demolish and Install	S.F.	2.04	2.29		4.33	Cost based on 26 gauge corrugated
Reinstall	S.F.		1.20		1.20	or ribbed steel roofing.
Minimum Charge	Job		182		182	
28 Gauge						
Demolish	S.F.		.79		.79	Includes material and labor to install
Install	S.F.	1.97	1.43		3.40	galvanized steel sheet metal roofing.
Demolish and Install	S.F.	1.97	2.22		4.19	Cost based on 28 gauge corrugated
Reinstall	S.F.		1.14		1.14	or ribbed steel roofing.
Minimum Charge	Job		182		182	
30 Gauge						
Demolish	S.F.		.79		.79	Includes material and labor to install
Install	S.F.	1.85	1.36		3.21	galvanized steel sheet metal roofing.
Demolish and Install	S.F.	1.85	2.15		4	Cost based on 30 gauge corrugated
Reinstall	S.F.		1.09		1.09	or ribbed steel roofing.
Minimum Charge	Job		182		182	

Standing Seam

Standing Seam	Unit	Material	Labor	Equip.	Total	Specification
Copper						
16 Ounce						
Demolish	Sq.		78.50		78.50	Includes material and labor to install
Install	Sq.	810	345		1155	copper standing seam metal roofing.
Demolish and Install	Sq.	810	423.50		1233.50	Cost based on 16 ounce copper
Reinstall	Sq.		277.42		277.42	roofing.
Minimum Charge	Job		225		225	
18 Ounce						
Demolish	Sq.		78.50		78.50	Includes material and labor to install
Install	Sq.	910	375		1285	copper standing seam metal roofing.
Demolish and Install	Sq.	910	453.50		1363.50	Cost based on 18 ounce copper
Reinstall	Sq.		300.53		300.53	roofing.
Minimum Charge	Job		225		225	
20 Ounce						
Demolish	Sq.		78.50		78.50	Includes material and labor to install
Install	Sq.	1000	410		1410	copper standing seam metal roofing.
Demolish and Install	Sq.	1000	488.50		1488.50	Cost based on 20 ounce copper
Reinstall	Sq.		327.85		327.85	roofing.
Stainless Steel						
26 Gauge						
Demolish	Sq.		78.50		78.50	Cost includes material and labor to
Install	Sq.	695	390		1085	install 26 gauge stainless steel
Demolish and Install	Sq.	695	468.50		1163.50	standing seam metal roofing.
Reinstall	Sq.		313.60		313.60	
Minimum Charge	Job		225		225	

Looking for your next job to bid?

Get up-to-date construction project information, plans and specs with SmartProject News from Reed Construction Data.

- Find projects bidding in your area
- Browse full project details, plans and specs
- Identify key project participants
- Track projects with e-mail notifications

Register for free access at <u>www.smartprojectnews.com</u>.

SmartProject News
Reed Construction Data

Roofing

Standing Seam

	Unit	Material	Labor	Equip.	Total	Specification
28 Gauge						
Demolish	Sq.		78.50		78.50	Includes material and labor to install
Install	Sq.	690	375		1065	standing seam metal roofing. Cost
Demolish and Install	Sq.	690	453.50		1143.50	based on 28 gauge stainless steel
Reinstall	Sq.		300.53		300.53	roofing.
Minimum Charge	Job		225		225	

Elastomeric Roofing

	Unit	Material	Labor	Equip.	Total	Specification
Neoprene						
1/16"						
Demolish	Sq.		27.50		27.50	Includes material and labor to install
Install	Sq.	287	174	32.50	493.50	neoprene membrane, fully adhered,
Demolish and Install	Sq.	287	201.50	32.50	521	1/16" thick.
Minimum Charge	Job		830	92.50	922.50	
GRM Membrane						
Demolish	Sq.		27.50		27.50	Includes material and labor to install
Install	Sq.	279	277	31	587	coal tar based elastomeric roofing
Demolish and Install	Sq.	279	304.50	31	614.50	membrane, polyester fiber reinforced.
Minimum Charge	Job		830	92.50	922.50	
Cant Strips						
3"						
Demolish	L.F.		.85		.85	Includes material and labor to install
Install	L.F.	1.10	1.12		2.22	cants 3" x 3", treated timber, cut
Demolish and Install	L.F.	1.10	1.97		3.07	diagonally.
Minimum Charge	Job		91		91	
4"						
Demolish	L.F.		.85		.85	Includes material and labor to install
Install	L.F.	2.20	1.12		3.32	cants 4" x 4", treated timber, cut
Demolish and Install	L.F.	2.20	1.97		4.17	diagonally.
Minimum Charge	Job		91		91	
Polyvinyl Chloride (PVC)						
45 mil (loose laid)						
Demolish	Sq.		27.50		27.50	Cost includes material and labor to
Install	Sq.	96.50	32.50	3.63	132.63	install 45 mil PVC elastomeric roofing,
Demolish and Install	Sq.	96.50	60	3.63	160.13	loose-laid with stone.
Minimum Charge	Job		830	92.50	922.50	
48 mil (loose laid)						
Demolish	Sq.		27.50		27.50	Cost includes material and labor to
Install	Sq.	112	32.50	3.63	148.13	install 48 mil PVC elastomeric roofing,
Demolish and Install	Sq.	112	60	3.63	175.63	loose-laid with stone.
Minimum Charge	Job		830	92.50	922.50	
60 mil (loose laid)						
Demolish	Sq.		27.50		27.50	Cost includes material and labor to
Install	Sq.	113	32.50	3.63	149.13	install 60 mil PVC elastomeric roofing,
Demolish and Install	Sq.	113	60	3.63	176.63	loose-laid with stone.
Minimum Charge	Job		830	92.50	922.50	
45 mil (attached)						
Demolish	Sq.		43.50		43.50	Cost includes material and labor to
Install	Sq.	84	64	7.10	155.10	install 45 mil PVC elastomeric roofing
Demolish and Install	Sq.	84	107.50	7.10	198.60	fully attached to roof deck.
Minimum Charge	Job		830	92.50	922.50	

Roofing

Elastomeric Roofing	Unit	Material	Labor	Equip.	Total	Specification
48 mil (attached)						Cost includes material and labor to
Demolish	Sq.		43.50		43.50	install 48 mil PVC elastomeric roofing
Install	Sq.	140	64	7.10	211.10	fully attached to roof deck.
Demolish and Install	Sq.	140	107.50	7.10	254.60	
Minimum Charge	Job		830	92.50	922.50	
60 mil (attached)						Cost includes material and labor to
Demolish	Sq.		43.50		43.50	install 60 mil PVC elastomeric roofing
Install	Sq.	141	64	7.10	212.10	fully attached to roof deck.
Demolish and Install	Sq.	141	107.50	7.10	255.60	
Minimum Charge	Job		830	92.50	922.50	
CSPE Type						
45 mil (loose laid w / stone)						Cost includes material and labor to
Demolish	Sq.		27.50		27.50	install 45 mil CSPE (chlorosulfonated
Install	Sq.	212	32.50	3.63	248.13	polyethylene-hypalon) roofing material
Demolish and Install	Sq.	212	60	3.63	275.63	loose laid on deck and ballasted with
Minimum Charge	Job		830	92.50	922.50	stone.
45 mil (attached at seams)						Cost includes material and labor to
Demolish	Sq.		32.50		32.50	install 45 mil CSPE (chlorosulfonated
Install	Sq.	205	47.50	5.30	257.80	polyethylene-hypalon) roofing material
Demolish and Install	Sq.	205	80	5.30	290.30	attached to deck at seams with batten
Minimum Charge	Job		830	92.50	922.50	strips.
45 mil (fully attached)						Cost includes material and labor to
Demolish	Sq.		43.50		43.50	install 45 mil CSPE (chlorosulfonated
Install	Sq.	204	64	7.10	275.10	polyethylene-hypalon) roofing material
Demolish and Install	Sq.	204	107.50	7.10	318.60	fully attached to deck.
Minimum Charge	Job		830	92.50	922.50	
EPDM Type						
45 mil (attached at seams)						Cost includes material and labor to
Demolish	Sq.		32.50		32.50	install 45 mil EPDM (ethylene
Install	Sq.	72	47.50	5.30	124.80	propylene diene monomer) roofing
Demolish and Install	Sq.	72	80	5.30	157.30	material attached to deck at seams.
Minimum Charge	Job		830	92.50	922.50	
45 mil (fully attached)						Cost includes material and labor to
Demolish	Sq.		43.50		43.50	install 45 mil EPDM (ethylene
Install	Sq.	111	64	7.10	182.10	propylene diene monomer) roofing
Demolish and Install	Sq.	111	107.50	7.10	225.60	material fully attached to deck.
Minimum Charge	Job		830	92.50	922.50	
45 mil (loose laid w / stone)						Cost includes material and labor to
Demolish	Sq.		27.50		27.50	install 45 mil EPDM (ethylene
Install	Sq.	81	32.50	3.63	117.13	propylene diene monomer) roofing
Demolish and Install	Sq.	81	60	3.63	144.63	material loose laid on deck and
Minimum Charge	Job		830	92.50	922.50	ballasted with stones (approx. 1/2 ton
						of stone per square).
60 mil (attached at seams)						Cost includes material and labor to
Demolish	Sq.		32.50		32.50	install 60 mil EPDM (ethylene
Install	Sq.	85.50	47.50	5.30	138.30	propylene diene monomer) roofing
Demolish and Install	Sq.	85.50	80	5.30	170.80	material attached to deck at seams.
Minimum Charge	Job		830	92.50	922.50	
60 mil (fully attached)						Cost includes material and labor to
Demolish	Sq.		43.50		43.50	install 60 mil EPDM (ethylene
Install	Sq.	124	64	7.10	195.10	propylene diene monomer) roofing
Demolish and Install	Sq.	124	107.50	7.10	238.60	material fully attached to deck.
Minimum Charge	Job		830	92.50	922.50	

Roofing

Elastomeric Roofing

	Unit	Material	Labor	Equip.	Total	Specification
60 mil (loose laid w / stone)						Cost includes material and labor to
Demolish	Sq.		27.50		27.50	install 60 mil EPDM (ethylene
Install	Sq.	95.50	32.50	3.63	131.63	propylene diene monomer) roofing
Demolish and Install	Sq.	95.50	60	3.63	159.13	material loose laid on deck and
Minimum Charge	Job		830	92.50	922.50	ballasted with stones (approx. 1/2 ton
						of stone per square).

Modified Bitumen Roofing

	Unit	Material	Labor	Equip.	Total	Specification
Fully Attached						
120 mil						
Demolish	Sq.		65		65	Cost includes material and labor to
Install	Sq.	92	8.10	1.53	101.63	install 120 mil modified bitumen
Demolish and Install	Sq.	92	73.10	1.53	166.63	roofing, fully attached to deck by
Minimum Charge	Job		91		91	torch.
150 mil						
Demolish	Sq.		65		65	Cost includes material and labor to
Install	Sq.	132	19.90	3.75	155.65	install 150 mil modified bitumen
Demolish and Install	Sq.	132	84.90	3.75	220.65	roofing, fully attached to deck by
Minimum Charge	Job		91		91	torch.
160 mil						
Demolish	Sq.		65		65	Cost includes material and labor to
Install	Sq.	106	21	3.92	130.92	install 160 mil modified bitumen
Demolish and Install	Sq.	106	86	3.92	195.92	roofing, fully attached to deck by
Minimum Charge	Job		91		91	torch.

Built-up Roofing

	Unit	Material	Labor	Equip.	Total	Specification
Emergency Repairs						
Install	Ea.	242	1700	320	2262	Minimum charge for work requiring
Minimum Charge	Job		1200	225	1425	hot asphalt.
Asphalt						
3-ply Asphalt						
Demolish	Sq.		67.50		67.50	Cost includes material and labor to
Install	Sq.	66	99.50	18.75	184.25	install 3-ply asphalt built-up roof
Demolish and Install	Sq.	66	167	18.75	251.75	including one 30 lb and two 15 lb
Minimum Charge	Job		1200	225	1425	layers of felt.
4-ply Asphalt						
Demolish	Sq.		80.50		80.50	Cost includes material and labor to
Install	Sq.	91	109	20.50	220.50	install 4-ply asphalt built-up roof
Demolish and Install	Sq.	91	189.50	20.50	301	including one 30 lb and three 15 lb
Minimum Charge	Job		1200	225	1425	layers of felt.
5-ply Asphalt						
Demolish	Sq.		106		106	Cost includes material and labor to
Install	Sq.	127	119	22.50	268.50	install 5-ply asphalt built-up roof
Demolish and Install	Sq.	127	225	22.50	374.50	including one 30 lb and four 15 lb
Minimum Charge	Job		1200	225	1425	layers of felt.

Built-up Roofing

Built-up Roofing		Unit	Material	Labor	Equip.	Total	Specification
Components / Accessories							
Flood Coat							
	Install	Sq.	23	56		79	Includes labor and material to install flood coat.
R / R Gravel and Flood Coat							
	Install	Sq.	29.50	182		211.50	Includes labor and material to install flood coat and gravel.
Aluminum UV Coat							
	Install	Sq.	31	208	23	262	Includes labor and material to install aluminum-based UV coating.
Gravel Coat							
	Demolish	Sq.		34		34	Includes labor and material to install gravel coat.
	Install	Sq.	6.35	30.50		36.85	
	Demolish and Install	Sq.	6.35	64.50		70.85	
Mineral Surface Cap Sheet							
	Install	Sq.	49.50	6.30		55.80	Cost includes labor and material to install 50 # mineral surfaced cap sheet.
Fibrated Aluminum UV Coating							
	Install	Sq.	35	56		91	Includes labor and material to install fibered aluminum-based UV coating.
Impregnated Walk							
1"							
	Install	S.F.	3.08	1.94		5.02	Cost includes labor and material to install 1" layer of asphalt coating.
1/2"							
	Install	S.F.	2.20	1.53		3.73	Cost includes labor and material to install 1/2" layer of asphalt coating.
3/4"							
	Install	S.F.	2.75	1.62		4.37	Cost includes labor and material to install 3/4" layer of asphalt coating.

| Doors | Roof Window | Double Hung Window |

Exterior Type Door		Unit	Material	Labor	Equip.	Total	Specification
Entry							
Flush (1-3/4″)							
	Demolish	Ea.		37.50		37.50	Cost includes material and labor to
	Install	Ea.	229	25		254	install 3′ x 6′ 8″ pre-hung 1-3/4″
	Demolish and Install	Ea.	229	62.50		291.50	door, including casing and stop,
	Reinstall	Ea.		25.23		25.23	hinges, jamb, aluminum sill,
	Clean	Ea.	5.20	12.45		17.65	weatherstripped.
	Paint	Ea.	8.65	49.50		58.15	
	Minimum Charge	Job		202		202	
Raised Panel							
	Demolish	Ea.		37.50		37.50	Cost includes material and labor to
	Install	Ea.	475	22.50		497.50	install 3′ x 6′ 8″ pre-hung 1-3/4″
	Demolish and Install	Ea.	475	60		535	door, jamb, including casing and
	Reinstall	Ea.		22.42		22.42	stop, hinges, aluminum sill,
	Clean	Ea.	5.20	12.45		17.65	weatherstripping.
	Paint	Ea.	8.65	49.50		58.15	
	Minimum Charge	Job		202		202	
Entry w / Lights							
Good Quality							
	Demolish	Ea.		37.50		37.50	Cost includes material and labor to
	Install	Ea.	330	50.50		380.50	install 3′ x 6′ 8″ pre-hung 1-3/4″
	Demolish and Install	Ea.	330	88		418	door, solid wood lower panel, with up
	Reinstall	Ea.		50.45		50.45	to 9-light glass panels, casing, sill,
	Clean	Ea.	5.20	12.45		17.65	weatherstripped.
	Paint	Ea.	6	23		29	
	Minimum Charge	Job		202		202	
Better Quality							
	Demolish	Ea.		37.50		37.50	Cost includes material and labor to
	Install	Ea.	350	50.50		400.50	install 3′ x 6′ 8″ pre-hung 1-3/4″ Ash
	Demolish and Install	Ea.	350	88		438	door, solid wood, raised panel door
	Reinstall	Ea.		50.45		50.45	without glass panels.
	Clean	Ea.	5.20	12.45		17.65	
	Paint	Ea.	8.65	49.50		58.15	
	Minimum Charge	Job		202		202	
Premium Quality							
	Demolish	Ea.		37.50		37.50	Cost includes material and labor to
	Install	Ea.	945	23.50		968.50	install 3′ x 6′ 8″ pre-hung 1-3/4″ Oak
	Demolish and Install	Ea.	945	61		1006	door, solid wood, raised panel door
	Reinstall	Ea.		23.74		23.74	without glass panels.
	Clean	Ea.	5.20	12.45		17.65	
	Paint	Ea.	8.65	49.50		58.15	
	Minimum Charge	Job		202		202	

Exterior Type Door		Unit	Material	Labor	Equip.	Total	Specification
Custom Quality							
	Demolish	Ea.		37.50		37.50	Cost includes material and labor to
	Install	Ea.	360	54		414	install 3' x 6' 8" pre-hung 1-3/4"
	Demolish and Install	Ea.	360	91.50		451.50	hand-made, solid wood, raised panel
	Reinstall	Ea.		53.81		53.81	door with custom stained glass.
	Clean	Ea.	.36	12.45		12.81	
	Paint	Ea.	2.22	115		117.22	
	Minimum Charge	Job		202		202	
Miami Style							
	Demolish	Ea.		37.50		37.50	Cost includes material and labor to
	Install	Ea.	216	23.50		239.50	install 3' x 6' 8" pre-hung 1-3/4"
	Demolish and Install	Ea.	216	61		277	lauan door of solid wood.
	Reinstall	Ea.		23.74		23.74	
	Clean	Ea.	.36	12.45		12.81	
	Paint	Ea.	8.65	49.50		58.15	
	Minimum Charge	Job		202		202	
French Style							
1-Light							
	Demolish	Ea.		37.50		37.50	Cost includes material and labor to
	Install	Ea.	650	29		679	install 3' x 6' 8" pre-hung 1-3/4"
	Demolish and Install	L.F.	650	66.50		716.50	french style door with 1 light.
	Reinstall	Ea.		28.83		28.83	
	Clean	Ea.	3.26	18.70		21.96	
	Paint	Ea.	9.55	86.50		96.05	
	Minimum Charge	Job		202		202	
9-Light							
	Demolish	Ea.		37.50		37.50	Cost includes material and labor to
	Install	Ea.	720.	29.		749.	install 3' x 6' 8" pre-hung 1-3/4"
	Demolish and Install	Ea.	720.	66.50		786.50	french style door with 9 lights.
	Reinstall	Ea.		28.83		28.83	
	Clean	Ea.	.72	25		25.72	
	Paint	Ea.	9.55	86.50		96.05	
	Minimum Charge	Job		202		202	
15-Light							
	Demolish	Ea.		41.50		41.50	Cost includes material and labor to
	Install	Ea.	690	57.50		747.50	install 3' x 6' 8" pre-hung 1-3/4"
	Demolish and Install	Ea.	690	99		789	french style door with 15 lights.
	Reinstall	Ea.		57.66		57.66	
	Clean	Ea.	.72	25		25.72	
	Paint	Ea.	9.55	86.50		96.05	
	Minimum Charge	Job		202		202	
Jamb							
Wood							
	Demolish	Ea.		22.50		22.50	Includes material and labor to install
	Install	Ea.	103	10.90		113.90	flat pine jamb with square cut heads
	Demolish and Install	Ea.	103	33.40		136.40	and rabbeted sides for 6' 8" high and
	Clean	Ea.	.17	7.50		7.67	3-9/16" door including trim sets for
	Paint	Ea.	6	23		29	both sides.
	Minimum Charge	Job		202		202	
Metal 6' 8" High							
	Demolish	Ea.		22.50		22.50	Cost includes material and labor to
	Install	Ea.	162	25		187	install 18 gauge hollow metal door
	Demolish and Install	Ea.	162	47.50		209.50	frame to fit a 4-1/2" jamb 6' 8" high
	Reinstall	Ea.		25.23		25.23	and up to 3' 6" opening.
	Clean	Ea.	1.09	6.25		7.34	
	Paint	Ea.	1.49	6.95		8.44	
	Minimum Charge	Job		202		202	

Exterior Doors and Windows

Exterior Type Door		Unit	Material	Labor	Equip.	Total	Specification
Metal 7' High							
	Demolish	Ea.		22.50		22.50	Cost includes material and labor to
	Install	Ea.	167	27		194	install 18 gauge hollow metal door
	Demolish and Install	Ea.	167	49.50		216.50	frame to fit a 4-1/2" jamb 7' high and
	Reinstall	Ea.		26.91		26.91	up to 3' 6" opening.
	Clean	Ea.	1.09	6.25		7.34	
	Paint	Ea.	1.49	6.95		8.44	
	Minimum Charge	Job		202		202	
Metal 8' High							
	Demolish	Ea.		22.50		22.50	Cost includes material and labor to
	Install	Ea.	206	33.50		239.50	install 18 gauge hollow metal door
	Demolish and Install	Ea.	206	56		262	frame to fit a 4-1/2" jamb 8' high and
	Reinstall	Ea.		33.63		33.63	up to 3' 6" opening.
	Clean	Ea.	1.53	7.50		9.03	
	Paint	Ea.	1.66	7.70		9.36	
	Minimum Charge	Job		202		202	
Metal 9' High							
	Demolish	Ea.		22.50		22.50	Cost includes material and labor to
	Install	Ea.	267	40.50		307.50	install 18 gauge hollow metal door
	Demolish and Install	Ea.	267	63		330	frame to fit a 4-1/2" jamb 9' high and
	Reinstall	Ea.		40.36		40.36	up to 3' 6" opening.
	Clean	Ea.	1.53	7.50		9.03	
	Paint	Ea.	1.66	7.70		9.36	
	Minimum Charge	Job		202		202	
Casing Trim							
Single Width							
	Demolish	Ea.		7.10		7.10	Cost includes material and labor to
	Install	Opng.	25	33.50		58.50	install 11/16" x 2-1/2" pine ranch
	Demolish and Install	Opng.	25	40.60		65.60	style casing for one side of a standard
	Reinstall	Opng.		26.91		26.91	door opening.
	Clean	Opng.	.74	2.99		3.73	
	Paint	Ea.	4.38	6.95		11.33	
	Minimum Charge	Job		202		202	
Double Width							
	Demolish	Ea.		8.45		8.45	Cost includes material and labor to
	Install	Opng.	29	40.50		69.50	install 11/16" x 2-1/2" pine ranch
	Demolish and Install	Opng.	29	48.95		77.95	style door casing for one side of a
	Reinstall	Opng.		32.29		32.29	double door opening.
	Clean	Opng.	.87	6		6.87	
	Paint	Ea.	4.38	7.85		12.23	
	Minimum Charge	Job		202		202	

Residential Metal Door		Unit	Material	Labor	Equip.	Total	Specification
Pre-hung, Steel-clad							
2' 8" x 6' 8"							
	Demolish	Ea.		37.50		37.50	Cost includes material and labor to
	Install	Ea.	253	50.50		303.50	install 2' x 6' 8" pre-hung 1-3/4" 24
	Demolish and Install	Ea.	253	88		341	gauge steel clad door with 4-1/2"
	Reinstall	Ea.		50.45		50.45	wood frame, trims, hinges, aluminum
	Clean	Ea.	5.20	12.45		17.65	sill, weatherstripped.
	Paint	Ea.	9.55	49.50		59.05	
	Minimum Charge	Job		202		202	

Exterior Doors and Windows

Residential Metal Door	Unit	Material	Labor	Equip.	Total	Specification
3' x 6' 8"						
Demolish	Ea.		37.50		37.50	Cost includes material and labor to
Install	Ea.	253	54		307	install 3' x 6' 8" pre-hung 1-3/4" 24
Demolish and Install	Ea.	253	91.50		344.50	gauge steel clad door with 4-1/2"
Reinstall	Ea.		53.81		53.81	wood frame, trims, hinges, aluminum
Clean	Ea.	5.20	12.45		17.65	sill, weatherstripped.
Paint	Ea.	9.55	49.50		59.05	
Minimum Charge	Job		202		202	

Metal Door	Unit	Material	Labor	Equip.	Total	Specification
2' 8" x 6' 8", 18 Gauge						
Demolish	Ea.		8		8	Cost includes material and labor to
Install	Ea.	525	25		550	install 18 gauge 2' 8" x 6' 8" steel
Demolish and Install	Ea.	525	33		558	door only, 1-3/4" thick, hinges.
Reinstall	Ea.		25.23		25.23	
Clean	Ea.	2.17	9.35		11.52	
Paint	Ea.	5.40	29		34.40	
Minimum Charge	Job		202		202	
3' x 6' 8", 18 Gauge						
Demolish	Ea.		8		8	Cost includes material and labor to
Install	Ea.	510	27		537	install 18 gauge 3' x 6' 8" steel door
Demolish and Install	Ea.	510	35		545	only, 1-3/4" thick, hinges.
Reinstall	Ea.		26.91		26.91	
Clean	Ea.	2.17	9.35		11.52	
Paint	Ea.	5.40	29		34.40	
Minimum Charge	Job		202		202	
2' 8" x 7', 18 Gauge						
Demolish	Ea.		8		8	Cost includes material and labor to
Install	Ea.	545	27		572	install 18 gauge 2' 8" x 7' steel door
Demolish and Install	Ea.	545	35		580	only, 1-3/4" thick, hinges.
Reinstall	Ea.		26.91		26.91	
Clean	Ea.	2.17	9.35		11.52	
Paint	Ea.	5.40	29		34.40	
Minimum Charge	Job		202		202	
3' x 7', 18 Gauge						
Demolish	Ea.		8		8	Cost includes material and labor to
Install	Ea.	535	29		564	install 18 gauge 3' x 7' steel door
Demolish and Install	Ea.	535	37		572	only, 1-3/4" thick, hinges.
Reinstall	Ea.		28.83		28.83	
Clean	Ea.	2.17	9.35		11.52	
Paint	Ea.	5.40	29		34.40	
Minimum Charge	Job		202		202	
3' 6" x 7', 18 Gauge						
Demolish	Ea.		8		8	Cost includes material and labor to
Install	Ea.	610	31		641	install 18 gauge 3' 6" x 7' steel door
Demolish and Install	Ea.	610	39		649	only, 1-3/4" thick, hinges.
Reinstall	Ea.		31.05		31.05	
Clean	Ea.	2.17	9.35		11.52	
Paint	Ea.	5.40	29		34.40	
Minimum Charge	Job		202		202	

Exterior Doors and Windows

Metal Door

Metal Door		Unit	Material	Labor	Equip.	Total	Specification
Casing Trim							
Single Width							
	Demolish	Ea.		7.10		7.10	Cost includes material and labor to
	Install	Opng.	25	33.50		58.50	install 11/16" x 2-1/2" pine ranch
	Demolish and Install	Opng.	25	40.60		65.60	style casing for one side of a standard
	Reinstall	Opng.		26.91		26.91	door opening.
	Clean	Opng.	.74	2.99		3.73	
	Paint	Ea.	4.38	6.95		11.33	
	Minimum Charge	Job		202		202	
Double Width							
	Demolish	Ea.		8.45		8.45	Cost includes material and labor to
	Install	Opng.	29	40.50		69.50	install 11/16" x 2-1/2" pine ranch
	Demolish and Install	Opng.	29	48.95		77.95	style door casing for one side of a
	Reinstall	Opng.		32.29		32.29	double door opening.
	Clean	Opng.	.87	6		6.87	
	Paint	Ea.	4.38	7.85		12.23	
	Minimum Charge	Job		202		202	

Solid Core Door

Solid Core Door		Unit	Material	Labor	Equip.	Total	Specification
Exterior Type							
Flush (1-3/4")							
	Demolish	Ea.		37.50		37.50	Cost includes material and labor to
	Install	Ea.	360	50.50		410.50	install 3' x 6' 8" pre-hung 1-3/4"
	Demolish and Install	Ea.	360	88		448	door, including casing and stop,
	Reinstall	Ea.		50.45		50.45	hinges, jamb, aluminum sill,
	Clean	Ea.	5.20	12.45		17.65	weatherstripped.
	Paint	Ea.	9.55	49.50		59.05	
	Minimum Charge	Job		202		202	
Raised Panel							
	Demolish	Ea.		37.50		37.50	Cost includes material and labor to
	Install	Ea.	475	22.50		497.50	install 3' x 6' 8" pre-hung 1-3/4"
	Demolish and Install	Ea.	475	60		535	door, jamb, including casing and
	Reinstall	Ea.		22.42		22.42	stop, hinges, aluminum sill,
	Clean	Ea.	5.20	12.45		17.65	weatherstripping.
	Paint	Ea.	9.55	115		124.55	
	Minimum Charge	Job		202		202	
Entry w / Lights							
	Demolish	Ea.		37.50		37.50	Cost includes material and labor to
	Install	Ea.	330	50.50		380.50	install 3' x 6' 8" pre-hung 1-3/4"
	Demolish and Install	Ea.	330	88		418	door, solid wood lower panel, with up
	Reinstall	Ea.		50.45		50.45	to 9-light glass panels, casing, sill,
	Clean	Ea.	5.20	12.45		17.65	weatherstripped.
	Paint	Ea.	2.22	115		117.22	
	Minimum Charge	Job		202		202	
Custom Entry							
	Demolish	Ea.		37.50		37.50	Cost includes material and labor to
	Install	Ea.	1650	80.50		1730.50	install prehung, fir, single glazed with
	Demolish and Install	Ea.	1650	118		1768	lead caming, 1-3/4" x 6' 8" x 3'
	Reinstall	Ea.		80.72		80.72	
	Clean	Ea.	5.20	12.45		17.65	
	Paint	Ea.	5.40	29		34.40	
	Minimum Charge	Job		202		202	

Exterior Doors and Windows

Solid Core Door		Unit	Material	Labor	Equip.	Total	Specification
Dutch Style							
	Demolish	Ea.		37.50		37.50	Includes material and labor to install
	Install	Ea.	745	67.50		812.50	dutch door, pine, 1-3/4" x 6' 8" x 2'
	Demolish and Install	Ea.	745	105		850	8" wide.
	Reinstall	Ea.		67.27		67.27	
	Clean	Ea.	5.20	12.45		17.65	
	Paint	Ea.	2.22	115		117.22	
	Minimum Charge	Job		202		202	
Miami Style							
	Demolish	Ea.		37.50		37.50	Cost includes material and labor to
	Install	Ea.	216	23.50		239.50	install 3' x 6' 8" pre-hung 1-3/4"
	Demolish and Install	Ea.	216	61		277	lauan door of solid wood.
	Reinstall	Ea.		23.74		23.74	
	Clean	Ea.	5.20	12.45		17.65	
	Paint	Ea.	8.65	49.50		58.15	
	Minimum Charge	Job		202		202	
French Style							
	Demolish	Ea.		41.50		41.50	Cost includes material and labor to
	Install	Ea.	690	57.50		747.50	install 3' x 6' 8" pre-hung 1-3/4"
	Demolish and Install	Ea.	690	99		789	french style door with 15 lights.
	Reinstall	Ea.		57.66		57.66	
	Clean	Ea.	.36	12.45		12.81	
	Paint	Ea.	6.50	173		179.50	
	Minimum Charge	Job		202		202	
Double							
	Demolish	Ea.		27.50		27.50	Includes material and labor to install a
	Install	Ea.	1450	101		1551	pre-hung double entry door including
	Demolish and Install	Ea.	1450	128.50		1578.50	frame and exterior trim.
	Clean	Ea.	.20	43.50		43.70	
	Paint	Ea.	19.10	173		192.10	
	Minimum Charge	Job		101		101	
Commercial Grade							
3' x 6' 8"							
	Demolish	Ea.		37.50		37.50	Includes material and labor to install
	Install	Ea.	305	23.50		328.50	flush solid core 1-3/4" hardwood
	Demolish and Install	Ea.	305	61		366	veneer 3' x 6' 8' door only.
	Reinstall	Ea.		23.74		23.74	
	Clean	Ea.	5.20	12.45		17.65	
	Paint	Ea.	8.95	29		37.95	
	Minimum Charge	Job		202		202	
3' 6" x 6' 8"							
	Demolish	Ea.		37.50		37.50	Includes material and labor to install
	Install	Ea.	415	23.50		438.50	flush solid core 1-3/4" hardwood
	Demolish and Install	Ea.	415	61		476	veneer 3' 6" x 6' 8' door only.
	Reinstall	Ea.		23.74		23.74	
	Clean	Ea.	5.20	12.45		17.65	
	Paint	Ea.	8.95	29		37.95	
	Minimum Charge	Job		202		202	
3' x 7'							
	Demolish	Ea.		37.50		37.50	Includes material and labor to install
	Install	Ea.	325	57.50		382.50	flush solid core 1-3/4" hardwood
	Demolish and Install	Ea.	325	95		420	veneer 3' x 7' door only.
	Reinstall	Ea.		57.66		57.66	
	Clean	Ea.	5.20	12.45		17.65	
	Paint	Ea.	8.95	29		37.95	
	Minimum Charge	Job		202		202	

Solid Core Door	Unit	Material	Labor	Equip.	Total	Specification
3' 6" x 7'						
Demolish	Ea.		37.50		37.50	Includes material and labor to install
Install	Ea.	445	29		474	flush solid core 1-3/4" hardwood
Demolish and Install	Ea.	445	66.50		511.50	veneer 3' 6" x 7' door only.
Reinstall	Ea.		28.83		28.83	
Clean	Ea.	5.20	12.45		17.65	
Paint	Ea.	8.95	29		37.95	
Minimum Charge	Job		202		202	
3' x 8'						
Demolish	Ea.		37.50		37.50	Includes material and labor to install
Install	Ea.	385	50.50		435.50	flush solid core 1-3/4" hardwood
Demolish and Install	Ea.	385	88		473	veneer 3' x 8' door only.
Reinstall	Ea.		50.45		50.45	
Clean	Ea.	6.20	18.70		24.90	
Paint	Ea.	8.95	29		37.95	
Minimum Charge	Job		202		202	
3' 6" x 8'						
Demolish	Ea.		37.50		37.50	Includes material and labor to install
Install	Ea.	470	50.50		520.50	flush solid core 1-3/4" hardwood
Demolish and Install	Ea.	470	88		558	veneer 3' 6" x 8' door only.
Reinstall	Ea.		50.45		50.45	
Clean	Ea.	6.20	18.70		24.90	
Paint	Ea.	8.95	29		37.95	
Minimum Charge	Job		202		202	
3' x 9'						
Demolish	Ea.		37.50		37.50	Includes material and labor to install
Install	Ea.	535	57.50		592.50	flush solid core 1-3/4" hardwood
Demolish and Install	Ea.	535	95		630	veneer 3' x 9' door only.
Reinstall	Ea.		57.66		57.66	
Clean	Ea.	6.20	18.70		24.90	
Paint	Ea.	8.95	29		37.95	
Minimum Charge	Job		202		202	
Stain						
Install	Ea.	9	38.50		47.50	Includes labor and material to stain
Minimum Charge	Job		173		173	exterior type door and trim on both sides.
Door Only (SC)						
2' 4" x 6' 8"						
Demolish	Ea.		8		8	Cost includes material and labor to
Install	Ea.	205	22.50		227.50	install 2' 4" x 6' 8" lauan solid core
Demolish and Install	Ea.	205	30.50		235.50	door slab.
Reinstall	Ea.		22.42		22.42	
Clean	Ea.	2.17	9.35		11.52	
Paint	Ea.	4.28	43.50		47.78	
Minimum Charge	Job		202		202	
2' 8" x 6' 8"						
Demolish	Ea.		8		8	Cost includes material and labor to
Install	Ea.	212	22.50		234.50	install 2' 8" x 6' 8" lauan solid core
Demolish and Install	Ea.	212	30.50		242.50	door slab.
Reinstall	Ea.		22.42		22.42	
Clean	Ea.	2.17	9.35		11.52	
Paint	Ea.	4.28	43.50		47.78	
Minimum Charge	Job		202		202	

Exterior Doors and Windows

Solid Core Door

	Unit	Material	Labor	Equip.	Total	Specification
3' x 6' 8"						
Demolish	Ea.		8		8	Cost includes material and labor to
Install	Ea.	219	23.50		242.50	install 3' x 6' 8" lauan solid core door
Demolish and Install	Ea.	219	31.50		250.50	slab.
Reinstall	Ea.		23.74		23.74	
Clean	Ea.	2.17	9.35		11.52	
Paint	Ea.	4.28	43.50		47.78	
Minimum Charge	Job		202		202	
3' 6" x 6' 8"						
Demolish	Ea.		8		8	Cost includes material and labor to
Install	Ea.	251	25		276	install 3' 6" x 6' 8" lauan solid core
Demolish and Install	Ea.	251	33		284	door slab.
Reinstall	Ea.		25.23		25.23	
Clean	Ea.	2.17	9.35		11.52	
Paint	Ea.	4.28	43.50		47.78	
Minimum Charge	Job		202		202	
Panel						
Demolish	Ea.		8		8	Cost includes material and labor to
Install	Ea.	184	47.50		231.50	install 3' x 6' 8" six (6) panel interior
Demolish and Install	Ea.	184	55.50		239.50	door.
Reinstall	Ea.		47.48		47.48	
Clean	Ea.	2.60	9.35		11.95	
Paint	Ea.	4.28	43.50		47.78	
Minimum Charge	Job		202		202	

Casing Trim
Single Width

	Unit	Material	Labor	Equip.	Total	Specification
Demolish	Ea.		7.10		7.10	Cost includes material and labor to
Install	Opng.	25	33.50		58.50	install 11/16" x 2-1/2" pine ranch
Demolish and Install	Opng.	25	40.60		65.60	style casing for one side of a standard
Reinstall	Opng.		26.91		26.91	door opening.
Clean	Opng.	.74	2.99		3.73	
Paint	Ea.	4.38	6.95		11.33	
Minimum Charge	Job		202		202	

Double Width

	Unit	Material	Labor	Equip.	Total	Specification
Demolish	Ea.		8.45		8.45	Cost includes material and labor to
Install	Opng.	29	40.50		69.50	install 11/16" x 2-1/2" pine ranch
Demolish and Install	Opng.	29	48.95		77.95	style door casing for one side of a
Reinstall	Opng.		32.29		32.29	double door opening.
Clean	Opng.	.87	6		6.87	
Paint	Ea.	4.38	7.85		12.23	
Minimum Charge	Job		202		202	

Components

	Unit	Material	Labor	Equip.	Total	Specification
Hardware						
Doorknob						
Demolish	Ea.		16		16	Includes material and labor to install
Install	Ea.	27.50	25		52.50	residential passage lockset, keyless
Demolish and Install	Ea.	27.50	41		68.50	bored type.
Reinstall	Ea.		20.18		20.18	
Clean	Ea.	.52	9.35		9.87	
Minimum Charge	Job		202		202	

Exterior Doors and Windows

Components		Unit	Material	Labor	Equip.	Total	Specification
Doorknob w / Lock							
	Demolish	Ea.		16		16	Includes material and labor to install
	Install	Ea.	43.50	25		68.50	privacy lockset.
	Demolish and Install	Ea.	43.50	41		84.50	
	Reinstall	Ea.		20.18		20.18	
	Clean	Ea.	.52	9.35		9.87	
	Minimum Charge	Job		202		202	
Lever Handle							
	Demolish	Ea.		16		16	Includes material and labor to install
	Install	Ea.	37.50	40.50		78	residential passage lockset, keyless
	Demolish and Install	Ea.	37.50	56.50		94	bored type with lever handle.
	Reinstall	Ea.		32.29		32.29	
	Clean	Ea.	.52	9.35		9.87	
	Minimum Charge	Job		202		202	
Deadbolt							
	Demolish	Ea.		14		14	Includes material and labor to install a
	Install	Ea.	67	29		96	deadbolt.
	Demolish and Install	Ea.	67	43		110	
	Reinstall	Ea.		23.06		23.06	
	Clean	Ea.	.52	9.35		9.87	
	Minimum Charge	Job		202		202	
Grip Handle Entry							
	Demolish	Ea.		12.80		12.80	Includes material and labor to install
	Install	Ea.	88	45		133	residential keyed entry lock set with
	Demolish and Install	Ea.	88	57.80		145.80	grip type handle.
	Reinstall	Ea.		35.88		35.88	
	Clean	Ea.	.52	9.35		9.87	
	Minimum Charge	Job		202		202	
Panic Device							
	Demolish	Ea.		33		33	Includes material and labor to install
	Install	Ea.	425	67.50		492.50	touch bar, low profile, exit only.
	Demolish and Install	Ea.	425	100.50		525.50	
	Reinstall	Ea.		53.81		53.81	
	Clean	Ea.	.26	16.60		16.86	
	Minimum Charge	Job		202		202	
Closer							
	Demolish	Ea.		8.40		8.40	Includes material and labor to install
	Install	Ea.	234	67.50		301.50	pneumatic heavy duty closer for
	Demolish and Install	Ea.	234	75.90		309.90	exterior type doors.
	Reinstall	Ea.		53.81		53.81	
	Clean	Ea.	.26	12.45		12.71	
	Minimum Charge	Job		202		202	
Peep-hole							
	Demolish	Ea.		7.40		7.40	Includes material and labor to install
	Install	Ea.	17.40	12.60		30	peep-hole for door.
	Demolish and Install	Ea.	17.40	20		37.40	
	Reinstall	Ea.		10.09		10.09	
	Clean	Ea.	.04	3.36		3.40	
	Minimum Charge	Job		202		202	
Exit Sign							
	Demolish	Ea.		22		22	Includes material and labor to install a
	Install	Ea.	105	54.50		159.50	wall mounted interior electric exit sign.
	Demolish and Install	Ea.	105	76.50		181.50	
	Reinstall	Ea.		43.72		43.72	
	Clean	Ea.	.04	6.85		6.89	
	Minimum Charge	Job		202		202	

Components		Unit	Material	Labor	Equip.	Total	Specification
Kickplate							Includes material and labor to install
	Demolish	Ea.		12.45		12.45	aluminum kickplate, 10" x 28".
	Install	Ea.	28.50	27		55.50	
	Demolish and Install	Ea.	28.50	39.45		67.95	
	Reinstall	Ea.		21.53		21.53	
	Clean	Ea.	.52	9.35		9.87	
	Minimum Charge	Job		202		202	
Threshold							Includes labor and material to install
	Install	L.F.	4.21	4.04		8.25	oak threshold.
	Minimum Charge	Job		101		101	
Weatherstripping							Includes labor and material to install
	Install	L.F.	.35	1.01		1.36	rubber weatherstripping for door.
	Minimum Charge	Job		101		101	
Metal Jamb							
6' 8" High							Cost includes material and labor to
	Demolish	Ea.		22.50		22.50	install 18 gauge hollow metal door
	Install	Ea.	162	25		187	frame to fit a 4-1/2" jamb 6' 8" high
	Demolish and Install	Ea.	162	47.50		209.50	and up to 3' 6" opening.
	Reinstall	Ea.		25.23		25.23	
	Clean	Ea.	1.09	6.25		7.34	
	Paint	Ea.	1.49	6.95		8.44	
	Minimum Charge	Job		202		202	
7' High							Cost includes material and labor to
	Demolish	Ea.		22.50		22.50	install 18 gauge hollow metal door
	Install	Ea.	167	27		194	frame to fit a 4-1/2" jamb 7' high and
	Demolish and Install	Ea.	167	49.50		216.50	up to 3' 6" opening.
	Reinstall	Ea.		26.91		26.91	
	Clean	Ea.	1.09	6.25		7.34	
	Paint	Ea.	1.49	6.95		8.44	
	Minimum Charge	Job		202		202	
8' High							Cost includes material and labor to
	Demolish	Ea.		22.50		22.50	install 18 gauge hollow metal door
	Install	Ea.	206	33.50		239.50	frame to fit a 4-1/2" jamb 8' high and
	Demolish and Install	Ea.	206	56		262	up to 3' 6" opening.
	Reinstall	Ea.		33.63		33.63	
	Clean	Ea.	1.53	7.50		9.03	
	Paint	Ea.	1.66	7.70		9.36	
	Minimum Charge	Job		202		202	
9' High							Cost includes material and labor to
	Demolish	Ea.		22.50		22.50	install 18 gauge hollow metal door
	Install	Ea.	267	40.50		307.50	frame to fit a 4-1/2" jamb 9' high and
	Demolish and Install	Ea.	267	63		330	up to 3' 6" opening.
	Reinstall	Ea.		40.36		40.36	
	Clean	Ea.	1.53	7.50		9.03	
	Paint	Ea.	1.66	7.70		9.36	
	Minimum Charge	Job		202		202	
Wood Jamb							Includes material and labor to install
	Demolish	Ea.		28		28	flat pine jamb with square cut heads
	Install	Ea.	103	10.90		113.90	and rabbeted sides for 6' 8" high and
	Demolish and Install	Ea.	103	38.90		141.90	3-9/16" door including trim sets for
	Clean	Ea.	.17	7.50		7.67	both sides.
	Paint	Ea.	6	23		29	
	Minimum Charge	Job		101		101	
Stain							Includes labor and material to stain
	Install	Ea.	6.20	29		35.20	single door and trim on both sides.
	Minimum Charge	Job		173		173	

Exterior Doors and Windows

Components		Unit	Material	Labor	Equip.	Total	Specification
Shave & Refit							
	Install	Ea.		33.50		33.50	Includes labor to shave and rework
	Minimum Charge	Job		101		101	door to fit opening at the job site.

Sliding Patio Door		Unit	Material	Labor	Equip.	Total	Specification
Aluminum							
6' Single Pane							
	Demolish	Ea.		56		56	Cost includes material and labor to
	Install	Ea.	495	202		697	install 6' x 6' 8" sliding anodized
	Demolish and Install	Ea.	495	258		753	aluminum patio door with single pane
	Reinstall	Ea.		161.44		161.44	tempered safety glass, anodized
	Clean	Ea.	3.26	18.70		21.96	frame, screen, weatherstripped.
	Minimum Charge	Job		202		202	
8' Single Pane							
	Demolish	Ea.		56		56	Cost includes material and labor to
	Install	Ea.	625	269		894	install 8' x 6' 8" sliding aluminum
	Demolish and Install	Ea.	625	325		950	patio door with single pane tempered
	Reinstall	Ea.		215.25		215.25	safety glass, anodized frame, screen,
	Clean	Ea.	3.26	18.70		21.96	weatherstripped.
	Minimum Charge	Job		202		202	
10' Single Pane							
	Demolish	Ea.		56		56	Cost includes material and labor to
	Install	Ea.	710	405		1115	install 10' x 6' 8" sliding aluminum
	Demolish and Install	Ea.	710	461		1171	patio door with single pane tempered
	Reinstall	Ea.		322.88		322.88	safety glass, anodized frame, screen,
	Clean	Ea.	3.26	18.70		21.96	weatherstripped.
	Minimum Charge	Job		202		202	
6' Insulated							
	Demolish	Ea.		56		56	Cost includes material and labor to
	Install	Ea.	985	202		1187	install 6' x 6' 8" sliding aluminum
	Demolish and Install	Ea.	985	258		1243	patio door with double insulated
	Reinstall	Ea.		161.44		161.44	tempered glass, baked-on enamel
	Clean	Ea.	3.26	18.70		21.96	finish, screen, weatherstripped.
	Minimum Charge	Job		202		202	
8' Insulated							
	Demolish	Ea.		56		56	Cost includes material and labor to
	Install	Ea.	1150	269		1419	install 8' x 6' 8" sliding aluminum
	Demolish and Install	Ea.	1150	325		1475	patio door with insulated tempered
	Reinstall	Ea.		215.25		215.25	glass, baked-on enamel finish, screen,
	Clean	Ea.	3.26	18.70		21.96	weatherstripped.
	Minimum Charge	Job		202		202	
10' Insulated							
	Demolish	Ea.		56		56	Cost includes material and labor to
	Install	Ea.	1425	405		1830	install 10' x 6' 8" sliding aluminum
	Demolish and Install	Ea.	1425	461		1886	patio door with double insulated
	Reinstall	Ea.		322.88		322.88	tempered glass, baked-on enamel
	Clean	Ea.	3.26	18.70		21.96	finish, screen, weatherstripped.
	Minimum Charge	Job		202		202	

Exterior Doors and Windows

Sliding Patio Door	Unit	Material	Labor	Equip.	Total	Specification
Vinyl						
6' Single Pane						
Demolish	Ea.		56		56	Cost includes material and labor to
Install	Ea.	460	202		662	install 6' x 6' 8" sliding vinyl patio
Demolish and Install	Ea.	460	258		718	door with single pane tempered safety
Reinstall	Ea.		161.44		161.44	glass, anodized frame, screen,
Clean	Ea.	3.26	18.70		21.96	weatherstripped.
Minimum Charge	Job		202		202	
8' Single Pane						
Demolish	Ea.		56		56	Cost includes material and labor to
Install	Ea.	640	269		909	install 8' x 6' 8" sliding vinyl patio
Demolish and Install	Ea.	640	325		965	door with single pane tempered safety
Reinstall	Ea.		215.25		215.25	glass, anodized frame, screen,
Clean	Ea.	3.26	18.70		21.96	weatherstripped.
Minimum Charge	Job		202		202	
10' Single Pane						
Demolish	Ea.		56		56	Cost includes material and labor to
Install	Ea.	695	405		1100	install 10' x 6' 8" sliding vinyl patio
Demolish and Install	Ea.	695	461		1156	door with single pane tempered safety
Reinstall	Ea.		322.88		322.88	glass, anodized frame, screen,
Clean	Ea.	3.26	18.70		21.96	weatherstripped.
Minimum Charge	Job		202		202	
6' Insulated						
Demolish	Ea.		56		56	Cost includes material and labor to
Install	Ea.	1200	202		1402	install 6' x 6' 8" sliding vinyl patio
Demolish and Install	Ea.	1200	258		1458	door with double insulated tempered
Reinstall	Ea.		161.44		161.44	glass, anodized frame, screen,
Clean	Ea.	3.26	18.70		21.96	weatherstripped.
Minimum Charge	Job		202		202	
8' Insulated						
Demolish	Ea.		56		56	Cost includes material and labor to
Install	Ea.	1000	269		1269	install 8' x 6' 8" sliding vinyl patio
Demolish and Install	Ea.	1000	325		1325	door with double insulated tempered
Reinstall	Ea.		215.25		215.25	glass, anodized frame, screen,
Clean	Ea.	3.26	18.70		21.96	weatherstripped.
Minimum Charge	Job		202		202	
10' Insulated						
Demolish	Ea.		56		56	Cost includes material and labor to
Install	Ea.	1800	202		2002	install 10' x 6' 8" sliding vinyl patio
Demolish and Install	Ea.	1800	258		2058	door with double insulated tempered
Reinstall	Ea.		161.44		161.44	glass, anodized frame, screen,
Clean	Ea.	3.26	18.70		21.96	weatherstripped.
Minimum Charge	Job		202		202	
Wood Framed						
6' Premium Insulated						
Demolish	Ea.		56		56	Cost includes material and labor to
Install	Ea.	1550	202		1752	install 6' x 6' 8" sliding wood patio
Demolish and Install	Ea.	1550	258		1808	door with pine frame, double insulated
Reinstall	Ea.		161.44		161.44	glass, screen, lock and dead bolt,
Clean	Ea.	3.26	18.70		21.96	weatherstripped. Add for casing and
Minimum Charge	Job		202		202	finishing.

Exterior Doors and Windows

Sliding Patio Door

Sliding Patio Door	Unit	Material	Labor	Equip.	Total	Specification
8' Premium Insulated						Cost includes material and labor to
Demolish	Ea.		56		56	install 8' x 6' 8" sliding wood patio
Install	Ea.	1950	269		2219	door with pine frame, double insulated
Demolish and Install	Ea.	1950	325		2275	glass, screen, lock and dead bolt,
Reinstall	Ea.		215.25		215.25	weatherstripped. Add for casing and
Clean	Ea.	3.26	18.70		21.96	finishing.
Minimum Charge	Job		202		202	
9' Premium Insulated						Cost includes material and labor to
Demolish	Ea.		56		56	install 9' x 6' 8" sliding wood patio
Install	Ea.	1950	269		2219	door with pine frame, double insulated
Demolish and Install	Ea.	1950	325		2275	glass, screen, lock and dead bolt,
Reinstall	Ea.		215.25		215.25	weatherstripped. Add for casing and
Clean	Ea.	3.26	18.70		21.96	finishing.
Minimum Charge	Job		202		202	
Stain						Includes labor and material to stain
Install	Ea.	9	38.50		47.50	exterior type door and trim on both
Minimum Charge	Job		173		173	sides.
Casing Trim						Cost includes material and labor to
Demolish	Ea.		8.45		8.45	install 11/16" x 2-1/2" pine ranch
Install	Opng.	29	40.50		69.50	style door casing for one side of a
Demolish and Install	Opng.	29	48.95		77.95	double door opening.
Reinstall	Opng.		32.29		32.29	
Clean	Opng.	.87	6		6.87	
Paint	Ea.	4.38	7.85		12.23	
Minimum Charge	Job		202		202	
Sliding Screen						Includes material and labor to install
Demolish	Ea.		8		8	sliding screen door, 6' 8" x 3'.
Install	Ea.	131	20		151	
Demolish and Install	Ea.	131	28		159	
Reinstall	Ea.		16.14		16.14	
Clean	Ea.	1.09	6.25		7.34	
Minimum Charge	Job		202		202	

Screen Door

Screen Door	Unit	Material	Labor	Equip.	Total	Specification
Aluminum						Includes material and labor to install
Demolish	Ea.		37.50		37.50	aluminum frame screen door with
Install	Ea.	125	57.50		182.50	fiberglass screen cloth, closer, hinges,
Demolish and Install	Ea.	125	95		220	latch.
Reinstall	Ea.		46.13		46.13	
Clean	Ea.	5.20	12.45		17.65	
Paint	Ea.	4.20	13.85		18.05	
Minimum Charge	Job		202		202	
Wood						Includes material and labor to install
Demolish	Ea.		37.50		37.50	wood screen door with aluminum cloth
Install	Ea.	246	67.50		313.50	screen. Frame and hardware not
Demolish and Install	Ea.	246	105		351	included.
Reinstall	Ea.		53.81		53.81	
Clean	Ea.	5.20	12.45		17.65	
Paint	Ea.	4.20	13.85		18.05	
Minimum Charge	Job		202		202	
Shave & Refit						Includes labor to shave and rework
Install	Ea.		33.50		33.50	door to fit opening at the job site.
Minimum Charge	Job		202		202	

Exterior Doors and Windows

Storm Door		Unit	Material	Labor	Equip.	Total	Specification
Good Grade							
	Demolish	Ea.		37.50		37.50	Includes material and labor to install
	Install	Ea.	210	57.50		267.50	aluminum frame storm door with
	Demolish and Install	Ea.	210	95		305	fiberglass screen cloth, upper glass
	Reinstall	Ea.		46.13		46.13	panel, closer, hinges, latch.
	Clean	Ea.	5.20	12.45		17.65	
	Paint	Ea.	4.20	13.85		18.05	
	Minimum Charge	Job		202		202	
Better Grade							
	Demolish	Ea.		37.50		37.50	Includes material and labor to install
	Install	Ea.	263	57.50		320.50	aluminum frame storm door with
	Demolish and Install	Ea.	263	95		358	fiberglass screen cloth, upper and
	Reinstall	Ea.		46.13		46.13	lower glass panel, closer, latch.
	Clean	Ea.	5.20	12.45		17.65	
	Paint	Ea.	4.20	13.85		18.05	
	Minimum Charge	Job		202		202	
Premium Grade							
	Demolish	Ea.		37.50		37.50	Includes material and labor to install
	Install	Ea.	288	57.50		345.50	aluminum frame storm door with
	Demolish and Install	Ea.	288	95		383	fiberglass screen cloth, upper and
	Reinstall	Ea.		46.13		46.13	lower glass panel, closer, latch.
	Clean	Ea.	5.20	12.45		17.65	
	Paint	Ea.	4.20	13.85		18.05	
	Minimum Charge	Job		202		202	
Insulated							
	Demolish	Ea.		37.50		37.50	Includes material and labor to install
	Install	Ea.	264	29		293	aluminum frame storm door with
	Demolish and Install	Ea.	264	66.50		330.50	fiberglass screen cloth, upper and
	Reinstall	Ea.		23.06		23.06	lower glass panel, closer, latch.
	Clean	Ea.	5.20	12.45		17.65	
	Paint	Ea.	4.20	13.85		18.05	
	Minimum Charge	Job		202		202	

Garage Door		Unit	Material	Labor	Equip.	Total	Specification
9' One Piece Metal							
	Demolish	Ea.		94.50		94.50	Includes material and labor to install
	Install	Ea.	460	101		561	one piece steel garage door 9' x 7'
	Demolish and Install	Ea.	460	195.50		655.50	primed including hardware.
	Reinstall	Ea.		80.72		80.72	
	Clean	Ea.	6.50	37.50		44	
	Paint	Ea.	8.80	86.50		95.30	
	Minimum Charge	Job		202		202	
16' One Piece Metal							
	Demolish	Ea.		112		112	Includes material and labor to install
	Install	Ea.	755	135		890	one piece steel garage door 16' x 7'
	Demolish and Install	Ea.	755	247		1002	primed including hardware.
	Reinstall	Ea.		107.63		107.63	
	Clean	Ea.	13	50		63	
	Paint	Ea.	17.60	99		116.60	
	Minimum Charge	Job		202		202	

Garage Door	Unit	Material	Labor	Equip.	Total	Specification
9' Metal Sectional						
Demolish	Ea.		94.50		94.50	Includes material and labor to install
Install	Ea.	690	153		843	sectional metal garage door 9' x 7'
Demolish and Install	Ea.	690	247.50		937.50	primed including hardware.
Reinstall	Ea.		122.30		122.30	
Clean	Ea.	6.65	42.50		49.15	
Paint	Ea.	17.60	99		116.60	
Minimum Charge	Job		202		202	
16' Metal Sectional						
Demolish	Ea.		112		112	Includes material and labor to install
Install	Ea.	835	269		1104	sectional metal garage door 16' x 7'
Demolish and Install	Ea.	835	381		1216	primed including hardware.
Reinstall	Ea.		215.25		215.25	
Clean	Ea.	13	50		63	
Paint	Ea.	17.60	99		116.60	
Minimum Charge	Job		202		202	
Metal / Steel Roll Up						
8' x 8' Steel						
Demolish	Ea.		128		128	Cost includes material and labor to
Install	Ea.	1175	620		1795	install 8' x 8' steel overhead roll-up,
Demolish and Install	Ea.	1175	748		1923	chain hoist operated service door.
Reinstall	Ea.		496.40		496.40	
Clean	Ea.	6.65	42.50		49.15	
Paint	Ea.	18.75	115		133.75	
Minimum Charge	Job		995		995	
10' x 10' Steel						
Demolish	Ea.		149		149	Cost includes material and labor to
Install	Ea.	1950	710		2660	install 10' x 10' steel overhead roll-up,
Demolish and Install	Ea.	1950	859		2809	chain hoist operated service door.
Reinstall	Ea.		567.31		567.31	
Clean	Ea.	10.40	60		70.40	
Paint	Ea.	29	115		144	
Minimum Charge	Job		995		995	
12' x 12' Steel						
Demolish	Ea.		179		179	Cost includes material and labor to
Install	Ea.	1975	825		2800	install 12' x 12' steel overhead roll-up,
Demolish and Install	Ea.	1975	1004		2979	chain hoist operated service door.
Reinstall	Ea.		661.87		661.87	
Clean	Ea.	14.95	66.50		81.45	
Paint	Ea.	42.50	139		181.50	
Minimum Charge	Job		995		995	
14' x 14' Steel						
Demolish	Ea.		224		224	Cost includes material and labor to
Install	Ea.	3250	1250		4500	install 14' x 14' steel overhead roll-up,
Demolish and Install	Ea.	3250	1474		4724	chain hoist operated service door.
Reinstall	Ea.		992.80		992.80	
Clean	Ea.	20.50	85.50		106	
Paint	Ea.	49	173		222	
Minimum Charge	Job		995		995	
18' x 18' Steel						
Demolish	Ea.		249		249	Cost includes material and labor to
Install	Opng.	3450	1650		5100	install 18' x 18' steel overhead roll-up,
Demolish and Install	Opng.	3450	1899		5349	chain hoist operated service door.
Reinstall	Opng.		1323.73		1323.73	
Clean	Ea.	20.50	50		70.50	
Paint	Ea.	95	345		440	
Minimum Charge	Job		995		995	
Automatic Motor						
Install	Ea.	510	40.50		550.50	Includes labor and material to install
Minimum Charge	Job		202		202	electric opener motor, 1/3 HP.

Exterior Doors and Windows

Garage Door		Unit	Material	Labor	Equip.	Total	Specification
9' One Piece Wood							
	Demolish	Ea.		94.50		94.50	Includes material and labor to install
	Install	Ea.	660	101		761	one piece wood garage door 9' x 7'
	Demolish and Install	Ea.	660	195.50		855.50	primed including hardware.
	Reinstall	Ea.		80.72		80.72	
	Clean	Ea.	6.50	37.50		44	
	Paint	Ea.	8.80	86.50		95.30	
	Minimum Charge	Job		202		202	
9' Wood Sectional							
	Demolish	Ea.		94.50		94.50	Includes material and labor to install
	Install	Ea.	990	101		1091	sectional wood garage door 9' x 7'
	Demolish and Install	Ea.	990	195.50		1185.50	unfinished including hardware.
	Reinstall	Ea.		80.72		80.72	
	Clean	Ea.	6.50	37.50		44	
	Paint	Ea.	8.80	86.50		95.30	
	Minimum Charge	Job		202		202	
16' Wood Sectional							
	Demolish	Ea.		112		112	Includes material and labor to install
	Install	Ea.	1700	135		1835	sectional fiberglass garage door 16' x
	Demolish and Install	Ea.	1700	247		1947	7' unfinished including hardware.
	Reinstall	Ea.		107.63		107.63	
	Clean	Ea.	13	50		63	
	Paint	Ea.	17.60	99		116.60	
	Minimum Charge	Job		202		202	
Electric Opener							
	Demolish	Ea.		66.50		66.50	Includes material and labor to install
	Install	Ea.	335	75.50		410.50	electric opener, 1/3 HP economy.
	Demolish and Install	Ea.	335	142		477	
	Reinstall	Ea.		60.58		60.58	
	Clean	Ea.	.26	16.60		16.86	
	Minimum Charge	Job		202		202	
Springs							
	Install	Pr.	61	101		162	Includes labor and material to replace
	Minimum Charge	Job		202		202	springs for garage door.

Commercial Metal Door		Unit	Material	Labor	Equip.	Total	Specification
Pre-hung Steel Door							
2' 8" x 6' 8"							
	Demolish	Ea.		56		56	Cost includes material and labor to
	Install	Ea.	700	25		725	install 2' 8" x 6' 8" pre-hung 1-3/4"
	Demolish and Install	Ea.	700	81		781	18 gauge steel door with steel frame,
	Reinstall	Ea.		25.23		25.23	hinges, aluminum sill,
	Clean	Ea.	5.20	12.45		17.65	weather-stripped.
	Paint	Ea.	5.40	29		34.40	
	Minimum Charge	Job		202		202	
3' x 6' 8"							
	Demolish	Ea.		56		56	Cost includes material and labor to
	Install	Ea.	655	27		682	install 3' x 6' 8" pre-hung 1-3/4" 18
	Demolish and Install	Ea.	655	83		738	gauge steel door with steel frame,
	Reinstall	Ea.		26.91		26.91	hinges, aluminum sill,
	Clean	Ea.	5.20	12.45		17.65	weather-stripped.
	Paint	Ea.	5.40	29		34.40	
	Minimum Charge	Job		202		202	

Commercial Metal Door		Unit	Material	Labor	Equip.	Total	Specification
3' 6" x 6' 8"							
	Demolish	Ea.		56		56	Cost includes material and labor to
	Install	Ea.	750	31		781	install 3' 6" x 6' 8" pre-hung 1-3/4"
	Demolish and Install	Ea.	750	87		837	18 gauge steel door with steel frame,
	Reinstall	Ea.		31.05		31.05	hinges, aluminum sill,
	Clean	Ea.	5.20	12.45		17.65	weather-stripped.
	Paint	Ea.	5.40	29		34.40	
	Minimum Charge	Job		202		202	
4' x 6' 8"							
	Demolish	Ea.		56		56	Cost includes material and labor to
	Install	Ea.	815	40.50		855.50	install 4' x 6' 8" pre-hung 1-3/4" 18
	Demolish and Install	Ea.	815	96.50		911.50	gauge steel door with steel frame,
	Reinstall	Ea.		40.36		40.36	hinges, aluminum sill,
	Clean	Ea.	5.20	12.45		17.65	weather-stripped.
	Paint	Ea.	5.40	29		34.40	
	Minimum Charge	Job		202		202	
Metal Jamb							
6' 8" High							
	Demolish	Ea.		22.50		22.50	Cost includes material and labor to
	Install	Ea.	162	25		187	install 18 gauge hollow metal door
	Demolish and Install	Ea.	162	47.50		209.50	frame to fit a 4-1/2" jamb 6' 8" high
	Reinstall	Ea.		25.23		25.23	and up to 3' 6" opening.
	Clean	Ea.	1.09	6.25		7.34	
	Paint	Ea.	1.49	6.95		8.44	
	Minimum Charge	Job		202		202	
7' High							
	Demolish	Ea.		22.50		22.50	Cost includes material and labor to
	Install	Ea.	167	27		194	install 18 gauge hollow metal door
	Demolish and Install	Ea.	167	49.50		216.50	frame to fit a 4-1/2" jamb 7' high and
	Reinstall	Ea.		26.91		26.91	up to 3' 6" opening.
	Clean	Ea.	1.09	6.25		7.34	
	Paint	Ea.	1.49	6.95		8.44	
	Minimum Charge	Job		202		202	
8' High							
	Demolish	Ea.		22.50		22.50	Cost includes material and labor to
	Install	Ea.	206	33.50		239.50	install 18 gauge hollow metal door
	Demolish and Install	Ea.	206	56		262	frame to fit a 4-1/2" jamb 8' high and
	Reinstall	Ea.		33.63		33.63	up to 3' 6" opening.
	Clean	Ea.	1.53	7.50		9.03	
	Paint	Ea.	1.66	7.70		9.36	
	Minimum Charge	Job		202		202	
9' High							
	Demolish	Ea.		22.50		22.50	Cost includes material and labor to
	Install	Ea.	267	40.50		307.50	install 18 gauge hollow metal door
	Demolish and Install	Ea.	267	63		330	frame to fit a 4-1/2" jamb 9' high and
	Reinstall	Ea.		40.36		40.36	up to 3' 6" opening.
	Clean	Ea.	1.53	7.50		9.03	
	Paint	Ea.	1.66	7.70		9.36	
	Minimum Charge	Job		202		202	
Hardware							
Doorknob w / Lock							
	Demolish	Ea.		16		16	Includes material and labor to install
	Install	Ea.	139	33.50		172.50	keyed entry lock set, bored type
	Demolish and Install	Ea.	139	49.50		188.50	including knob trim, strike and strike
	Reinstall	Ea.		26.91		26.91	box for standard commercial
	Clean	Ea.	.52	9.35		9.87	application.
	Minimum Charge	Job		202		202	

Exterior Doors and Windows

Commercial Metal Door

	Unit	Material	Labor	Equip.	Total	Specification
Lever Handle						
Demolish	Ea.		16		16	Includes material and labor to install
Install	Ea.	123	40.50		163.50	passage lockset, keyless bored type
Demolish and Install	Ea.	123	56.50		179.50	with lever handle, non-locking
Reinstall	Ea.		32.29		32.29	standard commercial latchset.
Clean	Ea.	.52	9.35		9.87	
Minimum Charge	Job		202		202	
Deadbolt						
Demolish	Ea.		14		14	Includes material and labor to install a
Install	Ea.	67	29		96	deadbolt.
Demolish and Install	Ea.	67	43		110	
Reinstall	Ea.		23.06		23.06	
Clean	Ea.	.52	9.35		9.87	
Minimum Charge	Job		202		202	
Panic Device						
Demolish	Ea.		33		33	Includes material and labor to install
Install	Ea.	425	67.50		492.50	touch bar, low profile, exit only.
Demolish and Install	Ea.	425	100.50		525.50	
Reinstall	Ea.		53.81		53.81	
Clean	Ea.	.26	16.60		16.86	
Minimum Charge	Job		202		202	
Closer						
Demolish	Ea.		8.40		8.40	Includes material and labor to install
Install	Ea.	251	67.50		318.50	pneumatic heavy duty model for
Demolish and Install	Ea.	251	75.90		326.90	exterior type doors.
Reinstall	Ea.		53.81		53.81	
Clean	Ea.	.26	12.45		12.71	
Minimum Charge	Job		202		202	
Peep-Hole						
Demolish	Ea.		7.40		7.40	Includes material and labor to install
Install	Ea.	17.40	12.60		30	peep-hole for door.
Demolish and Install	Ea.	17.40	20		37.40	
Reinstall	Ea.		10.09		10.09	
Clean	Ea.	.04	3.36		3.40	
Minimum Charge	Job		202		202	
Exit Sign						
Demolish	Ea.		22		22	Includes material and labor to install a
Install	Ea.	105	54.50		159.50	wall mounted interior electric exit sign.
Demolish and Install	Ea.	105	76.50		181.50	
Reinstall	Ea.		43.72		43.72	
Clean	Ea.	.04	6.85		6.89	
Minimum Charge	Job		202		202	
Kickplate						
Demolish	Ea.		12.45		12.45	Includes material and labor to install
Install	Ea.	53.50	27		80.50	stainless steel kickplate, 10" x 36".
Demolish and Install	Ea.	53.50	39.45		92.95	
Reinstall	Ea.		21.53		21.53	
Clean	Ea.	.52	9.35		9.87	
Minimum Charge	Job		202		202	

Aluminum Window

	Unit	Material	Labor	Equip.	Total	Specification
Single Hung Two Light						
2' x 2'						
Demolish	Ea.		21		21	Cost includes material and labor to
Install	Ea.	184	90.50		274.50	install 2' x 2' single hung, two light,
Demolish and Install	Ea.	184	111.50		295.50	double glazed aluminum window
Reinstall	Ea.		72.20		72.20	including screen.
Clean	Ea.	.06	7.80		7.86	
Minimum Charge	Job		248		248	

Aluminum Window	Unit	Material	Labor	Equip.	Total	Specification
2' x 2' 6"						
Demolish	Ea.		21		21	Cost includes material and labor to
Install	Ea.	76	90.50		166.50	install 2' x 2' 6" single hung, two
Demolish and Install	Ea.	76	111.50		187.50	light, double glazed aluminum
Reinstall	Ea.		72.20		72.20	window including screen.
Clean	Ea.	.06	7.80		7.86	
Minimum Charge	Job		248		248	
3' x 1' 6"						
Demolish	Ea.		21		21	Cost includes material and labor to
Install	Ea.	71.50	99.50		171	install 3' x 1' 6" single hung, two
Demolish and Install	Ea.	71.50	120.50		192	light, double glazed aluminum
Reinstall	Ea.		79.42		79.42	window including screen.
Clean	Ea.	.04	6.85		6.89	
Minimum Charge	Job		248		248	
3' x 2'						
Demolish	Ea.		21		21	Cost includes material and labor to
Install	Ea.	86	99.50		185.50	install 3' x 2' single hung, two light,
Demolish and Install	Ea.	86	120.50		206.50	double glazed aluminum window
Reinstall	Ea.		79.42		79.42	including screen.
Clean	Ea.	.04	6.85		6.89	
Minimum Charge	Job		248		248	
3' x 2' 6"						
Demolish	Ea.		21		21	Cost includes material and labor to
Install	Ea.	91.50	99.50		191	install 3' x 2' 6" single hung, two
Demolish and Install	Ea.	91.50	120.50		212	light, double glazed aluminum
Reinstall	Ea.		79.42		79.42	window including screen.
Clean	Ea.	.06	7.80		7.86	
Minimum Charge	Job		248		248	
3' x 3'						
Demolish	Ea.		21		21	Cost includes material and labor to
Install	Ea.	101	99.50		200.50	install 3' x 3' single hung, two light,
Demolish and Install	Ea.	101	120.50		221.50	double glazed aluminum window
Reinstall	Ea.		79.42		79.42	including screen.
Clean	Ea.	.06	7.80		7.86	
Minimum Charge	Job		248		248	
3' x 3' 6"						
Demolish	Ea.		21		21	Cost includes material and labor to
Install	Ea.	256	99.50		355.50	install 3' x 3' 6" single hung, two
Demolish and Install	Ea.	256	120.50		376.50	light, double glazed aluminum
Reinstall	Ea.		79.42		79.42	window including screen.
Clean	Ea.	.08	9.10		9.18	
Minimum Charge	Job		248		248	
3' x 4'						
Demolish	Ea.		21		21	Cost includes material and labor to
Install	Ea.	268	99.50		367.50	install 3' x 4' single hung, two light,
Demolish and Install	Ea.	268	120.50		388.50	double glazed aluminum window
Reinstall	Ea.		79.42		79.42	including screen.
Clean	Ea.	.08	9.10		9.18	
Minimum Charge	Job		248		248	
3' x 5'						
Demolish	Ea.		30		30	Cost includes material and labor to
Install	Ea.	129	99.50		228.50	install 3' x 5' single hung, two light,
Demolish and Install	Ea.	129	129.50		258.50	double glazed aluminum window
Reinstall	Ea.		79.42		79.42	including screen.
Clean	Ea.	.10	10.90		11	
Minimum Charge	Job		248		248	

Exterior Doors and Windows

Aluminum Window	Unit	Material	Labor	Equip.	Total	Specification
3' x 6'						
Demolish	Ea.		30		30	Cost includes material and labor to
Install	Ea.	365	110		475	install 3' x 6' single hung, two light,
Demolish and Install	Ea.	365	140		505	double glazed aluminum window
Reinstall	Ea.		88.25		88.25	including screen.
Clean	Ea.	.12	12.85		12.97	
Minimum Charge	Job		248		248	
Double Hung Two Light						
2' x 2'						
Demolish	Ea.		21		21	Cost includes material and labor to
Install	Ea.	122	90.50		212.50	install 2' x 2' double hung, two light,
Demolish and Install	Ea.	122	111.50		233.50	double glazed aluminum window
Reinstall	Ea.		72.20		72.20	including screen.
Clean	Ea.	.04	6.85		6.89	
Minimum Charge	Job		248		248	
2' x 2' 6"						
Demolish	Ea.		21		21	Cost includes material and labor to
Install	Ea.	132	90.50		222.50	install 2' x 2' 6" double hung, two
Demolish and Install	Ea.	132	111.50		243.50	light, double glazed aluminum
Reinstall	Ea.		72.20		72.20	window including screen.
Clean	Ea.	.04	6.85		6.89	
Minimum Charge	Job		248		248	
3' x 1' 6"						
Demolish	Ea.		21		21	Cost includes material and labor to
Install	Ea.	286	99.50		385.50	install 3' x 1' 6" double hung, two
Demolish and Install	Ea.	286	120.50		406.50	light, double glazed aluminum
Reinstall	Ea.		79.42		79.42	window including screen.
Clean	Ea.	.04	6.85		6.89	
Minimum Charge	Job		248		248	
3' x 2'						
Demolish	Ea.		21		21	Cost includes material and labor to
Install	Ea.	335	99.50		434.50	install 3' x 2' double hung, two light,
Demolish and Install	Ea.	335	120.50		455.50	double glazed aluminum window
Reinstall	Ea.		79.42		79.42	including screen.
Clean	Ea.	.04	6.85		6.89	
Minimum Charge	Job		248		248	
3' x 2' 6"						
Demolish	Ea.		21		21	Cost includes material and labor to
Install	Ea.	405	99.50		504.50	install 3' x 2' 6" double hung, two
Demolish and Install	Ea.	405	120.50		525.50	light, double glazed aluminum
Reinstall	Ea.		79.42		79.42	window including screen.
Clean	Ea.	.06	7.80		7.86	
Minimum Charge	Job		248		248	
3' x 3'						
Demolish	Ea.		21		21	Cost includes material and labor to
Install	Ea.	450	99.50		549.50	install 3' x 3' double hung, two light,
Demolish and Install	Ea.	450	120.50		570.50	double glazed aluminum window
Reinstall	Ea.		79.42		79.42	including screen.
Clean	Ea.	.06	7.80		7.86	
Minimum Charge	Job		248		248	
3' x 3' 6"						
Demolish	Ea.		21		21	Cost includes material and labor to
Install	Ea.	480	99.50		579.50	install 3' x 3' 6" double hung, two
Demolish and Install	Ea.	480	120.50		600.50	light, double glazed aluminum
Reinstall	Ea.		79.42		79.42	window including screen.
Clean	Ea.	.08	9.10		9.18	
Minimum Charge	Job		248		248	

Exterior Doors and Windows

Aluminum Window

	Unit	Material	Labor	Equip.	Total	Specification
3' x 4'						
Demolish	Ea.		21		21	Cost includes material and labor to
Install	Ea.	515	99.50		614.50	install 3' x 4' double hung, two light,
Demolish and Install	Ea.	515	120.50		635.50	double glazed aluminum window
Reinstall	Ea.		79.42		79.42	including screen.
Clean	Ea.	.08	9.10		9.18	
Minimum Charge	Job		248		248	
3' x 5'						
Demolish	Ea.		30		30	Cost includes material and labor to
Install	Ea.	565	99.50		664.50	install 3' x 5' double hung, two light,
Demolish and Install	Ea.	565	129.50		694.50	double glazed aluminum window
Reinstall	Ea.		79.42		79.42	including screen.
Clean	Ea.	.10	10.90		11	
Minimum Charge	Job		248		248	
3' x 6'						
Demolish	Ea.		30		30	Cost includes material and labor to
Install	Ea.	605	110		715	install 3' x 6' double hung, two light,
Demolish and Install	Ea.	605	140		745	double glazed aluminum window
Reinstall	Ea.		88.25		88.25	including screen.
Clean	Ea.	.12	12.85		12.97	
Minimum Charge	Job		248		248	

Sliding Sash

	Unit	Material	Labor	Equip.	Total	Specification
1' 6" x 3'						
Demolish	Ea.		21		21	Cost includes material and labor to
Install	Ea.	231	90.50		321.50	install 1' 6" x 3' sliding sash, two
Demolish and Install	Ea.	231	111.50		342.50	light, double glazed aluminum
Reinstall	Ea.		72.20		72.20	window including screen.
Clean	Ea.	.04	6.85		6.89	
Minimum Charge	Job		248		248	
2' x 2'						
Demolish	Ea.		21		21	Cost includes material and labor to
Install	Ea.	61.50	99.50		161	install 2' x 2' sliding sash, two light,
Demolish and Install	Ea.	61.50	120.50		182	double glazed aluminum window
Reinstall	Ea.		79.42		79.42	including screen.
Clean	Ea.	.04	6.85		6.89	
Minimum Charge	Job		248		248	
3' x 2'						
Demolish	Ea.		21		21	Cost includes material and labor to
Install	Ea.	244	99.50		343.50	install 3' x 2' sliding sash, two light,
Demolish and Install	Ea.	244	120.50		364.50	double glazed aluminum window
Reinstall	Ea.		79.42		79.42	including screen.
Clean	Ea.	.04	6.85		6.89	
Minimum Charge	Job		248		248	
3' x 2' 6"						
Demolish	Ea.		21		21	Cost includes material and labor to
Install	Ea.	83.50	99.50		183	install 3' x 2' 6" sliding sash, two
Demolish and Install	Ea.	83.50	120.50		204	light, double glazed aluminum
Reinstall	Ea.		79.42		79.42	window including screen.
Clean	Ea.	.06	7.80		7.86	
Minimum Charge	Job		248		248	
3' x 3'						
Demolish	Ea.		21		21	Cost includes material and labor to
Install	Ea.	294	99.50		393.50	install 3' x 3' sliding sash, two light,
Demolish and Install	Ea.	294	120.50		414.50	double glazed aluminum window
Reinstall	Ea.		79.42		79.42	including screen.
Clean	Ea.	.06	7.80		7.86	
Minimum Charge	Job		248		248	

Exterior Doors and Windows

Aluminum Window		Unit	Material	Labor	Equip.	Total	Specification
3' x 3' 6"							
	Demolish	Ea.		21		21	Cost includes material and labor to
	Install	Ea.	100	99.50		199.50	install 3' x 3' 6" sliding sash, two
	Demolish and Install	Ea.	100	120.50		220.50	light, double glazed aluminum
	Reinstall	Ea.		79.42		79.42	window including screen.
	Clean	Ea.	.08	9.10		9.18	
	Minimum Charge	Job		248		248	
3' x 4'							
	Demolish	Ea.		21		21	Cost includes material and labor to
	Install	Ea.	109	110		219	install 3' x 4' sliding sash, two light,
	Demolish and Install	Ea.	109	131		240	double glazed aluminum window
	Reinstall	Ea.		88.25		88.25	including screen.
	Clean	Ea.	.08	9.10		9.18	
	Minimum Charge	Job		248		248	
3' x 5'							
	Demolish	Ea.		30		30	Cost includes material and labor to
	Install	Ea.	139	110		249	install 3' x 5' sliding sash, two light,
	Demolish and Install	Ea.	139	140		279	double glazed aluminum window
	Reinstall	Ea.		88.25		88.25	including screen.
	Clean	Ea.	.10	10.90		11	
	Minimum Charge	Job		248		248	
4' x 5'							
	Demolish	Ea.		30		30	Cost includes material and labor to
	Install	Ea.	140	142		282	install 4' x 5' sliding sash, two light,
	Demolish and Install	Ea.	140	172		312	double glazed aluminum window
	Reinstall	Ea.		113.46		113.46	including screen.
	Clean	Ea.	.17	15.60		15.77	
	Minimum Charge	Job		248		248	
5' x 5'							
	Demolish	Ea.		30		30	Cost includes material and labor to
	Install	Ea.	340	142		482	install 5' x 5' sliding sash, two light,
	Demolish and Install	Ea.	340	172		512	double glazed aluminum window
	Reinstall	Ea.		113.46		113.46	including screen.
	Clean	Ea.	.17	15.60		15.77	
	Minimum Charge	Job		248		248	
Awning Sash							
26" x 26", 2 Light							
	Demolish	Ea.		21		21	Cost includes material and labor to
	Install	Ea.	295	110		405	install 26" x 26" two light awning,
	Demolish and Install	Ea.	295	131		426	double glazed aluminum window
	Reinstall	Ea.		88.25		88.25	including screen.
	Clean	Ea.	.06	7.80		7.86	
	Minimum Charge	Job		248		248	
26" x 37", 2 Light							
	Demolish	Ea.		21		21	Cost includes material and labor to
	Install	Ea.	335	110		445	install 26" x 37" two light awning,
	Demolish and Install	Ea.	335	131		466	double glazed aluminum window
	Reinstall	Ea.		88.25		88.25	including screen.
	Clean	Ea.	.06	7.80		7.86	
	Minimum Charge	Job		248		248	
38" x 26", 3 Light							
	Demolish	Ea.		21		21	Cost includes material and labor to
	Install	Ea.	380	110		490	install 38" x 26" three light awning,
	Demolish and Install	Ea.	380	131		511	double glazed aluminum window
	Reinstall	Ea.		88.25		88.25	including screen.
	Clean	Ea.	.08	9.10		9.18	
	Minimum Charge	Job		248		248	

Exterior Doors and Windows

Aluminum Window		Unit	Material	Labor	Equip.	Total	Specification
38" x 37", 3 Light							
	Demolish	Ea.		21		21	Cost includes material and labor to
	Install	Ea.	385	124		509	install 38" x 37" three light awning,
	Demolish and Install	Ea.	385	145		530	double glazed aluminum window
	Reinstall	Ea.		99.28		99.28	including screen.
	Clean	Ea.	.08	9.10		9.18	
	Minimum Charge	Job		248		248	
38" x 53", 3 Light							
	Demolish	Ea.		30		30	Cost includes material and labor to
	Install	Ea.	655	124		779	install 38" x 53" three light awning,
	Demolish and Install	Ea.	655	154		809	double glazed aluminum window
	Reinstall	Ea.		99.28		99.28	including screen.
	Clean	Ea.	.10	10.90		11	
	Minimum Charge	Job		248		248	
50" x 37", 4 Light							
	Demolish	Ea.		30		30	Cost includes material and labor to
	Install	Ea.	640	124		764	install 50" x 37" four light awning,
	Demolish and Install	Ea.	640	154		794	double glazed aluminum window
	Reinstall	Ea.		99.28		99.28	including screen.
	Clean	Ea.	.10	10.90		11	
	Minimum Charge	Job		248		248	
50" x 53", 4 Light							
	Demolish	Ea.		30		30	Cost includes material and labor to
	Install	Ea.	1100	142		1242	install 50" x 53" four light awning,
	Demolish and Install	Ea.	1100	172		1272	double glazed aluminum window
	Reinstall	Ea.		113.46		113.46	including screen.
	Clean	Ea.	.12	12.85		12.97	
	Minimum Charge	Job		248		248	
63" x 37", 5 Light							
	Demolish	Ea.		30		30	Cost includes material and labor to
	Install	Ea.	830	142		972	install 63" x 37" five light awning,
	Demolish and Install	Ea.	830	172		1002	double glazed aluminum window
	Reinstall	Ea.		113.46		113.46	including screen.
	Clean	Ea.	.12	12.85		12.97	
	Minimum Charge	Job		248		248	
63" x 53", 5 Light							
	Demolish	Ea.		30		30	Cost includes material and labor to
	Install	Ea.	1175	142		1317	install 63" x 53" five light awning,
	Demolish and Install	Ea.	1175	172		1347	double glazed aluminum window
	Reinstall	Ea.		113.46		113.46	including screen.
	Clean	Ea.	.17	15.60		15.77	
	Minimum Charge	Job		248		248	
Mullion Bars							
	Install	Ea.	12.95	39.50		52.45	Includes labor and material to install
	Minimum Charge	Job		248		248	mullions for sliding aluminum window.
Bay							
4' 8" x 6' 4"							
	Demolish	Ea.		22		22	Cost includes material and labor to
	Install	Ea.	1575	101		1676	install 4' 8" x 6' 4" angle bay double
	Demolish and Install	Ea.	1575	123		1698	hung unit, pine frame with aluminum
	Reinstall	Ea.		80.72		80.72	cladding, picture center sash,
	Clean	Ea.	.23	18.20		18.43	hardware, screens.
	Minimum Charge	Job		248		248	

Aluminum Window		Unit	Material	Labor	Equip.	Total	Specification
4' 8" x 7' 2"							
	Demolish	Ea.		22		22	Cost includes material and labor to
	Install	Ea.	1600	101		1701	install 4' 8" x 7' 2" angle bay double
	Demolish and Install	Ea.	1600	123		1723	hung unit, pine frame with aluminum
	Reinstall	Ea.		80.72		80.72	cladding, picture center sash,
	Clean	Ea.	.23	18.20		18.43	hardware, screens.
	Minimum Charge	Job		248		248	
4' 8" x 7' 10"							
	Demolish	Ea.		22		22	Cost includes material and labor to
	Install	Ea.	1650	101		1751	install 4' 8" x 7' 10" angle bay
	Demolish and Install	Ea.	1650	123		1773	double hung unit, pine frame with
	Reinstall	Ea.		80.72		80.72	aluminum cladding, picture center
	Clean	Ea.	.23	18.20		18.43	sash, hardware, screens.
	Minimum Charge	Job		248		248	
4' 8" x 8' 6"							
	Demolish	Ea.		25.50		25.50	Cost includes material and labor to
	Install	Ea.	1600	115		1715	install 4' 8" x 8' 6" angle bay double
	Demolish and Install	Ea.	1600	140.50		1740.50	hung unit, pine frame with aluminum
	Reinstall	Ea.		92.25		92.25	cladding, picture center sash,
	Clean	Ea.	.03	24.50		24.53	hardware, screens.
	Minimum Charge	Job		248		248	
4' 8" x 8' 10"							
	Demolish	Ea.		25.50		25.50	Cost includes material and labor to
	Install	Ea.	1625	115		1740	install 4' 8" x 8' 10" angle bay
	Demolish and Install	Ea.	1625	140.50		1765.50	double hung unit, pine frame with
	Reinstall	Ea.		92.25		92.25	aluminum cladding, picture center
	Clean	Ea.	.03	24.50		24.53	sash, hardware, screens.
	Minimum Charge	Job		248		248	
4' 8" x 9' 2"							
	Demolish	Ea.		25.50		25.50	Cost includes material and labor to
	Install	Ea.	1650	202		1852	install 4' 8" x 9' 2" angle bay double
	Demolish and Install	Ea.	1650	227.50		1877.50	hung unit, pine frame with aluminum
	Reinstall	Ea.		161.44		161.44	cladding, picture center sash,
	Clean	Ea.	.03	24.50		24.53	hardware, screens.
	Minimum Charge	Job		248		248	
4' 8" x 9' 10"							
	Demolish	Ea.		25.50		25.50	Cost includes material and labor to
	Install	Ea.	1725	202		1927	install 4' 8" x 9' 10" angle bay
	Demolish and Install	Ea.	1725	227.50		1952.50	double hung unit, pine frame with
	Reinstall	Ea.		161.44		161.44	aluminum cladding, picture center
	Clean	Ea.	.03	24.50		24.53	sash, hardware, screens.
	Minimum Charge	Job		248		248	
Casing							
	Demolish	Ea.		9.35		9.35	Cost includes material and labor to
	Install	Opng.	36	31		67	install 11/16" x 2-1/2" pine ranch
	Demolish and Install	Opng.	36	40.35		76.35	style window casing.
	Reinstall	Opng.		24.84		24.84	
	Clean	Opng.	.74	2.99		3.73	
	Paint	Ea.	4.38	6.95		11.33	
	Minimum Charge	Job		248		248	
Storm Window							
2' x 3' 6"							
	Demolish	Ea.		12.30		12.30	Includes material and labor to install
	Install	Ea.	82.50	27		109.50	residential aluminum storm window
	Demolish and Install	Ea.	82.50	39.30		121.80	with mill finish, 2' x 3' 5" high.
	Reinstall	Ea.		21.53		21.53	
	Clean	Ea.	.04	6.85		6.89	
	Minimum Charge	Job		248		248	

Exterior Doors and Windows

Aluminum Window

	Unit	Material	Labor	Equip.	Total	Specification
2' 6" x 5'						
Demolish	Ea.		12.30		12.30	Includes material and labor to install
Install	Ea.	93.50	29		122.50	residential aluminum storm window
Demolish and Install	Ea.	93.50	41.30		134.80	with mill finish, 2' 6" x 5' high.
Reinstall	Ea.		23.06		23.06	
Clean	Ea.	.08	9.10		9.18	
Minimum Charge	Job		248		248	
4' x 6'						
Demolish	Ea.		24		24	Includes material and labor to install
Install	Ea.	108	32.50		140.50	residential aluminum storm window, 4'
Demolish and Install	Ea.	108	56.50		164.50	x 6' high.
Reinstall	Ea.		25.83		25.83	
Clean	Ea.	.15	13.65		13.80	
Minimum Charge	Job		248		248	

Hardware

Weatherstripping

	Unit	Material	Labor	Equip.	Total	Specification
Install	L.F.	.42	3.36		3.78	Includes labor and material to install
Minimum Charge	Job		135		135	vinyl V strip weatherstripping for double-hung window.

Trim Set

	Unit	Material	Labor	Equip.	Total	Specification
Demolish	Ea.		9.35		9.35	Cost includes material and labor to
Install	Opng.	36	31		67	install 11/16" x 2-1/2" pine ranch
Demolish and Install	Opng.	36	40.35		76.35	style window casing.
Reinstall	Opng.		24.84		24.84	
Clean	Opng.	.74	2.99		3.73	
Paint	Ea.	4.38	6.95		11.33	
Minimum Charge	Job		202		202	

Vinyl Window

	Unit	Material	Labor	Equip.	Total	Specification
Double Hung						
2' x 2' 6"						
Demolish	Ea.		15.10		15.10	Cost includes material and labor to
Install	Ea.	217	54		271	install 2' x 2' 6" double hung, two
Demolish and Install	Ea.	217	69.10		286.10	light, vinyl window with screen.
Reinstall	Ea.		43.05		43.05	
Clean	Ea.	.04	6.85		6.89	
Minimum Charge	Job		135		135	
2' x 3' 6"						
Demolish	Ea.		15.10		15.10	Cost includes material and labor to
Install	Ea.	230	57.50		287.50	install 2' x 3' 6" double hung, two
Demolish and Install	Ea.	230	72.60		302.60	light, vinyl window with screen.
Reinstall	Ea.		46.13		46.13	
Clean	Ea.	.06	7.80		7.86	
Minimum Charge	Job		135		135	
2' 6" x 4' 6"						
Demolish	Ea.		15.10		15.10	Cost includes material and labor to
Install	Ea.	272	62		334	install 2' 6" x 4' 6" double hung, two
Demolish and Install	Ea.	272	77.10		349.10	light, vinyl window with screen.
Reinstall	Ea.		49.67		49.67	
Clean	Ea.	.08	9.10		9.18	
Minimum Charge	Job		135		135	
3' x 4'						
Demolish	Ea.		15.10		15.10	Includes material and labor to install
Install	Ea.	235	80.50		315.50	medium size double hung, 3' x 4',
Demolish and Install	Ea.	235	95.60		330.60	two light, vinyl window with screen.
Reinstall	Ea.		64.58		64.58	
Clean	Ea.	.08	9.10		9.18	
Minimum Charge	Job		135		135	

Exterior Doors and Windows

Vinyl Window		Unit	Material	Labor	Equip.	Total	Specification
3' x 4' 6"							
	Demolish	Ea.		18.45		18.45	Cost includes material and labor to
	Install	Ea.	305	89.50		394.50	install 3' x 4' 6" double hung, two
	Demolish and Install	Ea.	305	107.95		412.95	light, vinyl window with screen.
	Reinstall	Ea.		71.75		71.75	
	Clean	Ea.	.10	10.90		11	
	Minimum Charge	Job		135		135	
4' x 4' 6"							
	Demolish	Ea.		18.45		18.45	Cost includes material and labor to
	Install	Ea.	320	101		421	install 4' x 4' 6" double hung, two
	Demolish and Install	Ea.	320	119.45		439.45	light, vinyl window with screen.
	Reinstall	Ea.		80.72		80.72	
	Clean	Ea.	.12	12.85		12.97	
	Minimum Charge	Job		135		135	
4' x 6'							
	Demolish	Ea.		18.45		18.45	Includes material and labor to install
	Install	Ea.	370	115		485	large double hung, 4' x 6', two light,
	Demolish and Install	Ea.	370	133.45		503.45	vinyl window with screen.
	Reinstall	Ea.		92.25		92.25	
	Clean	Ea.	.17	15.60		15.77	
	Minimum Charge	Job		135		135	
Trim Set							
	Demolish	Ea.		9.35		9.35	Cost includes material and labor to
	Install	Opng.	36	31		67	install 11/16" x 2-1/2" pine ranch
	Demolish and Install	Opng.	36	40.35		76.35	style window casing.
	Reinstall	Opng.		24.84		24.84	
	Clean	Opng.	.74	2.99		3.73	
	Paint	Ea.	4.38	6.95		11.33	
	Minimum Charge	Job		248		248	

Wood Window		Unit	Material	Labor	Equip.	Total	Specification
2' 2" x 3' 4"							
	Demolish	Ea.		15.10		15.10	Cost includes material and labor to
	Install	Ea.	227	54		281	install 2' 2" x 3' 4" double hung, two
	Demolish and Install	Ea.	227	69.10		296.10	light, double glazed wood window
	Reinstall	Ea.		43.05		43.05	with screen.
	Clean	Ea.	.06	7.80		7.86	
	Paint	Ea.	2.74	14.45		17.19	
	Minimum Charge	Job		202		202	
2' 2" x 4' 4"							
	Demolish	Ea.		15.10		15.10	Cost includes material and labor to
	Install	Ea.	245	57.50		302.50	install 2' 2" x 4' 4" double hung, two
	Demolish and Install	Ea.	245	72.60		317.60	light, double glazed wood window
	Reinstall	Ea.		46.13		46.13	with screen.
	Clean	Ea.	.06	7.80		7.86	
	Paint	Ea.	2.74	14.45		17.19	
	Minimum Charge	Job		202		202	
2' 6" x 3' 4"							
	Demolish	Ea.		15.10		15.10	Cost includes material and labor to
	Install	Ea.	235	62		297	install 2' 6" x 3' 4" double hung, two
	Demolish and Install	Ea.	235	77.10		312.10	light, double glazed wood window
	Reinstall	Ea.		49.67		49.67	with screen.
	Clean	Ea.	.08	9.10		9.18	
	Paint	Ea.	3.51	17.30		20.81	
	Minimum Charge	Job		202		202	

Wood Window		Unit	Material	Labor	Equip.	Total	Specification
2' 6" x 4'							
	Demolish	Ea.		15.10		15.10	Cost includes material and labor to
	Install	Ea.	249	67.50		316.50	install 2' 6" x 4' double hung, two
	Demolish and Install	Ea.	249	82.60		331.60	light, double glazed wood window
	Reinstall	Ea.		53.81		53.81	with screen.
	Clean	Ea.	.08	9.10		9.18	
	Paint	Ea.	3.51	17.30		20.81	
	Minimum Charge	Job		202		202	
2' 6" x 4' 8"							
	Demolish	Ea.		15.10		15.10	Cost includes material and labor to
	Install	Ea.	268	67.50		335.50	install 2' 6" x 4' 8" double hung, two
	Demolish and Install	Ea.	268	82.60		350.60	light, double glazed wood window
	Reinstall	Ea.		53.81		53.81	with screen.
	Clean	Ea.	.08	9.10		9.18	
	Paint	Ea.	3.51	17.30		20.81	
	Minimum Charge	Job		202		202	
2' 10" x 3' 4"							
	Demolish	Ea.		15.10		15.10	Cost includes material and labor to
	Install	Ea.	241	80.50		321.50	install 2' 10" x 3' 4" double hung, two
	Demolish and Install	Ea.	241	95.60		336.60	light, double glazed wood window
	Reinstall	Ea.		64.58		64.58	with screen.
	Clean	Ea.	.08	9.10		9.18	
	Paint	Ea.	3.51	17.30		20.81	
	Minimum Charge	Job		202		202	
2' 10" x 4'							
	Demolish	Ea.		15.10		15.10	Cost includes material and labor to
	Install	Ea.	266	80.50		346.50	install 2' 10" x 4' double hung, two
	Demolish and Install	Ea.	266	95.60		361.60	light, double glazed wood window
	Reinstall	Ea.		64.58		64.58	with screen.
	Clean	Ea.	.08	9.10		9.18	
	Paint	Ea.	3.51	17.30		20.81	
	Minimum Charge	Job		202		202	
3' 7" x 3' 4"							
	Demolish	Ea.		15.10		15.10	Cost includes material and labor to
	Install	Ea.	273	89.50		362.50	install 3' 7" x 3' 4" double hung, two
	Demolish and Install	Ea.	273	104.60		377.60	light, double glazed wood window
	Reinstall	Ea.		71.75		71.75	with screen.
	Clean	Ea.	.08	9.10		9.18	
	Paint	Ea.	3.51	17.30		20.81	
	Minimum Charge	Job		202		202	
3' 7" x 5' 4"							
	Demolish	Ea.		18.45		18.45	Cost includes material and labor to
	Install	Ea.	350	89.50		439.50	install 3' 7" x 5' 4" double hung, two
	Demolish and Install	Ea.	350	107.95		457.95	light, double glazed wood window
	Reinstall	Ea.		71.75		71.75	with screen.
	Clean	Ea.	.17	15.60		15.77	
	Paint	Ea.	5.85	29		34.85	
	Minimum Charge	Job		202		202	
4' 3" x 5' 4"							
	Demolish	Ea.		18.45		18.45	Cost includes material and labor to
	Install	Ea.	545	101		646	install 4' 3" x 5' 4" double hung, two
	Demolish and Install	Ea.	545	119.45		664.45	light, double glazed wood window
	Reinstall	Ea.		80.72		80.72	with screen.
	Clean	Ea.	.17	15.60		15.77	
	Paint	Ea.	4.26	34.50		38.76	
	Minimum Charge	Job		202		202	

Wood Window		Unit	Material	Labor	Equip.	Total	Specification
Casement							
2' x 3' 4"							
	Demolish	Ea.		15.10		15.10	Cost includes material and labor to
	Install	Ea.	284	40.50		324.50	install 2' x 3' 4 " casement window
	Demolish and Install	Ea.	284	55.60		339.60	with 3/4" insulated glass, screens,
	Reinstall	Ea.		32.29		32.29	weatherstripping, hardware.
	Clean	Ea.	.06	7.80		7.86	
	Paint	Ea.	2.74	14.45		17.19	
	Minimum Charge	Job		405		405	
2' x 4'							
	Demolish	Ea.		15.10		15.10	Cost includes material and labor to
	Install	Ea.	305	45		350	install 2' x 4' casement window with
	Demolish and Install	Ea.	305	60.10		365.10	3/4" insulated glass, screens,
	Reinstall	Ea.		35.88		35.88	weatherstripping, hardware.
	Clean	Ea.	.06	7.80		7.86	
	Paint	Ea.	2.74	14.45		17.19	
	Minimum Charge	Job		405		405	
2' x 5'							
	Demolish	Ea.		15.10		15.10	Cost includes material and labor to
	Install	Ea.	335	47.50		382.50	install 2' x 5' casement window with
	Demolish and Install	Ea.	335	62.60		397.60	3/4" insulated glass, screens,
	Reinstall	Ea.		37.99		37.99	weatherstripping, hardware.
	Clean	Ea.	.08	9.10		9.18	
	Paint	Ea.	3.51	17.30		20.81	
	Minimum Charge	Job		405		405	
2' x 6'							
	Demolish	Ea.		15.10		15.10	Cost includes material and labor to
	Install	Ea.	330	50.50		380.50	install 2' x 6' casement window with
	Demolish and Install	Ea.	330	65.60		395.60	3/4" insulated glass, screens,
	Reinstall	Ea.		40.36		40.36	weatherstripping, hardware.
	Clean	Ea.	.08	9.10		9.18	
	Paint	Ea.	3.51	17.30		20.81	
	Minimum Charge	Job		405		405	
4' x 3' 4"							
	Demolish	Ea.		18.45		18.45	Cost includes material and labor to
	Install	Ea.	635	54		689	install 4' x 3' 4 " casement windows
	Demolish and Install	Ea.	635	72.45		707.45	with 3/4" insulated glass, screens,
	Reinstall	Ea.		43.05		43.05	weatherstripping, hardware.
	Clean	Ea.	.08	9.10		9.18	
	Paint	Ea.	2.13	17.30		19.43	
	Minimum Charge	Job		405		405	
4' x 4'							
	Demolish	Ea.		18.45		18.45	Cost includes material and labor to
	Install	Ea.	710	54		764	install 4' x 4' casement windows with
	Demolish and Install	Ea.	710	72.45		782.45	3/4" insulated glass, screens,
	Reinstall	Ea.		43.05		43.05	weatherstripping, hardware.
	Clean	Ea.	.12	12.85		12.97	
	Paint	Ea.	2.52	21.50		24.02	
	Minimum Charge	Job		405		405	
4' x 5'							
	Demolish	Ea.		18.45		18.45	Cost includes material and labor to
	Install	Ea.	805	57.50		862.50	install 4' x 5' casement windows with
	Demolish and Install	Ea.	805	75.95		880.95	3/4" insulated glass, screens,
	Reinstall	Ea.		46.13		46.13	weatherstripping, hardware.
	Clean	Ea.	.17	15.60		15.77	
	Paint	Ea.	3.29	29		32.29	
	Minimum Charge	Job		405		405	

Exterior Doors and Windows

Wood Window		Unit	Material	Labor	Equip.	Total	Specification
4' x 6'							
	Demolish	Ea.		18.45		18.45	Cost includes material and labor to
	Install	Ea.	910	67.50		977.50	install 4' x 6' casement windows with
	Demolish and Install	Ea.	910	85.95		995.95	3/4" insulated glass, screens,
	Reinstall	Ea.		53.81		53.81	weatherstripping, hardware.
	Clean	Ea.	.17	15.60		15.77	
	Paint	Ea.	3.87	34.50		38.37	
	Minimum Charge	Job		405		405	
Casement Bow							
4' 8" x 8' 1"							
	Demolish	Ea.		25.50		25.50	Includes material and labor to install
	Install	Ea.	1700	151		1851	casement bow window unit with 4
	Demolish and Install	Ea.	1700	176.50		1876.50	lights, pine frame, 1/2" insulated
	Reinstall	Ea.		121.08		121.08	glass, weatherstripping, hardware,
	Clean	Ea.	.23	18.20		18.43	screens.
	Paint	Ea.	7.15	69.50		76.65	
	Minimum Charge	Job		405		405	
4' 8" x 10'							
	Demolish	Ea.		25.50		25.50	Includes material and labor to install
	Install	Ea.	2100	202		2302	casement bow window unit with 5
	Demolish and Install	Ea.	2100	227.50		2327.50	lights, pine frame, 1/2" insulated
	Reinstall	Ea.		161.44		161.44	glass, weatherstripping, hardware,
	Clean	Ea.	.03	24.50		24.53	screens.
	Paint	Ea.	8.90	86.50		95.40	
	Minimum Charge	Job		405		405	
5' 4" x 8' 1"							
	Demolish	Ea.		25.50		25.50	Includes material and labor to install
	Install	Ea.	1825	151		1976	casement bow window unit with 4
	Demolish and Install	Ea.	1825	176.50		2001.50	lights, pine frame, 1/2" insulated
	Reinstall	Ea.		121.08		121.08	glass, weatherstripping, hardware,
	Clean	Ea.	.03	24.50		24.53	screens.
	Paint	Ea.	8.15	69.50		77.65	
	Minimum Charge	Job		405		405	
5' 4" x 10'							
	Demolish	Ea.		25.50		25.50	Includes material and labor to install
	Install	Ea.	2075	202		2277	casement bow window unit with 5
	Demolish and Install	Ea.	2075	227.50		2302.50	lights, pine frame, 1/2" insulated
	Reinstall	Ea.		161.44		161.44	glass, weatherstripping, hardware,
	Clean	Ea.	.03	24.50		24.53	screens.
	Paint	Ea.	10.30	86.50		96.80	
	Minimum Charge	Job		405		405	
6' x 8' 1"							
	Demolish	Ea.		25.50		25.50	Includes material and labor to install
	Install	Ea.	2100	202		2302	casement bow window unit with 5
	Demolish and Install	Ea.	2100	227.50		2327.50	lights, pine frame, 1/2" insulated
	Reinstall	Ea.		161.44		161.44	glass, weatherstripping, hardware,
	Clean	Ea.	.03	24.50		24.53	screens.
	Paint	Ea.	9.30	86.50		95.80	
	Minimum Charge	Job		405		405	
6' x 10'							
	Demolish	Ea.		25.50		25.50	Includes material and labor to install
	Install	Ea.	2175	202		2377	casement bow window unit with 5
	Demolish and Install	Ea.	2175	227.50		2402.50	lights, pine frame, 1/2" insulated
	Reinstall	Ea.		161.44		161.44	glass, weatherstripping, hardware,
	Clean	Ea.	.03	24.50		24.53	screens.
	Paint	Ea.	11.60	115		126.60	
	Minimum Charge	Job		405		405	

Exterior Doors and Windows

Wood Window		Unit	Material	Labor	Equip.	Total	Specification
Casing							
	Demolish	Ea.		9.35		9.35	Cost includes material and labor to
	Install	Opng.	36	31		67	install 11/16" x 2-1/2" pine ranch
	Demolish and Install	Opng.	36	40.35		76.35	style window casing.
	Reinstall	Opng.		24.84		24.84	
	Clean	Opng.	.74	2.99		3.73	
	Paint	Ea.	4.38	6.95		11.33	
	Minimum Charge	Job		248		248	
Trim Set							
	Demolish	Ea.		7.10		7.10	Cost includes material and labor to
	Install	Opng.	36	31		67	install 11/16" x 2-1/2" pine ranch
	Demolish and Install	Opng.	36	38.10		74.10	style window casing.
	Reinstall	Opng.		24.84		24.84	
	Clean	Opng.	.74	2.99		3.73	
	Paint	Ea.	4.38	6.95		11.33	
	Minimum Charge	Job		202		202	
Wood Picture Window							
3' 6" x 4'							
	Demolish	Ea.		18.45		18.45	Includes material and labor to install a
	Install	Ea.	450	67.50		517.50	wood framed picture window
	Demolish and Install	Ea.	450	85.95		535.95	including exterior trim.
	Clean	Ea.	.17	15.60		15.77	
	Paint	Ea.	3.06	26.50		29.56	
	Minimum Charge	Job		405		405	
4' x 4' 6"							
	Demolish	Ea.		18.45		18.45	Includes material and labor to install a
	Install	Ea.	570	73.50		643.50	wood framed picture window
	Demolish and Install	Ea.	570	91.95		661.95	including exterior trim.
	Clean	Ea.	.17	15.60		15.77	
	Paint	Ea.	3.06	26.50		29.56	
	Minimum Charge	Job		405		405	
5' x 4'							
	Demolish	Ea.		18.45		18.45	Includes material and labor to install a
	Install	Ea.	650	73.50		723.50	wood framed picture window
	Demolish and Install	Ea.	650	91.95		741.95	including exterior trim.
	Clean	Ea.	.17	15.60		15.77	
	Paint	Ea.	6.50	43.50		50	
	Minimum Charge	Job		405		405	
6' x 4' 6"							
	Demolish	Ea.		18.45		18.45	Includes material and labor to install a
	Install	Ea.	680	80.50		760.50	wood framed picture window
	Demolish and Install	Ea.	680	98.95		778.95	including exterior trim.
	Clean	Ea.	.17	15.60		15.77	
	Paint	Ea.	6.50	43.50		50	
	Minimum Charge	Job		405		405	

Window Screens		Unit	Material	Labor	Equip.	Total	Specification
Small							
	Demolish	Ea.		3.46		3.46	Includes material and labor to install
	Install	Ea.	19.25	12.25		31.50	small window screen, 4 S.F.
	Demolish and Install	Ea.	19.25	15.71		34.96	
	Reinstall	Ea.		9.78		9.78	
	Clean	Ea.	.52	6.25		6.77	
	Minimum Charge	Job		101		101	

Exterior Doors and Windows

Window Screens	Unit	Material	Labor	Equip.	Total	Specification
Standard Size						
Demolish	Ea.		3.46		3.46	Includes material and labor to install
Install	Ea.	47	12.25		59.25	medium window screen, 12 S.F.
Demolish and Install	Ea.	47	15.71		62.71	
Reinstall	Ea.		9.78		9.78	
Clean	Ea.	.52	6.25		6.77	
Minimum Charge	Job		101		101	
Large						
Demolish	Ea.		3.46		3.46	Includes material and labor to install
Install	Ea.	62.50	12.25		74.75	large window screen, 16 S.F.
Demolish and Install	Ea.	62.50	15.71		78.21	
Reinstall	Ea.		9.78		9.78	
Clean	Ea.	.52	6.25		6.77	
Minimum Charge	Job		101		101	

Window Glass	Unit	Material	Labor	Equip.	Total	Specification
Plate, Clear, 1/4"						
Demolish	S.F.		1.66		1.66	Includes material and labor to install
Install	S.F.	8.65	6.55		15.20	clear glass.
Demolish and Install	S.F.	8.65	8.21		16.86	
Reinstall	S.F.		5.23		5.23	
Clean	S.F.	.04	.17		.21	
Minimum Charge	Job		196		196	
Insulated						
Demolish	S.F.		1.66		1.66	Includes material and labor to install
Install	S.F.	14.50	11.20		25.70	insulated glass.
Demolish and Install	S.F.	14.50	12.86		27.36	
Reinstall	S.F.		8.96		8.96	
Clean	S.F.	.04	.17		.21	
Minimum Charge	Job		196		196	
Tinted						
Demolish	S.F.		1.66		1.66	Includes material and labor to install
Install	S.F.	8.10	6.05		14.15	tinted glass.
Demolish and Install	S.F.	8.10	7.71		15.81	
Reinstall	S.F.		4.82		4.82	
Clean	S.F.	.04	.17		.21	
Minimum Charge	Job		196		196	
Obscure / Florentine						
Demolish	S.F.		1.66		1.66	Includes material and labor to install
Install	S.F.	12.10	5.60		17.70	obscure glass.
Demolish and Install	S.F.	12.10	7.26		19.36	
Reinstall	S.F.		4.48		4.48	
Clean	S.F.	.04	.17		.21	
Minimum Charge	Job		196		196	
Laminated Safety						
Demolish	S.F.		1.66		1.66	Includes material and labor to install
Install	S.F.	12.70	8.70		21.40	clear laminated glass.
Demolish and Install	S.F.	12.70	10.36		23.06	
Reinstall	S.F.		6.97		6.97	
Clean	S.F.	.04	.17		.21	
Minimum Charge	Job		196		196	

Exterior Doors and Windows

Window Glass

Window Glass	Unit	Material	Labor	Equip.	Total	Specification
Wired						
Demolish	S.F.		1.66		1.66	Includes material and labor to install
Install	S.F.	19.55	5.80		25.35	rough obscure wire glass.
Demolish and Install	S.F.	19.55	7.46		27.01	
Reinstall	S.F.		4.65		4.65	
Clean	S.F.	.04	.17		.21	
Minimum Charge	Job		196		196	
Tempered						
Demolish	S.F.		1.66		1.66	Includes material and labor to install
Install	S.F.	8.65	6.55		15.20	clear glass.
Demolish and Install	S.F.	8.65	8.21		16.86	
Reinstall	S.F.		5.23		5.23	
Clean	S.F.	.04	.17		.21	
Minimum Charge	Job		196		196	
Stained						
Demolish	S.F.		1.66		1.66	Includes material and labor to install
Install	S.F.	65	6.55		71.55	stained glass.
Demolish and Install	S.F.	65	8.21		73.21	
Reinstall	S.F.		5.23		5.23	
Clean	S.F.	.04	.17		.21	
Minimum Charge	Job		196		196	
Etched						
Demolish	S.F.		1.66		1.66	Includes material and labor to install
Install	S.F.	53.50	6.55		60.05	etched glass.
Demolish and Install	S.F.	53.50	8.21		61.71	
Reinstall	S.F.		5.23		5.23	
Clean	S.F.	.04	.17		.21	
Minimum Charge	Job		196		196	
Wall Mirror						
Demolish	S.F.		1.66		1.66	Includes material and labor to install
Install	S.F.	10.30	6.25		16.55	distortion-free float glass mirror, 1/4"
Demolish and Install	S.F.	10.30	7.91		18.21	thick, cut and polished edges.
Reinstall	S.F.		5.02		5.02	
Clean	S.F.	.04	.17		.21	
Minimum Charge	Job		196		196	
Bullet Resistant						
Demolish	S.F.		1.66		1.66	Includes material and labor to install
Install	S.F.	121	78.50		199.50	bullet resistant clear laminated glass.
Demolish and Install	S.F.	121	80.16		201.16	
Reinstall	S.F.		62.72		62.72	
Clean	S.F.	.04	.17		.21	
Minimum Charge	Job		196		196	

Storefront System

Storefront System	Unit	Material	Labor	Equip.	Total	Specification
Clear Glass						
Stub Wall to 8'						
Demolish	S.F.		2.60		2.60	Includes material and labor to install
Install	S.F.	23.50	10.85		34.35	commercial grade 4-1/2" section,
Demolish and Install	S.F.	23.50	13.45		36.95	anodized aluminum with clear glass in
Reinstall	S.F.		8.66		8.66	upper section and safety glass in
Clean	S.F.	.01	.36		.37	lower section.
Minimum Charge	Job		248		248	

Exterior Doors and Windows

Storefront System	Unit	Material	Labor	Equip.	Total	Specification
Floor to 10'						
Demolish	S.F.		2.60		2.60	Includes material and labor to install
Install	S.F.	24	10.85		34.85	commercial grade 4-1/2" section,
Demolish and Install	S.F.	24	13.45		37.45	anodized aluminum with clear glass in
Reinstall	S.F.		8.66		8.66	upper section and safety glass in
Clean	S.F.	.01	.36		.37	lower section.
Minimum Charge	Job		248		248	
Polished Plate Glass						
Stub Wall to 9'						
Demolish	S.F.		2.60		2.60	Cost includes material and labor to
Install	S.F.	15.50	10.85		26.35	install 4' x 9' polished plate glass
Demolish and Install	S.F.	15.50	13.45		28.95	window built on 8" stub wall.
Reinstall	S.F.		8.66		8.66	
Clean	S.F.	.01	.36		.37	
Minimum Charge	Job		248		248	
Stub Wall to 13'						
Demolish	S.F.		2.60		2.60	Cost includes material and labor to
Install	S.F.	16.85	10.85		27.70	install 4' x 13' polished plate glass
Demolish and Install	S.F.	16.85	13.45		30.30	window built on 8" stub wall.
Reinstall	S.F.		8.66		8.66	
Clean	S.F.	.01	.36		.37	
Minimum Charge	Job		248		248	
Floor to 9'						
Demolish	S.F.		2.60		2.60	Cost includes material and labor to
Install	S.F.	17.40	10.85		28.25	install 4' x 9' polished plate glass
Demolish and Install	S.F.	17.40	13.45		30.85	window built on floor.
Reinstall	S.F.		8.66		8.66	
Clean	S.F.	.01	.36		.37	
Minimum Charge	Job		248		248	
Floor to 13'						
Demolish	S.F.		2.60		2.60	Cost includes material and labor to
Install	S.F.	18.60	10.85		29.45	install 4' x 13' polished plate glass
Demolish and Install	S.F.	18.60	13.45		32.05	window built on floor.
Reinstall	S.F.		8.66		8.66	
Clean	S.F.	.01	.36		.37	
Minimum Charge	Job		248		248	
Clear Plate Glass						
Floor to 9'						
Demolish	S.F.		2.60		2.60	Cost includes material and labor to
Install	S.F.	25	10.85		35.85	install 4' x 9' clear plate glass window
Demolish and Install	S.F.	25	13.45		38.45	built on floor.
Reinstall	S.F.		8.66		8.66	
Clean	S.F.	.01	.36		.37	
Minimum Charge	Job		248		248	
Floor to 11'						
Demolish	S.F.		2.60		2.60	Cost includes material and labor to
Install	S.F.	24	10.85		34.85	install 4' x 11' clear plate glass
Demolish and Install	S.F.	24	13.45		37.45	window built on floor.
Reinstall	S.F.		8.66		8.66	
Clean	S.F.	.01	.36		.37	
Minimum Charge	Job		248		248	
Floor to 13'						
Demolish	S.F.		2.60		2.60	Cost includes material and labor to
Install	S.F.	24	10.85		34.85	install 4' x 13' clear plate glass
Demolish and Install	S.F.	24	13.45		37.45	window built on floor.
Reinstall	S.F.		8.66		8.66	
Clean	S.F.	.01	.36		.37	
Minimum Charge	Job		248		248	

Exterior Doors and Windows

Storefront System		Unit	Material	Labor	Equip.	Total	Specification
Entrance							
Narrow Stile 3' x 7"							
	Demolish	Ea.		22.50		22.50	Cost includes material and labor to
	Install	Ea.	835	269		1104	install 3' x 7' narrow stile door, center
	Demolish and Install	Ea.	835	291.50		1126.50	pivot concealed closer.
	Reinstall	Ea.		215.25		215.25	
	Clean	Ea.	6.50	37.50		44	
	Minimum Charge	Job		248		248	
Tempered Glass							
	Demolish	Ea.		22.50		22.50	Cost includes material and labor to
	Install	Ea.	3275	535		3810	install 3' x 7' tempered glass door,
	Demolish and Install	Ea.	3275	557.50		3832.50	center pivot concealed closer,.
	Reinstall	Ea.		429.32		429.32	
	Clean	Ea.	6.50	37.50		44	
	Minimum Charge	Job		248		248	
Heavy Section							
	Demolish	Ea.		22.50		22.50	Includes material and labor to install
	Install	Ea.	1250	495		1745	wide stile door with 3' 6" x 7'
	Demolish and Install	Ea.	1250	517.50		1767.50	opening.
	Reinstall	Ea.		397.12		397.12	
	Clean	Ea.	1.30	12.45		13.75	
	Minimum Charge	Job		785		785	

Curtain Wall System		Unit	Material	Labor	Equip.	Total	Specification
Regular Weight							
Bronze Anodized							
	Demolish	S.F.		2.60		2.60	Includes material and labor to install
	Install	S.F.	38.50	10.85		49.35	structural curtain wall system with
	Demolish and Install	S.F.	38.50	13.45		51.95	bronze anodized frame of heavy
	Clean	S.F.	.01	.36		.37	weight, float glass.
	Minimum Charge	Job		202		202	
Black Anodized							
	Demolish	S.F.		2.60		2.60	Includes material and labor to install
	Install	S.F.	41.50	10.85		52.35	structural curtain wall system with
	Demolish and Install	S.F.	41.50	13.45		54.95	black anodized frame of regular
	Clean	S.F.	.01	.36		.37	weight, float glass.
	Minimum Charge	Job		202		202	
Heavy Weight							
Bronze Anodized							
	Demolish	S.F.		2.60		2.60	Includes material and labor to install
	Install	S.F.	38.50	10.85		49.35	structural curtain wall system with
	Demolish and Install	S.F.	38.50	13.45		51.95	bronze anodized frame of heavy
	Clean	S.F.	.01	.36		.37	weight, float glass.
	Minimum Charge	Job		202		202	
Black Anodized							
	Demolish	S.F.		2.60		2.60	Includes material and labor to install
	Install	S.F.	39.50	10.85		50.35	structural curtain wall system with
	Demolish and Install	S.F.	39.50	13.45		52.95	black anodized frame of heavy
	Clean	S.F.	.01	.36		.37	weight, float glass.
	Minimum Charge	Job		202		202	
Glass							
1" Insulated							
	Install	S.F.	17.20	10.45		27.65	Cost includes labor and material to
	Minimum Charge	Job		196		196	install 1" insulated glass.

Skylight	Unit	Material	Labor	Equip.	Total	Specification
Dome						
22″ x 22″						
Demolish	Ea.		76.50		76.50	Cost includes material and labor to
Install	Ea.	220	125		345	install 22″ x 22″ fixed dome skylight.
Demolish and Install	Ea.	220	201.50		421.50	
Reinstall	Ea.		100.01		100.01	
Clean	Ea.	.58	10.70		11.28	
Minimum Charge	Job		750		750	
22″ x 46″						
Demolish	Ea.		76.50		76.50	Cost includes material and labor to
Install	Ea.	252	150		402	install 22″ x 46″ fixed dome skylight.
Demolish and Install	Ea.	252	226.50		478.50	
Reinstall	Ea.		120.01		120.01	
Clean	Ea.		16.60		16.60	
Minimum Charge	Job		750		750	
30″ x 30″						
Demolish	Ea.		76.50		76.50	Cost includes material and labor to
Install	Ea.	253	125		378	install 30″ x 30″ fixed dome skylight.
Demolish and Install	Ea.	253	201.50		454.50	
Reinstall	Ea.		100.01		100.01	
Clean	Ea.		16.60		16.60	
Minimum Charge	Job		750		750	
30″ x 46″						
Demolish	Ea.		76.50		76.50	Cost includes material and labor to
Install	Ea.	320	150		470	install 30″ x 46″ fixed dome skylight.
Demolish and Install	Ea.	320	226.50		546.50	
Reinstall	Ea.		120.01		120.01	
Clean	Ea.		16.60		16.60	
Minimum Charge	Job		750		750	
Fixed						
22″ x 27″						
Demolish	Ea.		76.50		76.50	Includes material and labor to install
Install	Ea.	234	125		359	double glazed skylight, 22″ x 27″,
Demolish and Install	Ea.	234	201.50		435.50	fixed.
Reinstall	Ea.		100.01		100.01	
Clean	Ea.	.58	10.70		11.28	
Minimum Charge	Job		750		750	
22″ x 46″						
Demolish	Ea.		76.50		76.50	Includes material and labor to install
Install	Ea.	296	150		446	double glazed skylight, 22″ x 46″,
Demolish and Install	Ea.	296	226.50		522.50	fixed.
Reinstall	Ea.		120.01		120.01	
Clean	Ea.		16.60		16.60	
Minimum Charge	Job		750		750	
44″ x 46″						
Demolish	Ea.		76.50		76.50	Includes material and labor to install
Install	Ea.	440	150		590	double glazed skylight, 44″ x 46″,
Demolish and Install	Ea.	440	226.50		666.50	fixed.
Reinstall	Ea.		120.01		120.01	
Clean	Ea.		18.70		18.70	
Minimum Charge	Job		750		750	
Operable						
22″ x 27″						
Demolish	Ea.		76.50		76.50	Includes material and labor to install
Install	Ea.	340	125		465	double glazed skylight, 22″ x 27″,
Demolish and Install	Ea.	340	201.50		541.50	operable.
Reinstall	Ea.		100.01		100.01	
Clean	Ea.	.58	10.70		11.28	
Minimum Charge	Job		750		750	

Exterior Doors and Windows

Skylight

	Unit	Material	Labor	Equip.	Total	Specification
22″ x 46″						
Demolish	Ea.		76.50		76.50	Includes material and labor to install
Install	Ea.	400	150		550	double glazed skylight, 22″ x 46″,
Demolish and Install	Ea.	400	226.50		626.50	operable.
Reinstall	Ea.		120.01		120.01	
Clean	Ea.		16.60		16.60	
Minimum Charge	Job		750		750	
44″ x 46″						
Demolish	Ea.		76.50		76.50	Includes material and labor to install
Install	Ea.	875	150		1025	double glazed skylight, 44″ x 46″,
Demolish and Install	Ea.	875	226.50		1101.50	operable.
Reinstall	Ea.		120.01		120.01	
Clean	Ea.		18.70		18.70	
Minimum Charge	Job		750		750	

Industrial Steel Window

	Unit	Material	Labor	Equip.	Total	Specification
100% Fixed						
Demolish	S.F.		2.13		2.13	Includes material and labor to install
Install	S.F.	30.50	4.96		35.46	commercial grade steel windows,
Demolish and Install	S.F.	30.50	7.09		37.59	including glazing.
Reinstall	S.F.		3.97		3.97	
Clean	Ea.	.23	1.14		1.37	
Paint	S.F.	.15	.77		.92	
Minimum Charge	Job		248		248	
50% Vented						
Demolish	S.F.		2.13		2.13	Includes material and labor to install
Install	S.F.	56	4.96		60.96	commercial grade steel windows,
Demolish and Install	S.F.	56	7.09		63.09	including glazing.
Reinstall	S.F.		3.97		3.97	
Clean	Ea.	.23	1.14		1.37	
Paint	S.F.	.15	.77		.92	
Minimum Charge	Job		248		248	

Brick Veneer

Concrete Masonry Units

Masonry Wall	Unit	Material	Labor	Equip.	Total	Specification
Unreinforced CMU						
4″ x 8″ x 16″						
Demolish	S.F.		1.85		1.85	Includes material and labor to install
Install	S.F.	1.74	3.97		5.71	normal weight 4″ x 8″ x 16″ block.
Demolish and Install	S.F.	1.74	5.82		7.56	
Clean	S.F.	.09	.46		.55	
Paint	S.F.	.13	.79		.92	
Minimum Charge	Job		198		198	
6″ x 8″ x 16″						
Demolish	S.F.		1.96		1.96	Includes material and labor to install
Install	S.F.	2.40	4.16		6.56	normal weight 6″ x 8″ x 16″ block.
Demolish and Install	S.F.	2.40	6.12		8.52	
Clean	S.F.	.09	.46		.55	
Paint	S.F.	.13	.79		.92	
Minimum Charge	Job		198		198	
8″ x 8″ x 16″						
Demolish	S.F.		2.22		2.22	Includes material and labor to install
Install	S.F.	2.74	4.57		7.31	normal weight 8″ x 8″ x 16″ block.
Demolish and Install	S.F.	2.74	6.79		9.53	
Clean	S.F.	.09	.46		.55	
Paint	S.F.	.13	.79		.92	
Minimum Charge	Job		198		198	
12″ x 8″ x 16″						
Demolish	S.F.		2.22		2.22	Includes material and labor to install
Install	S.F.	3.87	6.95		10.82	normal weight 12″ x 8″ x 16″ block.
Demolish and Install	S.F.	3.87	9.17		13.04	
Clean	S.F.	.09	.46		.55	
Paint	S.F.	.13	.79		.92	
Minimum Charge	Job		198		198	
Reinforced CMU						
4″ x 8″ x 16″						
Demolish	S.F.		1.85	.91	2.76	Includes material and labor to install
Install	S.F.	1.88	4.06		5.94	normal weight 4″ x 8″ x 16″ block,
Demolish and Install	S.F.	1.88	5.91	.91	8.70	mortar and 1/2″ re-bar installed
Clean	S.F.	.09	.46		.55	vertically every 24″ O.C.
Paint	S.F.	.13	.79		.92	
Minimum Charge	Job		360		360	
6″ x 8″ x 16″						
Demolish	S.F.		1.94	.45	2.39	Includes material and labor to install
Install	S.F.	2.54	4.25		6.79	normal weight 6″ x 8″ x 16″ block,
Demolish and Install	S.F.	2.54	6.19	.45	9.18	mortar and 1/2″ re-bar installed
Clean	S.F.	.09	.46		.55	vertically every 24″ O.C.
Paint	S.F.	.13	.79		.92	
Minimum Charge	Job		360		360	

Masonry

Masonry Wall		Unit	Material	Labor	Equip.	Total	Specification
8″ x 8″ x 16″							
	Demolish	S.F.		2.05	.48	2.53	Includes material and labor to install
	Install	S.F.	2.88	4.63		7.51	normal weight 8″ x 8″ x 16″ block,
	Demolish and Install	S.F.	2.88	6.68	.48	10.04	mortar and 1/2″ re-bar installed
	Clean	S.F.	.09	.46		.55	vertically every 24″ O.C.
	Paint	S.F.	.13	.79		.92	
	Minimum Charge	Job		360		360	
12″ x 8″ x 16″							
	Demolish	S.F.		2.12	.49	2.61	Includes material and labor to install
	Install	S.F.	4.02	7.15		11.17	normal weight 12″ x 8″ x 16″ block,
	Demolish and Install	S.F.	4.02	9.27	.49	13.78	mortar and 1/2″ re-bar installed
	Clean	S.F.	.09	.46		.55	vertically every 24″ O.C.
	Paint	S.F.	.13	.79		.92	
	Minimum Charge	Job		360		360	
Structural Brick							
4″ Single Row							
	Demolish	S.F.		2.66		2.66	Cost includes material and labor to
	Install	S.F.	4.53	8.50		13.03	install 4″ red brick wall, running bond
	Demolish and Install	S.F.	4.53	11.16		15.69	with 3/8″ concave joints, mortar and
	Clean	S.F.	.09	.39		.48	ties.
	Paint	S.F.	.13	.79		.92	
	Minimum Charge	Job		360		360	
8″ Double Row							
	Demolish	S.F.		2.66		2.66	Cost includes material and labor to
	Install	S.F.	7.60	13.55		21.15	install 8″ red brick wall, running bond,
	Demolish and Install	S.F.	7.60	16.21		23.81	with 3/8″ concave joints, mortar and
	Clean	S.F.	.09	.39		.48	wall ties.
	Paint	S.F.	.13	.79		.92	
	Minimum Charge	Job		360		360	
12″ Triple Row							
	Demolish	S.F.		3.69		3.69	Cost includes material and labor to
	Install	S.F.	11.45	19.25		30.70	install 12″ red brick wall, running
	Demolish and Install	S.F.	11.45	22.94		34.39	bond, with 3/8″ concave joints,
	Clean	S.F.	.09	.39		.48	mortar and wall ties.
	Paint	S.F.	.13	.79		.92	
	Minimum Charge	Job		360		360	
Brick Veneer							
4″ Red Common							
	Demolish	S.F.		2.66		2.66	Cost includes material and labor to
	Install	S.F.	3.58	7.95		11.53	install 4″ common red face brick,
	Demolish and Install	S.F.	3.58	10.61		14.19	running bond with 3/8″ concave
	Clean	S.F.	.09	.39		.48	joints, mortar and wall ties.
	Paint	S.F.	.13	.79		.92	
	Minimum Charge	Job		198		198	
4″ Used							
	Demolish	S.F.		2.66		2.66	Cost includes material and labor to
	Install	S.F.	4.53	8.50		13.03	install 4″ red brick wall, running bond
	Demolish and Install	S.F.	4.53	11.16		15.69	with 3/8″ concave joints, mortar and
	Clean	S.F.	.09	.39		.48	ties.
	Paint	S.F.	.13	.79		.92	
	Minimum Charge	Job		198		198	

Masonry

Masonry Wall		Unit	Material	Labor	Equip.	Total	Specification
6" Jumbo							
	Demolish	S.F.		2.66		2.66	Cost includes material and labor to
	Install	S.F.	5.35	4.20		9.55	install 6" red jumbo brick veneer,
	Demolish and Install	S.F.	5.35	6.86		12.21	running bond with 3/8" concave
	Clean	S.F.	.09	.39		.48	joints, mortar and ties.
	Paint	S.F.	.13	.79		.92	
	Minimum Charge	Job		198		198	
Norman (11-1/2")							
	Demolish	S.F.		2.66		2.66	Cost includes material and labor to
	Install	S.F.	6.25	5.70		11.95	install 4" norman red brick wall,
	Demolish and Install	S.F.	6.25	8.36		14.61	running bond with 3/8" concave
	Clean	S.F.	.09	.39		.48	joints, mortar and ties.
	Paint	S.F.	.13	.79		.92	
	Minimum Charge	Job		198		198	
Glazed							
	Demolish	S.F.		2.66		2.66	Includes material, labor and
	Install	S.F.	18	8.70		26.70	equipment to install glazed brick.
	Demolish and Install	S.F.	18	11.36		29.36	
	Clean	S.F.	.09	.39		.48	
	Paint	S.F.	.13	.79		.92	
	Minimum Charge	Job		198		198	
Slumpstone							
6" x 4"							
	Demolish	S.F.		1.85		1.85	Cost includes material and labor to
	Install	S.F.	6	4.48		10.48	install 6" x 4" x 16" concrete slump
	Demolish and Install	S.F.	6	6.33		12.33	block.
	Clean	S.F.	.09	.46		.55	
	Paint	S.F.	.13	.79		.92	
	Minimum Charge	Job		198		198	
6" x 6"							
	Demolish	S.F.		1.96		1.96	Cost includes material and labor to
	Install	S.F.	5.25	4.62		9.87	install 6" x 6" x 16" concrete slump
	Demolish and Install	S.F.	5.25	6.58		11.83	block.
	Clean	S.F.	.09	.46		.55	
	Paint	S.F.	.13	.79		.92	
	Minimum Charge	Job		198		198	
8" x 6"							
	Demolish	S.F.		1.96		1.96	Cost includes material and labor to
	Install	S.F.	7.15	4.77		11.92	install 8" x 6" x 16" concrete slump
	Demolish and Install	S.F.	7.15	6.73		13.88	block.
	Clean	S.F.	.09	.46		.55	
	Paint	S.F.	.13	.79		.92	
	Minimum Charge	Job		198		198	
12" x 4"							
	Demolish	S.F.		1.85		1.85	Cost includes material and labor to
	Install	S.F.	12.55	5.50		18.05	install 12" x 4" x 16" concrete slump
	Demolish and Install	S.F.	12.55	7.35		19.90	block.
	Clean	S.F.	.09	.46		.55	
	Paint	S.F.	.13	.79		.92	
	Minimum Charge	Job		198		198	
12" x 6"							
	Demolish	S.F.		1.96		1.96	Cost includes material and labor to
	Install	S.F.	11.40	5.95		17.35	install 12" x 6" x 16" concrete slump
	Demolish and Install	S.F.	11.40	7.91		19.31	block.
	Clean	S.F.	.09	.46		.55	
	Paint	S.F.	.13	.79		.92	
	Minimum Charge	Job		198		198	

Masonry

Masonry Wall	Unit	Material	Labor	Equip.	Total	Specification
Stucco						
Three Coat						
Demolish	S.Y.		2.29		2.29	Includes material and labor to install
Install	S.Y.	3.89	8.60	.68	13.17	stucco on exterior masonry walls.
Demolish and Install	S.Y.	3.89	10.89	.68	15.46	
Clean	S.Y.		4.16		4.16	
Paint	S.F.	.28	.56		.84	
Minimum Charge	Job		180		180	
Three Coat w / Wire Mesh						
Demolish	S.Y.		4.16		4.16	Includes material and labor to install
Install	S.Y.	5.85	32.50	2.16	40.51	stucco on wire mesh over wood
Demolish and Install	S.Y.	5.85	36.66	2.16	44.67	framing.
Clean	S.Y.		4.16		4.16	
Paint	S.F.	.28	.56		.84	
Minimum Charge	Job		180		180	
Fill Cracks						
Install	S.F.	.43	2.87		3.30	Includes labor and material to fill-in
Minimum Charge	Job		180		180	hairline cracks up to 1/8" with filler, including sand and fill per S.F.
Furring						
1" x 2"						
Demolish	L.F.		.13		.13	Cost includes material and labor to
Install	L.F.	.28	.82		1.10	install 1" x 2" furring on masonry wall.
Demolish and Install	L.F.	.28	.95		1.23	
Minimum Charge	Job		202		202	
2" x 2"						
Demolish	L.F.		.14		.14	Cost includes material and labor to
Install	L.F.	.24	.90		1.14	install 2" x 2" furring on masonry wall.
Demolish and Install	L.F.	.24	1.04		1.28	
Minimum Charge	Job		202		202	
2" x 4"						
Demolish	L.F.		.16		.16	Cost includes material and labor to
Install	L.F.	.36	1.02		1.38	install 2" x 4" furring on masonry wall.
Demolish and Install	L.F.	.36	1.18		1.54	
Reinstall	L.F.		.82		.82	
Minimum Charge	Job		202		202	
Maintenance / Cleaning						
Repoint						
Install	S.F.	.58	4.96		5.54	Includes labor and material to cut and
Minimum Charge	Hr.		49.50		49.50	repoint brick, hard mortar, running bond.
Acid Etch						
Install	S.F.	.06	.71		.77	Includes labor and material to acid
Minimum Charge	Job		150	35	185	wash smooth brick.
Pressure Wash						
Clean	S.F.		1.02	.14	1.16	Includes labor and material to high
Minimum Charge	Job		150	35	185	pressure water wash masonry, average.
Waterproof						
Install	S.F.	.52	.73		1.25	Includes labor and material to install
Minimum Charge	Job		182		182	masory waterproofing.

Masonry

Chimney

Chimney		Unit	Material	Labor	Equip.	Total	Specification
Demo & Haul Exterior							
	Demolish	C.F.		5.45		5.45	Includes minimum labor and
	Minimum Charge	Job		166		166	equipment to remove masonry and haul debris to truck or dumpster.
Demo & Haul Interior							
	Demolish	C.F.		7.50		7.50	Includes minimum labor and
	Minimum Charge	Job		166		166	equipment to remove masonry and haul debris to truck or dumpster.
Install New (w / flue)							
Brick							
	Install	V.L.F.	37.50	45		82.50	Includes material and labor to install
	Minimum Charge	Job		198		198	brick chimney with flue from ground level up. Foundation not included.
Natural Stone							
	Install	L.F.	71	71.50		142.50	Includes labor and material to install
	Minimum Charge	Job		198		198	natural stone chimney.
Install From Roof Up							
Brick							
	Install	V.L.F.	37.50	45		82.50	Includes material and labor to install
	Minimum Charge	Job		198		198	brick chimney with flue from ground level up. Foundation not included.
Natural Stone							
	Install	L.F.	71	59.50		130.50	Includes labor and material to install
	Minimum Charge	Job		198		198	natural stone chimney.
Install Base Pad							
	Install	Ea.	259	222	1.07	482.07	Includes labor and material to replace
	Minimum Charge	Job		945	25.50	970.50	spread footing, 5' square x 16" deep.
Metal Cap							
	Install	Ea.	49	25		74	Includes labor and materials to install
	Minimum Charge	Job		202		202	bird and squirrel screens in a chimney flue.

Fireplace

Fireplace		Unit	Material	Labor	Equip.	Total	Specification
Common Brick							
30"							
	Demolish	Ea.		1175		1175	Includes material and labor to install a
	Install	Ea.	1900	3575		5475	complete unit which includes common
	Demolish and Install	Ea.	1900	4750		6650	brick, foundation, damper, flue lining
	Minimum Charge	Job		198		198	stack to 15' high and a 30" fire box.
36"							
	Demolish	Ea.		1175		1175	Includes material and labor to install a
	Install	Ea.	2000	3975		5975	complete unit which includes common
	Demolish and Install	Ea.	2000	5150		7150	brick, foundation, damper, flue lining
	Minimum Charge	Job		198		198	stack to 15' high and a 36" fire box.
42"							
	Demolish	Ea.		1175		1175	Includes material and labor to install a
	Install	Ea.	2200	4475		6675	complete unit which includes common
	Demolish and Install	Ea.	2200	5650		7850	brick, foundation, damper, flue lining
	Minimum Charge	Job		198		198	stack to 15' high and a 42" fire box.

Masonry

Fireplace	Unit	Material	Labor	Equip.	Total	Specification
48"						
Demolish	Ea.		1175		1175	Includes material and labor to install
Install	Ea.	2300	5100		7400	a complete unit which includes common
Demolish and Install	Ea.	2300	6275		8575	brick, foundation, damper, flue lining
Minimum Charge	Job		198		198	stack to 15' high and a 48" fire box.
Raised Hearth						
Brick Hearth						
Demolish	S.F.		5.20		5.20	Includes material and labor to install a
Install	S.F.	18.05	30		48.05	brick fireplace hearth based on 30" x
Demolish and Install	S.F.	18.05	35.20		53.25	29" opening.
Clean	S.F.	.09	.39		.48	
Minimum Charge	Job		198		198	
Marble Hearth / Facing						
Demolish	Ea.		33		33	Includes material and labor to install
Install	Ea.	730	121		851	marble fireplace hearth.
Demolish and Install	Ea.	730	154		884	
Reinstall	Ea.		96.47		96.47	
Clean	Ea.	26.50	6		32.50	
Minimum Charge	Job		198		198	
Breast (face) Brick						
Demolish	S.F.		5.20		5.20	Includes material and labor to install
Install	S.F.	4.61	8.30		12.91	standard red brick, running bond.
Demolish and Install	S.F.	4.61	13.50		18.11	
Clean	S.F.		1.02	.14	1.16	
Minimum Charge	Hr.		49.50		49.50	
Fire Box						
Demolish	Ea.		266		266	Includes material and labor to install
Install	Ea.	194	360		554	fireplace box only (110 brick).
Demolish and Install	Ea.	194	626		820	
Clean	Ea.	.20	13.65		13.85	
Minimum Charge	Hr.		49.50		49.50	
Natural Stone						
Demolish	S.F.		5.20		5.20	Includes material and labor to install
Install	S.F.	16.50	15.25		31.75	high priced stone, split or rock face.
Demolish and Install	S.F.	16.50	20.45		36.95	
Clean	S.F.	.09	.90		.99	
Minimum Charge	Job		360		360	
Slumpstone Veneer						
Demolish	S.F.		1.96		1.96	Cost includes material and labor to
Install	S.F.	7.15	4.77		11.92	install 8" x 6" x 16" concrete slump
Demolish and Install	S.F.	7.15	6.73		13.88	block.
Clean	S.F.	.09	.46		.55	
Paint	S.F.	.13	.79		.92	
Minimum Charge	Job		198		198	
Prefabricated						
Firebox						
Demolish	Ea.		47.50		47.50	Includes material and labor to install
Install	Ea.	1850	365		2215	up to 43" radiant heat, zero
Demolish and Install	Ea.	1850	412.50		2262.50	clearance, prefabricated fireplace.
Reinstall	Ea.		293.53		293.53	Flues, doors or blowers not included.
Clean	Ea.	2.60	18.70		21.30	
Minimum Charge	Job		202		202	

Masonry

Fireplace

	Unit	Material	Labor	Equip.	Total	Specification
Flue						
Demolish	V.L.F.		5.55		5.55	Includes material and labor to install
Install	V.L.F.	17	15.60		32.60	prefabricated chimney vent, 8″
Demolish and Install	V.L.F.	17	21.15		38.15	exposed metal flue.
Reinstall	V.L.F.		12.49		12.49	
Clean	L.F.	1.05	3.74		4.79	
Minimum Charge	Job		405		405	
Blower						
Demolish	Ea.		4.43		4.43	Includes material and labor to install
Install	Ea.	149	28		177	blower for metal fireplace flue.
Demolish and Install	Ea.	149	32.43		181.43	
Reinstall	Ea.		22.54		22.54	
Clean	Ea.	5.20	37.50		42.70	
Minimum Charge	Job		405		405	
Accessories						
Wood Mantle						
Demolish	L.F.		5.55		5.55	Includes material and labor to install
Install	L.F.	12	11.55		23.55	wood fireplace mantel.
Demolish and Install	L.F.	12	17.10		29.10	
Reinstall	L.F.		11.53		11.53	
Clean	Ea.	.04	.84		.88	
Paint	L.F.	.10	9.40		9.50	
Minimum Charge	Job		202		202	
Colonial Style						
Demolish	Ea.		50		50	Includes material and labor to install
Install	Opng.	1375	202		1577	wood fireplace mantel.
Demolish and Install	Opng.	1375	252		1627	
Reinstall	Opng.		201.80		201.80	
Clean	Ea.		.61		.61	
Paint	Ea.	16.95	130		146.95	
Minimum Charge	Job		202		202	
Modern Design						
Demolish	Ea.		50		50	Includes material and labor to install
Install	Opng.	450	80.50		530.50	wood fireplace mantel.
Demolish and Install	Opng.	450	130.50		580.50	
Reinstall	Opng.		80.72		80.72	
Clean	Ea.		.61		.61	
Paint	Ea.	16.95	130		146.95	
Minimum Charge	Job		202		202	
Glass Door Unit						
Demolish	Ea.		6.95		6.95	Includes material and labor to install a
Install	Ea.	375	8.25		383.25	fireplace glass door unit.
Demolish and Install	Ea.	375	15.20		390.20	
Reinstall	Ea.		8.26		8.26	
Clean	Ea.	.63	11.50		12.13	
Minimum Charge	Job		202		202	
Fire Screen						
Demolish	Ea.		3.46		3.46	Includes material and labor to install a
Install	Ea.	48	4.13		52.13	fireplace fire screen.
Demolish and Install	Ea.	48	7.59		55.59	
Reinstall	Ea.		4.13		4.13	
Clean	Ea.	.31	9.95		10.26	
Minimum Charge	Job		202		202	

Siding

Shingles

Board & Batten

Texture 1-11

Exterior Siding		Unit	Material	Labor	Equip.	Total	Specification
Trim							
1″ x 2″							
	Demolish	L.F.		.28		.28	Cost includes material and labor to
	Install	L.F.	.28	1.22		1.50	install 1″ x 2″ pine trim.
	Demolish and Install	L.F.	.28	1.50		1.78	
	Clean	L.F.	.01	.20		.21	
	Paint	L.F.	.02	.54		.56	
	Minimum Charge	Job		202		202	
1″ x 3″							
	Demolish	L.F.		.28		.28	Cost includes material and labor to
	Install	L.F.	.28	1.39		1.67	install 1″ x 3″ pine trim.
	Demolish and Install	L.F.	.28	1.67		1.95	
	Clean	L.F.	.01	.20		.21	
	Paint	L.F.	.02	.54		.56	
	Minimum Charge	Job		202		202	
1″ x 4″							
	Demolish	L.F.		.28		.28	Cost includes material and labor to
	Install	L.F.	.58	1.61		2.19	install 1″ x 4″ pine trim.
	Demolish and Install	L.F.	.58	1.89		2.47	
	Clean	L.F.	.02	.20		.22	
	Paint	L.F.	.02	.54		.56	
	Minimum Charge	Job		202		202	
1″ x 6″							
	Demolish	L.F.		.28		.28	Cost includes material and labor to
	Install	L.F.	.74	1.61		2.35	install 1″ x 6″ pine trim.
	Demolish and Install	L.F.	.74	1.89		2.63	
	Clean	L.F.	.02	.20		.22	
	Paint	L.F.	.07	.54		.61	
	Minimum Charge	Job		202		202	
1″ x 8″							
	Demolish	L.F.		.30		.30	Cost includes material and labor to
	Install	L.F.	1.07	2.02		3.09	install 1″ x 8″ pine trim.
	Demolish and Install	L.F.	1.07	2.32		3.39	
	Clean	L.F.	.04	.21		.25	
	Paint	L.F.	.07	.54		.61	
	Minimum Charge	Job		202		202	
Aluminum							
8″ Non-Insulated							
	Demolish	S.F.		.75		.75	Includes material and labor to install
	Install	S.F.	2.39	1.61		4	horizontal, colored clapboard, 8″ to
	Demolish and Install	S.F.	2.39	2.36		4.75	10″ wide, plain.
	Reinstall	S.F.		1.61		1.61	
	Clean	S.F.		.30		.30	
	Minimum Charge	Job		202		202	

Siding

Exterior Siding		Unit	Material	Labor	Equip.	Total	Specification
8″ Insulated							
	Demolish	S.F.		.75		.75	Includes material and labor to install
	Install	S.F.	2.55	1.61		4.16	horizontal, colored insulated
	Demolish and Install	S.F.	2.55	2.36		4.91	clapboard, 8″ wide, plain.
	Reinstall	S.F.		1.61		1.61	
	Clean	S.F.		.30		.30	
	Minimum Charge	Job		202		202	
12″ Non-Insulated							
	Demolish	S.F.		.75		.75	Includes material and labor to install
	Install	S.F.	2.39	1.38		3.77	horizontal, colored clapboard, plain.
	Demolish and Install	S.F.	2.39	2.13		4.52	
	Reinstall	S.F.		1.38		1.38	
	Clean	S.F.		.30		.30	
	Minimum Charge	Job		202		202	
12″ Insulated							
	Demolish	S.F.		.75		.75	Includes material and labor to install
	Install	S.F.	2.55	1.38		3.93	horizontal, colored insulated
	Demolish and Install	S.F.	2.55	2.13		4.68	clapboard, plain.
	Reinstall	S.F.		1.38		1.38	
	Clean	S.F.		.30		.30	
	Minimum Charge	Job		202		202	
Clapboard 8″ to 10″							
	Demolish	S.F.		.75		.75	Includes material and labor to install
	Install	S.F.	2.39	1.61		4	horizontal, colored clapboard, 8″ to
	Demolish and Install	S.F.	2.39	2.36		4.75	10″ wide, plain.
	Reinstall	S.F.		1.61		1.61	
	Clean	S.F.		.30		.30	
	Minimum Charge	Job		202		202	
Corner Strips							
	Demolish	L.F.		.39		.39	Includes material and labor to install
	Install	V.L.F.	3.51	1.61		5.12	corners for horizontal lapped
	Demolish and Install	V.L.F.	3.51	2		5.51	aluminum siding.
	Reinstall	V.L.F.		1.61		1.61	
	Clean	L.F.		.20		.20	
	Minimum Charge	Job		202		202	
Vinyl							
Non-Insulated							
	Demolish	S.F.		.59		.59	Cost includes material and labor to
	Install	S.F.	1.24	1.47		2.71	install 10″ non-insulated solid vinyl
	Demolish and Install	S.F.	1.24	2.06		3.30	siding.
	Reinstall	S.F.		1.17		1.17	
	Clean	S.F.		.30		.30	
	Minimum Charge	Job		202		202	
Insulated							
	Demolish	S.F.		.59		.59	Cost includes material and labor to
	Install	S.F.	2.98	2.02		5	install insulated solid vinyl siding
	Demolish and Install	S.F.	2.98	2.61		5.59	panels.
	Reinstall	S.F.		1.61		1.61	
	Clean	S.F.		.30		.30	
	Minimum Charge	Job		202		202	
Corner Strips							
	Demolish	L.F.		.37		.37	Cost includes material and labor to
	Install	L.F.	1.74	1.15		2.89	install corner posts for vinyl siding
	Demolish and Install	L.F.	1.74	1.52		3.26	panels.
	Reinstall	L.F.		.92		.92	
	Clean	L.F.		.20		.20	
	Minimum Charge	Job		202		202	

Siding

Exterior Siding		Unit	Material	Labor	Equip.	Total	Specification
Fiber Cement Siding							
4' x 8' Panel	Demolish	S.F.		.61		.61	Cost includes material and labor to
	Install	S.F.	.94	.88		1.82	install 4' x 8' fiber cement 7/16"
	Demolish and Install	S.F.	.94	1.49		2.43	thick.
	Clean	S.F.		.30		.30	
	Paint	S.F.	.25	1.17		1.42	
	Minimum Charge	Job		202		202	
Lap	Demolish	S.F.		.60		.60	Cost includes material and labor to
	Install	S.F.	1.03	1.60		2.63	install 8" or 12" fiber cement lap
	Demolish and Install	S.F.	1.03	2.20		3.23	siding 7/16" thick with wood grain
	Clean	S.F.		.30		.30	finish.
	Paint	S.F.	.25	1.17		1.42	
	Minimum Charge	Job		202		202	
Plywood Panel							
Douglas Fir (T-1-11)	Demolish	S.F.		.46		.46	Includes material and labor to install
	Install	S.F.	1.51	1.22		2.73	Douglas fir 4' x 8' plywood exterior
	Demolish and Install	S.F.	1.51	1.68		3.19	siding plain or patterns.
	Reinstall	S.F.		1.23		1.23	
	Clean	S.F.		.30		.30	
	Paint	S.F.	.25	1.17		1.42	
	Minimum Charge	Job		202		202	
Redwood	Demolish	S.F.		.46		.46	Includes material and labor to install
	Install	S.F.	2.11	1.22		3.33	redwood 4' x 8' plywood exterior
	Demolish and Install	S.F.	2.11	1.68		3.79	siding plain or patterns.
	Reinstall	S.F.		1.23		1.23	
	Clean	S.F.		.30		.30	
	Paint	S.F.	.25	1.17		1.42	
	Minimum Charge	Job		202		202	
Cedar	Demolish	S.F.		.46		.46	Cost includes material and labor to
	Install	S.F.	2.67	1.22		3.89	install 4' x 8' cedar plywood exterior
	Demolish and Install	S.F.	2.67	1.68		4.35	siding plain or patterns.
	Reinstall	S.F.		1.23		1.23	
	Clean	S.F.		.30		.30	
	Paint	S.F.	.25	1.17		1.42	
	Minimum Charge	Job		202		202	
Tongue and Groove							
Fir, Tongue and Groove	Demolish	S.F.		.83		.83	Includes material and labor to install
	Install	S.F.	2.56	1.22		3.78	fir tongue and groove exterior siding
	Demolish and Install	S.F.	2.56	2.05		4.61	1" x 8".
	Reinstall	S.F.		.98		.98	
	Clean	S.F.		.30		.30	
	Paint	S.F.	.25	1.17		1.42	
	Minimum Charge	Job		202		202	
Pine, Tongue and Groove	Demolish	S.F.		.83		.83	Includes labor and material to install
	Install	S.F.	2.42	1.22		3.64	Pine tongue and groove exterior
	Demolish and Install	S.F.	2.42	2.05		4.47	siding 1" x 8".
	Reinstall	S.F.		1.22		1.22	
	Clean	S.F.		.30		.30	
	Paint	S.F.	.25	1.17		1.42	
	Minimum Charge	Job		202		202	

Siding

Exterior Siding	Unit	Material	Labor	Equip.	Total	Specification
Cedar, Tongue and Groove						
Demolish	S.F.		.83		.83	Includes labor and material to install
Install	S.F.	4.27	1.83		6.10	cedar tongue and groove exterior
Demolish and Install	S.F.	4.27	2.66		6.93	siding 1″ x 8″.
Reinstall	S.F.		1.47		1.47	
Clean	S.F.		.30		.30	
Paint	S.F.	.25	1.17		1.42	
Minimum Charge	Job		202		202	
Redwood, Tongue and Groove						
Demolish	S.F.		.83		.83	Includes labor and material to install
Install	S.F.	2.79	1.83		4.62	redwood tongue and groove exterior
Demolish and Install	S.F.	2.79	2.66		5.45	siding 1″ x 4″.
Reinstall	S.F.		1.83		1.83	
Clean	S.F.		.30		.30	
Paint	S.F.	.25	1.17		1.42	
Minimum Charge	Job		202		202	
Board and Batten						
Fir						
Demolish	S.F.		.83		.83	Cost includes material and labor to
Install	S.F.	7.60	1.22		8.82	install 1″ x 8″ fir boards with 1″ x 3″
Demolish and Install	S.F.	7.60	2.05		9.65	battens.
Reinstall	S.F.		.98		.98	
Clean	S.F.		.30		.30	
Paint	S.F.	.25	1.17		1.42	
Minimum Charge	Job		202		202	
Pine						
Demolish	S.F.		.83		.83	Cost includes material and labor to
Install	S.F.	3.27	1.08		4.35	install 1″ x 10″ pine boards with 1″ x
Demolish and Install	S.F.	3.27	1.91		5.18	3″ battens.
Reinstall	S.F.		.86		.86	
Clean	S.F.		.30		.30	
Paint	S.F.	.25	1.17		1.42	
Minimum Charge	Job		202		202	
Cedar						
Demolish	S.F.		.83		.83	Cost includes material and labor to
Install	S.F.	2.68	1.08		3.76	install 1″ x 10″ cedar boards with 1″ x
Demolish and Install	S.F.	2.68	1.91		4.59	3″ battens.
Reinstall	S.F.		.86		.86	
Clean	S.F.		.30		.30	
Paint	S.F.	.25	1.17		1.42	
Minimum Charge	Job		202		202	
Redwood						
Demolish	S.F.		.83		.83	Cost includes material and labor to
Install	S.F.	5.60	1.08		6.68	install 1″ x 10″ redwood boards with
Demolish and Install	S.F.	5.60	1.91		7.51	1″ x 3″ battens.
Reinstall	S.F.		.86		.86	
Clean	S.F.		.30		.30	
Paint	S.F.	.25	1.17		1.42	
Minimum Charge	Job		202		202	
Wood Shingle						
Demolish	Sq.		77		77	Includes material and labor to install
Install	Sq.	178	179		357	wood shingles/shakes.
Demolish and Install	Sq.	178	256		434	
Clean	Sq.		31.50		31.50	
Paint	Sq.	15.90	104		119.90	
Minimum Charge	Job		202		202	

Siding

Exterior Siding	Unit	Material	Labor	Equip.	Total	Specification
Synthetic Stucco System						
Demolish	S.F.		2.77		2.77	Cost includes material and labor to
Install	S.F.	3.04	6.40	.51	9.95	install 2 coats of adhesive mixture,
Demolish and Install	S.F.	3.04	9.17	.51	12.72	glass fiber mesh, 1″ insulation board,
Clean	S.F.		.27		.27	and textured finish coat.
Paint	S.F.	.28	.56		.84	
Minimum Charge	Job		860	68	928	

Front-end Loader   **Bulldozer**

Grading

Grading		Unit	Material	Labor	Equip.	Total	Specification
Hand (fine)							
	Install	S.F.		.60		.60	Includes labor and material to install
	Minimum Charge	Job		150		150	fine grade for slab on grade, hand grade.
Machine (fine)							
	Install	S.Y.		.52	.44	.96	Includes labor and material to install
	Minimum Charge	Job		355	299	654	fine grade for roadway, base or leveling course.

Asphalt Paving

Asphalt Paving		Unit	Material	Labor	Equip.	Total	Specification
Seal Coat							
	Install	S.F.	.14	.11		.25	Includes labor and material to install
	Minimum Charge	Job		150		150	sealcoat for a small area.
Wearing Course							
	Install	S.F.	.17	.32	.25	.74	Cost includes labor and material to
	Minimum Charge	Job		150		150	install 1" thick wearing course.

Masonry Pavers

Masonry Pavers		Unit	Material	Labor	Equip.	Total	Specification
Natural Concrete							
Sand Base							
	Demolish	S.F.		3.32		3.32	Includes material and labor to install
	Install	S.F.	2.62	6.60		9.22	concrete pavers on sand base.
	Demolish and Install	S.F.	2.62	9.92		12.54	
	Reinstall	S.F.		5.29		5.29	
	Clean	S.F.		1.20		1.20	
	Minimum Charge	Job		198		198	
Mortar Base							
	Demolish	S.F.		5.50	1.96	7.46	Includes material and labor to install
	Install	S.F.	3.41	5.50		8.91	concrete pavers on mortar base.
	Demolish and Install	S.F.	3.41	11	1.96	16.37	
	Reinstall	S.F.		4.40		4.40	
	Clean	S.F.		1.09		1.09	
	Minimum Charge	Job		198		198	

Site Work

Masonry Pavers

Masonry Pavers		Unit	Material	Labor	Equip.	Total	Specification
Adobe							
Sand Base							
	Demolish	S.F.		3.32		3.32	Includes material and labor to install
	Install	S.F.	2.31	4.40		6.71	adobe pavers on sand base.
	Demolish and Install	S.F.	2.31	7.72		10.03	
	Reinstall	S.F.		3.52		3.52	
	Clean	S.F.		1.20		1.20	
	Minimum Charge	Job		198		198	
Mortar Base							
	Demolish	S.F.		5.50	1.96	7.46	Includes material and labor to install
	Install	S.F.	3.03	5.50		8.53	adobe pavers on mortar base.
	Demolish and Install	S.F.	3.03	11	1.96	15.99	
	Reinstall	S.F.		4.40		4.40	
	Clean	S.F.		1.09		1.09	
	Minimum Charge	Job		198		198	
Standard Brick							
Sand Base							
	Demolish	S.F.		3.32		3.32	Includes material and labor to install
	Install	S.F.	3.72	7.15		10.87	standard brick pavers on sand base.
	Demolish and Install	S.F.	3.72	10.47		14.19	
	Reinstall	S.F.		5.73		5.73	
	Clean	S.F.		1.20		1.20	
	Minimum Charge	Job		198		198	
Mortar Base							
	Demolish	S.F.		5.50	1.96	7.46	Includes material and labor to install
	Install	S.F.	5.90	9.90		15.80	standard brick pavers on mortar base.
	Demolish and Install	S.F.	5.90	15.40	1.96	23.26	
	Reinstall	S.F.		7.93		7.93	
	Clean	S.F.		1.09		1.09	
	Minimum Charge	Job		198		198	
Deluxe Brick							
Sand Base							
	Demolish	S.F.		3.32		3.32	Includes material and labor to install
	Install	S.F.	5.85	5.50		11.35	deluxe brick pavers on sand base.
	Demolish and Install	S.F.	5.85	8.82		14.67	
	Reinstall	S.F.		4.40		4.40	
	Clean	S.F.		1.20		1.20	
	Minimum Charge	Job		198		198	
Mortar Base							
	Demolish	S.F.		5.50	1.96	7.46	Includes material and labor to install
	Install	S.F.	6.60	9.90		16.50	deluxe brick pavers on mortar base.
	Demolish and Install	S.F.	6.60	15.40	1.96	23.96	
	Reinstall	S.F.		7.93		7.93	
	Clean	S.F.		1.09		1.09	
	Minimum Charge	Job		198		198	

Fencing

Fencing		Unit	Material	Labor	Equip.	Total	Specification
Block w / Footing							
4″							
	Demolish	S.F.		1.85		1.85	Cost includes material and labor to
	Install	S.F.	1.64	4.25		5.89	install 4″ non-reinforced concrete
	Demolish and Install	S.F.	1.64	6.10		7.74	block.
	Clean	S.F.	.15	1.27	.18	1.60	
	Paint	S.F.	.30	.66		.96	
	Minimum Charge	Job		198		198	

Site Work

Fencing

	Unit	Material	Labor	Equip.	Total	Specification
4" Reinforced						
Demolish	S.F.		1.85	.91	2.76	Cost includes material and labor to
Install	S.F.	1.78	4.30		6.08	install 4" reinforced concrete block.
Demolish and Install	S.F.	1.78	6.15	.91	8.84	
Clean	S.F.	.15	1.27	.18	1.60	
Paint	S.F.	.30	.66		.96	
Minimum Charge	Job		198		198	
6"						
Demolish	S.F.		1.96		1.96	Cost includes material and labor to
Install	S.F.	2.30	4.57		6.87	install 6" non-reinforced concrete
Demolish and Install	S.F.	2.30	6.53		8.83	block.
Clean	S.F.	.15	1.27	.18	1.60	
Paint	S.F.	.30	.66		.96	
Minimum Charge	Job		198		198	
6" Reinforced						
Demolish	S.F.		1.94	.45	2.39	Cost includes material and labor to
Install	S.F.	2.44	4.63		7.07	install 6" reinforced concrete block.
Demolish and Install	S.F.	2.44	6.57	.45	9.46	
Clean	S.F.	.15	1.27	.18	1.60	
Paint	S.F.	.30	.66		.96	
Minimum Charge	Job		198		198	
Cap for Block Wall						
Demolish	L.F.		2.08		2.08	Includes labor and equipment to install
Install	L.F.	19.30	9.55		28.85	precast concrete coping.
Demolish and Install	L.F.	19.30	11.63		30.93	
Clean	L.F.	.02	3.12		3.14	
Paint	S.F.	.30	.66		.96	
Minimum Charge	Job		198		198	
Block Pilaster						
Demolish	Ea.		143		143	Includes material and labor to install
Install	Ea.	78	143		221	block pilaster for fence.
Demolish and Install	Ea.	78	286		364	
Reinstall	Ea.		143.20		143.20	
Paint	Ea.	3.97	15.40		19.37	
Minimum Charge	Job		198		198	
Block w / o Footing						
4"						
Demolish	S.F.		1.85		1.85	Cost includes material and labor to
Install	S.F.	1.82	3.25		5.07	install 4" non-reinforced hollow
Demolish and Install	S.F.	1.82	5.10		6.92	lightweight block.
Clean	S.F.	.15	1.27	.18	1.60	
Paint	S.F.	.30	.66		.96	
Minimum Charge	Job		198		198	
4" Reinforced						
Demolish	S.F.		1.85	.91	2.76	Cost includes material and labor to
Install	S.F.	1.89	4.20		6.09	install 4" reinforced hollow lightweight
Demolish and Install	S.F.	1.89	6.05	.91	8.85	block.
Clean	S.F.	.15	1.27	.18	1.60	
Paint	S.F.	.30	.66		.96	
Minimum Charge	Job		198		198	
6"						
Demolish	S.F.		1.96		1.96	Cost includes material and labor to
Install	S.F.	2.61	3.58		6.19	install 6" non-reinforced hollow
Demolish and Install	S.F.	2.61	5.54		8.15	lightweight block.
Clean	S.F.	.15	1.27	.18	1.60	
Paint	S.F.	.30	.66		.96	
Minimum Charge	Job		198		198	

Fencing

	Unit	Material	Labor	Equip.	Total	Specification
6" Reinforced						
Demolish	S.F.		1.94	.45	2.39	Cost includes material and labor to
Install	S.F.	2.71	4.51		7.22	install 6" reinforced hollow lightweight
Demolish and Install	S.F.	2.71	6.45	.45	9.61	block.
Clean	S.F.	.15	1.27	.18	1.60	
Paint	S.F.	.30	.66		.96	
Minimum Charge	Job		198		198	
Cap for Block Wall						
Demolish	L.F.		2.08		2.08	Includes labor and equipment to install
Install	L.F.	19.30	9.55		28.85	precast concrete coping.
Demolish and Install	L.F.	19.30	11.63		30.93	
Clean	L.F.	.02	3.12		3.14	
Paint	S.F.	.30	.66		.96	
Minimum Charge	Job		198		198	
Block Pilaster						
Demolish	Ea.		143		143	Includes material and labor to install
Install	Ea.	78	143		221	block pilaster for fence.
Demolish and Install	Ea.	78	286		364	
Reinstall	Ea.		143.20		143.20	
Paint	Ea.	3.97	15.40		19.37	
Minimum Charge	Job		198		198	

Chain Link

	Unit	Material	Labor	Equip.	Total	Specification
3' High w / o Top Rail						
Demolish	L.F.		2.59	.92	3.51	Includes material and labor to install
Install	L.F.	3.61	1.74	.37	5.72	residential galvanized fence 3' high
Demolish and Install	L.F.	3.61	4.33	1.29	9.23	with 1-3/8" steel post 10' O.C. set
Reinstall	L.F.		1.39	.30	1.69	without concrete.
Clean	L.F.	.15	1.09		1.24	
Minimum Charge	Job		460		460	
4' High w / o Top Rail						
Demolish	L.F.		2.59	.92	3.51	Includes material and labor to install
Install	L.F.	4.71	2.15	.46	7.32	residential galvanized fence 4' high
Demolish and Install	L.F.	4.71	4.74	1.38	10.83	with 1-3/8" steel post 10' O.C. set
Reinstall	L.F.		1.72	.37	2.09	without concrete.
Clean	L.F.	.21	1.20		1.41	
Minimum Charge	Job		460		460	
5' High w / o Top Rail						
Demolish	L.F.		2.59	.92	3.51	Includes material and labor to install
Install	L.F.	5.10	2.81	.60	8.51	residential galvanized fence 5' high
Demolish and Install	L.F.	5.10	5.40	1.52	12.02	with 1-3/8" steel post 10' O.C. set
Reinstall	L.F.		2.25	.48	2.73	without concrete.
Clean	L.F.	.26	1.33		1.59	
Minimum Charge	Job		460		460	
3' High w / Top Rail						
Demolish	L.F.		2.76	.98	3.74	Includes material and labor to install
Install	L.F.	2.21	1.83	.39	4.43	residential galvanized fence 3' high
Demolish and Install	L.F.	2.21	4.59	1.37	8.17	with 1-3/8" steel post 10' O.C. set
Reinstall	L.F.		1.46	.31	1.77	without concrete.
Clean	L.F.	.15	1.11		1.26	
Minimum Charge	Job		460		460	
4' High w / Top Rail						
Demolish	L.F.		2.76	.98	3.74	Includes material and labor to install
Install	L.F.	5.20	2.28	.49	7.97	residential galvanized fence 4' high
Demolish and Install	L.F.	5.20	5.04	1.47	11.71	with 1-5/8" steel post 10' O.C. set
Reinstall	L.F.		1.83	.39	2.22	without concrete and 1-5/8" top rail
Clean	L.F.	.21	1.22		1.43	with sleeves.
Minimum Charge	Job		460		460	

Site Work

Fencing

	Unit	Material	Labor	Equip.	Total	Specification
5' High w / Top Rail						
Demolish	L.F.		2.76	.98	3.74	Includes material and labor to install
Install	L.F.	3.53	3.04	.66	7.23	residential galvanized fence 5' high
Demolish and Install	L.F.	3.53	5.80	1.64	10.97	with 1-5/8" steel post 10' O.C. set
Reinstall	L.F.		2.43	.52	2.95	without concrete and 1-5/8" top rail
Clean	L.F.	.26	1.36		1.62	with sleeves.
Minimum Charge	Job		460		460	
6' High w / Top Rail						
Demolish	L.F.		2.76	.98	3.74	Includes material and labor to install
Install	L.F.	6.55	4.56	.98	12.09	residential galvanized fence 6' high
Demolish and Install	L.F.	6.55	7.32	1.96	15.83	with 2" steel post 10' O.C. set without
Reinstall	L.F.		3.65	.79	4.44	concrete and 1-3/8" top rail with
Clean	L.F.	.31	1.53		1.84	sleeves.
Minimum Charge	Job		460		460	
Barbed Wire						
Demolish	L.F.		1.55		1.55	Cost includes material and labor to
Install	L.F.	.43	.60	.16	1.19	install 3 strand galvanized barbed
Demolish and Install	L.F.	.43	2.15	.16	2.74	wire fence.
Reinstall	L.F.		.48	.13	.61	
Minimum Charge	Job		460	340	800	
6' Redwood						
Demolish	L.F.		10.25		10.25	Cost includes material and labor to
Install	L.F.	29.50	7.30	1.57	38.37	install 6' high redwood fencing.
Demolish and Install	L.F.	29.50	17.55	1.57	48.62	
Reinstall	L.F.		5.84	1.26	7.10	
Clean	L.F.	.31	1.39		1.70	
Paint	L.F.	.65	3.65		4.30	
Minimum Charge	Job		460		460	
6' Red Cedar						
Demolish	L.F.		10.25		10.25	Cost includes material and labor to
Install	L.F.	17.75	7.30	1.57	26.62	install 6' cedar fence.
Demolish and Install	L.F.	17.75	17.55	1.57	36.87	
Reinstall	L.F.		5.84	1.26	7.10	
Clean	L.F.	.31	1.39		1.70	
Paint	L.F.	.65	3.65		4.30	
Minimum Charge	Job		460		460	
6' Shadowbox						
Demolish	L.F.		10.25		10.25	Cost includes material and labor to
Install	L.F.	13.30	6.10	1.31	20.71	install 6' pressure treated pine fence.
Demolish and Install	L.F.	13.30	16.35	1.31	30.96	
Reinstall	L.F.		4.87	1.05	5.92	
Clean	L.F.	.31	1.39		1.70	
Paint	L.F.	.65	3.65		4.30	
Minimum Charge	Job		460		460	
3' Picket						
Demolish	L.F.		10.25		10.25	Includes material, labor and
Install	L.F.	4.98	6.50	1.40	12.88	equipment to install pressure treated
Demolish and Install	L.F.	4.98	16.75	1.40	23.13	pine picket fence.
Reinstall	L.F.		5.22	1.12	6.34	
Clean	L.F.	.15	1.20		1.35	
Paint	L.F.	.33	1.98		2.31	
Minimum Charge	Job		460		460	

Fencing

Fencing	Unit	Material	Labor	Equip.	Total	Specification
Wrought Iron						
Demolish	L.F.		22		22	Cost includes material and labor to
Install	L.F.	31	12.35		43.35	install 5' high wrought iron fence with
Demolish and Install	L.F.	31	34.35		65.35	pickets at 4-1/2" O.C.
Reinstall	L.F.		9.86		9.86	
Clean	L.F.		1.20		1.20	
Paint	L.F.	.67	4.08		4.75	
Minimum Charge	Job		460		460	
Post						
Dirt Based Wood						
Demolish	Ea.		25.50		25.50	Includes material and labor to install
Install	Ea.	26.50	116		142.50	wood post set in earth.
Demolish and Install	Ea.	26.50	141.50		168	
Reinstall	Ea.		92.45		92.45	
Clean	Ea.		3.74		3.74	
Paint	Ea.	.72	1.39		2.11	
Minimum Charge	Job		460		460	
Concrete Based Wood						
Demolish	Ea.		36.50	13.05	49.55	Includes material and labor to install
Install	Ea.	16.40	154		170.40	wood post set in concrete.
Demolish and Install	Ea.	16.40	190.50	13.05	219.95	
Clean	Ea.		3.74		3.74	
Paint	Ea.	.72	1.39		2.11	
Minimum Charge	Job		460		460	
Block Pilaster						
Demolish	Ea.		143		143	Includes material and labor to install
Install	Ea.	78	143		221	block pilaster for fence.
Demolish and Install	Ea.	78	286		364	
Reinstall	Ea.		143.20		143.20	
Paint	Ea.	3.97	15.40		19.37	
Minimum Charge	Job		198		198	
Gate						
Chain Link						
Demolish	Ea.		34		34	Cost includes material and labor to
Install	Ea.	123	51.50		174.50	install 3' wide chain link pass gate
Demolish and Install	Ea.	123	85.50		208.50	and hardware.
Reinstall	Ea.		41.09		41.09	
Clean	Ea.		4.16		4.16	
Minimum Charge	Job		460		460	
Redwood						
Demolish	Ea.		29.50		29.50	Includes material, labor and
Install	Ea.	175	51.50		226.50	equipment to install redwood pass
Demolish and Install	Ea.	175	81		256	gate and hardware.
Reinstall	Ea.		41.09		41.09	
Clean	Ea.		4.16		4.16	
Paint	Ea.	1.07	6.95		8.02	
Minimum Charge	Job		460		460	
Red Cedar						
Demolish	Ea.		29.50		29.50	Cost includes material and labor to
Install	Ea.	85.50	51.50		137	install 3' wide red cedar pass gate
Demolish and Install	Ea.	85.50	81		166.50	and hardware.
Reinstall	Ea.		41.09		41.09	
Clean	Ea.		4.16		4.16	
Paint	Ea.	1.07	6.95		8.02	
Minimum Charge	Job		460		460	

Site Work

Fencing

	Unit	Material	Labor	Equip.	Total	Specification
Wrought Iron						
Demolish	Ea.		22		22	Includes material, labor and
Install	Ea.	201	116		317	equipment to install wrought iron gate
Demolish and Install	Ea.	201	138		339	with hardware.
Reinstall	Ea.		92.45		92.45	
Clean	Ea.		4.16		4.16	
Paint	Ea.	1.33	6.95		8.28	
Minimum Charge	Job		460		460	

| Fire-extinguishing System | Space Heater | Hot-air Furnace |

Plumbing		Unit	Material	Labor	Equip.	Total	Specification
Components							
3/4" Supply							
	Demolish	L.F.		2.57		2.57	Includes material and labor to install
	Install	L.F.	6.55	6.10		12.65	type L copper tubing including
	Demolish and Install	L.F.	6.55	8.67		15.22	couplings and hangers at 10' O.C.
	Reinstall	L.F.		6.08		6.08	
	Minimum Charge	Job		231		231	
1/2" Fixture Supply							
	Install	Ea.	64.50	154		218.50	Includes labor and materials to install
							supply pipe only to a plumbing fixture.
2" Single Vent Stack							
	Demolish	Ea.		43		43	Includes material and labor to install
	Install	Ea.	26.50	231		257.50	PVC vent stack pipe with couplings at
	Demolish and Install	Ea.	26.50	274		300.50	10' O.C.
	Reinstall	Ea.		231.20		231.20	
	Minimum Charge	Job		231		231	
4" Drain							
	Demolish	L.F.		3.43		3.43	Includes material and labor to install
	Install	L.F.	9.50	7.55		17.05	DVW type PVC pipe with couplings at
	Demolish and Install	L.F.	9.50	10.98		20.48	10' O.C. and 3 strap hangers per 10'
	Reinstall	L.F.		7.56		7.56	run.
	Minimum Charge	Job		231		231	
1-1/2" Drain							
	Demolish	L.F.		2.57		2.57	Includes material and labor to install
	Install	L.F.	3.17	4.92		8.09	DVW type PVC pipe with couplings at
	Demolish and Install	L.F.	3.17	7.49		10.66	10' O.C. and 3 strap hangers per 10'
	Reinstall	L.F.		4.92		4.92	run.
	Minimum Charge	Job		231		231	
Maintenance							
Flush Out / Unclog							
	Clean	Job		231		231	Minimum labor and equipment charge
	Minimum Charge	Job		231		231	to install water cooler.
Vent Cap							
Large							
	Demolish	Ea.		11.70		11.70	Includes labor and material to install a
	Install	Ea.	39	21		60	PVC plumbing pipe vent cap.
	Demolish and Install	Ea.	39	32.70		71.70	
	Clean	Ea.	.73	6.80		7.53	
	Paint	Ea.	.17	7.85		8.02	
	Minimum Charge	Job		116		116	

Plumbing		Unit	Material	Labor	Equip.	Total	Specification
Medium							
	Demolish	Ea.		11.70		11.70	Includes labor and material to install a
	Install	Ea.	33.50	20		53.50	PVC plumbing pipe vent cap.
	Demolish and Install	Ea.	33.50	31.70		65.20	
	Clean	Ea.	.73	6.80		7.53	
	Paint	Ea.	.17	7.85		8.02	
	Minimum Charge	Job		116		116	
Small							
	Demolish	Ea.		11.70		11.70	Includes material and labor to install a
	Install	Ea.	8.80	19.25		28.05	PVC plumbing pipe vent cap.
	Demolish and Install	Ea.	8.80	30.95		39.75	
	Clean	Ea.	.73	6.80		7.53	
	Paint	Ea.	.17	7.85		8.02	
	Minimum Charge	Job		116		116	

Plumbing		Unit	Material	Labor	Equip.	Total	Specification
Sump Pump							
1/4 HP							
	Demolish	Ea.		46		46	Includes material and labor to install a
	Install	Ea.	163	77		240	submersible sump pump.
	Demolish and Install	Ea.	163	123		286	
	Reinstall	Ea.		61.65		61.65	
	Clean	Ea.	1.82	18.70		20.52	
	Minimum Charge	Job		231		231	
1/3 HP							
	Demolish	Ea.		46		46	Includes material and labor to install a
	Install	Ea.	199	92.50		291.50	submersible sump pump.
	Demolish and Install	Ea.	199	138.50		337.50	
	Reinstall	Ea.		73.98		73.98	
	Clean	Ea.	1.82	18.70		20.52	
	Minimum Charge	Job		231		231	
1/2 HP							
	Demolish	Ea.		46		46	Includes material and labor to install a
	Install	Ea.	243	92.50		335.50	submersible sump pump.
	Demolish and Install	Ea.	243	138.50		381.50	
	Reinstall	Ea.		73.98		73.98	
	Clean	Ea.	1.82	18.70		20.52	
	Minimum Charge	Job		231		231	
Clean and Service							
	Clean	Ea.		29		29	Includes labor to clean and service a
	Minimum Charge	Job		231		231	sump pump.

Water Heater		Unit	Material	Labor	Equip.	Total	Specification
30 Gallon							
	Demolish	Ea.		145		145	Includes material and labor to install a
	Install	Ea.	635	210		845	30 gallon electric water heater.
	Demolish and Install	Ea.	635	355		990	
	Reinstall	Ea.		168.15		168.15	
	Clean	Ea.	1.82	18.70		20.52	
	Minimum Charge	Job		231		231	

Water Heater	Unit	Material	Labor	Equip.	Total	Specification
40 Gallon						
Demolish	Ea.		145		145	Includes material and labor to install a
Install	Ea.	675	231		906	40 gallon electric water heater.
Demolish and Install	Ea.	675	376		1051	
Reinstall	Ea.		184.96		184.96	
Clean	Ea.	1.82	18.70		20.52	
Minimum Charge	Job		231		231	
52 Gallon						
Demolish	Ea.		145		145	Includes material and labor to install a
Install	Ea.	760	231		991	52 gallon electric water heater.
Demolish and Install	Ea.	760	376		1136	
Reinstall	Ea.		184.96		184.96	
Clean	Ea.	1.82	18.70		20.52	
Minimum Charge	Job		231		231	
82 Gallon						
Demolish	Ea.		145		145	Includes material and labor to install
Install	Ea.	1125	289		1414	an 82 gallon electric water heater.
Demolish and Install	Ea.	1125	434		1559	
Reinstall	Ea.		231.20		231.20	
Clean	Ea.	1.82	18.70		20.52	
Minimum Charge	Job		231		231	
Gas-fired						
30 Gallon Gas-fired						
Demolish	Ea.		178		178	Includes material and labor to install a
Install	Ea.	985	231		1216	30 gallon gas water heater.
Demolish and Install	Ea.	985	409		1394	
Reinstall	Ea.		184.96		184.96	
Clean	Ea.	1.82	18.70		20.52	
Minimum Charge	Job		231		231	
30 Gallon Gas-fired, Flue						
Install	Ea.	39	66		105	Includes labor and materials to install
Minimum Charge	Job		231		231	a flue for a water heater (up to 50 gallon size).
40 Gallon Gas-fired						
Demolish	Ea.		178		178	Includes material and labor to install a
Install	Ea.	985	243		1228	40 gallon gas water heater.
Demolish and Install	Ea.	985	421		1406	
Reinstall	Ea.		194.69		194.69	
Clean	Ea.	1.82	18.70		20.52	
Minimum Charge	Job		231		231	
40 Gallon Gas-fired, Flue						
Install	Ea.	39	66		105	Includes labor and materials to install
Minimum Charge	Job		231		231	a flue for a water heater (up to 50 gallon size).
50 Gallon Gas-fired						
Demolish	Ea.		178		178	Includes material and labor to install a
Install	Ea.	1025	257		1282	50 gallon gas water heater.
Demolish and Install	Ea.	1025	435		1460	
Reinstall	Ea.		205.51		205.51	
Clean	Ea.	1.82	18.70		20.52	
Minimum Charge	Job		231		231	
50 Gallon Gas-fired, Flue						
Install	Ea.	39	66		105	Includes labor and materials to install
Minimum Charge	Job		231		231	a flue for a water heater (up to 50 gallon size).

Rough Mechanical

Water Heater

Water Heater	Unit	Material	Labor	Equip.	Total	Specification
Solar Hot Water System						
Water Heater						
Demolish	Ea.		116		116	Includes material and labor to install a
Install	Ea.	1125	310		1435	solar hot water heat exchanger
Demolish and Install	Ea.	1125	426		1551	storage tank, 100 gallon.
Reinstall	Ea.		246.61		246.61	
Minimum Charge	Job		233		233	
Solar Panel						
Demolish	S.F.		1.69		1.69	Includes material and labor to install
Install	S.F.	32.50	3.04		35.54	solar panel.
Demolish and Install	S.F.	32.50	4.73		37.23	
Reinstall	S.F.		2.43		2.43	
Minimum Charge	Job		233		233	
Repair Plumbing						
Install	Job		233		233	Includes 4 hour minimum labor charge
Minimum Charge	Job		233		233	for a steamfitter or pipefitter.
Insulating Wrap						
Demolish	Ea.		5.35		5.35	Includes material and labor to install
Install	Ea.	19.20	14.45		33.65	insulating wrap around a 100 gallon
Demolish and Install	Ea.	19.20	19.80		39	solar hot water heat exchanger
Reinstall	Ea.		11.56		11.56	storage tank.
Minimum Charge	Job		231		231	
Water Softener						
Demolish	Ea.		85.50		85.50	Includes material and labor to install a
Install	Ea.	1425	208		1633	14 GPM water softener.
Demolish and Install	Ea.	1425	293.50		1718.50	
Reinstall	Ea.		166.40		166.40	
Clean	Ea.	1.82	18.70		20.52	
Minimum Charge	Ea.		231		231	

Ductwork

Ductwork	Unit	Material	Labor	Equip.	Total	Specification
Galvanized, Square or Rectangular						
6"						
Demolish	L.F.		2.09		2.09	Includes material and labor to install
Install	L.F.	1.68	10		11.68	rectangular ductwork with a greatest
Demolish and Install	L.F.	1.68	12.09		13.77	dimension of 6".
Reinstall	L.F.		8.01		8.01	
Clean	L.F.		2.40		2.40	
Minimum Charge	Job		225		225	
8"						
Demolish	L.F.		2.09		2.09	Includes material and labor to install
Install	L.F.	2.23	12.90		15.13	rectangular ductwork with a greatest
Demolish and Install	L.F.	2.23	14.99		17.22	dimension of 8".
Reinstall	L.F.		10.30		10.30	
Clean	L.F.		3.21		3.21	
Minimum Charge	Job		225		225	
10"						
Demolish	L.F.		2.09		2.09	Includes material and labor to install
Install	L.F.	2.79	16.70		19.49	rectangular ductwork with a greatest
Demolish and Install	L.F.	2.79	18.79		21.58	dimension of 10".
Reinstall	L.F.		13.36		13.36	
Clean	L.F.		4.01		4.01	
Minimum Charge	Job		225		225	

Ductwork	Unit	Material	Labor	Equip.	Total	Specification
Galvanized, Spiral						
4"						
Demolish	L.F.		2.50		2.50	Cost includes material and labor to
Install	L.F.	1.95	2.25		4.20	install 4" diameter spiral pre-formed
Demolish and Install	L.F.	1.95	4.75		6.70	steel galvanized ductwork.
Reinstall	L.F.		1.80		1.80	
Clean	L.F.		1.26		1.26	
Minimum Charge	Job		225		225	
6"						
Demolish	L.F.		2.50		2.50	Cost includes material and labor to
Install	L.F.	1.95	2.90		4.85	install 6" diameter spiral pre-formed
Demolish and Install	L.F.	1.95	5.40		7.35	steel galvanized ductwork.
Reinstall	L.F.		2.32		2.32	
Clean	L.F.		1.89		1.89	
Minimum Charge	Job		225		225	
8"						
Demolish	L.F.		2.50		2.50	Cost includes material and labor to
Install	L.F.	2.59	4.06		6.65	install 8" diameter spiral pre-formed
Demolish and Install	L.F.	2.59	6.56		9.15	steel galvanized ductwork.
Reinstall	L.F.		3.25		3.25	
Clean	L.F.		2.52		2.52	
Minimum Charge	Job		225		225	
10"						
Demolish	L.F.		3.13		3.13	Cost includes material and labor to
Install	L.F.	3.23	5.05		8.28	install 10" diameter spiral pre-formed
Demolish and Install	L.F.	3.23	8.18		11.41	steel galvanized ductwork.
Reinstall	L.F.		4.06		4.06	
Clean	L.F.		3.15		3.15	
Minimum Charge	Job		225		225	
12"						
Demolish	L.F.		4.17		4.17	Cost includes material and labor to
Install	L.F.	3.88	6.75		10.63	install 12" diameter spiral pre-formed
Demolish and Install	L.F.	3.88	10.92		14.80	steel galvanized ductwork.
Reinstall	L.F.		5.41		5.41	
Clean	L.F.		3.78		3.78	
Minimum Charge	Job		225		225	
16"						
Demolish	L.F.		8.35		8.35	Cost includes material and labor to
Install	L.F.	5.85	13.55		19.40	install 16" diameter spiral pre-formed
Demolish and Install	L.F.	5.85	21.90		27.75	steel galvanized ductwork.
Reinstall	L.F.		10.82		10.82	
Clean	L.F.		5.05		5.05	
Minimum Charge	Job		225		225	
Flexible Fiberglass						
6" Non-insulated						
Demolish	L.F.		1.93		1.93	Cost includes material and labor to
Install	L.F.	1.68	2.90		4.58	install 6" diameter non-insulated
Demolish and Install	L.F.	1.68	4.83		6.51	flexible fiberglass fabric on corrosion
Reinstall	L.F.		2.32		2.32	resistant metal ductwork.
Clean	L.F.		1.89		1.89	
Minimum Charge	Job		225		225	
8" Non-insulated						
Demolish	L.F.		2.78		2.78	Cost includes material and labor to
Install	L.F.	2.31	4.06		6.37	install 8" diameter non-insulated
Demolish and Install	L.F.	2.31	6.84		9.15	flexible fiberglass fabric on corrosion
Reinstall	L.F.		3.25		3.25	resistant metal ductwork.
Clean	L.F.		2.52		2.52	
Minimum Charge	Job		225		225	

Rough Mechanical

Ductwork

	Unit	Material	Labor	Equip.	Total	Specification
10" Non-insulated						
Demolish	L.F.		3.58		3.58	Cost includes material and labor to
Install	L.F.	2.87	5.05		7.92	install 10" diameter non-insulated
Demolish and Install	L.F.	2.87	8.63		11.50	flexible fiberglass fabric on corrosion
Reinstall	L.F.		4.06		4.06	resistant metal ductwork.
Clean	L.F.		3.15		3.15	
Minimum Charge	Job		225		225	
12" Non-insulated						
Demolish	L.F.		5		5	Cost includes material and labor to
Install	L.F.	3.49	6.75		10.24	install 12" diameter non-insulated
Demolish and Install	L.F.	3.49	11.75		15.24	flexible fiberglass fabric on corrosion
Reinstall	L.F.		5.41		5.41	resistant metal ductwork.
Clean	L.F.		3.78		3.78	
Minimum Charge	Job		225		225	
4" Insulated						
Demolish	L.F.		1.47		1.47	Cost includes material and labor to
Install	L.F.	2.37	2.39		4.76	install 4" diameter insulated flexible
Demolish and Install	L.F.	2.37	3.86		6.23	fiberglass fabric on corrosion resistant
Reinstall	L.F.		1.91		1.91	metal ductwork.
Clean	L.F.		1.26		1.26	
Minimum Charge	Job		225		225	
6" Insulated						
Demolish	L.F.		1.93		1.93	Cost includes material and labor to
Install	L.F.	2.62	3.12		5.74	install 6" diameter insulated flexible
Demolish and Install	L.F.	2.62	5.05		7.67	fiberglass fabric on corrosion resistant
Reinstall	L.F.		2.50		2.50	metal ductwork.
Clean	L.F.		1.89		1.89	
Minimum Charge	Job		225		225	
8" Insulated						
Demolish	L.F.		2.78		2.78	Cost includes material and labor to
Install	L.F.	3.30	4.51		7.81	install 8" diameter insulated flexible
Demolish and Install	L.F.	3.30	7.29		10.59	fiberglass fabric on corrosion resistant
Reinstall	L.F.		3.61		3.61	metal ductwork.
Clean	L.F.		2.52		2.52	
Minimum Charge	Job		225		225	
10" Insulated						
Demolish	L.F.		3.58		3.58	Cost includes material and labor to
Install	L.F.	3.86	5.80		9.66	install 10" diameter insulated flexible
Demolish and Install	L.F.	3.86	9.38		13.24	fiberglass fabric on corrosion resistant
Reinstall	L.F.		4.64		4.64	metal ductwork.
Clean	L.F.		3.15		3.15	
Minimum Charge	Job		225		225	
12" Insulated						
Demolish	L.F.		5		5	Cost includes material and labor to
Install	L.F.	4.80	8.10		12.90	install 12" diameter insulated flexible
Demolish and Install	L.F.	4.80	13.10		17.90	fiberglass fabric on corrosion resistant
Reinstall	L.F.		6.49		6.49	metal ductwork.
Clean	L.F.		3.78		3.78	
Minimum Charge	Job		225		225	

Rough Mechanical

Heating		Unit	Material	Labor	Equip.	Total	Specification
Hot Water Baseboard							
	Demolish	L.F.		7.95		7.95	Includes material and labor to install
	Install	L.F.	8.30	14		22.30	baseboard radiation.
	Demolish and Install	L.F.	8.30	21.95		30.25	
	Reinstall	L.F.		11.19		11.19	
	Clean	L.F.	1.82	4.68		6.50	
	Minimum Charge	Job		231		231	
3'							
	Demolish	Ea.		25.50		25.50	Includes material and labor to install
	Install	Ea.	26.50	46.50		73	fin tube baseboard radiation in 3'
	Demolish and Install	Ea.	26.50	72		98.50	sections.
	Reinstall	Ea.		37.30		37.30	
	Clean	Ea.	.52	14.25		14.77	
	Minimum Charge	Job		231		231	
4'							
	Demolish	Ea.		34.50		34.50	Includes material and labor to install
	Install	Ea.	35	52.50		87.50	fin tube baseboard radiation in 4'
	Demolish and Install	Ea.	35	87		122	sections.
	Reinstall	Ea.		41.96		41.96	
	Clean	Ea.	1.05	18.70		19.75	
	Minimum Charge	Job		231		231	
5'							
	Demolish	Ea.		43		43	Includes material and labor to install
	Install	Ea.	44	60		104	fin tube baseboard radiation in 5'
	Demolish and Install	Ea.	44	103		147	sections.
	Reinstall	Ea.		47.95		47.95	
	Clean	Ea.	1.05	23		24.05	
	Minimum Charge	Job		231		231	
6'							
	Demolish	Ea.		51.50		51.50	Includes material and labor to install
	Install	Ea.	53	70		123	fin tube baseboard radiation in 6'
	Demolish and Install	Ea.	53	121.50		174.50	sections.
	Reinstall	Ea.		55.95		55.95	
	Clean	Ea.	1.05	27		28.05	
	Minimum Charge	Job		231		231	
7'							
	Demolish	Ea.		57		57	Includes material and labor to install
	Install	Ea.	61.50	92.50		154	fin tube baseboard radiation in 7'
	Demolish and Install	Ea.	61.50	149.50		211	sections.
	Reinstall	Ea.		73.98		73.98	
	Clean	Ea.	1.30	33		34.30	
	Minimum Charge	Job		231		231	
9'							
	Demolish	Ea.		85.50		85.50	Includes material and labor to install
	Install	Ea.	79	132		211	fin tube baseboard radiation in 9'
	Demolish and Install	Ea.	79	217.50		296.50	sections.
	Reinstall	Ea.		105.69		105.69	
	Clean	Ea.	2.08	42.50		44.58	
	Minimum Charge	Job		231		231	

Heating		Unit	Material	Labor	Equip.	Total	Specification
50 MBH							
	Demolish	Ea.		42		42	Includes material and labor to install a
	Install	Ea.	1325	120		1445	cabinet space heater with an output of
	Demolish and Install	Ea.	1325	162		1487	50 MBH.
	Reinstall	Ea.		95.91		95.91	
	Clean	Ea.	1.30	37.50		38.80	
	Minimum Charge	Job		233		233	

Rough Mechanical

Heating

Heating		Unit	Material	Labor	Equip.	Total	Specification
75 MBH							
	Demolish	Ea.		42		42	Includes material and labor to install a
	Install	Ea.	1350	140		1490	cabinet space heater with an output of
	Demolish and Install	Ea.	1350	182		1532	75 MBH.
	Reinstall	Ea.		111.89		111.89	
	Clean	Ea.	1.30	37.50		38.80	
	Minimum Charge	Job		233		233	
125 MBH							
	Demolish	Ea.		50.50		50.50	Includes material and labor to install a
	Install	Ea.	1650	168		1818	cabinet space heater with an output of
	Demolish and Install	Ea.	1650	218.50		1868.50	125 MBH.
	Reinstall	Ea.		134.27		134.27	
	Clean	Ea.	1.30	37.50		38.80	
	Minimum Charge	Job		233		233	
175 MBH							
	Demolish	Ea.		63		63	Includes material and labor to install a
	Install	Ea.	1875	240		2115	cabinet space heater with an output of
	Demolish and Install	Ea.	1875	303		2178	175 MBH.
	Reinstall	Ea.		191.82		191.82	
	Clean	Ea.	1.30	37.50		38.80	
	Minimum Charge	Job		233		233	

Furnace Unit

Furnace Unit		Unit	Material	Labor	Equip.	Total	Specification
Wall (gas-fired)							
25 MBH w / Thermostat							
	Demolish	Ea.		101		101	Includes material and labor to install a
	Install	Ea.	650	162		812	gas fired hot air furnace rated at 25
	Demolish and Install	Ea.	650	263		913	MBH.
	Reinstall	Ea.		129.87		129.87	
	Clean	Ea.	2.60	83		85.60	
	Minimum Charge	Job		233		233	
35 MBH w / Thermostat							
	Demolish	Ea.		101		101	Includes material and labor to install a
	Install	Ea.	775	180		955	gas fired hot air furnace rated at 35
	Demolish and Install	Ea.	775	281		1056	MBH.
	Reinstall	Ea.		144.30		144.30	
	Clean	Ea.	2.60	83		85.60	
	Minimum Charge	Job		233		233	
50 MBH w / Thermostat							
	Demolish	Ea.		101		101	Includes material and labor to install a
	Install	Ea.	1000	203		1203	gas fired hot air furnace rated at 50
	Demolish and Install	Ea.	1000	304		1304	MBH.
	Reinstall	Ea.		162.34		162.34	
	Clean	Ea.	2.60	83		85.60	
	Minimum Charge	Job		233		233	
60 MBH w / Thermostat							
	Demolish	Ea.		101		101	Includes material and labor to install a
	Install	Ea.	1125	225		1350	gas fired hot air furnace rated at 60
	Demolish and Install	Ea.	1125	326		1451	MBH.
	Reinstall	Ea.		180.37		180.37	
	Clean	Ea.	2.60	83		85.60	
	Minimum Charge	Job		233		233	

Furnace Unit	Unit	Material	Labor	Equip.	Total	Specification
Floor (gas-fired)						
30 MBH w / Thermostat						Includes material and labor to install a
Demolish	Ea.		101		101	gas fired hot air floor furnace rated at
Install	Ea.	890	162		1052	30 MBH.
Demolish and Install	Ea.	890	263		1153	
Reinstall	Ea.		129.87		129.87	
Clean	Ea.	2.60	83		85.60	
Minimum Charge	Job		233		233	
50 MBH w / Thermostat						Includes material and labor to install a
Demolish	Ea.		101		101	gas fired hot air floor furnace rated at
Install	Ea.	965	203		1168	50 MBH.
Demolish and Install	Ea.	965	304		1269	
Reinstall	Ea.		162.34		162.34	
Clean	Ea.	2.60	83		85.60	
Minimum Charge	Job		233		233	
Gas Forced Air						
50 MBH						Includes material and labor to install
Demolish	Ea.		101		101	an up flow gas fired hot air furnace
Install	Ea.	910	203		1113	rated at 50 MBH.
Demolish and Install	Ea.	910	304		1214	
Reinstall	Ea.		162.34		162.34	
Clean	Ea.	2.60	83		85.60	
Minimum Charge	Job		233		233	
80 MBH						Includes material and labor to install
Demolish	Ea.		101		101	an up flow gas fired hot air furnace
Install	Ea.	950	225		1175	rated at 80 MBH.
Demolish and Install	Ea.	950	326		1276	
Reinstall	Ea.		180.37		180.37	
Clean	Ea.	2.60	83		85.60	
Minimum Charge	Job		233		233	
100 MBH						Includes material and labor to install
Demolish	Ea.		101		101	an up flow gas fired hot air furnace
Install	Ea.	1125	254		1379	rated at 100 MBH.
Demolish and Install	Ea.	1125	355		1480	
Reinstall	Ea.		202.92		202.92	
Clean	Ea.	2.60	83		85.60	
Minimum Charge	Job		233		233	
120 MBH						Includes material and labor to install
Demolish	Ea.		101		101	an up flow gas fired hot air furnace
Install	Ea.	1250	271		1521	rated at 120 MBH.
Demolish and Install	Ea.	1250	372		1622	
Reinstall	Ea.		216.45		216.45	
Clean	Ea.	2.60	83		85.60	
Minimum Charge	Job		233		233	
Electric Forced Air						
31.4 MBH						Includes material and labor to install
Demolish	Ea.		101		101	an electric hot air furnace rated at
Install	Ea.	1725	229		1954	31.4 MBH.
Demolish and Install	Ea.	1725	330		2055	
Reinstall	Ea.		183.15		183.15	
Clean	Ea.	2.60	83		85.60	
Minimum Charge	Job		233		233	

Furnace Unit		Unit	Material	Labor	Equip.	Total	Specification
47.1 MBH							
	Demolish	Ea.		101		101	Includes material and labor to install
	Install	Ea.	1825	240		2065	an electric hot air furnace rated at
	Demolish and Install	Ea.	1825	341		2166	47.1 MBH.
	Reinstall	Ea.		191.67		191.67	
	Clean	Ea.	2.60	83		85.60	
	Minimum Charge	Job		233		233	
62.9 MBH							
	Demolish	Ea.		101		101	Includes material and labor to install
	Install	Ea.	1975	258		2233	an electric hot air furnace rated at
	Demolish and Install	Ea.	1975	359		2334	62.9 MBH.
	Reinstall	Ea.		206.04		206.04	
	Clean	Ea.	2.60	83		85.60	
	Minimum Charge	Job		233		233	
78.5 MBH							
	Demolish	Ea.		101		101	Includes material and labor to install
	Install	Ea.	2125	264		2389	an electric hot air furnace rated at
	Demolish and Install	Ea.	2125	365		2490	78.5 MBH.
	Reinstall	Ea.		211.32		211.32	
	Clean	Ea.	2.60	83		85.60	
	Minimum Charge	Job		233		233	
110 MBH							
	Demolish	Ea.		101		101	Includes material and labor to install
	Install	Ea.	2950	278		3228	an electric hot air furnace rated at
	Demolish and Install	Ea.	2950	379		3329	110 MBH.
	Reinstall	Ea.		222.75		222.75	
	Clean	Ea.	2.60	83		85.60	
	Minimum Charge	Job		233		233	
A/C Junction Box							
	Install	Ea.	62	109		171	Includes labor and materials to install
	Minimum Charge	Job		233		233	a heating system emergency shut-off switch. Cost includes up to 40 feet of non-metallic cable.

Boiler		Unit	Material	Labor	Equip.	Total	Specification
Gas-Fired							
60 MBH							
	Demolish	Ea.		850		850	Includes material and labor to install a
	Install	Ea.	3025	1525		4550	gas fired cast iron boiler rated at 60
	Demolish and Install	Ea.	3025	2375		5400	MBH.
	Reinstall	Ea.		1220.65		1220.65	
	Clean	Ea.	5.20	50		55.20	
	Minimum Charge	Job		233		233	
Gas-Fired							
125 MBH							
	Demolish	Ea.		2325		2325	Includes material and labor to install a
	Install	Ea.	4725	1875		6600	gas fired cast iron boiler rated at 125
	Demolish and Install	Ea.	4725	4200		8925	MBH.
	Reinstall	Ea.		1491.91		1491.91	
	Clean	Ea.	5.20	50		55.20	
	Minimum Charge	Job		233		233	

Rough Mechanical

Boiler

	Unit	Material	Labor	Equip.	Total	Specification
Gas-Fired						
400 MBH						
Demolish	Ea.		2325		2325	Includes material and labor to install a
Install	Ea.	5700	2625		8325	gas fired cast iron boiler rated at 400
Demolish and Install	Ea.	5700	4950		10650	MBH.
Reinstall	Ea.		2622.50		2622.50	
Clean	Ea.	5.20	50		55.20	
Minimum Charge	Job		233		233	

Heat Pump

	Unit	Material	Labor	Equip.	Total	Specification
2 Ton						
Demolish	Ea.		233		233	Includes material and labor to install a
Install	Ea.	2350	420		2770	2 ton heat pump.
Demolish and Install	Ea.	2350	653		3003	
Reinstall	Ea.		335.68		335.68	
Clean	Ea.	5.20	37.50		42.70	
Minimum Charge	Job		233		233	
3 Ton						
Demolish	Ea.		390		390	Includes material and labor to install a
Install	Ea.	2925	700		3625	3 ton heat pump.
Demolish and Install	Ea.	2925	1090		4015	
Reinstall	Ea.		559.47		559.47	
Clean	Ea.	5.20	37.50		42.70	
Minimum Charge	Job		233		233	
4 Ton						
Demolish	Ea.		585		585	Includes material and labor to install a
Install	Ea.	3475	1050		4525	4 ton heat pump.
Demolish and Install	Ea.	3475	1635		5110	
Reinstall	Ea.		839.20		839.20	
Clean	Ea.	5.20	37.50		42.70	
Minimum Charge	Job		233		233	
5 Ton						
Demolish	Ea.		935		935	Includes material and labor to install a
Install	Ea.	3775	1675		5450	5 ton heat pump.
Demolish and Install	Ea.	3775	2610		6385	
Reinstall	Ea.		1342.72		1342.72	
Clean	Ea.	5.20	37.50		42.70	
Minimum Charge	Job		233		233	
Thermostat						
Demolish	Ea.		12.95		12.95	Includes material and labor to install
Install	Ea.	161	58.50		219.50	an electric thermostat, 2 set back.
Demolish and Install	Ea.	161	71.45		232.45	
Reinstall	Ea.		46.64		46.64	
Clean	Ea.	.10	9.35		9.45	
Minimum Charge	Job		233		233	
A/C Junction Box						
Install	Ea.	625	335		960	Includes labor and materials to install
Minimum Charge	Job		219		219	a heat pump circuit including up to 40
						feet of non-metallic cable.

Heating	Unit	Material	Labor	Equip.	Total	Specification
Electric Baseboard						
Demolish	L.F.		6.05		6.05	Includes material and labor to install
Install	L.F.	14.95	14.55		29.50	electric baseboard heating elements.
Demolish and Install	L.F.	14.95	20.60		35.55	
Reinstall	L.F.		11.66		11.66	
Clean	L.F.	1.82	4.68		6.50	
Minimum Charge	Job		219		219	
2' 6"						
Demolish	Ea.		20		20	Includes material and labor to install a
Install	Ea.	44	54.50		98.50	2' 6" long section of electric
Demolish and Install	Ea.	44	74.50		118.50	baseboard heating elements.
Reinstall	Ea.		43.72		43.72	
Clean	Ea.	.52	11.50		12.02	
Minimum Charge	Job		219		219	
3'						
Demolish	Ea.		22		22	Includes material and labor to install a
Install	Ea.	50.50	54.50		105	3' long section of electric baseboard
Demolish and Install	Ea.	50.50	76.50		127	heating elements.
Reinstall	Ea.		43.72		43.72	
Clean	Ea.	.52	14.25		14.77	
Minimum Charge	Job		219		219	
4'						
Demolish	Ea.		24.50		24.50	Includes material and labor to install a
Install	Ea.	59.50	65.50		125	4' long section of electric baseboard
Demolish and Install	Ea.	59.50	90		149.50	heating elements.
Reinstall	Ea.		52.20		52.20	
Clean	Ea.	.21	3.12		3.33	
Minimum Charge	Job		219		219	
5'						
Demolish	Ea.		27		27	Includes material and labor to install a
Install	Ea.	75	76.50		151.50	5' long section of electric baseboard
Demolish and Install	Ea.	75	103.50		178.50	heating elements.
Reinstall	Ea.		61.36		61.36	
Clean	Ea.	1.05	23		24.05	
Minimum Charge	Job		219		219	
6'						
Demolish	Ea.		30.50		30.50	Includes material and labor to install a
Install	Ea.	81.50	87.50		169	6' long section of electric baseboard
Demolish and Install	Ea.	81.50	118		199.50	heating elements.
Reinstall	Ea.		69.95		69.95	
Clean	Ea.	.21	3.74		3.95	
Minimum Charge	Job		219		219	
8'						
Demolish	Ea.		40.50		40.50	Includes material and labor to install
Install	Ea.	101	109		210	an 8' long section of electric
Demolish and Install	Ea.	101	149.50		250.50	baseboard heating elements.
Reinstall	Ea.		87.44		87.44	
Clean	Ea.	.21	4.68		4.89	
Minimum Charge	Job		219		219	
10'						
Demolish	Ea.		48.50		48.50	Includes material and labor to install a
Install	Ea.	212	132		344	10' long section of electric baseboard
Demolish and Install	Ea.	212	180.50		392.50	heating elements.
Reinstall	Ea.		105.99		105.99	
Clean	Ea.	2.08	47		49.08	
Minimum Charge	Job		219		219	

Rough Mechanical

Heating

Electric Radiant Wall Panel	Unit	Material	Labor	Equip.	Total	Specification
Demolish	Ea.		32.50		32.50	Includes material and labor to install
Install	Ea.	430	87.50		517.50	an 18″ x 23″ electric radiant heat wall
Demolish and Install	Ea.	430	120		550	panel.
Reinstall	Ea.		69.95		69.95	
Clean	Ea.	.26	9.35		9.61	
Minimum Charge	Job		219		219	

Heating Control

Thermostat	Unit	Material	Labor	Equip.	Total	Specification
Demolish	Ea.		12.95		12.95	Includes material and labor to install
Install	Ea.	161	58.50		219.50	an electric thermostat, 2 set back.
Demolish and Install	Ea.	161	71.45		232.45	
Reinstall	Ea.		46.64		46.64	
Clean	Ea.	.10	9.35		9.45	
Minimum Charge	Job		233		233	

Air Conditioning

	Unit	Material	Labor	Equip.	Total	Specification
2 Ton						
Demolish	Ea.		430		430	Includes material and labor to install a
Install	Ea.	2175	725		2900	rooftop air conditioning unit, 2 ton.
Demolish and Install	Ea.	2175	1155		3330	No hoisting is included.
Reinstall	Ea.		724.07		724.07	
Clean	Ea.	5.20	37.50		42.70	
Minimum Charge	Job		233		233	
3 Ton						
Demolish	Ea.		430		430	Includes material and labor to install a
Install	Ea.	2275	955		3230	rooftop air conditioning unit, 3 ton.
Demolish and Install	Ea.	2275	1385		3660	No hoisting is included.
Reinstall	Ea.		954.72		954.72	
Clean	Ea.	5.20	37.50		42.70	
Minimum Charge	Job		233		233	
4 Ton						
Demolish	Ea.		430		430	Includes material and labor to install a
Install	Ea.	2700	1100		3800	rooftop air conditioning unit, 4 ton.
Demolish and Install	Ea.	2700	1530		4230	No hoisting is included.
Reinstall	Ea.		1107.12		1107.12	
Clean	Ea.	5.20	37.50		42.70	
Minimum Charge	Job		233		233	
5 Ton						
Demolish	Ea.		430		430	Includes material and labor to install a
Install	Ea.	2850	1200		4050	rooftop air conditioning unit, 5 ton.
Demolish and Install	Ea.	2850	1630		4480	No hoisting is included.
Reinstall	Ea.		1195.44		1195.44	
Clean	Ea.	5.20	37.50		42.70	
Minimum Charge	Job		233		233	
Compressor						
2 Ton						
Demolish	Ea.		390		390	Includes material and labor to install a
Install	Ea.	275	233		508	refrigeration compressor.
Demolish and Install	Ea.	275	623		898	
Reinstall	Ea.		186.56		186.56	
Clean	Ea.	5.20	37.50		42.70	
Minimum Charge	Job		233		233	

Rough Mechanical

Air Conditioning	Unit	Material	Labor	Equip.	Total	Specification
2.5 Ton						
Demolish	Ea.		390		390	Includes material and labor to install a
Install	Ea.	325	253		578	refrigeration compressor.
Demolish and Install	Ea.	325	643		968	
Reinstall	Ea.		202.12		202.12	
Clean	Ea.	5.20	37.50		42.70	
Minimum Charge	Job		233		233	
3 Ton						
Demolish	Ea.		390		390	Includes material and labor to install a
Install	Ea.	360	264		624	refrigeration compressor.
Demolish and Install	Ea.	360	654		1014	
Reinstall	Ea.		210.92		210.92	
Clean	Ea.	5.20	37.50		42.70	
Minimum Charge	Job		233		233	
4 Ton						
Demolish	Ea.		390		390	Includes material and labor to install a
Install	Ea.	455	212		667	refrigeration compressor.
Demolish and Install	Ea.	455	602		1057	
Reinstall	Ea.		169.60		169.60	
Clean	Ea.	5.20	37.50		42.70	
Minimum Charge	Job		233		233	
5 Ton						
Demolish	Ea.		390		390	Includes material and labor to install a
Install	Ea.	500	289		789	refrigeration compressor.
Demolish and Install	Ea.	500	679		1179	
Reinstall	Ea.		231.03		231.03	
Clean	Ea.	5.20	37.50		42.70	
Minimum Charge	Job		233		233	
Condensing Unit						
2 Ton Air-cooled						
Demolish	Ea.		111		111	Includes material and labor to install a
Install	Ea.	1475	400		1875	2 ton condensing unit.
Demolish and Install	Ea.	1475	511		1986	
Reinstall	Ea.		319.70		319.70	
Clean	Ea.	5.20	37.50		42.70	
Minimum Charge	Job		233		233	
2.5 Ton Air-cooled						
Demolish	Ea.		130		130	Includes material and labor to install a
Install	Ea.	1525	495		2020	2.5 ton condensing unit.
Demolish and Install	Ea.	1525	625		2150	
Reinstall	Ea.		394.92		394.92	
Clean	Ea.	5.20	37.50		42.70	
Minimum Charge	Job		233		233	
3 Ton Air-cooled						
Demolish	Ea.		155		155	Includes material and labor to install a
Install	Ea.	1550	645		2195	3 ton condensing unit.
Demolish and Install	Ea.	1550	800		2350	
Reinstall	Ea.		516.43		516.43	
Clean	Ea.	5.20	37.50		42.70	
Minimum Charge	Job		233		233	
4 Ton Air-cooled						
Demolish	Ea.		233		233	Includes material and labor to install a
Install	Ea.	2000	930		2930	4 ton condensing unit.
Demolish and Install	Ea.	2000	1163		3163	
Reinstall	Ea.		745.96		745.96	
Clean	Ea.	5.20	37.50		42.70	
Minimum Charge	Job		233		233	

Air Conditioning

Air Conditioning	Unit	Material	Labor	Equip.	Total	Specification
5 Ton Air-cooled						
Demolish	Ea.		350		350	Includes material and labor to install a
Install	Ea.	2450	1400		3850	5 ton condensing unit.
Demolish and Install	Ea.	2450	1750		4200	
Reinstall	Ea.		1118.93		1118.93	
Clean	Ea.	5.20	37.50		42.70	
Minimum Charge	Job		233		233	
Air Handler						
1,200 CFM						
Demolish	Ea.		280		280	Includes material and labor to install a
Install	Ea.	2725	645		3370	1200 CFM capacity air handling unit.
Demolish and Install	Ea.	2725	925		3650	
Reinstall	Ea.		516.43		516.43	
Clean	Ea.	5.20	37.50		42.70	
Minimum Charge	Job		233		233	
2,000 CFM						
Demolish	Ea.		280		280	Includes material and labor to install a
Install	Ea.	4575	765		5340	2000 CFM capacity air handling unit.
Demolish and Install	Ea.	4575	1045		5620	
Reinstall	Ea.		610.33		610.33	
Clean	Ea.	5.20	37.50		42.70	
Minimum Charge	Job		233		233	
3,000 CFM						
Demolish	Ea.		310		310	Includes material and labor to install a
Install	Ea.	5700	840		6540	3000 CFM capacity air handling unit.
Demolish and Install	Ea.	5700	1150		6850	
Reinstall	Ea.		671.36		671.36	
Clean	Ea.	5.20	37.50		42.70	
Minimum Charge	Job		233		233	
Evaporative Cooler						
4,300 CFM, 1/3 HP						
Demolish	Ea.		114		114	Includes material and labor to install
Install	Ea.	780	254		1034	an evaporative cooler.
Demolish and Install	Ea.	780	368		1148	
Reinstall	Ea.		202.92		202.92	
Clean	Ea.	2.08	37.50		39.58	
Minimum Charge	Job		233		233	
4,700 CFM, 1/2 HP						
Demolish	Ea.		114		114	Includes material and labor to install
Install	Ea.	780	262		1042	an evaporative cooler.
Demolish and Install	Ea.	780	376		1156	
Reinstall	Ea.		209.47		209.47	
Clean	Ea.	2.08	37.50		39.58	
Minimum Charge	Job		233		233	
5,600 CFM, 3/4 HP						
Demolish	Ea.		114		114	Includes material and labor to install
Install	Ea.	1550	271		1821	an evaporative cooler.
Demolish and Install	Ea.	1550	385		1935	
Reinstall	Ea.		216.45		216.45	
Clean	Ea.	2.08	37.50		39.58	
Minimum Charge	Job		233		233	
Master Cool Brand						
Demolish	Ea.		114		114	Includes material and labor to install
Install	Ea.	780	280		1060	an evaporative cooler.
Demolish and Install	Ea.	780	394		1174	
Reinstall	Ea.		223.91		223.91	
Clean	Ea.	2.08	37.50		39.58	
Minimum Charge	Job		233		233	

Air Conditioning		Unit	Material	Labor	Equip.	Total	Specification
Motor							
	Demolish	Ea.		64		64	Includes material and labor to install
	Install	Ea.	183	197		380	an evaporative cooler motor.
	Demolish and Install	Ea.	183	261		444	
	Reinstall	Ea.		157.76		157.76	
	Clean	Ea.	2.08	37.50		39.58	
	Minimum Charge	Job		233		233	
Water Pump							
	Demolish	Ea.		64		64	Includes material and labor to install
	Install	Ea.	51	113		164	an evaporative cooler water pump.
	Demolish and Install	Ea.	51	177		228	
	Reinstall	Ea.		90.16		90.16	
	Clean	Ea.	2.08	37.50		39.58	
	Minimum Charge	Job		233		233	
Fan Belt							
	Demolish	Ea.		12.85		12.85	Includes material and labor to install
	Install	Ea.	37	22.50		59.50	an evaporative cooler fan belt.
	Demolish and Install	Ea.	37	35.35		72.35	
	Reinstall	Ea.		18.03		18.03	
	Minimum Charge	Job		233		233	
Pads (4 ea.)							
	Demolish	Ea.		12.85		12.85	Includes material and labor to install
	Install	Ea.	22	56.50		78.50	pre-fabricated roof pads for an
	Demolish and Install	Ea.	22	69.35		91.35	evaporative cooler.
	Reinstall	Ea.		45.08		45.08	
	Clean	Ea.	2.08	37.50		39.58	
	Minimum Charge	Job		233		233	
Service call							
	Install	Job		225		225	Includes 4 hour minimum labor charge for an sheetmetal worker.
Window Mounted							
Low Output BTU							
	Install	Ea.	305	50.50		355.50	Includes material and labor to install a
	Reinstall	Ea.		40.36		40.36	window air conditioning unit.
	Clean	Ea.	.78	9.35		10.13	
	Minimum Charge	Job		233		233	
Mid-range Output BTU							
	Demolish	Ea.		35.50		35.50	Includes material and labor to install a
	Install	Ea.	475	67.50		542.50	window air conditioning unit.
	Demolish and Install	Ea.	475	103		578	
	Reinstall	Ea.		53.81		53.81	
	Clean	Ea.	.78	9.35		10.13	
	Minimum Charge	Job		233		233	
High Output BTU							
	Demolish	Ea.		45		45	Includes material and labor to install a
	Install	Ea.	595	67.50		662.50	window air conditioning unit.
	Demolish and Install	Ea.	595	112.50		707.50	
	Reinstall	Ea.		53.81		53.81	
	Clean	Ea.	.78	9.35		10.13	
	Minimum Charge	Job		233		233	
Hotel-type Hot / Cold							
	Demolish	Ea.		74.50		74.50	Includes material and labor to install
	Install	Ea.	1075	280		1355	packaged air conditioning unit,
	Demolish and Install	Ea.	1075	354.50		1429.50	15000 BTU cooling, 13900 BTU
	Reinstall	Ea.		223.79		223.79	heating.
	Clean	Ea.	1.05	18.70		19.75	
	Minimum Charge	Job		233		233	

Rough Mechanical

Air Conditioning

Air Conditioning	Unit	Material	Labor	Equip.	Total	Specification
Thermostat						
Demolish	Ea.		12.95		12.95	Includes material and labor to install
Install	Ea.	161	58.50		219.50	an electric thermostat, 2 set back.
Demolish and Install	Ea.	161	71.45		232.45	
Reinstall	Ea.		46.64		46.64	
Clean	Ea.	.10	9.35		9.45	
Minimum Charge	Job		233		233	
Concrete Pad						
Demolish	S.F.		2.08		2.08	Includes material and labor to install
Install	S.F.	2.45	4.57		7.02	air conditioner pad.
Demolish and Install	S.F.	2.45	6.65		9.10	
Reinstall	S.F.		3.65		3.65	
Clean	S.F.	.10	.60		.70	
Paint	S.F.	.17	.36		.53	
Minimum Charge	Job		233		233	
A/C Junction Box						
Install	Ea.	248	125		373	Includes labor and materials to install
Minimum Charge	Job		219		219	an air conditioning circuit including up to 40 feet of non-metallic cable.

Sprinkler System

Sprinkler System	Unit	Material	Labor	Equip.	Total	Specification
Exposed						
Wet Type						
Demolish	SF Flr.		.21		.21	Includes material and labor to install
Install	SF Flr.	1.27	2.01		3.28	an exposed wet pipe fire sprinkler
Demolish and Install	SF Flr.	1.27	2.22		3.49	system.
Reinstall	SF Flr.		2.01		2.01	
Minimum Charge	Job		231		231	
Dry Type						
Demolish	SF Flr.		.21		.21	Includes material and labor to install
Install	SF Flr.	1.45	2.01		3.46	an exposed dry pipe fire sprinkler
Demolish and Install	SF Flr.	1.45	2.22		3.67	system.
Reinstall	SF Flr.		2.01		2.01	
Minimum Charge	Job		231		231	
Concealed						
Wet Type						
Demolish	SF Flr.		.41		.41	Includes material and labor to install a
Install	SF Flr.	1.27	2.75		4.02	concealed wet pipe fire sprinkler
Demolish and Install	SF Flr.	1.27	3.16		4.43	system.
Reinstall	SF Flr.		2.75		2.75	
Minimum Charge	Job		231		231	
Dry Type						
Demolish	SF Flr.		.41		.41	Includes material and labor to install a
Install	SF Flr.	.01	2.75		2.76	concealed dry pipe fire sprinkler
Demolish and Install	SF Flr.	.01	3.16		3.17	system.
Reinstall	SF Flr.		2.75		2.75	
Minimum Charge	Job		231		231	

Junction Boxes		Cable				Switch Box

Electrical Per S.F.	Unit	Material	Labor	Equip.	Total	Specification
Residential						
Wiring, Lighting and Fixtures						
Install	S.F.	1.68	1.82		3.50	Includes labor and material to replace
Minimum Charge	Job		219		219	house wiring, lighting fixtures, and
						built-in appliances. Apply S.F. cost to
						floor area including garages but not
						basements.
Wiring Only						
Install	S.F.	.21	.72		.93	Includes labor and material to replace
						house wiring only. Apply S.F. cost to
						floor area including garages but not
						basements.

Main Service	Unit	Material	Labor	Equip.	Total	Specification
100 Amp.						
Demolish	Ea.		180		180	Cost includes material and labor to
Install	Ea.	615	365		980	install 100 Amp. residential service
Demolish and Install	Ea.	615	545		1160	panel including 12 breaker interior
Reinstall	Ea.		293.92		293.92	panel, 10 single pole breakers and
Clean	Ea.	.52	75		75.52	hook-up. Wiring is not included.
Minimum Charge	Job		219		219	
150 Amp.						
Demolish	Ea.		180		180	Cost includes material and labor to
Install	Ea.	950	425		1375	install 150 Amp. residential service,
Demolish and Install	Ea.	950	605		1555	incl. 20 breaker exterior panel, main
Reinstall	Ea.		339.57		339.57	switch, 1 GFI and 14 single pole
Clean	Ea.	.52	75		75.52	breakers, meter socket including
Minimum Charge	Job		219		219	hookup. Wiring is not included.
200 Amp.						
Demolish	Ea.		180		180	Cost includes material and labor to
Install	Ea.	1275	485		1760	install 200 Amp. residential service,
Demolish and Install	Ea.	1275	665		1940	incl. 20 breaker exterior panel, main
Reinstall	Ea.		388.62		388.62	switch, 1 GFI and 18 single pole
Clean	Ea.	.52	75		75.52	breakers, meter socket including
Minimum Charge	Job		219		219	hookup. Wiring is not included.

Rough Electrical

Main Service		Unit	Material	Labor	Equip.	Total	Specification
Masthead							
	Demolish	Ea.		30.50		30.50	Includes material and labor to install
	Install	Ea.	118	182		300	galvanized steel conduit including
	Demolish and Install	Ea.	118	212.50		330.50	masthead.
	Reinstall	Ea.		145.73		145.73	
	Minimum Charge	Job		219		219	
Allowance to Repair							
	Install	Job		219		219	Minimum labor charge for residential
	Minimum Charge	Job		219		219	wiring.

Wall Insulation

Floor Insulation		Unit	Material	Labor	Equip.	Total	Specification
Kraft Faced Batt							
3-1/2″ (R-13)							
	Demolish	S.F.		.14		.14	Cost includes material and labor to
	Install	S.F.	.35	.58		.93	install 3-1/2″ (R-13) kraft paper or foil
	Demolish and Install	S.F.	.35	.72		1.07	faced roll and batt fiberglass
	Minimum Charge	Job		202		202	insulation, joists 16″ O.C.
6″ (R-19)							
	Demolish	S.F.		.14		.14	Cost includes material and labor to
	Install	S.F.	.46	.67		1.13	install 6″ (R-19) kraft paper or foil
	Demolish and Install	S.F.	.46	.81		1.27	faced roll and batt fiberglass
	Minimum Charge	Job		202		202	insulation, joists 16″ O.C.
10″ (R-30)							
	Demolish	S.F.		.14		.14	Cost includes material and labor to
	Install	S.F.	.77	.81		1.58	install 10″ (R-30) kraft paper-faced roll
	Demolish and Install	S.F.	.77	.95		1.72	and batt fiberglass insulation, joists
	Minimum Charge	Job		202		202	16″ O.C.
12″ (R-38)							
	Demolish	S.F.		.14		.14	Cost includes material and labor to
	Install	S.F.	.94	.85		1.79	install 12″ (R-38) kraft paper-faced roll
	Demolish and Install	S.F.	.94	.99		1.93	and batt fiberglass insulation, joists
	Minimum Charge	Job		202		202	16″ O.C.
Foil Faced Batt							
3-1/2″ (R-13)							
	Demolish	S.F.		.14		.14	Cost includes material and labor to
	Install	S.F.	.35	.58		.93	install 3-1/2″ (R-13) kraft paper or foil
	Demolish and Install	S.F.	.35	.72		1.07	faced roll and batt fiberglass
	Minimum Charge	Job		202		202	insulation, joists 16″ O.C.
6″ (R-19)							
	Demolish	S.F.		.14		.14	Cost includes material and labor to
	Install	S.F.	.46	.67		1.13	install 6″ (R-19) kraft paper or foil
	Demolish and Install	S.F.	.46	.81		1.27	faced roll and batt fiberglass
	Minimum Charge	Job		202		202	insulation, joists 16″ O.C.
Unfaced Batt							
3-1/2″ (R-13)							
	Demolish	S.F.		.14		.14	Cost includes material and labor to
	Install	S.F.	.31	.67		.98	install 3-1/2″ (R-13) unfaced roll and
	Demolish and Install	S.F.	.31	.81		1.12	batt fiberglass insulation, joists 16″
	Minimum Charge	Job		202		202	O.C.

Insulation

Floor Insulation		Unit	Material	Labor	Equip.	Total	Specification
6″ (R-19)							
	Demolish	S.F.		.14		.14	Cost includes material and labor to
	Install	S.F.	.48	.81		1.29	install 6″ (R-19) unfaced roll and batt
	Demolish and Install	S.F.	.48	.95		1.43	fiberglass insulation, joists 16″ O.C.
	Minimum Charge	Job		202		202	
10″ (R-30)							
	Demolish	S.F.		.14		.14	Cost includes material and labor to
	Install	S.F.	.77	.90		1.67	install 10″ (R-30) unfaced roll and batt
	Demolish and Install	S.F.	.77	1.04		1.81	fiberglass insulation, joists 16″ O.C.
	Minimum Charge	Job		202		202	
12″ (R-38)							
	Demolish	S.F.		.14		.14	Cost includes material and labor to
	Install	S.F.	.80	.95		1.75	install 12″ (R-38) unfaced roll and batt
	Demolish and Install	S.F.	.80	1.09		1.89	fiberglass insulation, joists 16″ O.C.
	Minimum Charge	Job		202		202	
Rigid Board							
1/2″							
	Demolish	S.F.		.14		.14	Includes material and labor to install
	Install	S.F.	.32	.50		.82	rigid foam insulation board foil faced
	Demolish and Install	S.F.	.32	.64		.96	two sides.
	Minimum Charge	Job		202		202	
3/4″							
	Demolish	S.F.		.14		.14	Includes material and labor to install
	Install	S.F.	.36	.50		.86	rigid foam insulation board foil faced
	Demolish and Install	S.F.	.36	.64		1	two sides.
	Minimum Charge	Job		202		202	
1-1/2″							
	Demolish	S.F.		.14		.14	Includes material and labor to install
	Install	S.F.	.70	.54		1.24	rigid foam insulation board foil faced
	Demolish and Install	S.F.	.70	.68		1.38	two sides.
	Minimum Charge	Job		202		202	
Support Wire							
	Demolish	S.F.		.05		.05	Includes material and labor to install
	Install	S.F.	.01	.11		.12	friction fit support wire.
	Demolish and Install	S.F.	.01	.16		.17	
	Minimum Charge	Job		202		202	
Vapor Barrier							
	Demolish	S.F.		.07		.07	Cost includes material and labor to
	Install	S.F.	.03	.11		.14	install 4 mil polyethylene vapor barrier
	Demolish and Install	S.F.	.03	.18		.21	10′ wide sheets with 6″ overlaps.
	Minimum Charge	Job		202		202	

Wall Insulation		Unit	Material	Labor	Equip.	Total	Specification
Kraft Faced Batt							
3-1/2″ (R-13)							
	Demolish	S.F.		.13		.13	Cost includes material and labor to
	Install	S.F.	.30	.30		.60	install 3-1/2″ (R-13) kraft paper-faced
	Demolish and Install	S.F.	.30	.43		.73	roll and batt fiberglass insulation, joist
	Minimum Charge	Job		202		202	or studs 16″ O.C.
6″ (R-19)							
	Demolish	S.F.		.13		.13	Cost includes material and labor to
	Install	S.F.	.41	.30		.71	install 6″ (R-19) kraft paper-faced roll
	Demolish and Install	S.F.	.41	.43		.84	and batt fiberglass insulation, joist or
	Minimum Charge	Job		202		202	studs 16″ O.C.

Insulation

Wall Insulation

Wall Insulation		Unit	Material	Labor	Equip.	Total	Specification
10" (R-30)							
	Demolish	S.F.		.13		.13	Cost includes material and labor to
	Install	S.F.	.78	.35		1.13	install 10" (R-30) kraft paper-faced roll
	Demolish and Install	S.F.	.78	.48		1.26	and batt fiberglass insulation, joist or
	Minimum Charge	Job		202		202	studs 16" O.C.
12" (R-38)							
	Demolish	S.F.		.13		.13	Cost includes material and labor to
	Install	S.F.	1.05	.35		1.40	install 12" (R-38) kraft paper-faced roll
	Demolish and Install	S.F.	1.05	.48		1.53	and batt fiberglass insulation, joist or
	Minimum Charge	Job		202		202	studs 16" O.C.
Foil Faced Batt							
3-1/2" (R-13)							
	Demolish	S.F.		.13		.13	Cost includes material and labor to
	Install	S.F.	.59	.30		.89	install 3-1/2" (R-13) foil faced roll and
	Demolish and Install	S.F.	.59	.43		1.02	batt fiberglass insulation, joist or studs
	Minimum Charge	Job		202		202	16" O.C.
6" (R-19)							
	Demolish	S.F.		.13		.13	Cost includes material and labor to
	Install	S.F.	.85	.30		1.15	install 6" (R-19) foil faced roll and batt
	Demolish and Install	S.F.	.85	.43		1.28	fiberglass insulation, joist or studs 16"
	Minimum Charge	Job		202		202	O.C.
Unfaced Batt							
3-1/2" (R-13)							
	Demolish	S.F.		.13		.13	Cost includes material and labor to
	Install	S.F.	.31	.30		.61	install 3-1/2" (R-13) unfaced roll and
	Demolish and Install	S.F.	.31	.43		.74	batt fiberglass insulation, joist or studs
	Minimum Charge	Job		202		202	16" O.C.
6" (R-19)							
	Demolish	S.F.		.13		.13	Cost includes material and labor to
	Install	S.F.	.48	.35		.83	install 6" (R-19) unfaced roll and batt
	Demolish and Install	S.F.	.48	.48		.96	fiberglass insulation, joist or studs 16"
	Minimum Charge	Job		202		202	O.C.
10" (R-30)							
	Demolish	S.F.		.13		.13	Cost includes material and labor to
	Install	S.F.	.77	.35		1.12	install 10" (R-30) unfaced roll and batt
	Demolish and Install	S.F.	.77	.48		1.25	fiberglass insulation, joist or studs 16"
	Minimum Charge	Job		202		202	O.C.
12" (R-38)							
	Demolish	S.F.		.13		.13	Cost includes material and labor to
	Install	S.F.	.80	.40		1.20	install 12" (R-38) unfaced roll and batt
	Demolish and Install	S.F.	.80	.53		1.33	fiberglass insulation, joist or studs 16"
	Minimum Charge	Job		202		202	O.C.
Blown							
R-13							
	Demolish	S.F.		.13		.13	Includes material and labor to install
	Install	S.F.	.23	1.34	.47	2.04	fiberglass blown-in insulation in wall
	Demolish and Install	S.F.	.23	1.47	.47	2.17	with wood siding.
	Minimum Charge	Job		460	163	623	
R-19							
	Demolish	S.F.		.13		.13	Includes material and labor to install
	Install	S.F.	.35	1.54	.54	2.43	fiberglass blown-in insulation in wall
	Demolish and Install	S.F.	.35	1.67	.54	2.56	with wood siding.
	Minimum Charge	Job		460	163	623	

Insulation

Wall Insulation

Wall Insulation	Unit	Material	Labor	Equip.	Total	Specification
Rigid Board						
1/2″						
Demolish	S.F.		.17		.17	Includes material and labor to install
Install	S.F.	.32	.50		.82	rigid foam insulation board, foil faced,
Demolish and Install	S.F.	.32	.67		.99	two sides.
Minimum Charge	Job		202		202	
3/4″						
Demolish	S.F.		.17		.17	Includes material and labor to install
Install	S.F.	.36	.50		.86	rigid foam insulation board, foil faced,
Demolish and Install	S.F.	.36	.67		1.03	two sides.
Minimum Charge	Job		202		202	
1-1/2″						
Demolish	S.F.		.17		.17	Includes material and labor to install
Install	S.F.	.70	.55		1.25	rigid foam insulation board, foil faced,
Demolish and Install	S.F.	.70	.72		1.42	two sides.
Minimum Charge	Job		202		202	
Vapor Barrier						
Demolish	S.F.		.04		.04	Cost includes material and labor to
Install	S.F.	.03	.11		.14	install 4 mil polyethylene vapor barrier
Demolish and Install	S.F.	.03	.15		.18	10′ wide sheets with 6″ overlaps.
Minimum Charge	Job		202		202	

Ceiling Insulation

Ceiling Insulation	Unit	Material	Labor	Equip.	Total	Specification
Kraft Faced Batt						
3-1/2″ (R-13)						
Demolish	S.F.		.14		.14	Cost includes material and labor to
Install	S.F.	.30	.30		.60	install 3-1/2″ (R-13) kraft paper-faced
Demolish and Install	S.F.	.30	.44		.74	roll and batt fiberglass insulation, joist
Minimum Charge	Job		202		202	or studs 16″ O.C.
6″ (R-19)						
Demolish	S.F.		.14		.14	Cost includes material and labor to
Install	S.F.	.41	.30		.71	install 6″ (R-19) kraft paper-faced roll
Demolish and Install	S.F.	.41	.44		.85	and batt fiberglass insulation, joist or
Minimum Charge	Job		202		202	studs 16″ O.C.
10″ (R-30)						
Demolish	S.F.		.14		.14	Cost includes material and labor to
Install	S.F.	.78	.35		1.13	install 10″ (R-30) kraft paper-faced roll
Demolish and Install	S.F.	.78	.49		1.27	and batt fiberglass insulation, joist or
Minimum Charge	Job		202		202	studs 16″ O.C.
12″ (R-38)						
Demolish	S.F.		.14		.14	Cost includes material and labor to
Install	S.F.	1.05	.35		1.40	install 12″ (R-38) kraft paper-faced roll
Demolish and Install	S.F.	1.05	.49		1.54	and batt fiberglass insulation, joist or
Minimum Charge	Job		202		202	studs 16″ O.C.
Foil Faced Batt						
3-1/2″ (R-13)						
Demolish	S.F.		.14		.14	Cost includes material and labor to
Install	S.F.	.59	.30		.89	install 3-1/2″ (R-13) foil faced roll and
Demolish and Install	S.F.	.59	.44		1.03	batt fiberglass insulation, joist or studs
Minimum Charge	Job		202		202	16″ O.C.

Insulation

Ceiling Insulation		Unit	Material	Labor	Equip.	Total	Specification
6" (R-19)							
	Demolish	S.F.		.14		.14	Cost includes material and labor to
	Install	S.F.	.85	.30		1.15	install 6" (R-19) foil faced roll and batt
	Demolish and Install	S.F.	.85	.44		1.29	fiberglass insulation, joist or studs 16"
	Minimum Charge	Job		202		202	O.C.
Unfaced Batt							
3-1/2" (R-13)							
	Demolish	S.F.		.14		.14	Cost includes material and labor to
	Install	S.F.	.31	.30		.61	install 3-1/2" (R-13) unfaced roll and
	Demolish and Install	S.F.	.31	.44		.75	batt fiberglass insulation, joist or studs
	Minimum Charge	Job		202		202	16" O.C.
6" (R-19)							
	Demolish	S.F.		.14		.14	Cost includes material and labor to
	Install	S.F.	.48	.35		.83	install 6" (R-19) unfaced roll and batt
	Demolish and Install	S.F.	.48	.49		.97	fiberglass insulation, joist or studs 16"
	Minimum Charge	Job		202		202	O.C.
10" (R-30)							
	Demolish	S.F.		.14		.14	Cost includes material and labor to
	Install	S.F.	.77	.35		1.12	install 10" (R-30) unfaced roll and batt
	Demolish and Install	S.F.	.77	.49		1.26	fiberglass insulation, joist or studs 16"
	Minimum Charge	Job		202		202	O.C.
12" (R-38)							
	Demolish	S.F.		.14		.14	Cost includes material and labor to
	Install	S.F.	.80	.40		1.20	install 12" (R-38) unfaced roll and batt
	Demolish and Install	S.F.	.80	.54		1.34	fiberglass insulation, joist or studs 16"
	Minimum Charge	Job		202		202	O.C.
Blown							
5"							
	Demolish	S.F.		.42		.42	Includes material and labor to install
	Install	S.F.	.17	.24	.09	.50	fiberglass blown-in insulation.
	Demolish and Install	S.F.	.17	.66	.09	.92	
	Minimum Charge	Job		460	163	623	
6"							
	Demolish	S.F.		.42		.42	Includes material and labor to install
	Install	S.F.	.21	.31	.11	.63	fiberglass blown-in insulation.
	Demolish and Install	S.F.	.21	.73	.11	1.05	
	Minimum Charge	Job		460	163	623	
9"							
	Demolish	S.F.		.42		.42	Includes material and labor to install
	Install	S.F.	.29	.42	.15	.86	fiberglass blown-in insulation.
	Demolish and Install	S.F.	.29	.84	.15	1.28	
	Minimum Charge	Job		460	163	623	
12"							
	Demolish	S.F.		.42		.42	Includes material and labor to install
	Install	S.F.	.41	.62	.22	1.25	fiberglass blown-in insulation.
	Demolish and Install	S.F.	.41	1.04	.22	1.67	
	Minimum Charge	Job		460	163	623	
Rigid Board							
1/2"							
	Demolish	S.F.		.23		.23	Includes material and labor to install
	Install	S.F.	.32	.50		.82	rigid foam insulation board, foil faced,
	Demolish and Install	S.F.	.32	.73		1.05	two sides.
	Minimum Charge	Job		202		202	

Insulation

Ceiling Insulation

	Unit	Material	Labor	Equip.	Total	Specification
3/4"						
Demolish	S.F.		.23		.23	Includes material and labor to install
Install	S.F.	.36	.50		.86	rigid foam insulation board, foil faced,
Demolish and Install	S.F.	.36	.73		1.09	two sides.
Minimum Charge	Job		202		202	
1-1/2"						
Demolish	S.F.		.23		.23	Includes material and labor to install
Install	S.F.	.70	.55		1.25	rigid foam insulation board, foil faced,
Demolish and Install	S.F.	.70	.78		1.48	two sides.
Minimum Charge	Job		202		202	

Exterior Insulation

	Unit	Material	Labor	Equip.	Total	Specification
Rigid Board						
1/2"						
Demolish	S.F.		.13		.13	Includes material and labor to install
Install	S.F.	.32	.50		.82	rigid foam insulation board foil faced
Demolish and Install	S.F.	.32	.63		.95	two sides.
Minimum Charge	Job		202		202	
3/4"						
Demolish	S.F.		.13		.13	Includes material and labor to install
Install	S.F.	.36	.50		.86	rigid foam insulation board foil faced
Demolish and Install	S.F.	.36	.63		.99	two sides.
Minimum Charge	Job		202		202	
1-1/2"						
Demolish	S.F.		.13		.13	Includes material and labor to install
Install	S.F.	.70	.54		1.24	rigid foam insulation board foil faced
Demolish and Install	S.F.	.70	.67		1.37	two sides.
Minimum Charge	Job		202		202	
Vapor Barrier						
Demolish	S.F.		.07		.07	Cost includes material and labor to
Install	S.F.	.03	.11		.14	install 4 mil polyethylene vapor barrier
Demolish and Install	S.F.	.03	.18		.21	10' wide sheets with 6" overlaps.
Minimum Charge	Job		202		202	

Roof Insulation Board

	Unit	Material	Labor	Equip.	Total	Specification
Fiberglass						
3/4" Fiberglass						
Demolish	Sq.		43.50		43.50	Includes material and labor to install
Install	Sq.	58.50	30		88.50	fiberglass board insulation 3/4" thick,
Demolish and Install	Sq.	58.50	73.50		132	R-2.80 and C-0.36 values.
Minimum Charge	Job		202		202	
1" Fiberglass						
Demolish	Sq.		43.50		43.50	Includes material and labor to install
Install	Sq.	83.50	33.50		117	fiberglass board insulation 1" thick,
Demolish and Install	Sq.	83.50	77		160.50	R-4.20 and C-0.24 values.
Minimum Charge	Job		202		202	
1-3/8" Fiberglass						
Demolish	Sq.		43.50		43.50	Includes material and labor to install
Install	Sq.	132	36.50		168.50	fiberglass board insulation 1-3/8"
Demolish and Install	Sq.	132	80		212	thick, R-5.30 and C-0.19 values.
Minimum Charge	Job		202		202	

Insulation

Roof Insulation Board		Unit	Material	Labor	Equip.	Total	Specification
1-5/8" Fiberglass							
	Demolish	Sq.		43.50		43.50	Includes material and labor to install
	Install	Sq.	136	38.50		174.50	fiberglass board insulation 1-5/8"
	Demolish and Install	Sq.	136	82		218	thick, R-6.70 and C-0.15 values.
	Minimum Charge	Job		202		202	
2-1/4" Fiberglass							
	Demolish	Sq.		43.50		43.50	Includes material and labor to install
	Install	Sq.	162	42.50		204.50	fiberglass board insulation 2-1/4"
	Demolish and Install	Sq.	162	86		248	thick, R-8.30 and C-0.12 values.
	Minimum Charge	Job		202		202	
Perlite							
1" Perlite							
	Demolish	Sq.		43.50		43.50	Includes material and labor to install
	Install	Sq.	50.50	33.50		84	perlite board insulation 1" thick,
	Demolish and Install	Sq.	50.50	77		127.50	R-2.80 and C-0.36 values.
	Minimum Charge	Job		202		202	
4" Perlite							
	Demolish	Sq.		43.50		43.50	Includes material and labor to install
	Install	Sq.	202	64.50		266.50	perlite board insulation 4" thick,
	Demolish and Install	Sq.	202	108		310	R-10.0 and C-0.10 values.
	Minimum Charge	Job		202		202	
1-1/2" Perlite							
	Demolish	Sq.		43.50		43.50	Includes material and labor to install
	Install	Sq.	53	36.50		89.50	perlite board insulation 1-1/2" thick,
	Demolish and Install	Sq.	53	80		133	R-4.20 and C-0.24 values.
	Minimum Charge	Job		202		202	
2" Perlite							
	Demolish	Sq.		43.50		43.50	Includes material and labor to install
	Install	Sq.	88	45		133	perlite board insulation 2" thick,
	Demolish and Install	Sq.	88	88.50		176.50	R-5.30 and C-0.19 values.
	Minimum Charge	Job		202		202	
2-1/2" Perlite							
	Demolish	Sq.		43.50		43.50	Includes material and labor to install
	Install	Sq.	105	50.50		155.50	perlite board insulation 2-1/2" thick,
	Demolish and Install	Sq.	105	94		199	R-6.70 and C-0.15 values.
	Minimum Charge	Job		202		202	
3" Perlite							
	Demolish	Sq.		43.50		43.50	Includes material and labor to install
	Install	Sq.	152	54		206	perlite board insulation 3" thick,
	Demolish and Install	Sq.	152	97.50		249.50	R-8.30 and C-0.12 values.
	Minimum Charge	Job		202		202	
Polystyrene							
2" Polystyrene							
	Demolish	Sq.		43.50		43.50	Includes material and labor to install
	Install	Sq.	64	42.50		106.50	extruded polystyrene board, R5.0/ 2"
	Demolish and Install	Sq.	64	86		150	in thickness @25PSI compressive
	Minimum Charge	Job		202		202	strength.
1" Polystyrene							
	Demolish	Sq.		43.50		43.50	Includes material and labor to install
	Install	Sq.	32	29		61	extruded polystyrene board, R5.0/ 1"
	Demolish and Install	Sq.	32	72.50		104.50	in thickness @25PSI compressive
	Minimum Charge	Job		202		202	strength.
1-1/2" Polystyrene							
	Demolish	Sq.		43.50		43.50	Includes material and labor to install
	Install	Sq.	48	33.50		81.50	extruded polystyrene board, R5.0/
	Demolish and Install	Sq.	48	77		125	1-1/2" in thickness @25PSI
	Minimum Charge	Job		202		202	compressive strength.

Insulation

Roof Insulation Board	Unit	Material	Labor	Equip.	Total	Specification
Urethane						
3/4″ Urethane						
Demolish	Sq.		43.50		43.50	Includes material and labor to install
Install	Sq.	48.50	25		73.50	urethane board insulation 3/4″ thick,
Demolish and Install	Sq.	48.50	68.50		117	R-5.30 and C-0.19 values.
Minimum Charge	Job		202		202	
1″ Urethane						
Demolish	Sq.		43.50		43.50	Includes material and labor to install
Install	Sq.	56	27		83	urethane board insulation 1″ thick,
Demolish and Install	Sq.	56	70.50		126.50	R-6.70 and C-0.15 values.
Minimum Charge	Job		202		202	
1-1/2″ Urethane						
Demolish	Sq.		43.50		43.50	Includes material and labor to install
Install	Sq.	72.50	31		103.50	urethane board insulation 1-1/2″
Demolish and Install	Sq.	72.50	74.50		147	thick, R-10.1 and C-0.09 values.
Minimum Charge	Job		202		202	
2″ Urethane						
Demolish	Sq.		43.50		43.50	Includes material and labor to install
Install	Sq.	86	36.50		122.50	urethane board insulation 2″ thick,
Demolish and Install	Sq.	86	80		166	R-13.4 and C-0.06 values.
Minimum Charge	Job		202		202	

Gypsum Wallboard

Tile Ceiling

Gypsum Wallboard Ceiling

Wall Plaster		Unit	Material	Labor	Equip.	Total	Specification
Interior							
Cement							
	Demolish	S.Y.		5.55		5.55	Includes material and labor to install
	Install	S.Y.	14.15	23	1.84	38.99	cement plaster on interior wood
	Demolish and Install	S.Y.	14.15	28.55	1.84	44.54	framing with metal lath.
	Clean	S.Y.		2.72		2.72	
	Paint	S.Y.	1.95	4.62		6.57	
	Minimum Charge	Job		180		180	
Acoustic							
	Demolish	S.Y.		5.55		5.55	Includes material and labor to install
	Install	S.Y.	10.90	28	1.84	40.74	acoustical cement plaster on interior
	Demolish and Install	S.Y.	10.90	33.55	1.84	46.29	wood framing with metal lath.
	Clean	S.Y.		2.72		2.72	
	Paint	S.Y.	1.95	4.62		6.57	
	Minimum Charge	Job		180		180	
Gypsum							
	Demolish	S.Y.		5.55		5.55	Includes material and labor to install
	Install	S.Y.	10.10	23.50	1.56	35.16	gypsum wall or ceiling plaster on
	Demolish and Install	S.Y.	10.10	29.05	1.56	40.71	interior wood framing with metal lath.
	Clean	S.Y.		2.72		2.72	
	Paint	S.Y.	1.95	4.62		6.57	
	Minimum Charge	Job		180		180	
Stucco							
	Demolish	S.Y.		13.30		13.30	Includes material and labor to install
	Install	S.Y.	5.85	32.50	2.16	40.51	stucco on wire mesh over wood
	Demolish and Install	S.Y.	5.85	45.80	2.16	53.81	framing.
	Clean	S.Y.		2.72		2.72	
	Paint	S.Y.	1.95	4.62		6.57	
	Minimum Charge	Job		180		180	
Thin Coat							
Veneer							
	Demolish	S.Y.		5.55		5.55	Includes materials and labor to install
	Install	S.Y.	.86	4.29	.34	5.49	thin coat veneer plaster.
	Demolish and Install	S.Y.	.86	9.84	.34	11.04	
	Clean	S.Y.		2.72		2.72	
	Paint	S.Y.	1.95	4.62		6.57	
	Minimum Charge	Job		180		180	

Walls / Ceilings

Wall Plaster

Wall Plaster	Unit	Material	Labor	Equip.	Total	Specification
Lath						
Metal						
Demolish	S.Y.		1.30		1.30	Includes material and labor to install
Install	S.Y.	4.40	4.60		9	wire lath on steel framed walls.
Demolish and Install	S.Y.	4.40	5.90		10.30	
Clean	S.Y.		2.72		2.72	
Minimum Charge	Job		81		81	
Gypsum						
Demolish	S.Y.		1.30		1.30	Includes material and labor to install
Install	S.Y.	5.35	4.32		9.67	gypsum lath on walls.
Demolish and Install	S.Y.	5.35	5.62		10.97	
Clean	S.Y.		2.72		2.72	
Minimum Charge	Job		180		180	
Repairs						
Fill in Small Cracks						
Install	L.F.	.07	2.87		2.94	Includes labor and material to fill-in
Minimum Charge	Job		180		180	hairline cracks up to 1/8" with filler, sand and prep for paint.
Repair up to 1" Crack						
Install	L.F.	.26	3.59		3.85	Includes labor and material to fill-in
Minimum Charge	Job		180		180	hairline cracks up to 1" with filler, sand and prep for paint.
Patch Small Hole (2")						
Install	Ea.	.07	3.78		3.85	Includes labor and material to patch
Minimum Charge	Job		180		180	up to a 2" diameter hole in plaster.
Patch Large Hole						
Install	Ea.	8.05	120		128.05	Includes labor and material to patch
Minimum Charge	Job		180		180	up to a 20" diameter hole in plaster.
Patch Plaster Section						
Install	Ea.	2.31	3.59		5.90	Includes labor and material to repair
Minimum Charge	Job		180		180	section of plaster wall, area less than 20 S.F.
Repair Inside Corner						
Install	L.F.	3.20	9		12.20	Includes material and labor to patch
Minimum Charge	Job		180		180	plaster corners.

Ceiling Plaster

Ceiling Plaster	Unit	Material	Labor	Equip.	Total	Specification
Interior						
Cement						
Demolish	S.Y.		5.55		5.55	Includes material and labor to install
Install	S.Y.	14.15	23	1.84	38.99	cement plaster on interior wood
Demolish and Install	S.Y.	14.15	28.55	1.84	44.54	framing with metal lath.
Clean	S.Y.		2.85		2.85	
Paint	S.Y.	1.95	4.62		6.57	
Minimum Charge	Job		180		180	
Acoustic						
Demolish	S.Y.		5.55		5.55	Includes material and labor to install
Install	S.Y.	10.90	28	1.84	40.74	acoustical cement plaster on interior
Demolish and Install	S.Y.	10.90	33.55	1.84	46.29	wood framing with metal lath.
Clean	S.Y.		2.85		2.85	
Paint	S.Y.	1.95	4.62		6.57	
Minimum Charge	Job		180		180	

Walls / Ceilings

Ceiling Plaster

	Unit	Material	Labor	Equip.	Total	Specification
Gypsum						
Demolish	S.Y.		5.55		5.55	Includes material and labor to install
Install	S.Y.	10.10	23.50	1.56	35.16	gypsum wall or ceiling plaster on
Demolish and Install	S.Y.	10.10	29.05	1.56	40.71	interior wood framing with metal lath.
Clean	S.Y.		2.85		2.85	
Paint	S.Y.	1.95	4.62		6.57	
Minimum Charge	Job		180		180	
Stucco						
Demolish	S.Y.		13.30		13.30	Includes material and labor to install
Install	S.Y.	5.85	32.50	2.16	40.51	stucco on wire mesh over wood
Demolish and Install	S.Y.	5.85	45.80	2.16	53.81	framing.
Clean	S.Y.		2.85		2.85	
Paint	S.Y.	1.95	4.62		6.57	
Minimum Charge	Job		180		180	

Thin Coat

	Unit	Material	Labor	Equip.	Total	Specification
Veneer						
Demolish	S.Y.		5.55		5.55	Includes materials and labor to install
Install	S.Y.	.86	4.29	.34	5.49	thin coat veneer plaster.
Demolish and Install	S.Y.	.86	9.84	.34	11.04	
Clean	S.Y.		2.85		2.85	
Paint	S.Y.	1.95	4.62		6.57	
Minimum Charge	Job		180		180	

Lath

	Unit	Material	Labor	Equip.	Total	Specification
Metal						
Demolish	S.Y.		1.30		1.30	Includes material and labor to install
Install	S.Y.	4.40	5.75		10.15	wire lath on steel framed ceilings.
Demolish and Install	S.Y.	4.40	7.05		11.45	
Minimum Charge	Job		180		180	
Gypsum						
Demolish	S.Y.		1.30		1.30	Includes material and labor to install
Install	S.Y.	5.35	3.60		8.95	gypsum lath on ceilings.
Demolish and Install	S.Y.	5.35	4.90		10.25	
Minimum Charge	Job		180		180	

Repairs

	Unit	Material	Labor	Equip.	Total	Specification
Fill in Small Cracks						
Install	S.F.	.07	.65		.72	Includes labor and material to fill in
Minimum Charge	Job		360		360	hairline cracks up to 1/8" with filler, sand and prep for paint.

Gypsum Wallboard

	Unit	Material	Labor	Equip.	Total	Specification
Finished						
1/4"						
Demolish	S.F.		.33		.33	Cost includes material and labor to
Install	S.F.	.23	1.22		1.45	install 1/4" drywall, including joint
Demolish and Install	S.F.	.23	1.55		1.78	taping, premixed compound and
Clean	S.F.		.27		.27	screws.
Paint	S.F.	.20	.30		.50	
Minimum Charge	Job		202		202	
3/8"						
Demolish	S.F.		.33		.33	Cost includes material and labor to
Install	S.F.	.23	1.24		1.47	install 3/8" drywall including joint
Demolish and Install	S.F.	.23	1.57		1.80	tape, premixed compound and
Clean	S.F.		.27		.27	screws.
Paint	S.F.	.20	.30		.50	
Minimum Charge	Job		202		202	

Walls / Ceilings

Gypsum Wallboard

Gypsum Wallboard	Unit	Material	Labor	Equip.	Total	Specification
1/2″						
Demolish	S.F.		.33		.33	Cost includes material and labor to
Install	S.F.	.22	1.25		1.47	install 1/2″ drywall including joint
Demolish and Install	S.F.	.22	1.58		1.80	tape, premixed compound and
Clean	S.F.		.27		.27	screws.
Paint	S.F.	.20	.30		.50	
Minimum Charge	Job		202		202	
1/2″ Water Resistant						
Demolish	S.F.		.33		.33	Cost includes material and labor to
Install	S.F.	.35	1.06		1.41	install 1/2″ WR drywall including joint
Demolish and Install	S.F.	.35	1.39		1.74	tape, premixed compound and
Clean	S.F.		.27		.27	screws.
Paint	S.F.	.20	.30		.50	
Minimum Charge	Job		202		202	
1/2″ Fire-rated						
Demolish	S.F.		.33		.33	Cost includes material and labor to
Install	S.F.	.26	1.25		1.51	install 1/2″ FR drywall including
Demolish and Install	S.F.	.26	1.58		1.84	screws. Taping and finishing not
Clean	S.F.		.27		.27	included.
Paint	S.F.	.20	.30		.50	
Minimum Charge	Job		202		202	
5/8″						
Demolish	S.F.		.33		.33	Cost includes material and labor to
Install	S.F.	.29	1.20		1.49	install 5/8″ drywall including joint
Demolish and Install	S.F.	.29	1.53		1.82	tape, premixed compound and
Clean	S.F.		.27		.27	screws.
Paint	S.F.	.20	.30		.50	
Minimum Charge	Job		202		202	
5/8″ Fire-rated						
Demolish	S.F.		.33		.33	Cost includes material and labor to
Install	S.F.	.29	1.42		1.71	install 5/8″ FR drywall, including joint
Demolish and Install	S.F.	.29	1.75		2.04	taping, premixed compound and
Clean	S.F.		.27		.27	screws.
Paint	S.F.	.20	.30		.50	
Minimum Charge	Job		202		202	
2-hour fire-rated						
Demolish	S.F.		.83		.83	Cost includes material and labor to
Install	S.F.	.66	2.81		3.47	install 2 layers of 5/8″ type X drywall
Demolish and Install	S.F.	.66	3.64		4.30	including joint taping, premixed
Clean	S.F.		.27		.27	compound and screws.
Paint	S.F.	.20	.30		.50	
Minimum Charge	Job		202		202	
Unfinished						
1/4″						
Demolish	S.F.		.33		.33	Cost includes material and labor to
Install	S.F.	.20	.42		.62	install 1/4″ drywall including screws.
Demolish and Install	S.F.	.20	.75		.95	Taping and finishing not included.
Clean	S.F.		.27		.27	
Minimum Charge	Job		202		202	
3/8″						
Demolish	S.F.		.33		.33	Cost includes material and labor to
Install	S.F.	.20	.43		.63	install 3/8″ drywall including screws.
Demolish and Install	S.F.	.20	.76		.96	Tape, finish or texture is not included.
Clean	S.F.		.27		.27	
Minimum Charge	Job		202		202	

Gypsum Wallboard		Unit	Material	Labor	Equip.	Total	Specification
1/2″							
	Demolish	S.F.		.33		.33	Cost includes material and labor to
	Install	S.F.	.19	.43		.62	install 1/2″ drywall including screws.
	Demolish and Install	S.F.	.19	.76		.95	Taping and finishing not included.
	Clean	S.F.		.27		.27	
	Minimum Charge	Job		202		202	
1/2″ Water Resistant							
	Demolish	S.F.		.33		.33	Cost includes material and labor to
	Install	S.F.	.32	.43		.75	install 1/2″ WR drywall including
	Demolish and Install	S.F.	.32	.76		1.08	screws. Taping and finishing is not
	Clean	S.F.		.27		.27	included.
	Minimum Charge	Job		202		202	
1/2″ Fire-rated							
	Demolish	S.F.		.33		.33	Cost includes labor and material to
	Install	S.F.	.19	.29		.48	install 1/2″ FR drywall including
	Demolish and Install	S.F.	.19	.62		.81	screws. Tape, finish or texture is not
	Clean	S.F.		.27		.27	included.
	Minimum Charge	Job		202		202	
5/8″							
	Demolish	S.F.		.33		.33	Cost includes material and labor to
	Install	S.F.	.26	.48		.74	install 5/8″ drywall including screws.
	Demolish and Install	S.F.	.26	.81		1.07	Taping and finishing not included.
	Clean	S.F.		.27		.27	
	Minimum Charge	Job		202		202	
5/8″ Fire-rated							
	Demolish	S.F.		.33		.33	Cost includes material and labor to
	Install	S.F.	.26	.48		.74	install 5/8″ FR drywall including
	Demolish and Install	S.F.	.26	.81		1.07	screws. Taping and finishing not
	Clean	S.F.		.27		.27	included.
	Minimum Charge	Job		202		202	
2-hour Fire-rated							
	Demolish	S.F.		.83		.83	Cost includes material and labor to
	Install	S.F.	.66	2.81		3.47	install 2 layers of 5/8″ type X drywall
	Demolish and Install	S.F.	.66	3.64		4.30	including joint taping, premixed
	Clean	S.F.		.27		.27	compound and screws.
	Minimum Charge	Job		202		202	
Accessories							
Tape & Finish							
	Install	S.F.	.04	.40		.44	Includes labor and material for taping,
	Minimum Charge	Job		202		202	sanding and finish.
Texture							
Sprayed							
	Install	S.F.	.06	.43		.49	Includes labor and material to install
	Minimum Charge	Job		202		202	by spray, texture finish.
Trowel							
	Install	S.F.	.01	.23		.24	Includes labor and material to apply
	Minimum Charge	Job		202		202	hand troweled texture.
Patch Hole in Gypsum Wallboard							
	Install	S.F.	.42	54		54.42	Includes labor and material to patch a
	Minimum Charge	Job		202		202	one square foot area of damaged drywall.
Furring Strips							
	Demolish	S.F.		.08		.08	Cost includes material and labor to
	Install	S.F.	.21	.90		1.11	install 1″ x 2″ furring strips, 16″ O.C.
	Demolish and Install	S.F.	.21	.98		1.19	per S.F. of surface area to be covered.
	Minimum Charge	Job		101		101	

Ceramic Wall Tile	Unit	Material	Labor	Equip.	Total	Specification
Thin Set						
2″ x 2″						
Demolish	S.F.		1.11		1.11	Cost includes material and labor to
Install	S.F.	7	6.05		13.05	install 2″ x 2″ ceramic tile in organic
Demolish and Install	S.F.	7	7.16		14.16	adhesive including cutting and grout.
Clean	S.F.		.57		.57	
Minimum Charge	Job		181		181	
4-1/4″ x 4-1/4″						
Demolish	S.F.		1.11		1.11	Cost includes material and labor to
Install	S.F.	2.35	3.40		5.75	install 4-1/4″ x 4-1/4″ ceramic tile in
Demolish and Install	S.F.	2.35	4.51		6.86	organic adhesive including grout.
Clean	S.F.		.57		.57	
Minimum Charge	Job		181		181	
6″ x 6″						
Demolish	S.F.		1.11		1.11	Cost includes material and labor to
Install	S.F.	2.62	3.23		5.85	install 6″ x 6″ ceramic tile in organic
Demolish and Install	S.F.	2.62	4.34		6.96	adhesive including and grout.
Clean	S.F.		.57		.57	
Minimum Charge	Job		181		181	
8″ x 8″						
Demolish	S.F.		1.11		1.11	Cost includes material and labor to
Install	S.F.	4.49	2.88		7.37	install 8″ x 8″ ceramic tile in organic
Demolish and Install	S.F.	4.49	3.99		8.48	adhesive including cutting and grout.
Clean	S.F.		.57		.57	
Minimum Charge	Job		181		181	
Thick Set						
2″ x 2″						
Demolish	S.F.		1.33		1.33	Cost includes material and labor to
Install	S.F.	6.50	7.25		13.75	install 2″ x 2″ ceramic tile in mortar
Demolish and Install	S.F.	6.50	8.58		15.08	bed including cutting and grout.
Clean	S.F.		.57		.57	
Minimum Charge	Job		181		181	
4-1/4″ x 4-1/4″						
Demolish	S.F.		1.33		1.33	Cost includes material and labor to
Install	S.F.	8.15	7.25		15.40	install 4-1/4″ x 4-1/4″ ceramic tile in
Demolish and Install	S.F.	8.15	8.58		16.73	mortar bed including cutting and
Clean	S.F.		.57		.57	grout.
Minimum Charge	Job		181		181	
6″ x 6″						
Demolish	S.F.		1.33		1.33	Cost includes material and labor to
Install	S.F.	10.25	6.55		16.80	install 6″ x 6″ ceramic tile in mortar
Demolish and Install	S.F.	10.25	7.88		18.13	bed including cutting and grout.
Clean	S.F.		.57		.57	
Minimum Charge	Job		181		181	
8″ x 8″						
Demolish	S.F.		1.33		1.33	Cost includes material and labor to
Install	S.F.	11.75	6.05		17.80	install 8″ x 8″ ceramic tile in mortar
Demolish and Install	S.F.	11.75	7.38		19.13	bed including cutting and grout.
Clean	S.F.		.57		.57	
Minimum Charge	Job		181		181	
Re-grout						
Install	S.F.	.15	3.62		3.77	Includes material and labor to regrout
Minimum Charge	Job		181		181	ceramic tile walls.

Walls / Ceilings

Wall Tile		Unit	Material	Labor	Equip.	Total	Specification
Mirror							
Custom Cut Wall							
	Demolish	S.F.		.63		.63	Includes material and labor to install
	Install	S.F.	2.09	4.02		6.11	distortion-free float glass mirror, 1/8"
	Demolish and Install	S.F.	2.09	4.65		6.74	to 3/16" thick with cut and polished
	Clean	S.F.	.04	.17		.21	edges.
	Minimum Charge	Job		196		196	
Beveled Wall							
	Demolish	S.F.		.63		.63	Includes material and labor to install
	Install	S.F.	5.85	7.15		13	distortion-free float glass mirror, 1/8"
	Demolish and Install	S.F.	5.85	7.78		13.63	to 3/16" thick with beveled edges.
	Clean	S.F.	.04	.17		.21	
	Minimum Charge	Job		196		196	
Smoked Wall							
	Demolish	S.F.		.63		.63	Includes material and labor to install
	Install	S.F.	8.70	7.15		15.85	distortion-free smoked float glass
	Demolish and Install	S.F.	8.70	7.78		16.48	mirror, 1/8" to 3/16" thick with cut
	Clean	S.F.	.04	.17		.21	and polished edges.
	Minimum Charge	Job		196		196	
Marble							
Good Grade							
	Demolish	S.F.		2.08		2.08	Cost includes material and labor to
	Install	S.F.	9.85	15.70		25.55	install 3/8" x 12" x 12" marble tile in
	Demolish and Install	S.F.	9.85	17.78		27.63	mortar bed with grout.
	Clean	S.F.		.57		.57	
	Minimum Charge	Job		181		181	
Better Grade							
	Demolish	S.F.		2.08		2.08	Cost includes material and labor to
	Install	S.F.	10.45	15.70		26.15	install 3/8" x 12" x 12" marble, in
	Demolish and Install	S.F.	10.45	17.78		28.23	mortar bed with grout.
	Clean	S.F.		.57		.57	
	Minimum Charge	Job		181		181	
Premium Grade							
	Demolish	S.F.		2.08		2.08	Cost includes material and labor to
	Install	S.F.	20	15.70		35.70	install 3/8" x 12" x 12" marble, in
	Demolish and Install	S.F.	20	17.78		37.78	mortar bed with grout.
	Clean	S.F.		.57		.57	
	Minimum Charge	Job		181		181	
Glass Block							
	Demolish	S.F.		1.66		1.66	Cost includes material and labor to
	Install	S.F.	28	15.90		43.90	install 3-7/8" thick, 6" x 6" smooth
	Demolish and Install	S.F.	28	17.56		45.56	face glass block including mortar and
	Clean	S.F.		.57		.57	cleaning.
	Minimum Charge	Job		360		360	
Cork							
	Demolish	S.F.		.26		.26	Cost includes material and labor to
	Install	S.F.	4.92	1.45		6.37	install 3/16" thick cork tile and
	Demolish and Install	S.F.	4.92	1.71		6.63	installation.
	Clean	S.F.		.57		.57	
	Minimum Charge	Job		174		174	
Re-grout							
	Install	S.F.	.15	3.62		3.77	Includes material and labor to regrout
	Minimum Charge	Job		181		181	ceramic tile walls.

Walls / Ceilings

Wall Paneling

	Unit	Material	Labor	Equip.	Total	Specification
Plywood						
Good Grade						
Demolish	S.F.		.33		.33	Cost includes material and labor to
Install	S.F.	.98	1.61		2.59	install 4' x 8' x 1/4" paneling,
Demolish and Install	S.F.	.98	1.94		2.92	including nails and adhesive.
Clean	S.F.		.27		.27	
Paint	S.F.	.30	.66		.96	
Minimum Charge	Job		202		202	
Better Grade						
Demolish	S.F.		.33		.33	Cost includes material and labor to
Install	S.F.	1.49	1.92		3.41	install 4' x 8' x 1/4" plywood wall
Demolish and Install	S.F.	1.49	2.25		3.74	panel, including nails and adhesive.
Clean	S.F.		.27		.27	
Paint	S.F.	.30	.66		.96	
Minimum Charge	Job		202		202	
Premium Grade						
Demolish	S.F.		.33		.33	Cost includes material and labor to
Install	S.F.	2.17	2.31		4.48	install 4' x 8' x 1/4" plywood wall
Demolish and Install	S.F.	2.17	2.64		4.81	panel, including nails and adhesive.
Clean	S.F.		.27		.27	
Paint	S.F.	.30	.66		.96	
Minimum Charge	Job		202		202	
Hardboard						
Embossed Paneling						
Demolish	S.F.		.33		.33	Includes material and labor to install
Install	S.F.	.75	1.61		2.36	hardboard embossed paneling
Demolish and Install	S.F.	.75	1.94		2.69	including adhesives.
Clean	S.F.		.27		.27	
Minimum Charge	Job		202		202	
Plastic Molding						
Demolish	L.F.		.33		.33	Includes material and labor to install
Install	L.F.	.74	1.01		1.75	plastic trim for paneling.
Demolish and Install	L.F.	.74	1.34		2.08	
Clean	L.F.	.04	.18		.22	
Minimum Charge	Job		202		202	
Hardboard						
Embossed Brick						
Demolish	S.F.		.33		.33	Cost includes material and labor to
Install	S.F.	2.32	1.79		4.11	install 4' x 8' non-ceramic mineral
Demolish and Install	S.F.	2.32	2.12		4.44	brick-like veneer wall panels including
Clean	S.F.		.27		.27	adhesive.
Paint	S.F.	.22	.52		.74	
Minimum Charge	Job		202		202	
Embossed Ceramic Tile						
Demolish	S.F.		.33		.33	Includes material and labor to install
Install	S.F.	.75	1.61		2.36	hardboard embossed paneling
Demolish and Install	S.F.	.75	1.94		2.69	including adhesives.
Clean	S.F.		.27		.27	
Paint	S.F.	.22	.52		.74	
Minimum Charge	Job		202		202	
Pegboard						
Demolish	S.F.		.33		.33	Cost includes material and labor to
Install	S.F.	.46	1.61		2.07	install 4' x 8' x 1/4" pegboard panel,
Demolish and Install	S.F.	.46	1.94		2.40	including adhesive.
Clean	S.F.		.27		.27	
Paint	S.F.	.22	.52		.74	
Minimum Charge	Job		202		202	

Walls / Ceilings

Wall Paneling		Unit	Material	Labor	Equip.	Total	Specification
Furring Strips							
	Demolish	S.F.		.08		.08	Cost includes material and labor to
	Install	S.F.	.21	.90		1.11	install 1" x 2" furring strips, 16" O.C.
	Demolish and Install	S.F.	.21	.98		1.19	per S.F. of surface area to be covered.
	Minimum Charge	Job		202		202	
Molding							
Unfinished Base							
	Demolish	L.F.		.55		.55	Cost includes material and labor to
	Install	L.F.	.61	1.24		1.85	install 1/2" x 2-1/2" pine or birch
	Demolish and Install	L.F.	.61	1.79		2.40	base molding.
	Reinstall	L.F.		.99		.99	
	Clean	L.F.	.04	.17		.21	
	Paint	L.F.	.04	.38		.42	
	Minimum Charge	Job		202		202	
Unfinished Corner							
	Demolish	L.F.		.55		.55	Includes material and labor to install
	Install	L.F.	1.90	1.68		3.58	unfinished pine corner molding.
	Demolish and Install	L.F.	1.90	2.23		4.13	
	Reinstall	L.F.		1.35		1.35	
	Clean	Ea.	1.30	27.50		28.80	
	Paint	L.F.	.14	.55		.69	
	Minimum Charge	Job		202		202	
Unfinished Cove							
	Demolish	L.F.		.55		.55	Cost includes material and labor to
	Install	L.F.	2.06	1.49		3.55	install 3/4" x 3-1/2" unfinished pine
	Demolish and Install	L.F.	2.06	2.04		4.10	cove molding.
	Reinstall	L.F.		1.20		1.20	
	Clean	Ea.	1.30	27.50		28.80	
	Paint	L.F.	.14	.55		.69	
	Minimum Charge	Job		202		202	
Unfinished Crown							
	Demolish	L.F.		.66		.66	Includes material and labor to install
	Install	L.F.	2.53	1.61		4.14	unfinished pine crown molding.
	Demolish and Install	L.F.	2.53	2.27		4.80	
	Reinstall	L.F.		1.29		1.29	
	Clean	L.F.	.06	.23		.29	
	Paint	L.F.	.09	.37		.46	
	Minimum Charge	Job		202		202	
Prefinished Base							
	Demolish	L.F.		.55		.55	Cost includes material and labor to
	Install	L.F.	.82	1.29		2.11	install 9/16" x 3-5/16" prefinished
	Demolish and Install	L.F.	.82	1.84		2.66	base molding.
	Reinstall	L.F.		1.03		1.03	
	Clean	L.F.	.04	.18		.22	
	Paint	L.F.	.04	.38		.42	
	Minimum Charge	Job		202		202	
Prefinished Corner							
	Demolish	L.F.		.55		.55	Includes material and labor to install
	Install	L.F.	2.20	1.68		3.88	inside or outside prefinished corner
	Demolish and Install	L.F.	2.20	2.23		4.43	molding.
	Reinstall	L.F.		1.35		1.35	
	Clean	L.F.		.11		.11	
	Paint	L.F.	.14	.55		.69	
	Minimum Charge	Job		202		202	

Walls / Ceilings

Wall Paneling

	Unit	Material	Labor	Equip.	Total	Specification
Prefinished Crown						
Demolish	L.F.		.66		.66	Cost includes material and labor to
Install	L.F.	1.54	1.61		3.15	install 3/4" x 3-13/16" prefinished
Demolish and Install	L.F.	1.54	2.27		3.81	crown molding.
Reinstall	L.F.		1.29		1.29	
Clean	L.F.	.06	.23		.29	
Paint	L.F.	.09	.37		.46	
Minimum Charge	Job		202		202	

Wall Covering

	Unit	Material	Labor	Equip.	Total	Specification
Surface Prep						
Patch Walls						
Install	S.F.	.11	3.59		3.70	Includes labor and material to repair
Minimum Charge	Job		174		174	section of plaster wall, area less than
						20 S.F.
Sizing						
Install	S.F.	.07	.17		.24	Includes labor and materials to apply
Minimum Charge	Job		174		174	wall sizing.
Good Grade						
Walls						
Demolish	S.F.		.65		.65	Includes material and labor to install
Install	S.F.	.99	.73		1.72	pre-pasted, vinyl-coated wallcovering.
Demolish and Install	S.F.	.99	1.38		2.37	
Clean	S.F.	.01	.07		.08	
Minimum Charge	Job		174		174	
Ceiling						
Demolish	S.F.		.65		.65	Includes material and labor to install
Install	S.F.	.99	.73		1.72	pre-pasted, vinyl-coated wallcovering.
Demolish and Install	S.F.	.99	1.38		2.37	
Clean	S.F.	.04	.17		.21	
Minimum Charge	Job		174		174	
Better Grade						
Walls						
Demolish	S.F.		.65		.65	Includes material and labor to install
Install	S.F.	1.10	.73		1.83	pre-pasted, vinyl-coated wallcovering.
Demolish and Install	S.F.	1.10	1.38		2.48	
Clean	S.F.	.01	.07		.08	
Minimum Charge	Job		174		174	
Ceiling						
Demolish	S.F.		.65		.65	Includes material and labor to install
Install	S.F.	1.10	.73		1.83	pre-pasted, vinyl-coated wallcovering.
Demolish and Install	S.F.	1.10	1.38		2.48	
Clean	S.F.	.04	.17		.21	
Minimum Charge	Job		174		174	
Premium Grade						
Walls						
Demolish	S.F.		.81		.81	Includes material and labor to install
Install	S.F.	1.40	.73		2.13	pre-pasted, vinyl-coated wallcovering.
Demolish and Install	S.F.	1.40	1.54		2.94	
Clean	S.F.	.01	.07		.08	
Minimum Charge	Job		174		174	
Ceiling						
Demolish	S.F.		.81		.81	Includes material and labor to install
Install	S.F.	1.40	.73		2.13	pre-pasted, vinyl-coated wallcovering.
Demolish and Install	S.F.	1.40	1.54		2.94	
Clean	S.F.	.04	.17		.21	
Minimum Charge	Job		174		174	

Walls / Ceilings

Wall Covering

	Unit	Material	Labor	Equip.	Total	Specification
Mural						
Pre-printed						
Demolish	Ea.		104		104	Includes material and labor to install
Install	Ea.	262	262		524	wallcovering with a pre-printed mural.
Demolish and Install	Ea.	262	366		628	
Clean	Ea.		7.50		7.50	
Minimum Charge	Job		174		174	
Hand-painted						
Demolish	Ea.		104		104	Includes material and labor to install
Install	Ea.	525	530		1055	wallcovering with a hand-painted
Demolish and Install	Ea.	525	634		1159	mural.
Clean	Ea.		7.50		7.50	
Minimum Charge	Job		174		174	
Vinyl-coated						
Good Grade						
Demolish	Ea.		18.45		18.45	Includes material and labor to install
Install	Ea.	22	24.50		46.50	pre-pasted, vinyl-coated wallcovering.
Demolish and Install	Ea.	22	42.95		64.95	Based upon 30 S.F. rolls.
Clean	Ea.		7.50		7.50	
Minimum Charge	Job		174		174	
Better Grade						
Demolish	Ea.		18.45		18.45	Includes material and labor to install
Install	Ea.	29	24.50		53.50	pre-pasted, vinyl-coated wallcovering.
Demolish and Install	Ea.	29	42.95		71.95	Based upon 30 S.F. rolls.
Clean	Ea.		7.50		7.50	
Minimum Charge	Job		174		174	
Premium Grade						
Demolish	Ea.		18.45		18.45	Includes material and labor to install
Install	Ea.	51	24.50		75.50	pre-pasted, vinyl-coated wallcovering.
Demolish and Install	Ea.	51	42.95		93.95	Based upon 30 S.F. rolls.
Clean	Ea.		7.50		7.50	
Minimum Charge	Job		174		174	
Blank Underliner						
Demolish	Ea.		18.45		18.45	Includes material and labor to install
Install	Ea.	12.85	25		37.85	blank stock liner paper or bridging
Demolish and Install	Ea.	12.85	43.45		56.30	paper. Based upon 30 S.F. rolls.
Clean	Ea.		7.50		7.50	
Minimum Charge	Job		174		174	
Solid Vinyl						
Good Grade						
Demolish	Roll		21.50		21.50	Includes material and labor to install
Install	Ea.	29	24.50		53.50	pre-pasted, vinyl wallcovering. Based
Demolish and Install	Ea.	29	46		75	upon 30 S.F. rolls.
Clean	Ea.		7.50		7.50	
Minimum Charge	Job		174		174	
Better Grade						
Demolish	Roll		21.50		21.50	Includes material and labor to install
Install	Ea.	40.50	24.50		65	pre-pasted, vinyl wallcovering. Based
Demolish and Install	Ea.	40.50	46		86.50	upon 30 S.F. rolls.
Clean	Ea.		7.50		7.50	
Minimum Charge	Job		174		174	
Premium Grade						
Demolish	Roll		21.50		21.50	Includes material and labor to install
Install	Ea.	51.50	24.50		76	pre-pasted, vinyl wallcovering. Based
Demolish and Install	Ea.	51.50	46		97.50	upon 30 S.F. rolls.
Clean	Ea.		7.50		7.50	
Minimum Charge	Job		174		174	

Walls / Ceilings

Wall Covering	Unit	Material	Labor	Equip.	Total	Specification
Blank Underliner						
Demolish	Ea.		18.45		18.45	Includes material and labor to install
Install	Ea.	12.85	25		37.85	blank stock liner paper or bridging
Demolish and Install	Ea.	12.85	43.45		56.30	paper. Based upon 30 S.F. rolls.
Clean	Ea.		7.50		7.50	
Minimum Charge	Job		174		174	
Grasscloth / String						
Good Grade						
Demolish	Ea.		18.45		18.45	Includes material and labor to install
Install	Ea.	41.50	31.50		73	grasscloth or string wallcovering.
Demolish and Install	Ea.	41.50	49.95		91.45	Based upon 30 S.F. rolls.
Clean	Ea.		9.95		9.95	
Minimum Charge	Job		174		174	
Better Grade						
Demolish	Ea.		18.45		18.45	Includes material and labor to install
Install	Ea.	53.50	31.50		85	grasscloth or string wallcovering.
Demolish and Install	Ea.	53.50	49.95		103.45	Based upon 30 S.F. rolls.
Clean	Ea.		9.95		9.95	
Minimum Charge	Job		174		174	
Premium Grade						
Demolish	Ea.		18.45		18.45	Includes material and labor to install
Install	Ea.	68	31.50		99.50	grasscloth or string wallcovering.
Demolish and Install	Ea.	68	49.95		117.95	Based upon 30 S.F. rolls.
Clean	Ea.		9.95		9.95	
Minimum Charge	Job		174		174	
Blank Underliner						
Demolish	Ea.		18.45		18.45	Includes material and labor to install
Install	Ea.	12.85	25		37.85	blank stock liner paper or bridging
Demolish and Install	Ea.	12.85	43.45		56.30	paper. Based upon 30 S.F. rolls.
Clean	Ea.		7.50		7.50	
Minimum Charge	Job		174		174	
Designer						
Premium Grade						
Demolish	S.F.		.81		.81	Includes material and labor to install
Install	Ea.	128	36.50		164.50	paperback vinyl, untrimmed and
Demolish and Install	Ea.	128	37.31		165.31	hand-painted. Based upon 30 S.F.
Clean	Ea.		7.50		7.50	rolls.
Minimum Charge	Job		174		174	
Blank Underliner						
Demolish	Ea.		18.45		18.45	Includes material and labor to install
Install	Ea.	12.85	25		37.85	blank stock liner paper or bridging
Demolish and Install	Ea.	12.85	43.45		56.30	paper. Based upon 30 S.F. rolls.
Clean	Ea.		7.50		7.50	
Minimum Charge	Job		174		174	
Foil						
Demolish	Ea.		18.45		18.45	Includes material and labor to install
Install	Ea.	43.50	31.50		75	foil coated wallcovering. Based upon
Demolish and Install	Ea.	43.50	49.95		93.45	30 S.F. rolls.
Clean	Ea.		7.50		7.50	
Minimum Charge	Job		174		174	
Wallcovering Border						
Good Grade						
Demolish	L.F.		1.21		1.21	Includes material and labor install
Install	L.F.	2.17	1.34		3.51	vinyl-coated border 4" to 6" wide.
Demolish and Install	L.F.	2.17	2.55		4.72	
Clean	L.F.		.11		.11	
Minimum Charge	Job		174		174	

Walls / Ceilings

Wall Covering

	Unit	Material	Labor	Equip.	Total	Specification
Better Grade						
Demolish	L.F.		1.21		1.21	Includes material and labor install
Install	L.F.	2.90	1.34		4.24	vinyl-coated border 4″ to 6″ wide.
Demolish and Install	L.F.	2.90	2.55		5.45	
Clean	L.F.		.11		.11	
Minimum Charge	Job		174		174	
Premium Grade						
Demolish	L.F.		1.21		1.21	Includes material and labor install
Install	L.F.	3.64	1.34		4.98	vinyl-coated border 4″ to 6″ wide.
Demolish and Install	L.F.	3.64	2.55		6.19	
Clean	L.F.		.11		.11	
Minimum Charge	Job		174		174	

Acoustical Ceiling

	Unit	Material	Labor	Equip.	Total	Specification
Complete System						
2′ x 2′ Square Edge						
Demolish	S.F.		.55		.55	Includes material and labor to install
Install	S.F.	1.62	1.24		2.86	T-bar grid acoustical ceiling system,
Demolish and Install	S.F.	1.62	1.79		3.41	random pinhole 5/8″ thick square
Reinstall	S.F.		.99		.99	edge tile.
Clean	S.F.	.06	.23		.29	
Minimum Charge	Job		202		202	
2′ x 2′ Reveal Edge						
Demolish	S.F.		.55		.55	Includes material and labor to install
Install	S.F.	2.66	1.61		4.27	T-bar grid acoustical ceiling system,
Demolish and Install	S.F.	2.66	2.16		4.82	random pinhole 5/8″ thick reveal
Reinstall	S.F.		1.29		1.29	edge tile.
Clean	S.F.	.06	.23		.29	
Minimum Charge	Job		202		202	
2′ x 2′ Fire-rated						
Demolish	S.F.		.55		.55	Includes material and labor to install
Install	S.F.	3.04	1.24		4.28	T-bar grid FR acoustical ceiling system,
Demolish and Install	S.F.	3.04	1.79		4.83	random pinhole 5/8″ thick square
Reinstall	S.F.		.99		.99	edge tile.
Clean	S.F.	.06	.23		.29	
Minimum Charge	Job		202		202	
2′ x 4′ Square Edge						
Demolish	S.F.		.55		.55	Cost includes material and labor to
Install	S.F.	1.36	1.06		2.42	install 2′ x 4′ T-bar grid acoustical
Demolish and Install	S.F.	1.36	1.61		2.97	ceiling system, random pinhole 5/8″
Reinstall	S.F.		.85		.85	thick square edge tile.
Clean	S.F.	.06	.23		.29	
Minimum Charge	Job		202		202	
2′ x 4′ Reveal Edge						
Demolish	S.F.		.55		.55	Includes material and labor to install
Install	S.F.	2.66	1.47		4.13	T-bar grid acoustical ceiling system,
Demolish and Install	S.F.	2.66	2.02		4.68	random pinhole 5/8″ thick reveal
Reinstall	S.F.		1.17		1.17	edge tile.
Clean	S.F.	.06	.23		.29	
Minimum Charge	Job		202		202	
2′ x 4′ Fire-rated						
Demolish	S.F.		.55		.55	Includes material and labor to install
Install	S.F.	3.04	1.24		4.28	T-bar grid FR acoustical ceiling system,
Demolish and Install	S.F.	3.04	1.79		4.83	random pinhole 5/8″ thick square
Reinstall	S.F.		.99		.99	edge tile.
Clean	S.F.	.06	.23		.29	
Minimum Charge	Job		202		202	

Walls / Ceilings

Acoustical Ceiling

	Unit	Material	Labor	Equip.	Total	Specification
T-bar Grid						
2' x 2'						
Demolish	S.F.		.65		.65	Includes material and labor to install
Install	S.F.	.89	.62		1.51	T-bar grid acoustical ceiling
Demolish and Install	S.F.	.89	1.27		2.16	suspension system.
Reinstall	S.F.		.50		.50	
Clean	S.F.	.06	.23		.29	
Minimum Charge	Job		180		180	
2' x 4'						
Demolish	S.F.		.65		.65	Includes material and labor to install
Install	S.F.	.72	.50		1.22	T-bar grid acoustical ceiling
Demolish and Install	S.F.	.72	1.15		1.87	suspension system.
Reinstall	S.F.		.40		.40	
Clean	S.F.	.06	.23		.29	
Minimum Charge	Job		180		180	
Tile Panels						
2' x 2' Square Edge						
Demolish	S.F.		.18		.18	Includes material and labor to install
Install	S.F.	.65	.65		1.30	square edge panels 5/8" thick with
Demolish and Install	S.F.	.65	.83		1.48	pinhole pattern. T-bar grid not
Reinstall	S.F.		.52		.52	included.
Clean	S.F.	.06	.23		.29	
Minimum Charge	Job		202		202	
2' x 2' Reveal Edge						
Demolish	S.F.		.18		.18	Includes material and labor to install
Install	S.F.	1.60	.86		2.46	reveal edge panels 5/8" thick with
Demolish and Install	S.F.	1.60	1.04		2.64	pinhole pattern. T-bar grid not
Reinstall	S.F.		.69		.69	included.
Clean	S.F.	.06	.23		.29	
Minimum Charge	Job		202		202	
2' x 2' Fire-rated						
Demolish	S.F.		.18		.18	Includes material and labor to install
Install	S.F.	1.29	.60		1.89	FR square edge panels 5/8" thick with
Demolish and Install	S.F.	1.29	.78		2.07	pinhole pattern. T-bar grid not
Reinstall	S.F.		.48		.48	included.
Clean	S.F.	.06	.23		.29	
Minimum Charge	Job		202		202	
2' x 4' Square Edge						
Demolish	S.F.		.18		.18	Includes material and labor to install
Install	S.F.	.65	.65		1.30	square edge panels 5/8" thick with
Demolish and Install	S.F.	.65	.83		1.48	pinhole pattern. T-bar grid not
Reinstall	S.F.		.52		.52	included.
Clean	S.F.	.06	.23		.29	
Minimum Charge	Job		202		202	
2' x 4' Reveal Edge						
Demolish	S.F.		.18		.18	Includes material and labor to install
Install	S.F.	1.60	.86		2.46	reveal edge panels 5/8" thick with
Demolish and Install	S.F.	1.60	1.04		2.64	pinhole pattern. T-bar grid not
Reinstall	S.F.		.69		.69	included.
Clean	S.F.	.06	.23		.29	
Minimum Charge	Job		202		202	
2' x 4' Fire-rated						
Demolish	S.F.		.18		.18	Includes material and labor to install
Install	S.F.	1.29	.60		1.89	FR square edge panels 5/8" thick with
Demolish and Install	S.F.	1.29	.78		2.07	pinhole pattern. T-bar grid not
Reinstall	S.F.		.48		.48	included.
Clean	S.F.	.06	.23		.29	
Minimum Charge	Job		202		202	

Walls / Ceilings

Acoustical Ceiling		Unit	Material	Labor	Equip.	Total	Specification
Bleach Out Stains							
	Install	S.F.	.13	.30		.43	Includes labor and material to apply
	Minimum Charge	Job		202		202	laundry type chlorine bleach to remove light staining of acoustic tile material.
Adhesive Tile							
Good Grade							
	Demolish	S.F.		.74		.74	Cost includes material and labor to
	Install	S.F.	1.16	1.35		2.51	install 12" x 12" tile with embossed
	Demolish and Install	S.F.	1.16	2.09		3.25	texture pattern. Furring strips not
	Clean	S.F.	.04	.17		.21	included.
	Minimum Charge	Job		202		202	
Better Grade							
	Demolish	S.F.		.74		.74	Cost includes material and labor to
	Install	S.F.	1.65	1.35		3	install 12" x 12" tile with embossed
	Demolish and Install	S.F.	1.65	2.09		3.74	texture pattern. Furring strips not
	Clean	S.F.	.04	.17		.21	included.
	Minimum Charge	Job		202		202	
Premium Grade							
	Demolish	S.F.		.74		.74	Cost includes material and labor to
	Install	S.F.	5.45	1.35		6.80	install 12" x 12" tile with embossed
	Demolish and Install	S.F.	5.45	2.09		7.54	texture pattern. Furring strips not
	Clean	S.F.	.04	.17		.21	included.
	Minimum Charge	Job		202		202	
Bleach Out Stains							
	Install	S.F.	.13	.30		.43	Includes labor and material to apply
	Minimum Charge	Job		202		202	laundry type chlorine bleach to remove light staining of acoustic tile material.
Stapled Tile							
Good Grade							
	Demolish	S.F.		.44		.44	Cost includes material and labor to
	Install	S.F.	1.16	1.35		2.51	install 12" x 12" tile with embossed
	Demolish and Install	S.F.	1.16	1.79		2.95	texture pattern. Furring strips not
	Clean	S.F.	.04	.17		.21	included.
	Minimum Charge	Job		202		202	
Better Grade							
	Demolish	S.F.		.44		.44	Cost includes material and labor to
	Install	S.F.	1.65	1.35		3	install 12" x 12" tile with embossed
	Demolish and Install	S.F.	1.65	1.79		3.44	texture pattern. Furring strips not
	Clean	S.F.	.04	.17		.21	included.
	Minimum Charge	Job		202		202	
Premium Grade							
	Demolish	S.F.		.44		.44	Cost includes material and labor to
	Install	S.F.	5.45	1.35		6.80	install 12" x 12" tile with embossed
	Demolish and Install	S.F.	5.45	1.79		7.24	texture pattern. Furring strips not
	Clean	S.F.	.04	.17		.21	included.
	Minimum Charge	Job		202		202	
Bleach Out Stains							
	Install	S.F.	.13	.30		.43	Includes labor and material to apply
	Minimum Charge	Job		202		202	laundry type chlorine bleach to remove light staining of acoustic tile material.

Walls / Ceilings

Acoustical Ceiling		Unit	Material	Labor	Equip.	Total	Specification
Blown							
Scrape Off Existing							
	Install	S.F.		.62		.62	Includes labor and material to remove
	Minimum Charge	Job		202		202	existing blown acoustical ceiling material.
Seal Ceiling Gypsum Wallboard							
	Install	S.F.	.07	.30		.37	Includes labor and material to seal
	Minimum Charge	Job		173		173	existing drywall with shellac-based material.
Reblow Existing							
	Install	S.F.	.06	.43		.49	Includes labor and material to install
	Minimum Charge	Job		490	69	559	by spray, texture finish.
Bleach Out Stains							
	Install	S.F.	.13	.30		.43	Includes labor and material to apply
	Minimum Charge	Job		202		202	laundry type chlorine bleach to remove light staining of acoustic tile material.
New Blown							
	Install	S.F.	.06	.43		.49	Includes labor and material to install
	Minimum Charge	Job		173		173	by spray, texture finish.
Apply Glitter To							
	Install	S.F.	.17	.16		.33	Includes labor and material to apply
	Minimum Charge	Job		173		173	glitter material to existing or new drywall.
Furring Strips							
	Demolish	S.F.		.08		.08	Cost includes material and labor to
	Install	S.F.	.21	.90		1.11	install 1" x 2" furring strips, 16" O.C.
	Demolish and Install	S.F.	.21	.98		1.19	per S.F. of surface area to be covered.
	Minimum Charge	Job		101		101	

Finished Stair

Bi-Fold Door

Raised Panel Door

Hollow Core Door	Unit	Material	Labor	Equip.	Total	Specification
Pre-hung Wood						
1' 6" x 6' 8"						
Demolish	Ea.		37.50		37.50	Cost includes material and labor to
Install	Ea.	151	22.50		173.50	install 1' 6" x 6' 8" pre-hung 1-3/8"
Demolish and Install	Ea.	151	60		211	lauan door with split pine jamb
Reinstall	Ea.		22.42		22.42	including casing, stops, and hinges.
Clean	Ea.	5.20	12.45		17.65	
Paint	Ea.	8.65	49.50		58.15	
Minimum Charge	Job		202		202	
2' x 6' 8"						
Demolish	Ea.		37.50		37.50	Cost includes material and labor to
Install	Ea.	161	23.50		184.50	install 2' x 6' 8" pre-hung 1-3/8"
Demolish and Install	Ea.	161	61		222	lauan door with split pine jamb
Reinstall	Ea.		23.74		23.74	including casing, stops, and hinges.
Clean	Ea.	5.20	12.45		17.65	
Paint	Ea.	8.65	49.50		58.15	
Minimum Charge	Job		202		202	
2' 4" x 6' 8"						
Demolish	Ea.		37.50		37.50	Cost includes material and labor to
Install	Ea.	163	23.50		186.50	install 2' 4" x 6' 8" pre-hung 1-3/8"
Demolish and Install	Ea.	163	61		224	lauan door with split pine jamb
Reinstall	Ea.		23.74		23.74	including casing, stops, and hinges.
Clean	Ea.	5.20	12.45		17.65	
Paint	Ea.	8.65	49.50		58.15	
Minimum Charge	Job		202		202	
2' 6" x 6' 8"						
Demolish	Ea.		37.50		37.50	Cost includes material and labor to
Install	Ea.	167	23.50		190.50	install 2' 6" x 6' 8" pre-hung 1-3/8"
Demolish and Install	Ea.	167	61		228	lauan door with split pine jamb
Reinstall	Ea.		23.74		23.74	including casing, stops, and hinges.
Clean	Ea.	5.20	12.45		17.65	
Paint	Ea.	8.65	49.50		58.15	
Minimum Charge	Job		202		202	
2' 8" x 6' 8"						
Demolish	Ea.		37.50		37.50	Cost includes material and labor to
Install	Ea.	164	23.50		187.50	install 2' 8" x 6' 8" pre-hung 1-3/8"
Demolish and Install	Ea.	164	61		225	lauan door with split pine jamb,
Reinstall	Ea.		23.74		23.74	including casing, stop and hinges.
Clean	Ea.	5.20	12.45		17.65	
Paint	Ea.	8.65	49.50		58.15	
Minimum Charge	Job		202		202	

Finish Carpentry

Hollow Core Door

	Unit	Material	Labor	Equip.	Total	Specification
3' x 6' 8"						
Demolish	Ea.		37.50		37.50	Cost includes material and labor to
Install	Ea.	168	25		193	install 3' x 6' 8" pre-hung 1-3/8"
Demolish and Install	Ea.	168	62.50		230.50	lauan door with split pine jamb
Reinstall	Ea.		25.23		25.23	including casing, stops, and hinges.
Clean	Ea.	5.20	12.45		17.65	
Paint	Ea.	8.65	49.50		58.15	
Minimum Charge	Job		202		202	
Pocket Type						
Demolish	Ea.		56		56	Cost includes material and labor to
Install	Ea.	43	45		88	install 2' 8" x 6' 8" lauan door.
Demolish and Install	Ea.	43	101		144	
Reinstall	Ea.		44.84		44.84	
Clean	Ea.	5.20	12.45		17.65	
Paint	Ea.	8.65	49.50		58.15	
Minimum Charge	Job		202		202	
Stain						
Install	Ea.	6.20	29		35.20	Includes labor and material to stain
Minimum Charge	Job		173		173	single door and trim on both sides.
Pre-hung Masonite						
1' 6" x 6' 8"						
Demolish	Ea.		37.50		37.50	Cost includes material and labor to
Install	Ea.	207	22.50		229.50	install 1' 6" x 6' 8" pre-hung 1-3/8"
Demolish and Install	Ea.	207	60		267	masonite door with split pine jamb
Reinstall	Ea.		22.42		22.42	including casing, stops, and hinges.
Clean	Ea.	5.20	12.45		17.65	
Paint	Ea.	8.65	49.50		58.15	
Minimum Charge	Job		202		202	
2' x 6' 8"						
Demolish	Ea.		37.50		37.50	Cost includes material and labor to
Install	Ea.	215	23.50		238.50	install 2' x 6' 8" pre-hung 1-3/8"
Demolish and Install	Ea.	215	61		276	masonite door with split pine jamb
Reinstall	Ea.		23.74		23.74	including casing, stops, and hinges.
Clean	Ea.	5.20	12.45		17.65	
Paint	Ea.	8.65	49.50		58.15	
Minimum Charge	Job		202		202	
2' 4" x 6' 8"						
Demolish	Ea.		37.50		37.50	Cost includes material and labor to
Install	Ea.	218	23.50		241.50	install 2' 4" x 6' 8" pre-hung 1-3/8"
Demolish and Install	Ea.	218	61		279	masonite door with split pine jamb
Reinstall	Ea.		23.74		23.74	including casing, stops, and hinges.
Clean	Ea.	5.20	12.45		17.65	
Paint	Ea.	8.65	49.50		58.15	
Minimum Charge	Job		202		202	
2' 8" x 6' 8"						
Demolish	Ea.		37.50		37.50	Cost includes material and labor to
Install	Ea.	221	23.50		244.50	install 2' 8" x 6' 8" pre-hung 1-3/8"
Demolish and Install	Ea.	221	61		282	masonite door with split pine jamb
Reinstall	Ea.		23.74		23.74	including casing, stops, and hinges.
Clean	Ea.	5.20	12.45		17.65	
Paint	Ea.	8.65	49.50		58.15	
Minimum Charge	Job		202		202	
3' x 6' 8"						
Demolish	Ea.		37.50		37.50	Cost includes material and labor to
Install	Ea.	224	25		249	install 3' x 6' 8" pre-hung 1-3/8"
Demolish and Install	Ea.	224	62.50		286.50	masonite door with split pine jamb
Reinstall	Ea.		25.23		25.23	including casing, stops, and hinges.
Clean	Ea.	5.20	12.45		17.65	
Paint	Ea.	8.65	49.50		58.15	
Minimum Charge	Job		202		202	

Finish Carpentry

Hollow Core Door

	Unit	Material	Labor	Equip.	Total	Specification
Pocket Type						
Demolish	Ea.		56		56	Cost includes material and labor to
Install	Ea.	43	45		88	install 2' 8" x 6' 8" lauan door.
Demolish and Install	Ea.	43	101		144	
Reinstall	Ea.		44.84		44.84	
Clean	Ea.	5.20	12.45		17.65	
Paint	Ea.	8.65	49.50		58.15	
Minimum Charge	Job		202		202	
Stain						
Install	Ea.	6.20	29		35.20	Includes labor and material to stain
Minimum Charge	Job		173		173	single door and trim on both sides.
Hollow Core Door Only						
1' 6" x 6' 8'						
Demolish	Ea.		8		8	Cost includes material and labor to
Install	Ea.	43.50	21		64.50	install 1' 6" x 6' 8" lauan hollow core
Demolish and Install	Ea.	43.50	29		72.50	door slab.
Reinstall	Ea.		21.24		21.24	
Clean	Ea.	2.17	9.35		11.52	
Paint	Ea.	4.28	43.50		47.78	
Minimum Charge	Job		202		202	
2' x 6' 8'						
Demolish	Ea.		8		8	Cost includes material and labor to
Install	Ea.	47	22.50		69.50	install 2' x 6' 8" lauan hollow core
Demolish and Install	Ea.	47	30.50		77.50	door slab.
Reinstall	Ea.		22.42		22.42	
Clean	Ea.	2.17	9.35		11.52	
Paint	Ea.	4.28	43.50		47.78	
Minimum Charge	Job		202		202	
2' 4" x 6' 8'						
Demolish	Ea.		8		8	Cost includes material and labor to
Install	Ea.	50.50	22.50		73	install 2' 4" x 6' 8" lauan hollow core
Demolish and Install	Ea.	50.50	30.50		81	door slab.
Reinstall	Ea.		22.42		22.42	
Clean	Ea.	2.17	9.35		11.52	
Paint	Ea.	4.28	43.50		47.78	
Minimum Charge	Job		202		202	
2' 8" x 6' 8'						
Demolish	Ea.		8		8	Cost includes material and labor to
Install	Ea.	52.50	22.50		75	install 2' 8" x 6' 8" lauan hollow core
Demolish and Install	Ea.	52.50	30.50		83	door slab.
Reinstall	Ea.		22.42		22.42	
Clean	Ea.	2.17	9.35		11.52	
Paint	Ea.	4.28	43.50		47.78	
Minimum Charge	Job		202		202	
3' x 6' 8'						
Demolish	Ea.		8		8	Cost includes material and labor to
Install	Ea.	55	23.50		78.50	install 3' x 6' 8" lauan hollow core
Demolish and Install	Ea.	55	31.50		86.50	door slab.
Reinstall	Ea.		23.74		23.74	
Clean	Ea.	2.17	9.35		11.52	
Paint	Ea.	4.28	43.50		47.78	
Minimum Charge	Job		202		202	
Pocket Type						
Demolish	Ea.		8		8	Cost includes material and labor to
Install	Ea.	43	45		88	install 2' 8" x 6' 8" lauan door.
Demolish and Install	Ea.	43	53		96	
Reinstall	Ea.		44.84		44.84	
Clean	Ea.	2.17	9.35		11.52	
Paint	Ea.	4.28	43.50		47.78	
Minimum Charge	Job		202		202	

Finish Carpentry

Hollow Core Door

	Unit	Material	Labor	Equip.	Total	Specification
Stain						
Install	Ea.	3.44	38.50		41.94	Includes labor and materials to stain a
Minimum Charge	Job		173		173	flush style door on both sides by
						brush.
Casing Trim						
Single Width						
Demolish	Ea.		7.10		7.10	Cost includes material and labor to
Install	Opng.	25	33.50		58.50	install 11/16" x 2-1/2" pine ranch
Demolish and Install	Opng.	25	40.60		65.60	style casing for one side of a standard
Reinstall	Opng.		26.91		26.91	door opening.
Clean	Opng.	.74	2.99		3.73	
Paint	Ea.	4.38	6.95		11.33	
Minimum Charge	Job		202		202	
Double Width						
Demolish	Ea.		8.45		8.45	Cost includes material and labor to
Install	Opng.	29	40.50		69.50	install 11/16" x 2-1/2" pine ranch
Demolish and Install	Opng.	29	48.95		77.95	style door casing for one side of a
Reinstall	Opng.		32.29		32.29	double door opening.
Clean	Opng.	.87	6		6.87	
Paint	Ea.	4.38	7.85		12.23	
Minimum Charge	Job		202		202	
Hardware						
Doorknob w / Lock						
Demolish	Ea.		16		16	Includes material and labor to install
Install	Ea.	43.50	25		68.50	privacy lockset.
Demolish and Install	Ea.	43.50	41		84.50	
Reinstall	Ea.		20.18		20.18	
Clean	Ea.	.52	9.35		9.87	
Minimum Charge	Job		202		202	
Doorknob						
Demolish	Ea.		16		16	Includes material and labor to install
Install	Ea.	27.50	25		52.50	residential passage lockset, keyless
Demolish and Install	Ea.	27.50	41		68.50	bored type.
Reinstall	Ea.		20.18		20.18	
Clean	Ea.	.52	9.35		9.87	
Minimum Charge	Job		202		202	
Deadbolt						
Demolish	Ea.		14		14	Includes material and labor to install a
Install	Ea.	67	29		96	deadbolt.
Demolish and Install	Ea.	67	43		110	
Reinstall	Ea.		23.06		23.06	
Clean	Ea.	.52	9.35		9.87	
Minimum Charge	Job		202		202	
Lever Handle						
Demolish	Ea.		16		16	Includes material and labor to install
Install	Ea.	37.50	40.50		78	residential passage lockset, keyless
Demolish and Install	Ea.	37.50	56.50		94	bored type with lever handle.
Reinstall	Ea.		32.29		32.29	
Clean	Ea.	.52	9.35		9.87	
Minimum Charge	Job		202		202	
Closer						
Demolish	Ea.		8.40		8.40	Includes material and labor to install
Install	Ea.	144	62		206	pneumatic light duty closer for interior
Demolish and Install	Ea.	144	70.40		214.40	type doors.
Reinstall	Ea.		49.67		49.67	
Clean	Ea.	.26	12.45		12.71	
Minimum Charge	Job		202		202	

Finish Carpentry

Hollow Core Door

Hollow Core Door	Unit	Material	Labor	Equip.	Total	Specification
Push Plate						
Demolish	Ea.		12.45		12.45	Includes material and labor to install
Install	Ea.	23.50	33.50		57	bronze push-pull plate.
Demolish and Install	Ea.	23.50	45.95		69.45	
Reinstall	Ea.		26.91		26.91	
Clean	Ea.	.52	9.35		9.87	
Minimum Charge	Job		202		202	
Kickplate						
Demolish	Ea.		12.45		12.45	Includes material and labor to install
Install	Ea.	28.50	27		55.50	aluminum kickplate, 10" x 28".
Demolish and Install	Ea.	28.50	39.45		67.95	
Reinstall	Ea.		21.53		21.53	
Clean	Ea.	.52	9.35		9.87	
Minimum Charge	Job		202		202	
Exit Sign						
Demolish	Ea.		22		22	Includes material and labor to install a
Install	Ea.	105	54.50		159.50	wall mounted interior electric exit sign.
Demolish and Install	Ea.	105	76.50		181.50	
Reinstall	Ea.		43.72		43.72	
Clean	Ea.	.04	6.85		6.89	
Minimum Charge	Job		202		202	
Jamb						
Demolish	Ea.		28		28	Includes material and labor to install
Install	Ea.	103	10.90		113.90	flat pine jamb with square cut heads
Demolish and Install	Ea.	103	38.90		141.90	and rabbeted sides for 6' 8" high and
Clean	Ea.	.17	7.50		7.67	3-9/16" door including trim sets for
Paint	Ea.	6	23		29	both sides.
Minimum Charge	Job		202		202	
Shave & Refit						
Install	Ea.		33.50		33.50	Includes labor to shave and rework
Minimum Charge	Job		202		202	door to fit opening at the job site.

Solid Core Door

Solid Core Door	Unit	Material	Labor	Equip.	Total	Specification
Pre-hung Wood						
2' 4" x 6' 8"						
Demolish	Ea.		37.50		37.50	Cost includes material and labor to
Install	Ea.	241	23.50		264.50	install 2' 4" x 6' 8" pre-hung 1-3/4"
Demolish and Install	Ea.	241	61		302	door, 4-1/2" split jamb, including
Reinstall	Ea.		23.74		23.74	casing and stop, hinges, aluminum sill,
Clean	Ea.	5.20	12.45		17.65	weatherstripping.
Paint	Ea.	9.55	49.50		59.05	
Minimum Charge	Job		202		202	
2' 6" x 6' 8"						
Demolish	Ea.		37.50		37.50	Cost includes material and labor to
Install	Ea.	237	23.50		260.50	install 2' 6" x 6' 8" pre-hung 1-3/4"
Demolish and Install	Ea.	237	61		298	door, 4-1/2" split jamb, including
Reinstall	Ea.		23.74		23.74	casing and stop, hinges, aluminum sill,
Clean	Ea.	5.20	12.45		17.65	weatherstripping.
Paint	Ea.	9.55	49.50		59.05	
Minimum Charge	Job		202		202	

Finish Carpentry

Solid Core Door

Solid Core Door	Unit	Material	Labor	Equip.	Total	Specification
2′ 8″ x 6′ 8″						
Demolish	Ea.		37.50		37.50	Cost includes material and labor to
Install	Ea.	220	23.50		243.50	install 2′ 8″ x 6′ 8″ pre-hung 1-3/4″
Demolish and Install	Ea.	220	61		281	door, 4-1/2″ split jamb, including
Reinstall	Ea.		23.74		23.74	casing and stop, hinges, aluminum sill,
Clean	Ea.	5.20	12.45		17.65	weatherstripping.
Paint	Ea.	9.55	49.50		59.05	
Minimum Charge	Job		202		202	
3′ x 6′ 8″						
Demolish	Ea.		37.50		37.50	Cost includes material and labor to
Install	Ea.	229	25		254	install 3′ x 6′ 8″ pre-hung 1-3/4″
Demolish and Install	Ea.	229	62.50		291.50	door, including casing and stop,
Reinstall	Ea.		25.23		25.23	hinges, jamb, aluminum sill,
Clean	Ea.	5.20	12.45		17.65	weatherstripped.
Paint	Ea.	9.55	49.50		59.05	
Minimum Charge	Job		202		202	
3′ 6″ x 6′ 8″						
Demolish	Ea.		37.50		37.50	Cost includes material and labor to
Install	Ea.	385	27		412	install 3′ 6″ x 6′ 8″ pre-hung 1-3/4″
Demolish and Install	Ea.	385	64.50		449.50	door, 4-1/2″ split jamb, including
Reinstall	Ea.		26.91		26.91	casing and stop, hinges, aluminum sill,
Clean	Ea.	5.20	12.45		17.65	weatherstripping.
Paint	Ea.	9.55	49.50		59.05	
Minimum Charge	Job		202		202	
Raised Panel						
Demolish	Ea.		37.50		37.50	Cost includes material and labor to
Install	Ea.	475	22.50		497.50	install 3′ x 6′ 8″ pre-hung 1-3/4″
Demolish and Install	Ea.	475	60		535	door, jamb, including casing and
Reinstall	Ea.		22.42		22.42	stop, hinges, aluminum sill,
Clean	Ea.	5.20	12.45		17.65	weatherstripping.
Paint	Ea.	9.55	115		124.55	
Minimum Charge	Job		202		202	
Stain						
Install	Ea.	6.20	29		35.20	Includes labor and material to stain
Minimum Charge	Job		173		173	single door and trim on both sides.

Bifold Door

Bifold Door	Unit	Material	Labor	Equip.	Total	Specification
Wood, Single						
3′						
Demolish	Ea.		28		28	Cost includes material and labor to
Install	Ea.	62	62		124	install 3′ wide solid wood bi-fold door
Demolish and Install	Ea.	62	90		152	not including jamb, trim, track, and
Reinstall	Ea.		62.09		62.09	hardware.
Clean	Ea.	5.20	12.45		17.65	
Paint	Ea.	8.65	49.50		58.15	
Minimum Charge	Job		202		202	
5′						
Demolish	Ea.		28		28	Includes material and labor to install
Install	Ea.	111	73.50		184.50	pair of 2′ 6″ wide solid wood bi-fold
Demolish and Install	Ea.	111	101.50		212.50	doors not including jamb, trim, track,
Reinstall	Ea.		73.38		73.38	and hardware.
Clean	Ea.	2.28	21.50		23.78	
Paint	Ea.	29.50	86.50		116	
Minimum Charge	Job		202		202	

Finish Carpentry

Bifold Door

	Unit	Material	Labor	Equip.	Total	Specification
6'						
Demolish	Ea.		28		28	Includes material and labor to install
Install	Ea.	140	80.50		220.50	pair of 3' wide solid wood bi-fold
Demolish and Install	Ea.	140	108.50		248.50	doors not including jamb, trim, track,
Reinstall	Ea.		80.72		80.72	and hardware.
Clean	Ea.	2.60	25		27.60	
Paint	Ea.	29.50	86.50		116	
Minimum Charge	Job		202		202	
8'						
Demolish	Ea.		28		28	Includes material and labor to install
Install	Ea.	215	89.50		304.50	pair of 4' wide solid wood bi-fold
Demolish and Install	Ea.	215	117.50		332.50	doors not including jamb, trim, track,
Reinstall	Ea.		89.69		89.69	and hardware.
Clean	Ea.	3.58	30		33.58	
Paint	Ea.	15.45	86.50		101.95	
Minimum Charge	Job		202		202	

Mirrored

	Unit	Material	Labor	Equip.	Total	Specification
6'						
Demolish	Ea.		28		28	Includes material and labor to install
Install	Ea.	450	45		495	pair of 3' wide mirrored bi-fold doors
Demolish and Install	Ea.	450	73		523	including jamb, trim, track, and
Reinstall	Ea.		44.84		44.84	hardware.
Clean	Ea.	2.60	12.45		15.05	
Minimum Charge	Job		202		202	
8'						
Demolish	Ea.		28		28	Includes material and labor to install
Install	Ea.	710	67.50		777.50	pair of 4' wide mirrored bi-fold doors
Demolish and Install	Ea.	710	95.50		805.50	including jamb, trim, track, and
Reinstall	Ea.		67.27		67.27	hardware.
Clean	Ea.	3.58	14.95		18.53	
Minimum Charge	Job		202		202	

Louvered

	Unit	Material	Labor	Equip.	Total	Specification
3'						
Demolish	Ea.		28		28	Cost includes material and labor to
Install	Ea.	217	62		279	install 3' wide louvered bi-fold door
Demolish and Install	Ea.	217	90		307	not including jamb, trim, track, and
Reinstall	Ea.		62.09		62.09	hardware.
Clean	Ea.	5.20	12.45		17.65	
Paint	Ea.	8.65	49.50		58.15	
Minimum Charge	Job		202		202	
5'						
Demolish	Ea.		28		28	Includes material and labor to install
Install	Ea.	282	73.50		355.50	pair of 2' 6" wide louvered wood
Demolish and Install	Ea.	282	101.50		383.50	bi-fold doors not including jamb, trim,
Reinstall	Ea.		73.38		73.38	track, and hardware.
Clean	Ea.	2.28	21.50		23.78	
Paint	Ea.	29.50	86.50		116	
Minimum Charge	Job		202		202	
6'						
Demolish	Ea.		28		28	Includes material and labor to install
Install	Ea.	315	80.50		395.50	pair of 3' wide louvered wood bi-fold
Demolish and Install	Ea.	315	108.50		423.50	doors not including jamb, trim, track,
Reinstall	Ea.		80.72		80.72	and hardware.
Clean	Ea.	2.60	25		27.60	
Paint	Ea.	29.50	86.50		116	
Minimum Charge	Job		202		202	

Finish Carpentry

Bifold Door		Unit	Material	Labor	Equip.	Total	Specification
8'							
	Demolish	Ea.		28		28	Includes material and labor to install
	Install	Ea.	485	80.50		565.50	pair of 4' wide solid wood bi-fold
	Demolish and Install	Ea.	485	108.50		593.50	doors not including jamb, trim, track,
	Reinstall	Ea.		80.72		80.72	and hardware.
	Clean	Ea.	12.40	21.50		33.90	
	Paint	Ea.	15.45	86.50		101.95	
	Minimum Charge	Job		202		202	
Accordion Type							
	Demolish	S.F.		.98		.98	Includes material and labor to install
	Install	Ea.	31	80.50		111.50	vinyl folding accordion closet doors,
	Demolish and Install	Ea.	31	81.48		112.48	including track and frame.
	Reinstall	Ea.		80.72		80.72	
	Clean	S.F.	.01	.36		.37	
	Minimum Charge	Job		202		202	
Casing Trim							
Single Width							
	Demolish	Ea.		7.10		7.10	Cost includes material and labor to
	Install	Opng.	25	33.50		58.50	install 11/16" x 2-1/2" pine ranch
	Demolish and Install	Opng.	25	40.60		65.60	style casing for one side of a standard
	Reinstall	Opng.		26.91		26.91	door opening.
	Clean	Opng.	.74	2.99		3.73	
	Paint	Ea.	4.38	6.95		11.33	
	Minimum Charge	Job		202		202	
Double Width							
	Demolish	Ea.		8.45		8.45	Cost includes material and labor to
	Install	Opng.	29	40.50		69.50	install 11/16" x 2-1/2" pine ranch
	Demolish and Install	Opng.	29	48.95		77.95	style door casing for one side of a
	Reinstall	Opng.		32.29		32.29	double door opening.
	Clean	Opng.	.87	6		6.87	
	Paint	Ea.	4.38	7.85		12.23	
	Minimum Charge	Job		202		202	
Jamb							
	Demolish	Ea.		28		28	Includes material and labor to install
	Install	Ea.	103	10.90		113.90	flat pine jamb with square cut heads
	Demolish and Install	Ea.	103	38.90		141.90	and rabbeted sides for 6' 8" high and
	Clean	Ea.	.17	7.50		7.67	3-9/16" door including trim sets for
	Paint	Ea.	6	23		29	both sides.
	Minimum Charge	Job		101		101	
Stain							
	Install	Ea.	6.20	29		35.20	Includes labor and material to stain
	Minimum Charge	Job		173		173	single door and trim on both sides.
Shave & Refit							
	Install	Ea.		33.50		33.50	Includes labor to shave and rework
	Minimum Charge	Job		101		101	door to fit opening at the job site.

Finish Carpentry

Louver Door		Unit	Material	Labor	Equip.	Total	Specification
Full							
2' x 6' 8"							
	Demolish	Ea.		8		8	Cost includes material and labor to
	Install	Ea.	198	40.50		238.50	install 2' x 6' 8" pine full louver door,
	Demolish and Install	Ea.	198	48.50		246.50	jamb, hinges.
	Reinstall	Ea.		40.36		40.36	
	Clean	Ea.	9.65	37.50		47.15	
	Paint	Ea.	8.65	49.50		58.15	
	Minimum Charge	Job		202		202	
2' 8" x 6' 8"							
	Demolish	Ea.		8		8	Cost includes material and labor to
	Install	Ea.	219	40.50		259.50	install 2' 8" x 6' 8" pine full louver
	Demolish and Install	Ea.	219	48.50		267.50	door, jamb, hinges.
	Reinstall	Ea.		40.36		40.36	
	Clean	Ea.	9.65	37.50		47.15	
	Paint	Ea.	8.65	49.50		58.15	
	Minimum Charge	Job		202		202	
3' x 6' 8"							
	Demolish	Ea.		8		8	Cost includes material and labor to
	Install	Ea.	248	42.50		290.50	install 3' x 6' 8" pine full louver door,
	Demolish and Install	Ea.	248	50.50		298.50	jamb, hinges.
	Reinstall	Ea.		42.48		42.48	
	Clean	Ea.	9.65	37.50		47.15	
	Paint	Ea.	8.65	49.50		58.15	
	Minimum Charge	Job		202		202	
Half							
2' x 6' 8"							
	Demolish	Ea.		8		8	Cost includes material and labor to
	Install	Ea.	320	40.50		360.50	install 2' x 6' 8" pine half louver door,
	Demolish and Install	Ea.	320	48.50		368.50	jamb, hinges.
	Reinstall	Ea.		40.36		40.36	
	Clean	Ea.	9.65	37.50		47.15	
	Paint	Ea.	8.65	49.50		58.15	
	Minimum Charge	Job		202		202	
2' 8" x 6' 8"							
	Demolish	Ea.		8		8	Cost includes material and labor to
	Install	Ea.	345	40.50		385.50	install 2' 8" x 6' 8" pine half louver
	Demolish and Install	Ea.	345	48.50		393.50	door, jamb, hinges.
	Reinstall	Ea.		40.36		40.36	
	Clean	Ea.	9.65	37.50		47.15	
	Paint	Ea.	8.65	49.50		58.15	
	Minimum Charge	Job		202		202	
3' x 6' 8"							
	Demolish	Ea.		8		8	Cost includes material and labor to
	Install	Ea.	360	42.50		402.50	install 3' x 6' 8" pine half louver door,
	Demolish and Install	Ea.	360	50.50		410.50	jamb, hinges.
	Reinstall	Ea.		42.48		42.48	
	Clean	Ea.	9.65	37.50		47.15	
	Paint	Ea.	8.65	49.50		58.15	
	Minimum Charge	Job		202		202	
Jamb							
	Demolish	Ea.		28		28	Includes material and labor to install
	Install	Ea.	103	10.90		113.90	flat pine jamb with square cut heads
	Demolish and Install	Ea.	103	38.90		141.90	and rabbeted sides for 6' 8" high and
	Clean	Ea.	.17	7.50		7.67	3-9/16" door including trim sets for
	Paint	Ea.	6	23		29	both sides.
	Minimum Charge	Job		101		101	

Finish Carpentry

Louver Door

Louver Door		Unit	Material	Labor	Equip.	Total	Specification
Stain							Includes labor and material to stain single door and trim on both sides.
	Install	Ea.	6.20	29		35.20	
	Minimum Charge	Job		173		173	
Shave & Refit							Includes labor to shave and rework door to fit opening at the job site.
	Install	Ea.		33.50		33.50	
	Minimum Charge	Job		173		173	

Bypass Sliding Door

Bypass Sliding Door		Unit	Material	Labor	Equip.	Total	Specification
Wood							
5'							Includes material and labor to install pair of 2' 6" wide lauan hollow core wood bi-pass doors with jamb, track hardware.
	Demolish	Ea.		37.50		37.50	
	Install	Opng.	205	73.50		278.50	
	Demolish and Install	Opng.	205	111		316	
	Reinstall	Opng.		73.38		73.38	
	Clean	Ea.	2.28	21.50		23.78	
	Paint	Ea.	29.50	86.50		116	
	Minimum Charge	Job		202		202	
6'							Includes material and labor to install pair of 3' wide lauan hollow core wood bi-pass doors with jamb, track and hardware.
	Demolish	Ea.		37.50		37.50	
	Install	Opng.	230	80.50		310.50	
	Demolish and Install	Opng.	230	118		348	
	Reinstall	Opng.		80.72		80.72	
	Clean	Ea.	2.60	25		27.60	
	Paint	Ea.	29.50	86.50		116	
	Minimum Charge	Job		202		202	
8'							Includes material and labor to install pair of 4' wide lauan hollow core wood bi-pass doors with jamb, track and hardware.
	Demolish	Ea.		37.50		37.50	
	Install	Opng.	345	101		446	
	Demolish and Install	Opng.	345	138.50		483.50	
	Reinstall	Opng.		100.90		100.90	
	Clean	Ea.	3.58	30		33.58	
	Paint	Ea.	15.45	86.50		101.95	
	Minimum Charge	Job		202		202	
Mirrored							
6'							Includes material and labor to install pair of 3' wide mirrored bi-pass doors with jamb, trim, track hardware.
	Demolish	Ea.		37.50		37.50	
	Install	Opng.	268	80.50		348.50	
	Demolish and Install	Opng.	268	118		386	
	Reinstall	Opng.		80.72		80.72	
	Clean	Ea.	2.60	12.45		15.05	
	Minimum Charge	Job		202		202	
8'							Includes material and labor to install pair of 4' wide mirrored bi-pass doors with jamb, trim, track hardware.
	Demolish	Ea.		37.50		37.50	
	Install	Opng.	470	89.50		559.50	
	Demolish and Install	Opng.	470	127		597	
	Reinstall	Opng.		89.69		89.69	
	Clean	Ea.	3.58	14.95		18.53	
	Minimum Charge	Job		202		202	

Finish Carpentry

Bypass Sliding Door

Bypass Sliding Door	Unit	Material	Labor	Equip.	Total	Specification
Casing Trim						
Single Width						
Demolish	Ea.		7.10		7.10	Cost includes material and labor to
Install	Opng.	25	33.50		58.50	install 11/16″ x 2-1/2″ pine ranch
Demolish and Install	Opng.	25	40.60		65.60	style casing for one side of a standard
Reinstall	Opng.		26.91		26.91	door opening.
Clean	Opng.	.74	2.99		3.73	
Paint	Ea.	4.38	6.95		11.33	
Minimum Charge	Job		202		202	
Double Width						
Demolish	Ea.		8.45		8.45	Cost includes material and labor to
Install	Opng.	29	40.50		69.50	install 11/16″ x 2-1/2″ pine ranch
Demolish and Install	Opng.	29	48.95		77.95	style door casing for one side of a
Reinstall	Opng.		32.29		32.29	double door opening.
Clean	Opng.	.87	6		6.87	
Paint	Ea.	4.38	7.85		12.23	
Minimum Charge	Job		202		202	
Jamb						
Demolish	Ea.		28		28	Includes material and labor to install
Install	Ea.	103	10.90		113.90	flat pine jamb with square cut heads
Demolish and Install	Ea.	103	38.90		141.90	and rabbeted sides for 6′ 8″ high and
Clean	Ea.	.17	7.50		7.67	3-9/16″ door including trim sets for
Paint	Ea.	6	23		29	both sides.
Minimum Charge	Job		101		101	
Stain						
Install	Ea.	6.20	29		35.20	Includes labor and material to stain
Minimum Charge	Job		173		173	single door and trim on both sides.
Shave & Refit						
Install	Ea.		33.50		33.50	Includes labor to shave and rework
Minimum Charge	Job		101		101	door to fit opening at the job site.

Base Molding

Base Molding	Unit	Material	Labor	Equip.	Total	Specification
One Piece						
1-5/8″						
Demolish	L.F.		.55		.55	Includes material and labor to install
Install	L.F.	.41	1.19		1.60	pine or birch base molding.
Demolish and Install	L.F.	.41	1.74		2.15	
Reinstall	L.F.		.96		.96	
Clean	L.F.	.04	.17		.21	
Paint	L.F.	.04	.38		.42	
Minimum Charge	Job		202		202	
2-1/2″						
Demolish	L.F.		.55		.55	Cost includes material and labor to
Install	L.F.	.61	1.24		1.85	install 1/2″ x 2-1/2″ pine or birch
Demolish and Install	L.F.	.61	1.79		2.40	base molding.
Reinstall	L.F.		.99		.99	
Clean	L.F.	.04	.17		.21	
Paint	L.F.	.04	.38		.42	
Minimum Charge	Job		202		202	

Finish Carpentry

Base Molding		Unit	Material	Labor	Equip.	Total	Specification
3-1/2"							
	Demolish	L.F.		.55		.55	Cost includes material and labor to
	Install	L.F.	1.71	1.29		3	install 9/16" x 3-1/2" pine or birch
	Demolish and Install	L.F.	1.71	1.84		3.55	base molding.
	Reinstall	L.F.		1.03		1.03	
	Clean	L.F.	.04	.17		.21	
	Paint	L.F.	.07	.41		.48	
	Minimum Charge	Job		202		202	
6"							
	Demolish	L.F.		.55		.55	Cost includes material and labor to
	Install	L.F.	.81	1.41		2.22	install 1" x 6" pine or birch base
	Demolish and Install	L.F.	.81	1.96		2.77	molding.
	Reinstall	L.F.		1.13		1.13	
	Clean	L.F.	.04	.25		.29	
	Paint	L.F.	.09	.52		.61	
	Minimum Charge	Job		202		202	
8"							
	Demolish	L.F.		.66		.66	Cost includes material and labor to
	Install	L.F.	1.10	1.55		2.65	install 1" x 8" pine or birch base
	Demolish and Install	L.F.	1.10	2.21		3.31	molding.
	Reinstall	L.F.		1.24		1.24	
	Clean	L.F.	.06	.30		.36	
	Paint	L.F.	.10	.58		.68	
	Minimum Charge	Job		202		202	
Premium / Custom Grade							
	Demolish	L.F.		.66		.66	Includes material and labor to install
	Install	L.F.	4.20	3.88		8.08	custom 2 or 3 piece oak or other
	Demolish and Install	L.F.	4.20	4.54		8.74	hardwood, stain grade trim.
	Reinstall	L.F.		3.10		3.10	
	Clean	L.F.	.06	.30		.36	
	Paint	L.F.	.11	.58		.69	
	Minimum Charge	Job		202		202	
One Piece Oak							
1-5/8"							
	Demolish	L.F.		.55		.55	Cost includes material and labor to
	Install	L.F.	.71	1.19		1.90	install 1/2" x 1-5/8" oak base
	Demolish and Install	L.F.	.71	1.74		2.45	molding.
	Reinstall	L.F.		.96		.96	
	Clean	L.F.	.04	.17		.21	
	Paint	L.F.	.11	.51		.62	
	Minimum Charge	Job		202		202	
2-1/2"							
	Demolish	L.F.		.55		.55	Cost includes material and labor to
	Install	L.F.	1.07	1.22		2.29	install 1/2" x 2-1/2" oak base
	Demolish and Install	L.F.	1.07	1.77		2.84	molding.
	Reinstall	L.F.		.97		.97	
	Clean	L.F.	.04	.17		.21	
	Paint	L.F.	.11	.52		.63	
	Minimum Charge	Job		202		202	
3-1/2"							
	Demolish	L.F.		.55		.55	Cost includes material and labor to
	Install	L.F.	2.62	1.24		3.86	install 1/2" x 3-1/2" oak base
	Demolish and Install	L.F.	2.62	1.79		4.41	molding.
	Reinstall	L.F.		.99		.99	
	Clean	L.F.	.04	.17		.21	
	Paint	L.F.	.11	.53		.64	
	Minimum Charge	Job		202		202	

Finish Carpentry

Base Molding

	Unit	Material	Labor	Equip.	Total	Specification
6"						
Demolish	L.F.		.55		.55	Cost includes material and labor to
Install	L.F.	4.77	1.41		6.18	install 1" x 6" oak base molding.
Demolish and Install	L.F.	4.77	1.96		6.73	
Reinstall	L.F.		1.13		1.13	
Clean	L.F.	.06	.30		.36	
Paint	L.F.	.12	.55		.67	
Minimum Charge	Job		202		202	
8"						
Demolish	L.F.		.66		.66	Cost includes material and labor to
Install	L.F.	6.45	1.55		8	install 1" x 8" oak base molding.
Demolish and Install	L.F.	6.45	2.21		8.66	
Reinstall	L.F.		1.24		1.24	
Clean	L.F.	.06	.30		.36	
Paint	L.F.	.12	.58		.70	
Minimum Charge	Job		202		202	

Vinyl Base Molding

	Unit	Material	Labor	Equip.	Total	Specification
2-1/2"						
Demolish	L.F.		.55		.55	Cost includes material and labor to
Install	L.F.	1.10	1.15		2.25	install 2-1/2" vinyl or rubber cove
Demolish and Install	L.F.	1.10	1.70		2.80	base including adhesive.
Reinstall	L.F.		1.15		1.15	
Clean	L.F.		.27		.27	
Minimum Charge	Job		182		182	
4"						
Demolish	L.F.		.55		.55	Cost includes material and labor to
Install	L.F.	1.19	1.15		2.34	install 4" vinyl or rubber cove base
Demolish and Install	L.F.	1.19	1.70		2.89	including adhesive.
Reinstall	L.F.		1.15		1.15	
Clean	L.F.		.27		.27	
Minimum Charge	Job		182		182	
6"						
Demolish	L.F.		.55		.55	Cost includes material and labor to
Install	L.F.	1.65	1.15		2.80	install 6" vinyl or rubber cove base
Demolish and Install	L.F.	1.65	1.70		3.35	including adhesive.
Reinstall	L.F.		1.15		1.15	
Clean	L.F.		.27		.27	
Minimum Charge	Job		182		182	

Prefinished

	Unit	Material	Labor	Equip.	Total	Specification
Demolish	L.F.		.55		.55	Cost includes material and labor to
Install	L.F.	.82	1.29		2.11	install 9/16" x 3-5/16" prefinished
Demolish and Install	L.F.	.82	1.84		2.66	base molding.
Reinstall	L.F.		1.03		1.03	
Clean	L.F.	.04	.18		.22	
Paint	L.F.	.07	.41		.48	
Minimum Charge	Job		202		202	

Shoe

	Unit	Material	Labor	Equip.	Total	Specification
Demolish	L.F.		.55		.55	Includes material and labor to install
Install	L.F.	.41	1.19		1.60	pine or birch base molding.
Demolish and Install	L.F.	.41	1.74		2.15	
Reinstall	L.F.		.96		.96	
Clean	L.F.	.04	.17		.21	
Paint	L.F.	.14	.55		.69	
Minimum Charge	Job		202		202	

Finish Carpentry

Base Molding

Base Molding		Unit	Material	Labor	Equip.	Total	Specification
Carpeted							Includes material and labor to install
	Demolish	L.F.		.22		.22	carpet baseboard with adhesive.
	Install	L.F.	1.49	2.19		3.68	
	Demolish and Install	L.F.	1.49	2.41		3.90	
	Reinstall	L.F.		1.75		1.75	
	Clean	L.F.		.11		.11	
	Minimum Charge	Job		181		181	
Ceramic Tile							Includes material and labor to install
	Demolish	L.F.		1.21		1.21	thin set ceramic tile cove base
	Install	L.F.	4.19	5.05		9.24	including grout.
	Demolish and Install	L.F.	4.19	6.26		10.45	
	Clean	L.F.		.57		.57	
	Minimum Charge	Job		181		181	
Quarry Tile							Includes material and labor to install
	Demolish	L.F.		1.21		1.21	quarry tile base including grout.
	Install	L.F.	5.85	5.90		11.75	
	Demolish and Install	L.F.	5.85	7.11		12.96	
	Clean	L.F.		.57		.57	
	Minimum Charge	Job		181		181	
Caulk and Renail							Includes labor and material to renail
	Install	L.F.	.01	.63		.64	base and caulk where necessary.
	Minimum Charge	Job		202		202	

Molding

Molding		Unit	Material	Labor	Equip.	Total	Specification
Oak Base							Cost includes material and labor to
	Demolish	L.F.		.55		.55	install 1/2" x 2-1/2" oak base
	Install	L.F.	1.07	1.22		2.29	molding.
	Demolish and Install	L.F.	1.07	1.77		2.84	
	Reinstall	L.F.		.97		.97	
	Clean	L.F.	.04	.17		.21	
	Paint	L.F.	.11	.52		.63	
	Minimum Charge	Job		202		202	
Shoe							Includes material and labor to install
	Demolish	L.F.		.55		.55	pine or birch base molding.
	Install	L.F.	.41	1.19		1.60	
	Demolish and Install	L.F.	.41	1.74		2.15	
	Reinstall	L.F.		.96		.96	
	Clean	L.F.	.04	.17		.21	
	Paint	L.F.	.14	.55		.69	
	Minimum Charge	Job		202		202	
Quarter Round							Includes material and labor to install
	Demolish	L.F.		.55		.55	pine base quarter round molding.
	Install	L.F.	.66	1.58		2.24	
	Demolish and Install	L.F.	.66	2.13		2.79	
	Reinstall	L.F.		1.27		1.27	
	Clean	L.F.	.04	.17		.21	
	Paint	L.F.	.10	.87		.97	
	Minimum Charge	Job		202		202	
Chair Rail							Cost includes material and labor to
	Demolish	L.F.		.55		.55	install 5/8" x 2-1/2" oak chair rail
	Install	L.F.	1.57	1.49		3.06	molding.
	Demolish and Install	L.F.	1.57	2.04		3.61	
	Reinstall	L.F.		1.20		1.20	
	Clean	L.F.	.04	.17		.21	
	Paint	L.F.	.10	.87		.97	
	Minimum Charge	Job		202		202	

Finish Carpentry

Molding

	Unit	Material	Labor	Equip.	Total	Specification
Crown						
Demolish	L.F.		.55		.55	Includes material and labor to install
Install	L.F.	2.53	1.61		4.14	unfinished pine crown molding.
Demolish and Install	L.F.	2.53	2.16		4.69	
Reinstall	L.F.		1.29		1.29	
Clean	L.F.	.06	.23		.29	
Paint	L.F.	.10	.87		.97	
Minimum Charge	Job		202		202	
Cove						
Demolish	L.F.		.55		.55	Cost includes material and labor to
Install	L.F.	2.05	1.58		3.63	install 1/2" x 2-3/4" pine cove
Demolish and Install	L.F.	2.05	2.13		4.18	molding.
Reinstall	L.F.		1.27		1.27	
Clean	L.F.	.04	.17		.21	
Paint	L.F.	.10	.87		.97	
Minimum Charge	Job		202		202	
Corner						
Demolish	L.F.		.55		.55	Includes material and labor to install
Install	L.F.	1.60	.63		2.23	inside or outside pine corner molding.
Demolish and Install	L.F.	1.60	1.18		2.78	
Reinstall	L.F.		.50		.50	
Clean	L.F.	.04	.17		.21	
Paint	L.F.	.10	.87		.97	
Minimum Charge	Job		202		202	
Picture						
Demolish	L.F.		.55		.55	Cost includes material and labor to
Install	L.F.	1.46	1.68		3.14	install 9/16" x 2-1/2" pine casing.
Demolish and Install	L.F.	1.46	2.23		3.69	
Reinstall	L.F.		1.35		1.35	
Clean	L.F.	.04	.17		.21	
Paint	L.F.	.10	.87		.97	
Minimum Charge	Job		202		202	
Single Cased Opening						
Demolish	Ea.		28		28	Includes material and labor to install
Install	Ea.	26	25		51	flat pine jamb with square cut heads
Demolish and Install	Ea.	26	53		79	and rabbeted sides for 6' 8" high
Clean	Ea.	.36	6.25		6.61	opening including trim sets for both
Paint	Ea.	1.16	8.65		9.81	sides.
Minimum Charge	Job		202		202	
Double Cased Opening						
Demolish	Ea.		28		28	Includes material and labor to install
Install	Ea.	51.50	29		80.50	flat pine jamb with square cut heads
Demolish and Install	Ea.	51.50	57		108.50	and rabbeted sides for 6' 8" high
Clean	Ea.	.42	7.30		7.72	opening including trim sets for both
Paint	Ea.	1.34	10.20		11.54	sides.
Minimum Charge	Job		202		202	

Window Trim Set

	Unit	Material	Labor	Equip.	Total	Specification
Single						
Demolish	Ea.		7.40		7.40	Cost includes material and labor to
Install	Opng.	42	40.50		82.50	install 11/16" x 2-1/2" pine ranch
Demolish and Install	Opng.	42	47.90		89.90	style window casing.
Reinstall	Opng.		32.29		32.29	
Clean	Ea.	.52	4.27		4.79	
Paint	Ea.	1.08	8.25		9.33	
Minimum Charge	Job		202		202	

Finish Carpentry

Window Trim Set

	Unit	Material	Labor	Equip.	Total	Specification
Double						
Demolish	Ea.		8.30		8.30	Cost includes material and labor to
Install	Ea.	54.50	50.50		105	install 11/16" x 2-1/2" pine ranch
Demolish and Install	Ea.	54.50	58.80		113.30	style trim for casing one side of a
Reinstall	Ea.		40.36		40.36	double window opening.
Clean	Ea.	.92	4.99		5.91	
Paint	Ea.	1.82	13.85		15.67	
Minimum Charge	Job		202		202	
Triple						
Demolish	Ea.		9.50		9.50	Cost includes material and labor to
Install	Opng.	69	67.50		136.50	install 11/16" x 2-1/2" pine ranch
Demolish and Install	Opng.	69	77		146	style trim for casing one side of a
Reinstall	Opng.		53.81		53.81	triple window opening.
Clean	Ea.	1.30	6		7.30	
Paint	Ea.	2.54	19.25		21.79	
Minimum Charge	Job		202		202	
Window Casing Per L.F.						
Demolish	L.F.		.55		.55	Cost includes material and labor to
Install	L.F.	1.46	1.68		3.14	install 11/16" x 2-1/2" pine ranch
Demolish and Install	L.F.	1.46	2.23		3.69	style trim for casing.
Reinstall	L.F.		1.35		1.35	
Clean	L.F.	.04	.17		.21	
Paint	L.F.	.10	.87		.97	
Minimum Charge	Job		202		202	

Window Sill

	Unit	Material	Labor	Equip.	Total	Specification
Wood						
Demolish	L.F.		.55		.55	Includes material and labor to install
Install	L.F.	2.50	2.02		4.52	flat, wood window stool.
Demolish and Install	L.F.	2.50	2.57		5.07	
Reinstall	L.F.		1.61		1.61	
Clean	L.F.	.04	.17		.21	
Paint	L.F.	.10	.87		.97	
Minimum Charge	Job		202		202	
Marble						
Demolish	L.F.		.83		.83	Includes material and labor to install
Install	L.F.	9.85	8.40		18.25	marble window sills, 6" x 3/4" thick.
Demolish and Install	L.F.	9.85	9.23		19.08	
Reinstall	L.F.		6.74		6.74	
Clean	L.F.	.04	.17		.21	
Minimum Charge	Job		181		181	

Shelving

	Unit	Material	Labor	Equip.	Total	Specification
Pine						
18"						
Demolish	L.F.		.95		.95	Cost includes material and labor to
Install	L.F.	7	4.25		11.25	install 1" thick custom shelving board
Demolish and Install	L.F.	7	5.20		12.20	18" wide.
Reinstall	L.F.		3.40		3.40	
Clean	L.F.	.08	.50		.58	
Paint	L.F.	1.31	.55		1.86	
Minimum Charge	Job		202		202	

Finish Carpentry

Shelving

Shelving		Unit	Material	Labor	Equip.	Total	Specification
24"							
	Demolish	L.F.		.95		.95	Cost includes material and labor to
	Install	L.F.	9.35	4.75		14.10	install 1" thick custom shelving board.
	Demolish and Install	L.F.	9.35	5.70		15.05	
	Reinstall	L.F.		3.80		3.80	
	Clean	L.F.	.10	.75		.85	
	Paint	L.F.	1.78	.73		2.51	
	Minimum Charge	Job		202		202	
Particle Board							
	Demolish	L.F.		.87		.87	Cost includes material and labor to
	Install	L.F.	1.42	2.12		3.54	install 3/4" thick particle shelving
	Demolish and Install	L.F.	1.42	2.99		4.41	board 18" wide.
	Reinstall	L.F.		1.70		1.70	
	Clean	L.F.	.08	.50		.58	
	Paint	S.F.	.12	.81		.93	
	Minimum Charge	Job		202		202	
Plywood							
	Demolish	L.F.		.87		.87	Cost includes material and labor to
	Install	L.F.	.99	6.20		7.19	install 3/4" thick plywood shelving
	Demolish and Install	L.F.	.99	7.07		8.06	board.
	Reinstall	L.F.		4.97		4.97	
	Clean	L.F.	.08	.50		.58	
	Paint	S.F.	.12	.81		.93	
	Minimum Charge	Job		202		202	
Hardwood (oak)							
	Demolish	L.F.		.87		.87	Includes material and labor to install
	Install	L.F.	5.15	2.78		7.93	oak shelving, 1" x 12", incl. cleats and
	Demolish and Install	L.F.	5.15	3.65		8.80	bracing.
	Reinstall	L.F.		2.23		2.23	
	Clean	L.F.	.08	.50		.58	
	Paint	S.F.	.12	.81		.93	
	Minimum Charge	Job		202		202	
Custom Bookcase							
	Demolish	L.F.		11.10		11.10	Includes material and labor to install
	Install	L.F.	36	40.50		76.50	custom modular bookcase unit with
	Demolish and Install	L.F.	36	51.60		87.60	clear pine faced frames, shelves 12"
	Reinstall	L.F.		32.29		32.29	O.C., 7' high, 8" deep.
	Clean	L.F.	2.08	10.70		12.78	
	Paint	L.F.	1.40	26.50		27.90	
	Minimum Charge	Job		202		202	
Glass							
	Demolish	L.F.		.87		.87	Includes material and labor to install
	Install	L.F.	31.50	2.78		34.28	glass shelving, 1" x 12", incl. cleats
	Demolish and Install	L.F.	31.50	3.65		35.15	and bracing.
	Reinstall	L.F.		2.23		2.23	
	Clean	L.F.	.09	.46		.55	
	Minimum Charge	Job		196		196	

Closet Shelving

Closet Shelving		Unit	Material	Labor	Equip.	Total	Specification
Closet Shelf and Rod							
	Demolish	L.F.		.87		.87	Cost includes material and labor to
	Install	L.F.	2.45	6.75		9.20	install 1" thick custom shelving board
	Demolish and Install	L.F.	2.45	7.62		10.07	18" wide and 1" diameter clothes pole
	Reinstall	L.F.		5.38		5.38	with brackets 3' O.C.
	Clean	L.F.	.06	.37		.43	
	Paint	L.F.	.21	.87		1.08	
	Minimum Charge	Job		202		202	

Finish Carpentry

Closet Shelving

Closet Shelving	Unit	Material	Labor	Equip.	Total	Specification
Clothing Rod						
Demolish	L.F.		.58		.58	Includes material and labor to install
Install	L.F.	2.12	2.02		4.14	fir closet pole, 1-5/8" diameter.
Demolish and Install	L.F.	2.12	2.60		4.72	
Reinstall	L.F.		1.61		1.61	
Clean	L.F.	.06	.51		.57	
Paint	L.F.	.20	.94		1.14	
Minimum Charge	Job		202		202	

Stair Assemblies

Stair Assemblies	Unit	Material	Labor	Equip.	Total	Specification
Straight Hardwood						
Demolish	Ea.		390		390	Includes material and labor to install
Install	Flight	1125	269		1394	factory cut and assembled straight
Demolish and Install	Flight	1125	659		1784	closed box stairs with oak treads and
Clean	Flight	5.20	25.50		30.70	prefinished stair rail with balusters.
Paint	Flight	18.30	46		64.30	
Minimum Charge	Job		202		202	
Clear Oak Tread						
Demolish	Ea.		10.20		10.20	Includes material and labor to install
Install	Ea.	82.50	22.50		105	1-1/4" thick clear oak treads per riser.
Demolish and Install	Ea.	82.50	32.70		115.20	
Clean	Ea.	.17	2.55		2.72	
Paint	Ea.	.62	2.57		3.19	
Minimum Charge	Job		202		202	
Landing						
Demolish	S.F.		3.46		3.46	Includes material and labor to install
Install	S.F.	9.90	22.50		32.40	clear oak landing.
Demolish and Install	S.F.	9.90	25.96		35.86	
Clean	S.F.		.37		.37	
Paint	S.F.	.39	.86		1.25	
Minimum Charge	Job		202		202	
Refinish / Stain						
Install	S.F.	1.28	2.30		3.58	Includes labor and material to sand
Minimum Charge	Job		173		173	and finish (3 passes) with two coats of
						urethane on a new floor.
Spiral Hardwood						
Demolish	Ea.		390		390	Cost includes material and labor to
Install	Flight	4000	540		4540	install 4' - 6' diameter spiral stairs with
Demolish and Install	Flight	4000	930		4930	oak treads, factory cut and assembled
Clean	Flight	5.20	25.50		30.70	with double handrails.
Paint	Flight	18.30	46		64.30	
Minimum Charge	Job		202		202	

Stairs

Stairs	Unit	Material	Labor	Equip.	Total	Specification
Disappearing						
Demolish	Ea.		21		21	Includes material and labor to install a
Install	Ea.	239	115		354	folding staircase.
Demolish and Install	Ea.	239	136		375	
Reinstall	Ea.		92.25		92.25	
Clean	Ea.	.78	18.70		19.48	
Minimum Charge	Job		202		202	

Finish Carpentry

Stair Components

	Unit	Material	Labor	Equip.	Total	Specification
Handrail w / Balusters						
Demolish	L.F.		2.77		2.77	Includes material and labor to install
Install	L.F.	40.50	8.40		48.90	prefinished assembled stair rail with
Demolish and Install	L.F.	40.50	11.17		51.67	brackets, turned balusters and newel.
Clean	L.F.	1.05	2.06		3.11	
Paint	L.F.	1.99	4.08		6.07	
Minimum Charge	Job		202		202	
Bannister						
Demolish	L.F.		2.77		2.77	Includes material and labor to install
Install	L.F.	38	6.75		44.75	built-up oak railings.
Demolish and Install	L.F.	38	9.52		47.52	
Clean	L.F.	1.05	1.87		2.92	
Paint	L.F.	1.99	3.15		5.14	
Minimum Charge	Job		202		202	

Wall and Base Cabinets

Countertop

Wall Cabinets	Unit	Material	Labor	Equip.	Total	Specification
Good Grade Laminated						
12″ Wide, 1 Door						
Demolish	Ea.		8.30		8.30	Includes material and labor to install
Install	Ea.	153	36.50		189.50	good modular unit with melamine
Demolish and Install	Ea.	153	44.80		197.80	laminated to particle board, in
Reinstall	Ea.		29.35		29.35	textured colors or wood grain print
Clean	Ea.	.78	5.75		6.53	finish, hinges and pulls.
Paint	Ea.	.59	12.35		12.94	
Minimum Charge	Job		202		202	
15″ Wide, 1 Door						
Demolish	Ea.		10.40		10.40	Includes material and labor to install
Install	Ea.	172	37.50		209.50	good modular unit with melamine
Demolish and Install	Ea.	172	47.90		219.90	laminated to particle board, in
Reinstall	Ea.		30.18		30.18	textured colors or wood grain print
Clean	Ea.	.98	7.10		8.08	finish, hinges and pulls.
Paint	Ea.	.75	15.75		16.50	
Minimum Charge	Job		202		202	
18″ Wide, 1 Door						
Demolish	Ea.		12.55		12.55	Includes material and labor to install
Install	Ea.	189	38.50		227.50	good modular unit with melamine
Demolish and Install	Ea.	189	51.05		240.05	laminated to particle board, in
Reinstall	Ea.		30.90		30.90	textured colors or wood grain print
Clean	Ea.	1.17	8.55		9.72	finish, hinges and pulls.
Paint	Ea.	.89	18.25		19.14	
Minimum Charge	Job		202		202	
21″ Wide, 1 Door						
Demolish	Ea.		14.45		14.45	Includes material and labor to install
Install	Ea.	198	39		237	good modular unit with melamine
Demolish and Install	Ea.	198	53.45		251.45	laminated to particle board, in
Reinstall	Ea.		31.35		31.35	textured colors or wood grain print
Clean	Ea.	1.36	9.95		11.31	finish, hinges and pulls.
Paint	Ea.	1.05	21.50		22.55	
Minimum Charge	Job		202		202	
24″ w / Blind Corner						
Demolish	Ea.		16.60		16.60	Includes material and labor to install
Install	Ea.	220	40		260	good modular unit with melamine
Demolish and Install	Ea.	220	56.60		276.60	laminated to particle board, in
Reinstall	Ea.		31.81		31.81	textured colors or wood grain print
Clean	Ea.	1.56	11.50		13.06	finish, hinges and pulls.
Paint	Ea.	1.19	24.50		25.69	
Minimum Charge	Job		202		202	

Cabinets and Countertops

Wall Cabinets

	Unit	Material	Labor	Equip.	Total	Specification
27″ Wide, 2 Door						
Demolish	Ea.		18.45		18.45	Includes material and labor to install
Install	Ea.	242	41		283	good modular unit with melamine
Demolish and Install	Ea.	242	59.45		301.45	laminated to particle board, in
Reinstall	Ea.		32.61		32.61	textured colors or wood grain print
Clean	Ea.	1.76	13		14.76	finish, hinges and pulls.
Paint	Ea.	1.35	29		30.35	
Minimum Charge	Job		202		202	
30″ Wide, 2 Door						
Demolish	Ea.		21		21	Includes material and labor to install
Install	Ea.	251	42		293	good modular unit with melamine
Demolish and Install	Ea.	251	63		314	laminated to particle board, in
Reinstall	Ea.		33.46		33.46	textured colors or wood grain print
Clean	Ea.	1.95	14.25		16.20	finish, hinges and pulls.
Paint	Ea.	1.50	31.50		33	
Minimum Charge	Job		202		202	
36″ Wide, 2 Door						
Demolish	Ea.		24.50		24.50	Includes material and labor to install
Install	Ea.	287	43		330	good modular unit with melamine
Demolish and Install	Ea.	287	67.50		354.50	laminated to particle board, in
Reinstall	Ea.		34.35		34.35	textured colors or wood grain print
Clean	Ea.	2.34	17.60		19.94	finish, hinges and pulls.
Paint	Ea.	1.80	38.50		40.30	
Minimum Charge	Job		202		202	
48″ Wide, 2 Door						
Demolish	Ea.		33		33	Includes material and labor to install
Install	Ea.	360	44		404	good modular unit with melamine
Demolish and Install	Ea.	360	77		437	laminated to particle board, in
Reinstall	Ea.		35.10		35.10	textured colors or wood grain print
Clean	Ea.	3.12	23		26.12	finish, hinges and pulls.
Paint	Ea.	2.40	49.50		51.90	
Minimum Charge	Job		202		202	
Above-Appliance						
Demolish	Ea.		21		21	Includes material and labor to install
Install	Ea.	168	32.50		200.50	good modular unit with melamine
Demolish and Install	Ea.	168	53.50		221.50	laminated to particle board, in
Reinstall	Ea.		26.04		26.04	textured colors or wood grain print
Clean	Ea.	1.95	14.25		16.20	finish, hinges and pulls.
Paint	Ea.	1.50	31.50		33	
Minimum Charge	Job		202		202	

Better Grade Wood

	Unit	Material	Labor	Equip.	Total	Specification
12″ Wide, 1 Door						
Demolish	Ea.		8.30		8.30	Includes material and labor to install
Install	Ea.	204	36.50		240.50	custom modular unit with solid
Demolish and Install	Ea.	204	44.80		248.80	hardwood faced frames, hardwood
Reinstall	Ea.		29.35		29.35	door frames and drawer fronts,
Clean	Ea.	.78	5.75		6.53	hardwood veneer on raised door
Paint	Ea.	.59	13.30		13.89	panels, hinges and pulls.
Minimum Charge	Job		202		202	
15″ Wide, 1 Door						
Demolish	Ea.		10.40		10.40	Includes material and labor to install
Install	Ea.	229	37.50		266.50	custom modular unit with solid
Demolish and Install	Ea.	229	47.90		276.90	hardwood faced frames, hardwood
Reinstall	Ea.		30.18		30.18	door frames and drawer fronts,
Clean	Ea.	.98	7.10		8.08	hardwood veneer on raised door
Paint	Ea.	.75	16.50		17.25	panels, hinges and pulls.
Minimum Charge	Job		202		202	

Cabinets and Countertops

Wall Cabinets	Unit	Material	Labor	Equip.	Total	Specification
18″ Wide, 1 Door						
Demolish	Ea.		12.55		12.55	Includes material and labor to install
Install	Ea.	252	38.50		290.50	custom modular unit with solid
Demolish and Install	Ea.	252	51.05		303.05	hardwood faced frames, hardwood
Reinstall	Ea.		30.90		30.90	door frames and drawer fronts,
Clean	Ea.	1.17	8.55		9.72	hardwood veneer on raised door
Paint	Ea.	.89	20.50		21.39	panels, hinges and pulls.
Minimum Charge	Job		202		202	
21″ Wide, 1 Door						
Demolish	Ea.		14.45		14.45	Includes material and labor to install
Install	Ea.	264	39		303	custom modular unit with solid
Demolish and Install	Ea.	264	53.45		317.45	hardwood faced frames, hardwood
Reinstall	Ea.		31.35		31.35	door frames and drawer fronts,
Clean	Ea.	1.36	9.95		11.31	hardwood veneer on raised door
Paint	Ea.	1.05	23		24.05	panels, hinges and pulls.
Minimum Charge	Job		202		202	
24″ w / Blind Corner						
Demolish	Ea.		16.60		16.60	Includes material and labor to install
Install	Ea.	294	40		334	custom modular unit with solid
Demolish and Install	Ea.	294	56.60		350.60	hardwood faced frames, hardwood
Reinstall	Ea.		31.81		31.81	door frames and drawer fronts,
Clean	Ea.	1.56	11.50		13.06	hardwood veneer on raised door
Paint	Ea.	1.19	26.50		27.69	panels, hinges and pulls.
Minimum Charge	Job		202		202	
27″ Wide, 2 Door						
Demolish	Ea.		18.45		18.45	Includes material and labor to install
Install	Ea.	325	41		366	custom modular unit with solid
Demolish and Install	Ea.	325	59.45		384.45	hardwood faced frames, hardwood
Reinstall	Ea.		32.61		32.61	door frames and drawer fronts,
Clean	Ea.	1.76	13		14.76	hardwood veneer on raised door
Paint	Ea.	1.35	29		30.35	panels, hinges and pulls.
Minimum Charge	Job		202		202	
30″ Wide, 2 Door						
Demolish	Ea.		21		21	Includes material and labor to install
Install	Ea.	335	42		377	custom modular unit with solid
Demolish and Install	Ea.	335	63		398	hardwood faced frames, hardwood
Reinstall	Ea.		33.46		33.46	door frames and drawer fronts,
Clean	Ea.	1.95	14.25		16.20	hardwood veneer on raised door
Paint	Ea.	1.50	34.50		36	panels, hinges and pulls.
Minimum Charge	Job		202		202	
36″ Wide, 2 Door						
Demolish	Ea.		24.50		24.50	Includes material and labor to install
Install	Ea.	385	43		428	custom modular unit with solid
Demolish and Install	Ea.	385	67.50		452.50	hardwood faced frames, hardwood
Reinstall	Ea.		34.35		34.35	door frames and drawer fronts,
Clean	Ea.	2.34	17.60		19.94	hardwood veneer on raised door
Paint	Ea.	1.80	38.50		40.30	panels, hinges and pulls.
Minimum Charge	Job		202		202	
48″ Wide, 2 Door						
Demolish	Ea.		33		33	Includes material and labor to install
Install	Ea.	475	44		519	custom modular unit with solid
Demolish and Install	Ea.	475	77		552	hardwood faced frames, hardwood
Reinstall	Ea.		35.10		35.10	door frames and drawer fronts,
Clean	Ea.	3.12	23		26.12	hardwood veneer on raised door
Paint	Ea.	2.40	49.50		51.90	panels, hinges and pulls.
Minimum Charge	Job		202		202	

Cabinets and Countertops

Wall Cabinets		Unit	Material	Labor	Equip.	Total	Specification
Above-appliance							
	Demolish	Ea.		21		21	Includes material and labor to install
	Install	Ea.	226	32.50		258.50	custom modular unit with solid
	Demolish and Install	Ea.	226	53.50		279.50	hardwood faced frames, hardwood
	Reinstall	Ea.		26.04		26.04	door frames and drawer fronts,
	Clean	Ea.	1.95	14.25		16.20	hardwood veneer on raised door
	Paint	Ea.	1.50	34.50		36	panels, hinges and pulls.
	Minimum Charge	Job		202		202	
Premium Grade Wood							
12″ Wide, 1 Door							
	Demolish	Ea.		8.30		8.30	Includes material and labor to install
	Install	Ea.	244	36.50		280.50	premium modular unit with solid
	Demolish and Install	Ea.	244	44.80		288.80	hardwood faced frames, hardwood
	Reinstall	Ea.		29.35		29.35	door frames and drawer fronts,
	Clean	Ea.	.78	5.75		6.53	hardwood veneer on raised door
	Paint	Ea.	.59	14.45		15.04	panels, hinges and pulls.
	Minimum Charge	Job		202		202	
15″ Wide, 1 Door							
	Demolish	Ea.		10.40		10.40	Includes material and labor to install
	Install	Ea.	305	37.50		342.50	premium modular unit with solid
	Demolish and Install	Ea.	305	47.90		352.90	hardwood faced frames, hardwood
	Reinstall	Ea.		30.18		30.18	door frames and drawer fronts,
	Clean	Ea.	.98	7.10		8.08	hardwood veneer on raised door
	Paint	Ea.	.75	18.25		19	panels, hinges and pulls.
	Minimum Charge	Job		202		202	
18″ Wide, 1 Door							
	Demolish	Ea.		12.55		12.55	Includes material and labor to install
	Install	Ea.	305	38.50		343.50	premium modular unit with solid
	Demolish and Install	Ea.	305	51.05		356.05	hardwood faced frames, hardwood
	Reinstall	Ea.		30.90		30.90	door frames and drawer fronts,
	Clean	Ea.	1.17	8.55		9.72	hardwood veneer on raised door
	Paint	Ea.	.89	21.50		22.39	panels, hinges and pulls.
	Minimum Charge	Job		202		202	
21″ Wide, 1 Door							
	Demolish	Ea.		14.45		14.45	Includes material and labor to install
	Install	Ea.	315	39		354	premium modular unit with solid
	Demolish and Install	Ea.	315	53.45		368.45	hardwood faced frames, hardwood
	Reinstall	Ea.		31.35		31.35	door frames and drawer fronts,
	Clean	Ea.	1.36	9.95		11.31	hardwood veneer on raised door
	Paint	Ea.	1.05	24.50		25.55	panels, hinges and pulls.
	Minimum Charge	Job		202		202	
24″ w / Blind Corner							
	Demolish	Ea.		16.60		16.60	Includes material and labor to install
	Install	Ea.	350	40		390	premium modular unit with solid
	Demolish and Install	Ea.	350	56.60		406.60	hardwood faced frames, hardwood
	Reinstall	Ea.		31.81		31.81	door frames and drawer fronts,
	Clean	Ea.	1.56	11.50		13.06	hardwood veneer on raised door
	Paint	Ea.	1.19	29		30.19	panels, hinges and pulls.
	Minimum Charge	Job		202		202	
27″ Wide, 2 Door							
	Demolish	Ea.		18.45		18.45	Includes material and labor to install
	Install	Ea.	325	41		366	premium modular unit with solid
	Demolish and Install	Ea.	325	59.45		384.45	hardwood faced frames, hardwood
	Reinstall	Ea.		32.61		32.61	door frames and drawer fronts,
	Clean	Ea.	1.76	13		14.76	hardwood veneer on raised door
	Paint	Ea.	1.35	31.50		32.85	panels, hinges and pulls.
	Minimum Charge	Job		202		202	

Cabinets and Countertops

Wall Cabinets	Unit	Material	Labor	Equip.	Total	Specification
30″ Wide, 2 Door						
Demolish	Ea.		21		21	Includes material and labor to install
Install	Ea.	400	42		442	premium modular unit with solid
Demolish and Install	Ea.	400	63		463	hardwood faced frames, hardwood
Reinstall	Ea.		33.46		33.46	door frames and drawer fronts,
Clean	Ea.	1.95	14.25		16.20	hardwood veneer on raised door
Paint	Ea.	1.50	34.50		36	panels, hinges and pulls.
Minimum Charge	Job		202		202	
36″ Wide, 2 Door						
Demolish	Ea.		24.50		24.50	Includes material and labor to install
Install	Ea.	455	43		498	premium modular unit with solid
Demolish and Install	Ea.	455	67.50		522.50	hardwood faced frames, hardwood
Reinstall	Ea.		34.35		34.35	door frames and drawer fronts,
Clean	Ea.	2.34	17.60		19.94	hardwood veneer on raised door
Paint	Ea.	1.80	43.50		45.30	panels, hinges and pulls.
Minimum Charge	Job		202		202	
48″ Wide, 2 Door						
Demolish	Ea.		33		33	Includes material and labor to install
Install	Ea.	570	44		614	premium modular unit with solid
Demolish and Install	Ea.	570	77		647	hardwood faced frames, hardwood
Reinstall	Ea.		35.10		35.10	door frames and drawer fronts,
Clean	Ea.	3.12	23		26.12	hardwood veneer on raised door
Paint	Ea.	2.40	57.50		59.90	panels, hinges and pulls.
Minimum Charge	Job		202		202	
Above-appliance						
Demolish	Ea.		21		21	Includes material and labor to install
Install	Ea.	271	32.50		303.50	premium modular unit with solid
Demolish and Install	Ea.	271	53.50		324.50	hardwood faced frames, hardwood
Reinstall	Ea.		26.04		26.04	door frames and drawer fronts,
Clean	Ea.	1.95	14.25		16.20	hardwood veneer on raised door
Paint	Ea.	1.50	34.50		36	panels, hinges, pulls.
Minimum Charge	Job		202		202	
Premium Hardwood						
12″ Wide, 1 Door						
Demolish	Ea.		8.30		8.30	Includes material and labor to install
Install	Ea.	267	36.50		303.50	premium hardwood modular unit with
Demolish and Install	Ea.	267	44.80		311.80	solid hardwood faced frames, drawer
Reinstall	Ea.		29.35		29.35	fronts, and door panels, steel drawer
Clean	Ea.	.78	5.75		6.53	guides, hinges, pulls, laminated
Paint	Ea.	.59	15.75		16.34	interior.
Minimum Charge	Job		202		202	
15″ Wide, 1 Door						
Demolish	Ea.		10.40		10.40	Includes material and labor to install
Install	Ea.	400	37.50		437.50	premium hardwood modular unit with
Demolish and Install	Ea.	400	47.90		447.90	solid hardwood faced frames, drawer
Reinstall	Ea.		30.18		30.18	fronts, and door panels, steel drawer
Clean	Ea.	.98	7.10		8.08	guides, hinges, pulls, laminated
Paint	Ea.	.75	19.25		20	interior.
Minimum Charge	Job		202		202	
18″ Wide, 1 Door						
Demolish	Ea.		12.55		12.55	Includes material and labor to install
Install	Ea.	330	38.50		368.50	premium hardwood modular unit with
Demolish and Install	Ea.	330	51.05		381.05	solid hardwood faced frames, drawer
Reinstall	Ea.		30.90		30.90	fronts, and door panels, steel drawer
Clean	Ea.	1.17	8.55		9.72	guides, hinges, pulls, laminated
Paint	Ea.	.89	23		23.89	interior.
Minimum Charge	Job		202		202	

211

Cabinets and Countertops

Wall Cabinets

	Unit	Material	Labor	Equip.	Total	Specification
21″ Wide, 1 Door						
Demolish	Ea.		14.45		14.45	Includes material and labor to install
Install	Ea.	345	39		384	premium hardwood modular unit with
Demolish and Install	Ea.	345	53.45		398.45	solid hardwood faced frames, drawer
Reinstall	Ea.		31.35		31.35	fronts, and door panels, steel drawer
Clean	Ea.	1.36	9.95		11.31	guides, hinges, pulls, laminated
Paint	Ea.	1.05	26.50		27.55	interior.
Minimum Charge	Job		202		202	
24″ w / Blind Corner						
Demolish	Ea.		16.60		16.60	Includes material and labor to install
Install	Ea.	385	40		425	premium hardwood modular unit with
Demolish and Install	Ea.	385	56.60		441.60	solid hardwood faced frames, drawer
Reinstall	Ea.		31.81		31.81	fronts, and door panels, steel drawer
Clean	Ea.	1.56	11.50		13.06	guides, hinges, pulls, laminated
Paint	Ea.	1.19	31.50		32.69	interior.
Minimum Charge	Job		202		202	
27″ Wide, 2 Door						
Demolish	Ea.		18.45		18.45	Includes material and labor to install
Install	Ea.	425	41		466	premium hardwood modular unit with
Demolish and Install	Ea.	425	59.45		484.45	solid hardwood faced frames, drawer
Reinstall	Ea.		32.61		32.61	fronts, and door panels, steel drawer
Clean	Ea.	1.76	13		14.76	guides, hinges, pulls, laminated
Paint	Ea.	1.35	34.50		35.85	interior.
Minimum Charge	Job		202		202	
30″ Wide, 2 Door						
Demolish	Ea.		21		21	Includes material and labor to install
Install	Ea.	440	42		482	premium hardwood modular unit with
Demolish and Install	Ea.	440	63		503	solid hardwood faced frames, drawer
Reinstall	Ea.		33.46		33.46	fronts, and door panels, steel drawer
Clean	Ea.	1.95	14.25		16.20	guides, hinges, pulls, laminated
Paint	Ea.	1.50	38.50		40	interior.
Minimum Charge	Job		202		202	
36″ Wide, 2 Door						
Demolish	Ea.		24.50		24.50	Includes material and labor to install
Install	Ea.	500	43		543	premium hardwood modular unit with
Demolish and Install	Ea.	500	67.50		567.50	solid hardwood faced frames, drawer
Reinstall	Ea.		34.35		34.35	fronts, and door panels, steel drawer
Clean	Ea.	2.34	17.60		19.94	guides, hinges, pulls, laminated
Paint	Ea.	1.80	49.50		51.30	interior.
Minimum Charge	Job		202		202	
48″ Wide, 2 Door						
Demolish	Ea.		33		33	Includes material and labor to install
Install	Ea.	620	44		664	premium hardwood modular unit with
Demolish and Install	Ea.	620	77		697	solid hardwood faced frames, drawer
Reinstall	Ea.		35.10		35.10	fronts, and door panels, steel drawer
Clean	Ea.	3.12	23		26.12	guides, hinges, pulls, laminated
Paint	Ea.	2.40	57.50		59.90	interior.
Minimum Charge	Job		202		202	
Above-appliance						
Demolish	Ea.		21		21	Includes material and labor to install
Install	Ea.	295	32.50		327.50	premium hardwood modular unit with
Demolish and Install	Ea.	295	53.50		348.50	solid hardwood faced frames, drawer
Reinstall	Ea.		26.04		26.04	fronts, and door panels, steel drawer
Clean	Ea.	1.95	14.25		16.20	guides, hinges, pulls, laminated
Paint	Ea.	1.50	38.50		40	interior.
Minimum Charge	Job		202		202	

Cabinets and Countertops

Wall Cabinets		Unit	Material	Labor	Equip.	Total	Specification
Medicine Cabinet							
Good Grade							
	Demolish	Ea.		13.85		13.85	Cost includes material and labor to
	Install	Ea.	187	29		216	install 14" x 18" recessed medicine
	Demolish and Install	Ea.	187	42.85		229.85	cabinet with stainless steel frame,
	Reinstall	Ea.		23.06		23.06	mirror. Light not included.
	Clean	Ea.	.04	13.65		13.69	
	Paint	Ea.	1.78	21.50		23.28	
	Minimum Charge	Job		202		202	
Good Grade Lighted							
	Demolish	Ea.		13.85		13.85	Cost includes material and labor to
	Install	Ea.	430	33.50		463.50	install 14" x 18" recessed medicine
	Demolish and Install	Ea.	430	47.35		477.35	cabinet with stainless steel frame,
	Reinstall	Ea.		26.91		26.91	mirror and light.
	Clean	Ea.	.04	13.65		13.69	
	Paint	Ea.	1.78	21.50		23.28	
	Minimum Charge	Job		202		202	
Better Grade							
	Demolish	Ea.		13.85		13.85	Includes material and labor to install
	Install	Ea.	221	29		250	recessed medicine cabinet with
	Demolish and Install	Ea.	221	42.85		263.85	polished chrome frame and mirror.
	Reinstall	Ea.		23.06		23.06	Light not included.
	Clean	Ea.	.04	13.65		13.69	
	Paint	Ea.	1.78	21.50		23.28	
	Minimum Charge	Job		202		202	
Better Grade Lighted							
	Demolish	Ea.		13.85		13.85	Includes material and labor to install
	Install	Ea.	460	33.50		493.50	recessed medicine cabinet with
	Demolish and Install	Ea.	460	47.35		507.35	polished chrome frame, mirror and
	Reinstall	Ea.		26.91		26.91	light.
	Clean	Ea.	.04	13.65		13.69	
	Paint	Ea.	1.78	21.50		23.28	
	Minimum Charge	Job		202		202	
Premium Grade							
	Demolish	Ea.		13.85		13.85	Cost includes material and labor to
	Install	Ea.	285	29		314	install 14" x 24" recessed medicine
	Demolish and Install	Ea.	285	42.85		327.85	cabinet with beveled mirror, frameless
	Reinstall	Ea.		23.06		23.06	swing door. Light not included.
	Clean	Ea.	.04	13.65		13.69	
	Paint	Ea.	1.78	21.50		23.28	
	Minimum Charge	Job		202		202	
Premium Grade Light							
	Demolish	Ea.		13.85		13.85	Cost includes material and labor to
	Install	Ea.	530	33.50		563.50	install 36" x 30" surface mounted
	Demolish and Install	Ea.	530	47.35		577.35	medicine cabinet with beveled tri-view
	Reinstall	Ea.		26.91		26.91	mirror, frameless swing door and light.
	Clean	Ea.	.04	13.65		13.69	
	Paint	Ea.	1.78	21.50		23.28	
	Minimum Charge	Job		202		202	
Bath Mirror							
	Demolish	Ea.		10.40		10.40	Cost includes material and labor to
	Install	Ea.	52.50	20		72.50	install 18" x 24" surface mount mirror
	Demolish and Install	Ea.	52.50	30.40		82.90	with stainless steel frame.
	Reinstall	Ea.		16.14		16.14	
	Clean	Ea.	.04	.91		.95	
	Minimum Charge	Job		202		202	

Cabinets and Countertops

Wall Cabinets		Unit	Material	Labor	Equip.	Total	Specification
Garage							
	Demolish	L.F.		8.30		8.30	Includes material and labor to install
	Install	L.F.	77	20		97	good modular unit with melamine
	Demolish and Install	L.F.	77	28.30		105.30	laminated to particle board, in
	Reinstall	L.F.		16.14		16.14	textured colors or wood grain print
	Clean	L.F.	.78	5.75		6.53	finish, hinges and pulls.
	Paint	L.F.	.59	12.35		12.94	
	Minimum Charge	Job		202		202	
Strip and Refinish							
	Install	L.F.	3.98	43.50		47.48	Includes labor and material to strip,
	Minimum Charge	Job		173		173	prep and refinish exterior of cabinets.

Tall Cabinets		Unit	Material	Labor	Equip.	Total	Specification
Good Grade Laminated							
	Demolish	L.F.		14.80		14.80	Includes material and labor to install
	Install	L.F.	205	45		250	custom modular unit with solid
	Demolish and Install	L.F.	205	59.80		264.80	hardwood faced frames, hardwood
	Reinstall	L.F.		35.88		35.88	door frames and drawer fronts,
	Clean	L.F.	2.08	10.70		12.78	hardwood veneer on raised door
	Paint	L.F.	1.40	24.50		25.90	panels, hinges and pulls.
	Minimum Charge	Job		202		202	
Better Grade Wood							
	Demolish	L.F.		14.80		14.80	Includes material and labor to install
	Install	L.F.	295	45		340	custom modular unit with solid
	Demolish and Install	L.F.	295	59.80		354.80	hardwood faced frames, hardwood
	Reinstall	L.F.		35.88		35.88	door frames and drawer fronts,
	Clean	L.F.	2.08	10.70		12.78	hardwood veneer on raised door
	Paint	L.F.	1.40	26.50		27.90	panels, hinges and pulls.
	Minimum Charge	Job		202		202	
Premium Grade Wood							
	Demolish	L.F.		14.80		14.80	Includes material and labor to install
	Install	L.F.	420	45		465	premium modular unit with solid
	Demolish and Install	L.F.	420	59.80		479.80	hardwood faced frames, hardwood
	Reinstall	L.F.		35.88		35.88	door frames and drawer fronts,
	Clean	L.F.	2.08	10.70		12.78	hardwood veneer on raised door
	Paint	L.F.	1.40	29		30.40	panels, hinges and pulls.
	Minimum Charge	Job		202		202	
Premium Hardwood							
	Demolish	L.F.		14.80		14.80	Includes material and labor to install
	Install	L.F.	590	45		635	premium hardwood modular unit with
	Demolish and Install	L.F.	590	59.80		649.80	solid hardwood faced frames, drawer
	Reinstall	L.F.		35.88		35.88	fronts, and door panels, steel drawer
	Clean	L.F.	2.08	10.70		12.78	guides, hinges and pulls, laminated
	Paint	L.F.	1.40	31.50		32.90	interior.
	Minimum Charge	Job		202		202	

Cabinets and Countertops

Tall Cabinets	Unit	Material	Labor	Equip.	Total	Specification
Single Oven, 27″ Wide						
Good Grade Laminated						
Demolish	Ea.		33		33	Includes material and labor to install
Install	Ea.	710	101		811	good modular unit with melamine
Demolish and Install	Ea.	710	134		844	laminated to particle board, in
Reinstall	Ea.		80.72		80.72	textured colors or wood grain print
Clean	Ea.	6.50	18.70		25.20	finish, hinges and pulls.
Paint	Ea.	2.34	55.50		57.84	
Minimum Charge	Job		202		202	
Better Grade Veneer						
Demolish	Ea.		33		33	Includes material and labor to install
Install	Ea.	1275	101		1376	custom modular unit with solid
Demolish and Install	Ea.	1275	134		1409	hardwood faced frames, hardwood
Reinstall	Ea.		80.72		80.72	door frames and drawer fronts,
Clean	Ea.	6.50	18.70		25.20	hardwood veneer on raised door
Paint	Ea.	2.34	59.50		61.84	panels, hinges and pulls.
Minimum Charge	Job		202		202	
Premium Grade Veneer						
Demolish	Ea.		33		33	Includes material and labor to install
Install	Ea.	1125	101		1226	premium modular unit with solid
Demolish and Install	Ea.	1125	134		1259	hardwood faced frames, hardwood
Reinstall	Ea.		80.72		80.72	door frames and drawer fronts,
Clean	Ea.	6.50	18.70		25.20	hardwood veneer on raised door
Paint	Ea.	2.34	65.50		67.84	panels, hinges and pulls.
Minimum Charge	Job		202		202	
Premium Hardwood						
Demolish	Ea.		33		33	Includes material and labor to install
Install	Ea.	1250	101		1351	premium hardwood modular unit with
Demolish and Install	Ea.	1250	134		1384	solid hardwood faced frames, drawer
Reinstall	Ea.		80.72		80.72	fronts, and door panels, steel drawer
Clean	Ea.	6.50	18.70		25.20	guides, hinges and pulls, laminated
Paint	Ea.	2.34	70.50		72.84	interior.
Minimum Charge	Job		202		202	
Single Oven, 30″ Wide						
Good Grade Laminated						
Demolish	Ea.		33		33	Includes material and labor to install
Install	Ea.	875	101		976	good modular unit with melamine
Demolish and Install	Ea.	875	134		1009	laminated to particle board, in
Reinstall	Ea.		80.72		80.72	textured colors or wood grain print
Clean	Ea.	6.50	18.70		25.20	finish, hinges and pulls.
Paint	Ea.	2.34	55.50		57.84	
Minimum Charge	Job		202		202	
Better Grade Veneer						
Demolish	Ea.		33		33	Includes material and labor to install
Install	Ea.	925	101		1026	custom modular unit with solid
Demolish and Install	Ea.	925	134		1059	hardwood faced frames, hardwood
Reinstall	Ea.		80.72		80.72	door frames and drawer fronts,
Clean	Ea.	6.50	18.70		25.20	hardwood veneer on raised door
Paint	Ea.	2.34	55.50		57.84	panels, hinges and pulls.
Minimum Charge	Job		202		202	

Cabinets and Countertops

Tall Cabinets	Unit	Material	Labor	Equip.	Total	Specification
Premium Grade Veneer						Includes material and labor to install
Demolish	Ea.		33		33	premium modular unit with solid
Install	Ea.	1000	101		1101	hardwood faced frames, hardwood
Demolish and Install	Ea.	1000	134		1134	door frames and drawer fronts,
Reinstall	Ea.		80.72		80.72	hardwood veneer on raised door
Clean	Ea.	6.50	18.70		25.20	panels, hinges and pulls.
Paint	Ea.	2.34	55.50		57.84	
Minimum Charge	Job		202		202	
Premium Hardwood						Includes material and labor to install
Demolish	Ea.		33		33	premium hardwood modular unit with
Install	Ea.	1075	101		1176	solid hardwood faced frames, drawer
Demolish and Install	Ea.	1075	134		1209	fronts, and door panels, steel drawer
Reinstall	Ea.		80.72		80.72	guides, hinges and pulls, laminated
Clean	Ea.	6.50	18.70		25.20	interior.
Paint	Ea.	2.34	55.50		57.84	
Minimum Charge	Job		202		202	
Utility 18″ W x 12″ D						
Good Grade Laminated						Includes material and labor to install
Demolish	Ea.		33		33	good modular unit with melamine
Install	Ea.	415	80.50		495.50	laminated to particle board, in
Demolish and Install	Ea.	415	113.50		528.50	textured colors or wood grain print
Reinstall	Ea.		64.58		64.58	finish, hinges and pulls.
Clean	Ea.	1.53	9.05		10.58	
Paint	Ea.	.89	21.50		22.39	
Minimum Charge	Job		202		202	
Better Grade Veneer						Includes material and labor to install
Demolish	Ea.		33		33	custom modular unit with solid
Install	Ea.	550	80.50		630.50	hardwood faced frames, hardwood
Demolish and Install	Ea.	550	113.50		663.50	door frames and drawer fronts,
Reinstall	Ea.		64.58		64.58	hardwood veneer on raised door
Clean	Ea.	1.53	9.05		10.58	panels, hinges and pulls.
Paint	Ea.	.89	23		23.89	
Minimum Charge	Job		202		202	
Premium Grade Veneer						Includes material and labor to install
Demolish	Ea.		33		33	premium modular unit with solid
Install	Ea.	665	80.50		745.50	hardwood faced frames, hardwood
Demolish and Install	Ea.	665	113.50		778.50	door frames and drawer fronts,
Reinstall	Ea.		64.58		64.58	hardwood veneer on raised door
Clean	Ea.	1.53	9.05		10.58	panels, hinges and pulls.
Paint	Ea.	.89	26.50		27.39	
Minimum Charge	Job		202		202	
Premium Hardwood						Includes material and labor to install
Demolish	Ea.		33		33	premium hardwood modular unit with
Install	Ea.	725	80.50		805.50	solid hardwood faced frames, drawer
Demolish and Install	Ea.	725	113.50		838.50	fronts, and door panels, steel drawer
Reinstall	Ea.		64.58		64.58	guides, hinges and pulls, laminated
Clean	Ea.	1.53	9.05		10.58	interior.
Paint	Ea.	.89	29		29.89	
Minimum Charge	Job		202		202	

Cabinets and Countertops

Tall Cabinets	Unit	Material	Labor	Equip.	Total	Specification
Utility 24″ W x 24″ D						
Good Grade Laminated						
Demolish	Ea.		33		33	Includes material and labor to install
Install	Ea.	585	101		686	good modular unit with melamine
Demolish and Install	Ea.	585	134		719	laminated to particle board, in
Reinstall	Ea.		80.72		80.72	textured colors or wood grain print
Clean	Ea.	2	11.95		13.95	finish, hinges and pulls.
Paint	Ea.	1.19	29		30.19	
Minimum Charge	Job		202		202	
Better Grade Veneer						
Demolish	Ea.		33		33	Includes material and labor to install
Install	Ea.	775	101		876	custom modular unit with solid
Demolish and Install	Ea.	775	134		909	hardwood faced frames, hardwood
Reinstall	Ea.		80.72		80.72	door frames and drawer fronts,
Clean	Ea.	2	11.95		13.95	hardwood veneer on raised door
Paint	Ea.	1.19	31.50		32.69	panels, hinges and pulls.
Minimum Charge	Job		202		202	
Premium Grade Veneer						
Demolish	Ea.		33		33	Includes material and labor to install
Install	Ea.	930	101		1031	premium modular unit with solid
Demolish and Install	Ea.	930	134		1064	hardwood faced frames, hardwood
Reinstall	Ea.		80.72		80.72	door frames and drawer fronts,
Clean	Ea.	2	11.95		13.95	hardwood veneer on raised door
Paint	Ea.	1.19	34.50		35.69	panels, hinges and pulls.
Minimum Charge	Job		202		202	
Premium Hardwood						
Demolish	Ea.		33		33	Includes material and labor to install
Install	Ea.	1025	101		1126	premium hardwood modular unit with
Demolish and Install	Ea.	1025	134		1159	solid hardwood faced frames, drawer
Reinstall	Ea.		80.72		80.72	fronts, and door panels, steel drawer
Clean	Ea.	2	11.95		13.95	guides, hinges and pulls, laminated
Paint	Ea.	1.19	38.50		39.69	interior.
Minimum Charge	Job		202		202	
Plain Shelves						
Install	Ea.	28	22.50		50.50	Includes labor and material to install
Rotating Shelves						tall cabinet shelving, per set.
Install	Ea.	138	20		158	Includes labor and material to install
Strip and Refinish						lazy susan shelving for wall cabinet.
Install	L.F.	8	69.50		77.50	Includes labor and material to strip,
Minimum Charge	Job		173		173	prep and refinish exterior of cabinets.
Stain						
Install	L.F.	.24	3.15		3.39	Includes labor and material to replace
Minimum Charge	Job		173		173	normal prep and stain on doors and
						exterior cabinets.

Cabinets and Countertops

Base Cabinets	Unit	Material	Labor	Equip.	Total	Specification
Good Grade Laminated						
12" w, 1 Door, 1 Drawer						
Demolish	Ea.		8.30		8.30	Includes material and labor to install
Install	Ea.	189	32.50		221.50	good modular unit with melamine
Demolish and Install	Ea.	189	40.80		229.80	laminate, textured colors or wood
Reinstall	Ea.		26.04		26.04	grain print finish including hinges and
Clean	Ea.	1.05	6		7.05	pulls.
Paint	Ea.	.59	14.45		15.04	
Minimum Charge	Job		202		202	
15" w, 1 Door, 1 Drawer						
Demolish	Ea.		10.40		10.40	Includes material and labor to install
Install	Ea.	197	33.50		230.50	good modular unit with melamine
Demolish and Install	Ea.	197	43.90		240.90	laminate, textured colors or wood
Reinstall	Ea.		26.91		26.91	grain print finish including hinges and
Clean	Ea.	1.30	7.50		8.80	pulls.
Paint	Ea.	.75	18.25		19	
Minimum Charge	Job		202		202	
18" w, 1 Door, 1 Drawer						
Demolish	Ea.		12.30		12.30	Includes material and labor to install
Install	Ea.	213	34.50		247.50	good modular unit with melamine
Demolish and Install	Ea.	213	46.80		259.80	laminate, textured colors or wood
Reinstall	Ea.		27.72		27.72	grain print finish including hinges and
Clean	Ea.	1.53	9.05		10.58	pulls.
Paint	Ea.	.89	21.50		22.39	
Minimum Charge	Job		202		202	
21" w, 1 Door, 1 Drawer						
Demolish	Ea.		14.45		14.45	Includes material and labor to install
Install	Ea.	224	35.50		259.50	good modular unit with melamine
Demolish and Install	Ea.	224	49.95		273.95	laminate, textured colors or wood
Reinstall	Ea.		28.45		28.45	grain print finish including hinges and
Clean	Ea.	1.86	10.70		12.56	pulls.
Paint	Ea.	1.05	24.50		25.55	
Minimum Charge	Job		202		202	
24" w, 1 Door, 1 Drawer						
Demolish	Ea.		16.60		16.60	Includes material and labor to install
Install	Ea.	257	36		293	good modular unit with melamine
Demolish and Install	Ea.	257	52.60		309.60	laminate, textured colors or wood
Reinstall	Ea.		28.96		28.96	grain print finish including hinges and
Clean	Ea.	2	11.95		13.95	pulls.
Paint	Ea.	1.19	29		30.19	
Minimum Charge	Job		202		202	
30" Wide Sink Base						
Demolish	Ea.		21		21	Includes material and labor to install
Install	Ea.	252	37.50		289.50	good modular unit with melamine
Demolish and Install	Ea.	252	58.50		310.50	laminate, textured colors or wood
Reinstall	Ea.		30.18		30.18	grain print finish including hinges and
Clean	Ea.	2.60	14.95		17.55	pulls.
Paint	Ea.	1.50	34.50		36	
Minimum Charge	Job		202		202	
36" Wide Sink Base						
Demolish	Ea.		25.50		25.50	Includes material and labor to install
Install	Ea.	284	40		324	good modular unit with melamine
Demolish and Install	Ea.	284	65.50		349.50	laminate, textured colors or wood
Reinstall	Ea.		31.81		31.81	grain print finish including hinges and
Clean	Ea.	2.89	17.60		20.49	pulls.
Paint	Ea.	1.80	43.50		45.30	
Minimum Charge	Job		202		202	

Cabinets and Countertops

Base Cabinets	Unit	Material	Labor	Equip.	Total	Specification
36" Blind Corner						
Demolish	Ea.		25.50		25.50	Includes material and labor to install
Install	Ea.	445	45		490	good modular unit with melamine
Demolish and Install	Ea.	445	70.50		515.50	laminate, textured colors or wood
Reinstall	Ea.		35.88		35.88	grain print finish including hinges and
Clean	Ea.	2.89	17.60		20.49	pulls.
Paint	Ea.	1.80	43.50		45.30	
Minimum Charge	Job		202		202	
42" w, 2 Door, 2 Drawer						
Demolish	Ea.		30		30	Includes material and labor to install
Install	Ea.	350	41		391	good modular unit with melamine
Demolish and Install	Ea.	350	71		421	laminate, textured colors or wood
Reinstall	Ea.		32.61		32.61	grain print finish including hinges and
Clean	Ea.	3.72	21.50		25.22	pulls.
Paint	Ea.	2.07	49.50		51.57	
Minimum Charge	Job		202		202	
Clean Interior						
Clean	L.F.	1.05	4.53		5.58	Includes labor and materials to clean
Minimum Charge	Job		150		150	the interior of a 27" cabinet.
Better Grade Wood						
12" w, 1 Door, 1 Drawer						
Demolish	Ea.		8.30		8.30	Includes material and labor to install
Install	Ea.	252	32.50		284.50	custom modular unit including solid
Demolish and Install	Ea.	252	40.80		292.80	hardwood faced frames, hardwood
Reinstall	Ea.		26.04		26.04	door frames and drawer fronts,
Clean	Ea.	1.05	6		7.05	hardwood veneer on raised door
Paint	Ea.	.59	15.75		16.34	panels, hinges and pulls.
Minimum Charge	Job		202		202	
15" w, 1 Door, 1 Drawer						
Demolish	Ea.		10.40		10.40	Includes material and labor to install
Install	Ea.	262	33.50		295.50	custom modular unit including solid
Demolish and Install	Ea.	262	43.90		305.90	hardwood faced frames, hardwood
Reinstall	Ea.		26.91		26.91	door frames and drawer fronts,
Clean	Ea.	1.30	7.50		8.80	hardwood veneer on raised door
Paint	Ea.	.75	20.50		21.25	panels, hinges and pulls.
Minimum Charge	Job		202		202	
18" w, 1 Door, 1 Drawer						
Demolish	Ea.		12.30		12.30	Includes material and labor to install
Install	Ea.	285	34.50		319.50	custom modular unit including solid
Demolish and Install	Ea.	285	46.80		331.80	hardwood faced frames, hardwood
Reinstall	Ea.		27.72		27.72	door frames and drawer fronts,
Clean	Ea.	1.53	9.05		10.58	hardwood veneer on raised door
Paint	Ea.	.89	23		23.89	panels, hinges and pulls.
Minimum Charge	Job		202		202	
21" w, 1 Door, 1 Drawer						
Demolish	Ea.		14.45		14.45	Includes material and labor to install
Install	Ea.	299	35.50		334.50	custom modular unit including solid
Demolish and Install	Ea.	299	49.95		348.95	hardwood faced frames, hardwood
Reinstall	Ea.		28.45		28.45	door frames and drawer fronts,
Clean	Ea.	1.86	10.70		12.56	hardwood veneer on raised door
Paint	Ea.	1.05	26.50		27.55	panels, hinges and pulls.
Minimum Charge	Job		202		202	

Cabinets and Countertops

Base Cabinets		Unit	Material	Labor	Equip.	Total	Specification
24″ w, 1 Door, 1 Drawer							
	Demolish	Ea.		16.60		16.60	Includes material and labor to install
	Install	Ea.	340	36		376	custom modular unit including solid
	Demolish and Install	Ea.	340	52.60		392.60	hardwood faced frames, hardwood
	Reinstall	Ea.		28.96		28.96	door frames and drawer fronts,
	Clean	Ea.	2	11.95		13.95	hardwood veneer on raised door
	Paint	Ea.	1.19	31.50		32.69	panels, hinges and pulls.
	Minimum Charge	Job		202		202	
30″ Wide Sink Base							
	Demolish	Ea.		21		21	Includes material and labor to install
	Install	Ea.	335	37.50		372.50	custom modular unit including solid
	Demolish and Install	Ea.	335	58.50		393.50	hardwood faced frames, hardwood
	Reinstall	Ea.		30.18		30.18	door frames and drawer fronts,
	Clean	Ea.	2.60	14.95		17.55	hardwood veneer on raised door
	Paint	Ea.	1.50	38.50		40	panels, hinges and pulls.
	Minimum Charge	Job		202		202	
36″ Wide Sink Base							
	Demolish	Ea.		25.50		25.50	Includes material and labor to install
	Install	Ea.	380	40		420	custom modular unit including solid
	Demolish and Install	Ea.	380	65.50		445.50	hardwood faced frames, hardwood
	Reinstall	Ea.		31.81		31.81	door frames and drawer fronts,
	Clean	Ea.	2.89	17.60		20.49	hardwood veneer on raised door
	Paint	Ea.	1.80	49.50		51.30	panels, hinges and pulls.
	Minimum Charge	Job		202		202	
36″ Blind Corner							
	Demolish	Ea.		25.50		25.50	Includes material and labor to install
	Install	Ea.	595	45		640	custom modular unit including solid
	Demolish and Install	Ea.	595	70.50		665.50	hardwood faced frames, hardwood
	Reinstall	Ea.		35.88		35.88	door frames and drawer fronts,
	Clean	Ea.	2.89	17.60		20.49	hardwood veneer on raised door
	Paint	Ea.	1.80	49.50		51.30	panels, hinges and pulls.
	Minimum Charge	Job		202		202	
42″ w, 2 Door, 2 Drawer							
	Demolish	Ea.		30		30	Includes material and labor to install
	Install	Ea.	470	41		511	modular unit including solid hardwood
	Demolish and Install	Ea.	470	71		541	faced frames, hardwood door frames
	Reinstall	Ea.		32.61		32.61	and drawer fronts, hardwood veneer
	Clean	Ea.	3.72	21.50		25.22	on raised door panels, hinges and
	Paint	Ea.	2.07	57.50		59.57	pulls.
	Minimum Charge	Job		202		202	
Clean Interior							
	Clean	L.F.	1.05	4.53		5.58	Includes labor and materials to clean
	Minimum Charge	Job		150		150	the interior of a 27″ cabinet.
Premium Grade Wood							
12″ w, 1 Door, 1 Drawer							
	Demolish	Ea.		8.30		8.30	Includes material and labor to install
	Install	Ea.	305	16.25		321.25	premium hardwood modular unit with
	Demolish and Install	Ea.	305	24.55		329.55	solid hardwood faced frames, drawer
	Reinstall	Ea.		13.02		13.02	fronts, and door panels, steel drawer
	Clean	Ea.	1.05	6		7.05	guides, hinges, pulls and laminated
	Paint	Ea.	.59	17.30		17.89	interior.
	Minimum Charge	Job		202		202	

Cabinets and Countertops

Base Cabinets		Unit	Material	Labor	Equip.	Total	Specification
15" w, 1 Door, 1 Drawer							
	Demolish	Ea.		10.40		10.40	Includes material and labor to install
	Install	Ea.	315	33.50		348.50	premium modular unit including solid
	Demolish and Install	Ea.	315	43.90		358.90	hardwood faced frames, hardwood
	Reinstall	Ea.		26.91		26.91	door frames and drawer fronts,
	Clean	Ea.	1.30	7.50		8.80	hardwood veneer on raised door
	Paint	Ea.	.75	21.50		22.25	panels, hinges and pulls.
	Minimum Charge	Job		202		202	
18" w, 1 Door, 1 Drawer							
	Demolish	Ea.		12.30		12.30	Includes material and labor to install
	Install	Ea.	340	34.50		374.50	premium modular unit including solid
	Demolish and Install	Ea.	340	46.80		386.80	hardwood faced frames, hardwood
	Reinstall	Ea.		27.72		27.72	door frames and drawer fronts,
	Clean	Ea.	1.53	9.05		10.58	hardwood veneer on raised door
	Paint	Ea.	.89	26.50		27.39	panels, hinges and pulls.
	Minimum Charge	Job		202		202	
21" w, 1 Door, 1 Drawer							
	Demolish	Ea.		14.45		14.45	Includes material and labor to install
	Install	Ea.	365	35.50		400.50	premium modular unit including solid
	Demolish and Install	Ea.	365	49.95		414.95	hardwood faced frames, hardwood
	Reinstall	Ea.		28.45		28.45	door frames and drawer fronts,
	Clean	Ea.	1.86	10.70		12.56	hardwood veneer on raised door
	Paint	Ea.	1.05	29		30.05	panels, hinges and pulls.
	Minimum Charge	Job		202		202	
24" w, 1 Door, 1 Drawer							
	Demolish	Ea.		16.60		16.60	Includes material and labor to install
	Install	Ea.	415	36		451	premium modular unit including solid
	Demolish and Install	Ea.	415	52.60		467.60	hardwood faced frames, hardwood
	Reinstall	Ea.		28.96		28.96	door frames and drawer fronts,
	Clean	Ea.	2	11.95		13.95	hardwood veneer on raised door
	Paint	Ea.	1.19	34.50		35.69	panels, hinges and pulls.
	Minimum Charge	Job		202		202	
30" Wide Sink Base							
	Demolish	Ea.		21		21	Includes material and labor to install
	Install	Ea.	400	37.50		437.50	premium modular unit including solid
	Demolish and Install	Ea.	400	58.50		458.50	hardwood faced frames, hardwood
	Reinstall	Ea.		30.18		30.18	door frames and drawer fronts,
	Clean	Ea.	2.60	14.95		17.55	hardwood veneer on raised door
	Paint	Ea.	1.50	43.50		45	panels, hinges and pulls.
	Minimum Charge	Job		202		202	
36" Wide Sink Base							
	Demolish	Ea.		25.50		25.50	Includes material and labor to install
	Install	Ea.	455	40		495	premium modular unit including solid
	Demolish and Install	Ea.	455	65.50		520.50	hardwood faced frames, hardwood
	Reinstall	Ea.		31.81		31.81	door frames and drawer fronts,
	Clean	Ea.	2.89	17.60		20.49	hardwood veneer on raised door
	Paint	Ea.	1.80	49.50		51.30	panels, hinges and pulls.
	Minimum Charge	Job		202		202	
36" Blind Corner							
	Demolish	Ea.		25.50		25.50	Includes material and labor to install
	Install	Ea.	710	45		755	premium modular unit including solid
	Demolish and Install	Ea.	710	70.50		780.50	hardwood faced frames, hardwood
	Reinstall	Ea.		35.88		35.88	door frames and drawer fronts,
	Clean	Ea.	2.89	17.60		20.49	hardwood veneer on raised door
	Paint	Ea.	1.80	49.50		51.30	panels, hinges and pulls.
	Minimum Charge	Job		202		202	

Cabinets and Countertops

Base Cabinets	Unit	Material	Labor	Equip.	Total	Specification
42″ w, 2 Door, 2 Drawer						
Demolish	Ea.		30		30	Includes material and labor to install
Install	Ea.	620	41		661	premium modular unit including solid
Demolish and Install	Ea.	620	71		691	hardwood faced frames, hardwood
Reinstall	Ea.		32.61		32.61	door frames and drawer fronts,
Clean	Ea.	3.72	21.50		25.22	hardwood veneer on raised door
Paint	Ea.	2.07	57.50		59.57	panels, hinges and pulls.
Minimum Charge	Job		202		202	
Clean Interior						
Clean	L.F.	1.05	4.53		5.58	Includes labor and materials to clean
Minimum Charge	Job		150		150	the interior of a 27″ cabinet.

Premium Hardwood

	Unit	Material	Labor	Equip.	Total	Specification
12″ w, 1 Door, 1 Drawer						
Demolish	Ea.		8.30		8.30	Includes material and labor to install
Install	Ea.	330	32.50		362.50	premium hardwood modular unit with
Demolish and Install	Ea.	330	40.80		370.80	solid hardwood faced frames, drawer
Reinstall	Ea.		26.04		26.04	fronts, and door panels, steel drawer
Clean	Ea.	1.05	6		7.05	guides, hinges, pulls and laminated
Paint	Ea.	.59	19.25		19.84	interior.
Minimum Charge	Job		202		202	
15″ w, 1 Door, 1 Drawer						
Demolish	Ea.		10.40		10.40	Includes material and labor to install
Install	Ea.	340	33.50		373.50	premium hardwood modular unit with
Demolish and Install	Ea.	340	43.90		383.90	solid hardwood faced frames, drawer
Reinstall	Ea.		26.91		26.91	fronts, and door panels, steel drawer
Clean	Ea.	1.30	7.50		8.80	guides, hinges, pulls and laminated
Paint	Ea.	.75	24.50		25.25	interior.
Minimum Charge	Job		202		202	
18″ w, 1 Door, 1 Drawer						
Demolish	Ea.		12.30		12.30	Includes material and labor to install
Install	Ea.	375	34.50		409.50	premium hardwood modular unit with
Demolish and Install	Ea.	375	46.80		421.80	solid hardwood faced frames, drawer
Reinstall	Ea.		27.72		27.72	fronts, and door panels, steel drawer
Clean	Ea.	1.53	9.05		10.58	guides, hinges, pulls and laminated
Paint	Ea.	.89	29		29.89	interior.
Minimum Charge	Job		202		202	
21″ w, 1 Door, 1 Drawer						
Demolish	Ea.		14.45		14.45	Includes material and labor to install
Install	Ea.	390	35.50		425.50	premium hardwood modular unit with
Demolish and Install	Ea.	390	49.95		439.95	solid hardwood faced frames, drawer
Reinstall	Ea.		28.45		28.45	fronts, and door panels, steel drawer
Clean	Ea.	1.86	10.70		12.56	guides, hinges, pulls and laminated
Paint	Ea.	1.05	31.50		32.55	interior.
Minimum Charge	Job		202		202	
24″ w, 1 Door, 1 Drawer						
Demolish	Ea.		16.60		16.60	Includes material and labor to install
Install	Ea.	450	36		486	premium hardwood modular unit with
Demolish and Install	Ea.	450	52.60		502.60	solid hardwood faced frames, drawer
Reinstall	Ea.		28.96		28.96	fronts, and door panels, steel drawer
Clean	Ea.	2	11.95		13.95	guides, hinges and pulls, laminated
Paint	Ea.	1.19	38.50		39.69	interior.
Minimum Charge	Job		202		202	

Cabinets and Countertops

Base Cabinets		Unit	Material	Labor	Equip.	Total	Specification
30″ Wide Sink Base							
	Demolish	Ea.		21		21	Includes material and labor to install
	Install	Ea.	440	37.50		477.50	premium hardwood modular unit with
	Demolish and Install	Ea.	440	58.50		498.50	solid hardwood faced frames, drawer
	Reinstall	Ea.		30.18		30.18	fronts, and door panels, steel drawer
	Clean	Ea.	2.60	14.95		17.55	guides, hinges, pulls and laminated
	Paint	Ea.	1.50	43.50		45	interior.
	Minimum Charge	Job		202		202	
36″ Wide Sink Base							
	Demolish	Ea.		25.50		25.50	Includes material and labor to install
	Install	Ea.	495	40		535	premium hardwood modular unit with
	Demolish and Install	Ea.	495	65.50		560.50	solid hardwood faced frames, drawer
	Reinstall	Ea.		31.81		31.81	fronts, and door panels, steel drawer
	Clean	Ea.	2.89	17.60		20.49	guides, hinges, pulls and laminated
	Paint	Ea.	1.80	57.50		59.30	interior.
	Minimum Charge	Job		202		202	
36″ Blind Corner							
	Demolish	Ea.		25.50		25.50	Includes material and labor to install
	Install	Ea.	775	45		820	premium hardwood modular unit with
	Demolish and Install	Ea.	775	70.50		845.50	solid hardwood faced frames, drawer
	Reinstall	Ea.		35.88		35.88	fronts, and door panels, steel drawer
	Clean	Ea.	2.89	17.60		20.49	guides, hinges, pulls and laminated
	Paint	Ea.	1.80	57.50		59.30	interior.
	Minimum Charge	Job		202		202	
42″ w, 2 Door, 2 Drawer							
	Demolish	Ea.		30		30	Includes material and labor to install
	Install	Ea.	820	41		861	premium hardwood modular unit with
	Demolish and Install	Ea.	820	71		891	solid hardwood faced frames, drawer
	Reinstall	Ea.		32.61		32.61	fronts, and door panels, steel drawer
	Clean	Ea.	3.72	21.50		25.22	guides, hinges, pulls and laminated
	Paint	Ea.	2.07	69.50		71.57	interior.
	Minimum Charge	Job		202		202	
Clean Interior							
	Clean	L.F.	1.05	4.53		5.58	Includes labor and materials to clean
	Minimum Charge	Job		150		150	the interior of a 27″ cabinet.
Island							
24″ Wide							
	Demolish	Ea.		16.60		16.60	Includes material and labor to install
	Install	Ea.	530	33.50		563.50	custom modular unit with solid
	Demolish and Install	Ea.	530	50.10		580.10	hardwood faced frames, hardwood
	Reinstall	Ea.		26.91		26.91	door frames and drawer fronts,
	Clean	Ea.	2.89	17.60		20.49	hardwood veneer on raised door
	Paint	Ea.	1.78	49.50		51.28	panels, hinges and pulls.
	Minimum Charge	Job		202		202	
30″ Wide							
	Demolish	Ea.		21		21	Includes material and labor to install
	Install	Ea.	570	42		612	custom modular unit with solid
	Demolish and Install	Ea.	570	63		633	hardwood faced frames, hardwood
	Reinstall	Ea.		33.63		33.63	door frames and drawer fronts,
	Clean	Ea.	3.72	21.50		25.22	hardwood veneer on raised door
	Paint	Ea.	2.24	57.50		59.74	panels, hinges and pulls.
	Minimum Charge	Job		202		202	

Cabinets and Countertops

Base Cabinets		Unit	Material	Labor	Equip.	Total	Specification
36″ Wide							
	Demolish	Ea.		25.50		25.50	Includes material and labor to install
	Install	Ea.	860	50.50		910.50	custom modular unit with solid
	Demolish and Install	Ea.	860	76		936	hardwood faced frames, hardwood
	Reinstall	Ea.		40.36		40.36	door frames and drawer fronts,
	Clean	Ea.	4.33	27		31.33	hardwood veneer on raised door
	Paint	Ea.	2.71	69.50		72.21	panels, hinges and pulls.
	Minimum Charge	Job		202		202	
48″ Wide							
	Demolish	Ea.		33		33	Includes material and labor to install
	Install	Ea.	1050	67.50		1117.50	custom modular unit with solid
	Demolish and Install	Ea.	1050	100.50		1150.50	hardwood faced frames, hardwood
	Reinstall	Ea.		53.81		53.81	door frames and drawer fronts,
	Clean	Ea.	5.20	33		38.20	hardwood veneer on raised door
	Paint	Ea.	3.11	86.50		89.61	panels, hinges and pulls.
	Minimum Charge	Job		202		202	
60″ Wide							
	Demolish	Ea.		37		37	Includes material and labor to install
	Install	Ea.	1150	84		1234	custom modular unit with solid
	Demolish and Install	Ea.	1150	121		1271	hardwood faced frames, hardwood
	Reinstall	Ea.		67.27		67.27	door frames and drawer fronts,
	Clean	Ea.	6.50	42.50		49	hardwood veneer on raised door
	Paint	Ea.	3.11	115		118.11	panels, hinges and pulls.
	Minimum Charge	Job		202		202	
Clean Interior							
	Clean	L.F.	1.05	4.53		5.58	Includes labor and materials to clean
	Minimum Charge	Job		150		150	the interior of a 27″ cabinet.
Liquor Bar							
	Demolish	L.F.		8.30		8.30	Includes material and labor to install
	Install	L.F.	163	40.50		203.50	custom modular unit with solid
	Demolish and Install	L.F.	163	48.80		211.80	hardwood faced frames, hardwood
	Reinstall	L.F.		32.29		32.29	door frames and drawer fronts,
	Clean	L.F.	1.05	6.25		7.30	hardwood veneer on raised door
	Paint	L.F.	4.77	15.75		20.52	panels, hinges and pulls.
	Minimum Charge	Job		202		202	
Clean Interior							
	Clean	L.F.	1.05	4.53		5.58	Includes labor and materials to clean
	Minimum Charge	Job		150		150	the interior of a 27″ cabinet.
Seal Interior							
	Install	L.F.	.47	5.70		6.17	Includes labor and materials to seal a
	Minimum Charge	Job		173		173	cabinet interior.
Back Bar							
	Demolish	L.F.		8.30		8.30	Includes material and labor to install
	Install	L.F.	163	40.50		203.50	custom modular unit with solid
	Demolish and Install	L.F.	163	48.80		211.80	hardwood faced frames, hardwood
	Reinstall	L.F.		32.29		32.29	door frames and drawer fronts,
	Clean	L.F.	1.05	6.25		7.30	hardwood veneer on raised door
	Paint	L.F.	4.77	15.75		20.52	panels, hinges and pulls.
	Minimum Charge	Job		202		202	
Clean Interior							
	Clean	L.F.	1.05	4.53		5.58	Includes labor and materials to clean
	Minimum Charge	Job		150		150	the interior of a 27″ cabinet.

Cabinets and Countertops

Base Cabinets		Unit	Material	Labor	Equip.	Total	Specification
Seal Interior							
	Install	L.F.	.47	5.70		6.17	Includes labor and materials to seal a
	Minimum Charge	Job		173		173	cabinet interior.
Storage (garage)							
	Demolish	L.F.		8.30		8.30	Includes material and labor to install
	Install	L.F.	122	40.50		162.50	good modular unit with melamine
	Demolish and Install	L.F.	122	48.80		170.80	laminate, textured colors or wood
	Reinstall	L.F.		32.29		32.29	grain print finish including hinges and
	Clean	L.F.	1.05	6.25		7.30	pulls.
	Paint	L.F.	4.77	15.75		20.52	
	Minimum Charge	Job		202		202	
Clean Interior							
	Clean	L.F.	1.05	4.53		5.58	Includes labor and materials to clean
	Minimum Charge	Job		150		150	the interior of a 27" cabinet.
Seal Interior							
	Install	L.F.	.47	5.70		6.17	Includes labor and materials to seal a
	Minimum Charge	Job		173		173	cabinet interior.
Built-in Desk							
	Demolish	L.F.		8.30		8.30	Includes material and labor to install
	Install	L.F.	163	40.50		203.50	custom modular unit with solid
	Demolish and Install	L.F.	163	48.80		211.80	hardwood faced frames, hardwood
	Reinstall	L.F.		32.29		32.29	door frames and drawer fronts,
	Clean	L.F.	1.05	6.25		7.30	hardwood veneer on raised door
	Paint	L.F.	4.77	15.75		20.52	panels, hinges and pulls.
	Minimum Charge	Job		202		202	
Built-in Bookcase							
	Demolish	L.F.		11.10		11.10	Includes material and labor to install
	Install	L.F.	36	40.50		76.50	custom modular bookcase unit with
	Demolish and Install	L.F.	36	51.60		87.60	clear pine faced frames, shelves 12"
	Reinstall	L.F.		32.29		32.29	O.C., 7' high, 8" deep.
	Clean	L.F.	2.08	10.70		12.78	
	Paint	L.F.	1.40	26.50		27.90	
	Minimum Charge	Job		202		202	
Strip and Refinish							
	Install	L.F.	3.98	43.50		47.48	Includes labor and material to strip,
	Minimum Charge	Job		173		173	prep and refinish exterior of cabinets.
Stain							
	Install	L.F.	.55	1.61		2.16	Includes labor and material to stain
	Minimum Charge	Job		202		202	door and exterior of cabinets.

Countertop		Unit	Material	Labor	Equip.	Total	Specification
Laminated							
With Splash							
	Demolish	L.F.		5.55		5.55	Includes material and labor to install
	Install	L.F.	35	14.40		49.40	one piece laminated top with 4"
	Demolish and Install	L.F.	35	19.95		54.95	backsplash.
	Reinstall	L.F.		11.53		11.53	
	Clean	L.F.	.13	.75		.88	
	Minimum Charge	Job		202		202	

Cabinets and Countertops

Countertop		Unit	Material	Labor	Equip.	Total	Specification
Roll Top							
	Demolish	L.F.		5.55		5.55	Includes material and labor to install
	Install	L.F.	12.10	13.45		25.55	one piece laminated top with rolled
	Demolish and Install	L.F.	12.10	19		31.10	drip edge (post formed) and
	Reinstall	L.F.		10.76		10.76	backsplash.
	Clean	L.F.	.19	1.13		1.32	
	Minimum Charge	Job		202		202	
Ceramic Tile							
	Demolish	S.F.		2.77		2.77	Cost includes material and labor to
	Install	S.F.	18.15	8.05		26.20	install 4-1/4" x 4-1/4" to 6" x 6"
	Demolish and Install	S.F.	18.15	10.82		28.97	glazed tile set in mortar bed and grout
	Clean	S.F.	.09	.57		.66	on particle board substrate.
	Minimum Charge	Job		181		181	
Cultured Marble							
	Demolish	L.F.		5.55		5.55	Includes material and labor to install
	Install	L.F.	49.50	39.50		89	marble countertop, 24" wide, no
	Demolish and Install	L.F.	49.50	45.05		94.55	backsplash.
	Reinstall	L.F.		31.71		31.71	
	Clean	L.F.	.19	1.13		1.32	
	Minimum Charge	Job		181		181	
With Splash							
	Demolish	L.F.		5.55		5.55	Includes material and labor to install
	Install	L.F.	57	39.50		96.50	marble countertop, 24" wide, with
	Demolish and Install	L.F.	57	45.05		102.05	backsplash.
	Reinstall	L.F.		31.71		31.71	
	Clean	L.F.	.19	1.13		1.32	
	Minimum Charge	Job		181		181	
Quarry Tile							
	Demolish	S.F.		2.77		2.77	Includes material and labor to install
	Install	S.F.	8.80	8.05		16.85	quarry tile countertop with no
	Demolish and Install	S.F.	8.80	10.82		19.62	backsplash.
	Clean	S.F.	.09	.57		.66	
	Minimum Charge	Job		181		181	
With Splash							
	Demolish	S.F.		2.77		2.77	Includes material and labor to install
	Install	S.F.	11.60	8.95		20.55	quarry tile countertop with backsplash.
	Demolish and Install	S.F.	11.60	11.72		23.32	
	Clean	S.F.	.09	.57		.66	
	Minimum Charge	Job		181		181	
Butcher Block							
	Demolish	S.F.		2.77		2.77	Includes material and labor to install
	Install	S.F.	40.50	7.20		47.70	solid laminated maple countertop with
	Demolish and Install	S.F.	40.50	9.97		50.47	no backsplash.
	Reinstall	S.F.		5.77		5.77	
	Clean	S.F.	.02	.23		.25	
	Minimum Charge	Job		202		202	
Solid Surface							
	Demolish	L.F.		5.55		5.55	Includes material and labor to install
	Install	L.F.	49	29		78	solid surface counter top 22" deep.
	Demolish and Install	L.F.	49	34.55		83.55	
	Reinstall	L.F.		23.06		23.06	
	Clean	L.F.	.19	1.13		1.32	
	Minimum Charge	Job		202		202	

Cabinets and Countertops

Vanity Cabinets	Unit	Material	Labor	Equip.	Total	Specification
Good Grade Laminated						
24" Wide, 2 Door						
Demolish	Ea.		16.60		16.60	Includes material and labor to install
Install	Ea.	187	40.50		227.50	modular unit with melamine laminated
Demolish and Install	Ea.	187	57.10		244.10	to particle board, textured colors or
Reinstall	Ea.		32.29		32.29	wood grain print finish, hinges and
Clean	Ea.	2	11.95		13.95	pulls.
Paint	Ea.	1.19	29		30.19	
Minimum Charge	Job		202		202	
30" Wide, 2 Door						
Demolish	Ea.		21		21	Includes material and labor to install
Install	Ea.	216	50.50		266.50	modular unit with melamine laminated
Demolish and Install	Ea.	216	71.50		287.50	to particle board, textured colors or
Reinstall	Ea.		40.36		40.36	wood grain print finish, hinges and
Clean	Ea.	2.60	14.95		17.55	pulls.
Paint	Ea.	1.50	34.50		36	
Minimum Charge	Job		202		202	
36" Wide, 2 Door						
Demolish	Ea.		25.50		25.50	Includes material and labor to install
Install	Ea.	287	60.50		347.50	modular unit with melamine laminated
Demolish and Install	Ea.	287	86		373	to particle board, textured colors or
Reinstall	Ea.		48.44		48.44	wood grain print finish, hinges and
Clean	Ea.	2.89	17.60		20.49	pulls.
Paint	Ea.	1.80	43.50		45.30	
Minimum Charge	Job		202		202	
42" w, 3 Doors / Drawer						
Demolish	Ea.		30		30	Includes material and labor to install
Install	Ea.	415	65		480	modular unit with melamine laminated
Demolish and Install	Ea.	415	95		510	to particle board, textured colors or
Reinstall	Ea.		52.16		52.16	wood grain print finish, hinges and
Clean	Ea.	3.72	21.50		25.22	pulls.
Paint	Ea.	2.07	49.50		51.57	
Minimum Charge	Job		202		202	
48" w, 3 Doors / Drawer						
Demolish	Ea.		33		33	Includes material and labor to install
Install	Ea.	340	70.50		410.50	modular unit with melamine laminated
Demolish and Install	Ea.	340	103.50		443.50	to particle board, textured colors or
Reinstall	Ea.		56.50		56.50	wood grain print finish, hinges and
Clean	Ea.	5.20	33		38.20	pulls.
Paint	Ea.	3.11	86.50		89.61	
Minimum Charge	Job		202		202	
Clean Interior						
Install	L.F.	1.05	6.25		7.30	Includes labor and materials to clean
Minimum Charge	Job		150		150	base cabinetry.
Better Grade Wood						
24" Wide, 2 Door						
Demolish	Ea.		16.60		16.60	Includes material and labor to install
Install	Ea.	250	40.50		290.50	custom modular unit with solid
Demolish and Install	Ea.	250	57.10		307.10	hardwood faced frames, hardwood
Reinstall	Ea.		32.29		32.29	door frames and drawer fronts,
Clean	Ea.	2	11.95		13.95	hardwood veneer on raised door
Paint	Ea.	1.19	31.50		32.69	panels, hinges and pulls.
Minimum Charge	Job		202		202	

Cabinets and Countertops

Vanity Cabinets	Unit	Material	Labor	Equip.	Total	Specification
30″ Wide, 2 Door						
Demolish	Ea.		21		21	Includes material and labor to install
Install	Ea.	288	50.50		338.50	custom modular unit with solid
Demolish and Install	Ea.	288	71.50		359.50	hardwood faced frames, hardwood
Reinstall	Ea.		40.36		40.36	door frames and drawer fronts,
Clean	Ea.	2.60	14.95		17.55	hardwood veneer on raised door
Paint	Ea.	1.50	38.50		40	panels, hinges and pulls.
Minimum Charge	Job		202		202	
36″ Wide, 2 Door						
Demolish	Ea.		25.50		25.50	Includes material and labor to install
Install	Ea.	385	60.50		445.50	custom modular unit with solid
Demolish and Install	Ea.	385	86		471	hardwood faced frames, hardwood
Reinstall	Ea.		48.44		48.44	door frames and drawer fronts,
Clean	Ea.	2.89	17.60		20.49	hardwood veneer on raised door
Paint	Ea.	1.80	49.50		51.30	panels, hinges and pulls.
Minimum Charge	Job		202		202	
42″ w, 3 Doors / Drawer						
Demolish	Ea.		30		30	Includes material and labor to install
Install	Ea.	415	65		480	custom modular unit with solid
Demolish and Install	Ea.	415	95		510	hardwood faced frames, hardwood
Reinstall	Ea.		52.16		52.16	door frames and drawer fronts,
Clean	Ea.	3.72	21.50		25.22	hardwood veneer on raised door
Paint	Ea.	2.07	57.50		59.57	panels, hinges and pulls.
Minimum Charge	Job		202		202	
48″ w, 3 Doors / Drawer						
Demolish	Ea.		33		33	Includes material and labor to install
Install	Ea.	455	70.50		525.50	custom modular unit with solid
Demolish and Install	Ea.	455	103.50		558.50	hardwood faced frames, hardwood
Reinstall	Ea.		56.50		56.50	door frames and drawer fronts,
Clean	Ea.	5.20	33		38.20	hardwood veneer on raised door
Paint	Ea.	3.11	86.50		89.61	panels, hinges and pulls.
Minimum Charge	Job		202		202	
Clean Interior						
Install	L.F.	1.05	6.25		7.30	Includes labor and materials to clean
Minimum Charge	Job		150		150	base cabinetry.
Premium Grade Wood						
24″ Wide, 2 Door						
Demolish	Ea.		16.60		16.60	Includes material and labor to install
Install	Ea.	286	40.50		326.50	premium modular unit with solid
Demolish and Install	Ea.	286	57.10		343.10	hardwood faced frames, hardwood
Reinstall	Ea.		32.29		32.29	door frames and drawer fronts,
Clean	Ea.	2	11.95		13.95	hardwood veneer on raised door
Paint	Ea.	1.19	34.50		35.69	panels, hinges and pulls.
Minimum Charge	Job		202		202	
30″ Wide, 2 Door						
Demolish	Ea.		21		21	Includes material and labor to install
Install	Ea.	330	50.50		380.50	premium modular unit with solid
Demolish and Install	Ea.	330	71.50		401.50	hardwood faced frames, hardwood
Reinstall	Ea.		40.36		40.36	door frames and drawer fronts,
Clean	Ea.	2.60	14.95		17.55	hardwood veneer on raised door
Paint	Ea.	1.50	43.50		45	panels, hinges and pulls.
Minimum Charge	Job		202		202	

Cabinets and Countertops

Vanity Cabinets	Unit	Material	Labor	Equip.	Total	Specification
36″ Wide, 2 Door						
Demolish	Ea.		25.50		25.50	Includes material and labor to install
Install	Ea.	440	60.50		500.50	premium modular unit with solid
Demolish and Install	Ea.	440	86		526	hardwood faced frames, hardwood
Reinstall	Ea.		48.44		48.44	door frames and drawer fronts,
Clean	Ea.	2.89	17.60		20.49	hardwood veneer on raised door
Paint	Ea.	1.80	49.50		51.30	panels, hinges and pulls.
Minimum Charge	Job		202		202	
42″ w, 3 Doors / Drawer						
Demolish	Ea.		30		30	Includes material and labor to install
Install	Ea.	475	65		540	premium modular unit with solid
Demolish and Install	Ea.	475	95		570	hardwood faced frames, hardwood
Reinstall	Ea.		52.16		52.16	door frames and drawer fronts,
Clean	Ea.	3.72	21.50		25.22	hardwood veneer on raised door
Paint	Ea.	2.07	57.50		59.57	panels, hinges and pulls.
Minimum Charge	Job		202		202	
48″ w, 3 Doors / Drawer						
Demolish	Ea.		33		33	Includes material and labor to install
Install	Ea.	530	70.50		600.50	premium modular unit with solid
Demolish and Install	Ea.	530	103.50		633.50	hardwood faced frames, hardwood
Reinstall	Ea.		56.50		56.50	door frames and drawer fronts,
Clean	Ea.	5.20	33		38.20	hardwood veneer on raised door
Paint	Ea.	3.11	86.50		89.61	panels, hinges and pulls.
Minimum Charge	Job		202		202	
Clean Interior						
Install	L.F.	1.05	6.25		7.30	Includes labor and materials to clean
Minimum Charge	Job		150		150	base cabinetry.
Premium Hardwood						
24″ Wide, 2 Door						
Demolish	Ea.		16.60		16.60	Includes material and labor to install
Install	Ea.	310	40.50		350.50	premium modular unit with solid
Demolish and Install	Ea.	310	57.10		367.10	hardwood faced frames, hardwood
Reinstall	Ea.		32.29		32.29	door frames and drawer fronts,
Clean	Ea.	2	11.95		13.95	hardwood veneer on raised door
Paint	Ea.	1.19	38.50		39.69	panels, hinges and pulls.
Minimum Charge	Job		202		202	
30″ Wide, 2 Door						
Demolish	Ea.		21		21	Includes material and labor to install
Install	Ea.	580	50.50		630.50	premium modular unit with solid
Demolish and Install	Ea.	580	71.50		651.50	hardwood faced frames, hardwood
Reinstall	Ea.		40.36		40.36	door frames and drawer fronts,
Clean	Ea.	2.60	14.95		17.55	hardwood veneer on raised door
Paint	Ea.	1.50	43.50		45	panels, hinges and pulls.
Minimum Charge	Job		202		202	
36″ Wide, 2 Door						
Demolish	Ea.		25.50		25.50	Includes material and labor to install
Install	Ea.	765	60.50		825.50	premium modular unit with solid
Demolish and Install	Ea.	765	86		851	hardwood faced frames, hardwood
Reinstall	Ea.		48.44		48.44	door frames and drawer fronts,
Clean	Ea.	2.89	17.60		20.49	hardwood veneer on raised door
Paint	Ea.	1.80	57.50		59.30	panels, hinges and pulls.
Minimum Charge	Job		202		202	

Cabinets and Countertops

Vanity Cabinets	Unit	Material	Labor	Equip.	Total	Specification
42″ w, 3 Doors / Drawer						
Demolish	Ea.		30		30	Includes material and labor to install
Install	Ea.	545	65		610	premium modular unit with solid
Demolish and Install	Ea.	545	95		640	hardwood faced frames, hardwood
Reinstall	Ea.		52.16		52.16	door frames and drawer fronts,
Clean	Ea.	3.72	21.50		25.22	hardwood veneer on raised door
Paint	Ea.	2.07	69.50		71.57	panels, hinges and pulls.
Minimum Charge	Job		202		202	
48″ w, 3 Doors / Drawer						
Demolish	Ea.		33		33	Includes material and labor to install
Install	Ea.	595	70.50		665.50	premium modular unit with solid
Demolish and Install	Ea.	595	103.50		698.50	hardwood faced frames, hardwood
Reinstall	Ea.		56.50		56.50	door frames and drawer fronts,
Clean	Ea.	5.20	33		38.20	hardwood veneer on raised door
Paint	Ea.	3.11	86.50		89.61	panels, hinges and pulls.
Minimum Charge	Job		202		202	
Clean Interior						
Install	L.F.	1.05	6.25		7.30	Includes labor and materials to clean
Minimum Charge	Job		150		150	base cabinetry.
Strip and Refinish						
Install	L.F.	3.98	43.50		47.48	Includes labor and material to strip,
Minimum Charge	Job		173		173	prep and refinish exterior of cabinets.

Vanity Cabinet Tops	Unit	Material	Labor	Equip.	Total	Specification
Cultured Marble Top						
Demolish	L.F.		5.55		5.55	Includes material and labor to install
Install	L.F.	45	23.50		68.50	cultured marble vanity top with
Demolish and Install	L.F.	45	29.05		74.05	integral sink, 22″ deep.
Reinstall	L.F.		18.65		18.65	
Clean	L.F.	.19	1.13		1.32	
Minimum Charge	Job		181		181	
Laminated Top						
Demolish	L.F.		3.32		3.32	Includes material and labor to install
Install	L.F.	35	14.40		49.40	one piece laminated top with 4″
Demolish and Install	L.F.	35	17.72		52.72	backsplash.
Reinstall	L.F.		11.53		11.53	
Clean	L.F.	.13	.75		.88	
Minimum Charge	Job		202		202	
Solid Surface						
Demolish	L.F.		5.55		5.55	Includes material and labor to install
Install	L.F.	68	30		98	solid surface vanity top with integral
Demolish and Install	L.F.	68	35.55		103.55	sink installed, 22″ deep.
Reinstall	L.F.		23.92		23.92	
Clean	L.F.	.19	1.13		1.32	
Minimum Charge	Job		202		202	

Roller Handle   Paint Brush

Paint Preparation, Walls		Unit	Material	Labor	Equip.	Total	Specification
Cover / Protect Floors							
	Install	S.F.	.54	.13		.67	Includes material and labor to install
	Minimum Charge	Job		174		174	plastic masking sheet on large uninterrupted areas.
Cover / Protect Walls							
	Install	S.F.	.03	.13		.16	Includes material and labor to install
	Minimum Charge	Job		174		174	plastic masking sheet on walls.
Clean Walls							
Light							
	Clean	S.F.		.11		.11	Includes labor to wash gypsum
	Minimum Charge	Job		174		174	drywall or plaster wall surfaces.
Heavy							
	Clean	S.F.		.14		.14	Includes labor and material for heavy
	Minimum Charge	Job		174		174	cleaning (multiple applications) with detergent and solvent.
Prep Walls							
	Paint	S.F.	.04	.17		.21	Includes labor and material to prepare
	Minimum Charge	Job		174		174	for painting including scraping, patching and puttying.
Sand Walls							
	Paint	S.F.		.11		.11	Includes labor to sand gypsum drywall
	Minimum Charge	Job		174		174	wall surfaces.
Seal Walls							
Large Area							
	Paint	S.F.	.07	.26		.33	Includes labor and material to paint
	Minimum Charge	Job		174		174	with primer / sealer by roller.
Spot							
	Paint	S.F.	.07	.30		.37	Includes labor and material to seal
	Minimum Charge	Job		174		174	existing drywall with shellac-based material.

Paint Preparation, Ceilings		Unit	Material	Labor	Equip.	Total	Specification
Cover / Protect Floors							
	Install	S.F.	.54	.13		.67	Includes material and labor to install
	Minimum Charge	Job		174		174	plastic masking sheet on large uninterrupted areas.

Painting

Paint Preparation, Ceilings

Paint Preparation, Ceilings		Unit	Material	Labor	Equip.	Total	Specification
Cover / Protect Walls							
	Install	S.F.	.03	.13		.16	Includes material and labor to install
	Minimum Charge	Job		174		174	plastic masking sheet on walls.
Prep Ceiling							
	Paint	S.F.	.07	.65		.72	Includes labor and material to fill in
	Minimum Charge	Job		174		174	hairline cracks up to 1/8" with filler, sand and prep for paint.
Sand Ceiling							
	Paint	S.F.		.16		.16	Includes labor to sand gypsum drywall
	Minimum Charge	Job		174		174	ceiling surfaces.
Seal Ceiling							
Large Area							
	Paint	S.F.	.11	.27		.38	Includes labor and material to paint
	Minimum Charge	Job		173		173	ceiling, one coat flat latex.
Spot							
	Paint	S.F.	.07	.30		.37	Includes labor and material to seal
	Minimum Charge	Job		173		173	existing drywall with shellac-based material.

Paint / Texture, Walls

Paint / Texture, Walls		Unit	Material	Labor	Equip.	Total	Specification
Texture Walls							
Spray							
	Install	S.F.	.06	.43		.49	Includes labor and material to install
	Minimum Charge	Job		173		173	by spray, texture finish.
Trowel							
	Install	S.F.	.01	.23		.24	Includes labor and material to apply
	Minimum Charge	Job		173		173	hand troweled texture.
Paint Walls 1 Coat							
	Paint	S.F.	.11	.27		.38	Includes labor and material to paint,
	Minimum Charge	Job		173		173	one coat flat latex.
Paint Walls 2 Coats							
	Paint	S.F.	.12	.43		.55	Includes labor and material to paint,
	Minimum Charge	Job		173		173	two coats flat latex.
Paint Walls 3 Coats							
	Paint	S.F.	.18	.53		.71	Includes labor and material to paint,
	Minimum Charge	Job		173		173	three coats flat latex.
Clean and Seal							
	Paint	S.F.	.44	.92		1.36	Includes labor and material to do light
	Minimum Charge	Job		173		173	cleaning, sealing with 2 coats of latex paint.

Paint / Texture, Ceilings

Paint / Texture, Ceilings		Unit	Material	Labor	Equip.	Total	Specification
Texture Ceiling							
Spray							
	Install	S.F.	.06	.43		.49	Includes labor and material to install
	Minimum Charge	Job		173		173	by spray, texture finish.
Trowel							
	Install	S.F.	.01	.23		.24	Includes labor and material to apply
	Minimum Charge	Job		173		173	hand troweled texture.

Painting

Paint / Texture, Ceilings		Unit	Material	Labor	Equip.	Total	Specification
Paint Ceiling, 1 Coat							
	Paint	S.F.	.11	.27		.38	Includes labor and material to paint
	Minimum Charge	Job		173		173	ceiling, one coat flat latex.
Paint Ceiling, 2 Coats							
	Paint	S.F.	.22	.43		.65	Includes labor and material to paint
	Minimum Charge	Job		173		173	two coats flat latex paint.
Paint Ceiling, 3 Coats							
	Paint	S.F.	.34	.51		.85	Includes labor and material to paint
	Minimum Charge	Job		173		173	ceiling, three coats flat latex.
Clean and Seal							
	Paint	S.F.	.34	.73		1.07	Includes labor and material for light
	Minimum Charge	Job		173		173	cleaning, sealing and paint 3 coats of
							flat latex paint.

Plank Flooring	Wood Strip Flooring	Tile Flooring

Wood Plank Flooring	Unit	Material	Labor	Equip.	Total	Specification
Maple						
2-1/4"						
Demolish	S.F.		1.33		1.33	Includes material and labor to install
Install	S.F.	3.94	2.01		5.95	unfinished T&G maple flooring,
Demolish and Install	S.F.	3.94	3.34		7.28	25/32" thick, 2-1/4" wide, random
Reinstall	S.F.		1.61		1.61	3' to 16' lengths including felt
Clean	S.F.		.37		.37	underlayment, nailed in place over
Paint	S.F.	1.28	2.30		3.58	prepared subfloor.
Minimum Charge	Job		202		202	
3-1/4"						
Demolish	S.F.		1.33		1.33	Includes material and labor to install
Install	S.F.	3.78	2.01		5.79	unfinished T&G maple flooring,
Demolish and Install	S.F.	3.78	3.34		7.12	33/32" thick, 3-1/4" wide, random
Reinstall	S.F.		1.61		1.61	3' to 16' lengths including felt
Clean	S.F.		.37		.37	underlayment, nailed in place over
Paint	S.F.	1.28	2.30		3.58	prepared subfloor.
Minimum Charge	Job		202		202	
Sand and Finish						
Install	S.F.	.86	.75		1.61	Includes labor and material to sand (3
Minimum Charge	Job		202		202	passes) and finish and two coats of
						urethane existing floor.
Oak						
2-1/4"						
Demolish	S.F.		1.33		1.33	Includes material and labor to install
Install	S.F.	3.73	2.01		5.74	unfinished T&G oak flooring, 25/32"
Demolish and Install	S.F.	3.73	3.34		7.07	thick, 2-1/4" wide, random 3' to 16'
Reinstall	S.F.		1.61		1.61	lengths including felt underlayment,
Clean	S.F.		.37		.37	nailed in place over prepared
Paint	S.F.	1.28	2.30		3.58	subfloor.
Minimum Charge	Job		202		202	
3-1/4"						
Demolish	S.F.		1.33		1.33	Includes material and labor to install
Install	S.F.	4.50	1.43		5.93	unfinished T&G oak flooring, 25/32"
Demolish and Install	S.F.	4.50	2.76		7.26	thick, 3-1/4" wide, random 3' to 16'
Reinstall	S.F.		1.14		1.14	lengths including felt underlayment,
Clean	S.F.		.37		.37	nailed in place over prepared
Paint	S.F.	1.28	2.30		3.58	subfloor.
Minimum Charge	Job		202		202	

Wood Plank Flooring		Unit	Material	Labor	Equip.	Total	Specification
Sand and Finish							
	Install	S.F.	1.28	2.30		3.58	Includes labor and material to sand
	Minimum Charge	Job		202		202	and finish (3 passes) with two coats of
							urethane on a new floor.
Walnut							
3″ to 7″							
	Demolish	S.F.		1.33		1.33	Includes material and labor to install
	Install	S.F.	9.50	1.43		10.93	unfinished T&G walnut flooring,
	Demolish and Install	S.F.	9.50	2.76		12.26	25/32″ thick, random 3′ to 16′
	Reinstall	S.F.		1.14		1.14	lengths including felt underlayment,
	Clean	S.F.		.37		.37	nailed in place over prepared
	Paint	S.F.	1.28	2.30		3.58	subfloor.
	Minimum Charge	Job		202		202	
Sand and Finish							
	Install	S.F.	1.28	2.30		3.58	Includes labor and material to sand
	Minimum Charge	Job		202		202	and finish (3 passes) with two coats of
							urethane on a new floor.
Pine							
2-1/4″							
	Demolish	S.F.		1.33		1.33	Includes material and labor to install
	Install	S.F.	7.60	1.52		9.12	unfinished T&G pine flooring, 25/32″
	Demolish and Install	S.F.	7.60	2.85		10.45	thick, 2-1/4″ wide, random 3′ to 16′
	Reinstall	S.F.		1.22		1.22	lengths including felt underlayment,
	Clean	S.F.		.37		.37	nailed in place over prepared
	Paint	S.F.	.86	.75		1.61	subfloor.
	Minimum Charge	Job		202		202	
Sand and Finish							
	Install	S.F.	1.28	2.30		3.58	Includes labor and material to sand
	Minimum Charge	Job		202		202	and finish (3 passes) with two coats of
							urethane on a new floor.
Prefinished Oak							
2-1/4″							
	Demolish	S.F.		1.33		1.33	Includes material and labor to install
	Install	S.F.	4.05	2.01		6.06	prefinished T&G oak flooring, 2-1/4″
	Demolish and Install	S.F.	4.05	3.34		7.39	wide, random 3′ to 16′ lengths
	Reinstall	S.F.		1.61		1.61	including felt underlayment, nailed in
	Clean	S.F.		.37		.37	place over prepared subfloor.
	Minimum Charge	Job		202		202	
3-1/4″							
	Demolish	S.F.		1.33		1.33	Includes material and labor to install
	Install	S.F.	4.50	1.85		6.35	prefinished T&G oak flooring, 25/32″
	Demolish and Install	S.F.	4.50	3.18		7.68	thick, 3″ to 7″ wide, random 3′ to 16′
	Reinstall	S.F.		1.48		1.48	lengths including felt underlayment,
	Clean	S.F.		.37		.37	nailed in place over prepared
	Minimum Charge	Job		202		202	subfloor.
Sand and Finish New							
	Install	S.F.	.86	1.01		1.87	Includes labor and material to sand (3
	Minimum Charge	Job		202		202	passes) and finish, two coats of
							urethane, new floor.
Refinish Existing							
	Install	S.F.	.86	.75		1.61	Includes labor and material to sand (3
	Minimum Charge	Job		202		202	passes) and finish and two coats of
							urethane existing floor.

Flooring

Wood Plank Flooring

Wood Plank Flooring		Unit	Material	Labor	Equip.	Total	Specification
Urethane Coat							
	Install	S.F.	.17	.18		.35	Includes labor and material to install
	Minimum Charge	Job		202		202	two coats of urethane, on existing floor.
Clean and Wax							
	Clean	S.F.	.02	.23		.25	Includes labor and material to wash
	Minimum Charge	Job		202		202	and wax a hardwood floor.
Underlayment Per S.F.							
	Demolish	S.F.		.59		.59	Cost includes material and labor to
	Install	S.F.	.76	.54		1.30	install 1/4" lauan subfloor, standard
	Demolish and Install	S.F.	.76	1.13		1.89	interior grade, nailed every 6".
	Clean	S.F.		.29		.29	
	Minimum Charge	Job		202		202	

Wood Parquet Tile Floor

Wood Parquet Tile Floor		Unit	Material	Labor	Equip.	Total	Specification
Oak							
9" x 9"							
	Demolish	S.F.		1		1	Includes material and labor to install
	Install	S.F.	4.96	3.23		8.19	prefinished oak 9" x 9" parquet block
	Demolish and Install	S.F.	4.96	4.23		9.19	flooring, 5/16" thick, installed in
	Reinstall	S.F.		2.58		2.58	mastic.
	Clean	S.F.		.37		.37	
	Paint	S.F.	1.28	2.30		3.58	
	Minimum Charge	Job		202		202	
13" x 13"							
	Demolish	S.F.		1		1	Includes material and labor to install
	Install	S.F.	9.35	2.52		11.87	prefinished oak 13" x 13" parquet
	Demolish and Install	S.F.	9.35	3.52		12.87	block flooring, 5/16" thick, installed in
	Reinstall	S.F.		2.02		2.02	mastic.
	Clean	S.F.		.37		.37	
	Paint	S.F.	1.28	2.30		3.58	
	Minimum Charge	Job		202		202	
Cherry							
9" x 9"							
	Demolish	S.F.		1		1	Includes material and labor to install
	Install	S.F.	8.55	3.23		11.78	prefinished cherry 9" x 9" parquet
	Demolish and Install	S.F.	8.55	4.23		12.78	block flooring, 5/16" thick, installed in
	Reinstall	S.F.		3.23		3.23	mastic.
	Clean	S.F.		.37		.37	
	Paint	S.F.	1.28	2.30		3.58	
	Minimum Charge	Job		202		202	
13" x 13"							
	Demolish	S.F.		1		1	Includes material and labor to install
	Install	S.F.	9.75	2.52		12.27	prefinished cherry 13" x 13" parquet
	Demolish and Install	S.F.	9.75	3.52		13.27	block flooring, 5/16" thick, installed in
	Reinstall	S.F.		2.52		2.52	mastic.
	Clean	S.F.		.37		.37	
	Paint	S.F.	1.28	2.30		3.58	
	Minimum Charge	Job		202		202	

Flooring

Wood Parquet Tile Floor

Wood Parquet Tile Floor	Unit	Material	Labor	Equip.	Total	Specification
Walnut						
9" x 9"						
Demolish	S.F.		1		1	Includes material and labor to install
Install	S.F.	5.40	3.23		8.63	prefinished walnut 9" x 9" parquet
Demolish and Install	S.F.	5.40	4.23		9.63	flooring in mastic.
Reinstall	S.F.		2.58		2.58	
Clean	S.F.		.37		.37	
Paint	S.F.	1.28	2.30		3.58	
Minimum Charge	Job		202		202	
13" x 13"						
Demolish	S.F.		1		1	Includes material and labor to install
Install	S.F.	10	2.52		12.52	prefinished walnut 13" x 13" parquet
Demolish and Install	S.F.	10	3.52		13.52	block flooring, 5/16" thick, installed in
Reinstall	S.F.		2.52		2.52	mastic.
Clean	S.F.		.37		.37	
Paint	S.F.	1.28	2.30		3.58	
Minimum Charge	Job		202		202	
Acrylic Impregnated						
Oak 12" x 12"						
Demolish	S.F.		1		1	Includes material and labor to install
Install	S.F.	8.45	2.88		11.33	red oak 12" x 12" acrylic
Demolish and Install	S.F.	8.45	3.88		12.33	impregnated parquet block flooring,
Reinstall	S.F.		2.88		2.88	5/16" thick, installed in mastic.
Clean	S.F.		.37		.37	
Minimum Charge	Job		202		202	
Cherry 12" x 12"						
Demolish	S.F.		1		1	Includes material and labor to install
Install	S.F.	11.95	2.88		14.83	prefinished cherry 12" x 12" acrylic
Demolish and Install	S.F.	11.95	3.88		15.83	impregnated parquet block flooring,
Reinstall	S.F.		2.88		2.88	5/16" thick, installed in mastic.
Clean	S.F.		.37		.37	
Minimum Charge	Job		202		202	
Ash 12" x 12"						
Demolish	S.F.		1		1	Includes material and labor to install
Install	S.F.	10.75	2.88		13.63	ash 12" x 12" acrylic impregnated
Demolish and Install	S.F.	10.75	3.88		14.63	parquet block flooring, 5/16" thick in
Reinstall	S.F.		2.88		2.88	mastic.
Clean	S.F.		.37		.37	
Minimum Charge	Job		202		202	
Teak						
Demolish	S.F.		1		1	Includes material and labor to install
Install	S.F.	8.55	2.52		11.07	prefinished teak parquet block
Demolish and Install	S.F.	8.55	3.52		12.07	flooring, 5/16" thick, and installed in
Reinstall	S.F.		2.52		2.52	mastic.
Clean	S.F.		.37		.37	
Paint	S.F.	1.28	2.30		3.58	
Minimum Charge	Job		202		202	
Clean and Wax						
Clean	S.F.	.02	.23		.25	Includes labor and material to wash
Minimum Charge	Job		202		202	and wax a hardwood floor.

Flooring

Ceramic Tile Flooring

Ceramic Tile Flooring		Unit	Material	Labor	Equip.	Total	Specification
Economy Grade							
	Demolish	S.F.		.99		.99	Cost includes material and labor to
	Install	S.F.	7.55	7.10		14.65	install 4-1/4" x 4-1/4" ceramic tile in
	Demolish and Install	S.F.	7.55	8.09		15.64	mortar bed including grout.
	Clean	S.F.		.57		.57	
	Minimum Charge	Job		181		181	
Average Grade							
	Demolish	S.F.		.99		.99	Cost includes material and labor to
	Install	S.F.	11	7.25		18.25	install 4-1/4" x 4-1/4" ceramic tile in
	Demolish and Install	S.F.	11	8.24		19.24	mortar bed including grout.
	Clean	S.F.		.57		.57	
	Minimum Charge	Job		181		181	
Premium Grade							
	Demolish	S.F.		.99		.99	Cost includes material and labor to
	Install	S.F.	12.10	7.25		19.35	install 4-1/4" x 4-1/4" ceramic tile in
	Demolish and Install	S.F.	12.10	8.24		20.34	mortar bed including grout.
	Clean	S.F.		.57		.57	
	Minimum Charge	Job		181		181	
Re-grout							
	Install	S.F.	.15	2.89		3.04	Includes material and labor to regrout
	Minimum Charge	Job		181		181	tile floors.

Hard Tile Flooring

Hard Tile Flooring		Unit	Material	Labor	Equip.	Total	Specification
Thick Set Paver							
Brick							
	Demolish	S.F.		2.08		2.08	Cost includes material and labor to
	Install	S.F.	.92	17.05		17.97	install 6" x 12" adobe brick paver with
	Demolish and Install	S.F.	.92	19.13		20.05	1/2" mortar joints.
	Clean	S.F.		.57		.57	
	Minimum Charge	Job		181		181	
Mexican Red							
	Demolish	S.F.		2.08		2.08	Cost includes material and labor to
	Install	S.F.	1.52	7.55		9.07	install 12" x 12" red Mexican paver
	Demolish and Install	S.F.	1.52	9.63		11.15	tile in mortar bed with grout.
	Clean	S.F.		.57		.57	
	Minimum Charge	Job		181		181	
Saltillo							
	Demolish	S.F.		.99		.99	Cost includes material and labor to
	Install	S.F.	1.52	7.55		9.07	install 12" x 12" saltillo tile in mortar
	Demolish and Install	S.F.	1.52	8.54		10.06	bed with grout.
	Clean	S.F.		.57		.57	
	Minimum Charge	Job		181		181	
Marble							
Premium Grade							
	Demolish	S.F.		.99		.99	Cost includes material and labor to
	Install	S.F.	20	15.70		35.70	install 3/8" x 12" x 12" marble, in
	Demolish and Install	S.F.	20	16.69		36.69	mortar bed with grout.
	Clean	S.F.		.57		.57	
	Minimum Charge	Job		181		181	

Flooring

Hard Tile Flooring

	Unit	Material	Labor	Equip.	Total	Specification
Terrazzo						
Gray Cement						
Demolish	S.F.		1.32		1.32	Cost includes material and labor to
Install	S.F.	3.21	8.75	3.54	15.50	install 1-3/4" terrazzo , #1 and #2
Demolish and Install	S.F.	3.21	10.07	3.54	16.82	chips in gray Portland cement.
Clean	S.F.		.57		.57	
Minimum Charge	Job		330	133	463	
White Cement						
Demolish	S.F.		1.32		1.32	Cost includes material and labor to
Install	S.F.	3.65	8.75	3.54	15.94	install 1-3/4" terrazzo, #1 and #2
Demolish and Install	S.F.	3.65	10.07	3.54	17.26	chips in white Portland cement.
Clean	S.F.		.57		.57	
Minimum Charge	Job		330	133	463	
Non-skid Gray						
Demolish	S.F.		1.32		1.32	Cost includes material and labor to
Install	S.F.	5.85	10.95	4.43	21.23	install 1-3/4" terrazzo, #1 and #2
Demolish and Install	S.F.	5.85	12.27	4.43	22.55	chips in gray Portland cement with
Clean	S.F.		.57		.57	light non-skid abrasive.
Minimum Charge	Job		330	133	463	
Non-skid White						
Demolish	S.F.		1.32		1.32	Cost includes material and labor to
Install	S.F.	6.45	10.95	4.43	21.83	install 1-3/4" terrazzo, #1 and #2
Demolish and Install	S.F.	6.45	12.27	4.43	23.15	chips in white Portland cement with
Clean	S.F.		.57		.57	light non-skid abrasive.
Minimum Charge	Job		330	133	463	
Gray w / Brass Divider						
Demolish	S.F.		1.33		1.33	Cost includes material and labor to
Install	S.F.	9	11.95	4.83	25.78	install 1-3/4" terrazzo, #1 and #2
Demolish and Install	S.F.	9	13.28	4.83	27.11	chips in gray Portland cement with
Clean	S.F.		.57		.57	brass strips 2' O.C. each way.
Minimum Charge	Job		330	133	463	
Clean						
Clean	S.F.	.22	.38		.60	Includes labor and material to clean
Minimum Charge	Job		330	133	463	terrazzo flooring.
Slate						
Demolish	S.F.		1.19		1.19	Includes material and labor to install
Install	S.F.	7.50	3.59		11.09	slate tile flooring in thin set with grout.
Demolish and Install	S.F.	7.50	4.78		12.28	
Clean	S.F.		.57		.57	
Minimum Charge	Job		181		181	
Granite						
Demolish	S.F.		.98		.98	Includes material and labor to install
Install	S.F.	20	3.62		23.62	granite tile flooring in thin set with
Demolish and Install	S.F.	20	4.60		24.60	grout.
Reinstall	S.F.		3.62		3.62	
Clean	S.F.		.57		.57	
Minimum Charge	Job		181		181	
Re-grout						
Install	S.F.	.15	2.89		3.04	Includes material and labor to regrout
Minimum Charge	Job		181		181	tile floors.

Flooring

Sheet Vinyl Per S.F.

Sheet Vinyl Per S.F.		Unit	Material	Labor	Equip.	Total	Specification
Economy Grade							
	Demolish	S.F.		.47		.47	Includes material and labor to install
	Install	S.F.	2.26	1.13		3.39	resilient sheet vinyl flooring.
	Demolish and Install	S.F.	2.26	1.60		3.86	
	Clean	S.F.		.37		.37	
	Minimum Charge	Job		181		181	
Average Grade							
	Demolish	S.F.		.47		.47	Includes material and labor to install
	Install	S.F.	3.57	1.13		4.70	resilient sheet vinyl flooring.
	Demolish and Install	S.F.	3.57	1.60		5.17	
	Clean	S.F.		.37		.37	
	Minimum Charge	Job		181		181	
Premium Grade							
	Demolish	S.F.		.47		.47	Includes material and labor to install
	Install	S.F.	5.70	1.13		6.83	resilient sheet vinyl flooring.
	Demolish and Install	S.F.	5.70	1.60		7.30	
	Clean	S.F.		.37		.37	
	Minimum Charge	Job		181		181	
Clean and Wax							
	Clean	S.F.	.02	.19		.21	Includes labor and material to wash
	Minimum Charge	Job		181		181	and wax a vinyl tile floor.

Sheet Vinyl

Sheet Vinyl		Unit	Material	Labor	Equip.	Total	Specification
Economy Grade							
	Demolish	S.Y.		4.29		4.29	Includes material and labor to install
	Install	S.Y.	20.50	10.20		30.70	no wax sheet vinyl flooring.
	Demolish and Install	S.Y.	20.50	14.49		34.99	
	Clean	S.Y.		2.60		2.60	
	Minimum Charge	Job		181		181	
Average Grade							
	Demolish	S.Y.		4.29		4.29	Includes material and labor to install
	Install	S.Y.	32	10.20		42.20	no wax sheet vinyl flooring.
	Demolish and Install	S.Y.	32	14.49		46.49	
	Clean	S.Y.		2.60		2.60	
	Minimum Charge	Job		181		181	
Premium Grade							
	Demolish	S.Y.		4.29		4.29	Includes material and labor to install
	Install	S.Y.	51.50	10.20		61.70	no wax sheet vinyl flooring.
	Demolish and Install	S.Y.	51.50	14.49		65.99	
	Clean	S.Y.		2.60		2.60	
	Minimum Charge	Job		181		181	
Clean and Wax							
	Clean	S.F.	.02	.19		.21	Includes labor and material to wash
	Minimum Charge	Job		181		181	and wax a vinyl tile floor.

Vinyl Tile

Vinyl Tile		Unit	Material	Labor	Equip.	Total	Specification
Economy Grade							
	Demolish	S.F.		.66		.66	Includes material and labor to install
	Install	S.F.	3.30	.72		4.02	no wax 12″ x 12″ vinyl tile.
	Demolish and Install	S.F.	3.30	1.38		4.68	
	Clean	S.F.		.37		.37	
	Minimum Charge	Job		181		181	

Flooring

Vinyl Tile		Unit	Material	Labor	Equip.	Total	Specification
Average Grade							
	Demolish	S.F.		.66		.66	Includes material and labor to install
	Install	S.F.	6.80	.72		7.52	no wax 12″ x 12″ vinyl tile.
	Demolish and Install	S.F.	6.80	1.38		8.18	
	Clean	S.F.		.37		.37	
	Minimum Charge	Job		181		181	
Premium Grade							
	Demolish	S.F.		.66		.66	Includes material and labor to install
	Install	S.F.	14.85	.72		15.57	no wax 12″ x 12″ vinyl tile.
	Demolish and Install	S.F.	14.85	1.38		16.23	
	Clean	S.F.		.37		.37	
	Minimum Charge	Job		181		181	
Clean and Wax							
	Clean	S.F.	.02	.19		.21	Includes labor and material to wash
	Minimum Charge	Job		181		181	and wax a vinyl tile floor.

Carpeting Per S.F.		Unit	Material	Labor	Equip.	Total	Specification
Economy Grade							
	Demolish	S.F.		.07		.07	Includes material and labor to install
	Install	S.F.	1.42	.70		2.12	carpet including tack strips and hot
	Demolish and Install	S.F.	1.42	.77		2.19	melt tape on seams.
	Clean	S.F.		.52		.52	
	Minimum Charge	Job		181		181	
Average Grade							
	Demolish	S.F.		.07		.07	Includes material and labor to install
	Install	S.F.	1.67	.70		2.37	carpet including tack strips and hot
	Demolish and Install	S.F.	1.67	.77		2.44	melt tape on seams.
	Clean	S.F.		.52		.52	
	Minimum Charge	Job		181		181	
Premium Grade							
	Demolish	S.F.		.07		.07	Includes material and labor to install
	Install	S.F.	2.94	.70		3.64	carpet including tack strips and hot
	Demolish and Install	S.F.	2.94	.77		3.71	melt tape on seams.
	Clean	S.F.		.52		.52	
	Minimum Charge	Job		181		181	
Indoor/Outdoor							
	Demolish	S.F.		.07		.07	Includes material and labor to install
	Install	S.F.	1.09	.85		1.94	indoor-outdoor carpet.
	Demolish and Install	S.F.	1.09	.92		2.01	
	Clean	S.F.		.52		.52	
	Minimum Charge	Job		181		181	
100% Wool							
Average Grade							
	Demolish	S.F.		.07		.07	Includes material and labor to install
	Install	S.F.	10.40	.72		11.12	carpet including tack strips and hot
	Demolish and Install	S.F.	10.40	.79		11.19	melt tape on seams.
	Clean	S.F.		.52		.52	
	Minimum Charge	Job		181		181	
Premium Grade							
	Demolish	S.F.		.07		.07	Includes material and labor to install
	Install	S.F.	11.50	.72		12.22	carpet including tack strips and hot
	Demolish and Install	S.F.	11.50	.79		12.29	melt tape on seams.
	Clean	S.F.		.52		.52	
	Minimum Charge	Job		181		181	

Flooring

Carpeting Per S.F.

Carpeting Per S.F.		Unit	Material	Labor	Equip.	Total	Specification
Luxury Grade							
	Demolish	S.F.		.07		.07	Includes material and labor to install
	Install	S.F.	16.10	.72		16.82	carpet including tack strips and hot
	Demolish and Install	S.F.	16.10	.79		16.89	melt tape on seams.
	Clean	S.F.		.52		.52	
	Minimum Charge	Job		181		181	
Berber							
Average Grade							
	Demolish	S.F.		.07		.07	Includes material and labor to install
	Install	S.F.	3.83	.85		4.68	carpet including tack strips and hot
	Demolish and Install	S.F.	3.83	.92		4.75	melt tape on seams.
	Clean	S.F.		.52		.52	
	Minimum Charge	Job		181		181	
Premium Grade							
	Demolish	S.F.		.07		.07	Includes material and labor to install
	Install	S.F.	7.75	.85		8.60	carpet including tack strips and hot
	Demolish and Install	S.F.	7.75	.92		8.67	melt tape on seams.
	Clean	S.F.		.52		.52	
	Minimum Charge	Job		181		181	

Carpeting

Carpeting		Unit	Material	Labor	Equip.	Total	Specification
Indoor/Outdoor							
	Demolish	S.Y.		1.11		1.11	Includes material and labor to install
	Install	S.Y.	9.80	7.70		17.50	indoor-outdoor carpet.
	Demolish and Install	S.Y.	9.80	8.81		18.61	
	Reinstall	S.Y.		6.15		6.15	
	Clean	S.Y.		4.68		4.68	
	Minimum Charge	Job		181		181	
Economy Grade							
	Demolish	S.Y.		1.11		1.11	Includes material and labor to install
	Install	S.Y.	12.80	6.35		19.15	carpet including tack strips and hot
	Demolish and Install	S.Y.	12.80	7.46		20.26	melt tape on seams.
	Reinstall	S.Y.		5.08		5.08	
	Clean	S.Y.		4.68		4.68	
	Minimum Charge	Job		181		181	
Average Grade							
	Demolish	S.Y.		1.11		1.11	Includes material and labor to install
	Install	S.Y.	15	6.35		21.35	carpet including tack strips and hot
	Demolish and Install	S.Y.	15	7.46		22.46	melt tape on seams.
	Reinstall	S.Y.		5.08		5.08	
	Clean	S.Y.		4.68		4.68	
	Minimum Charge	Job		181		181	
Premium Grade							
	Demolish	S.Y.		1.11		1.11	Includes material and labor to install
	Install	S.Y.	26.50	6.35		32.85	carpet including tack strips and hot
	Demolish and Install	S.Y.	26.50	7.46		33.96	melt tape on seams.
	Reinstall	S.Y.		5.08		5.08	
	Clean	S.Y.		4.68		4.68	
	Minimum Charge	Job		181		181	

243

Flooring

Carpeting

Carpeting	Unit	Material	Labor	Equip.	Total	Specification
100% Wool						
Average Grade						
Demolish	S.Y.		1.11		1.11	Includes material and labor to install
Install	S.Y.	93.50	6.45		99.95	wool carpet including tack strips and
Demolish and Install	S.Y.	93.50	7.56		101.06	hot melt tape on seams.
Reinstall	S.Y.		5.17		5.17	
Clean	S.Y.		4.68		4.68	
Minimum Charge	Job		181		181	
Premium Grade						
Demolish	S.Y.		1.11		1.11	Includes material and labor to install
Install	S.Y.	103	6.45		109.45	carpet including tack strips and hot
Demolish and Install	S.Y.	103	7.56		110.56	melt tape on seams.
Reinstall	S.Y.		5.17		5.17	
Clean	S.Y.		4.68		4.68	
Minimum Charge	Job		181		181	
Luxury Grade						
Demolish	S.Y.		1.11		1.11	Includes material and labor to install
Install	S.Y.	145	6.45		151.45	carpet including tack strips and hot
Demolish and Install	S.Y.	145	7.56		152.56	melt tape on seams.
Reinstall	S.Y.		5.17		5.17	
Clean	S.Y.		4.68		4.68	
Minimum Charge	Job		181		181	
Berber						
Average Grade						
Demolish	S.Y.		1.11		1.11	Includes material and labor to install
Install	S.Y.	34.50	7.70		42.20	berber carpet including tack strips and
Demolish and Install	S.Y.	34.50	8.81		43.31	hot melt tape on seams.
Reinstall	S.Y.		6.15		6.15	
Clean	S.Y.		4.68		4.68	
Minimum Charge	Job		181		181	
Premium Grade						
Demolish	S.Y.		1.11		1.11	Includes material and labor to install
Install	S.Y.	70	7.70		77.70	carpet including tack strips and hot
Demolish and Install	S.Y.	70	8.81		78.81	melt tape on seams.
Reinstall	S.Y.		6.15		6.15	
Clean	S.Y.		4.68		4.68	
Minimum Charge	Job		181		181	

Carpet Pad Per S.F.	Unit	Material	Labor	Equip.	Total	Specification
Urethane						
Demolish	S.F.		.02		.02	Includes material and labor to install
Install	S.F.	.56	.27		.83	urethane carpet pad.
Demolish and Install	S.F.	.56	.29		.85	
Minimum Charge	Job		181		181	
Foam Rubber Slab						
Demolish	S.F.		.02		.02	Includes material and labor to install
Install	S.F.	.61	.27		.88	carpet pad, 3/8" thick foam rubber.
Demolish and Install	S.F.	.61	.29		.90	
Minimum Charge	Job		181		181	
Waffle						
Demolish	S.F.		.02		.02	Includes material and labor to install
Install	S.F.	.41	.03		.44	rubber waffle carpet pad.
Demolish and Install	S.F.	.41	.05		.46	
Minimum Charge	Job		181		181	

Flooring

Carpet Pad Per S.F.

Carpet Pad Per S.F.	Unit	Material	Labor	Equip.	Total	Specification
Jute						
Demolish	S.F.		.02		.02	Includes material and labor to install
Install	S.F.	.75	.24		.99	jute hair carpet pad.
Demolish and Install	S.F.	.75	.26		1.01	
Minimum Charge	Job		181		181	
Rebound						
Demolish	S.F.		.02		.02	Includes material and labor to install
Install	S.F.	.34	.20		.54	rebound carpet pad.
Demolish and Install	S.F.	.34	.22		.56	
Minimum Charge	Job		181		181	

Carpet Pad

Carpet Pad	Unit	Material	Labor	Equip.	Total	Specification
Urethane						
Demolish	S.Y.		.19		.19	Includes material and labor to install
Install	S.Y.	5.05	2.41		7.46	urethane carpet pad.
Demolish and Install	S.Y.	5.05	2.60		7.65	
Reinstall	S.Y.		1.93		1.93	
Minimum Charge	Job		181		181	
Foam Rubber Slab						
Demolish	S.Y.		.19		.19	Includes material and labor to install
Install	S.Y.	5.45	2.41		7.86	rubber slab carpet pad.
Demolish and Install	S.Y.	5.45	2.60		8.05	
Reinstall	S.Y.		1.93		1.93	
Minimum Charge	Job		181		181	
Waffle						
Demolish	S.Y.		.19		.19	Includes material and labor to install
Install	S.Y.	3.65	.27		3.92	rubber waffle carpet pad.
Demolish and Install	S.Y.	3.65	.46		4.11	
Reinstall	S.Y.		.21		.21	
Minimum Charge	Job		181		181	
Jute						
Demolish	S.Y.		.19		.19	Includes material and labor to install
Install	S.Y.	6.75	2.13		8.88	jute hair carpet pad.
Demolish and Install	S.Y.	6.75	2.32		9.07	
Reinstall	S.Y.		1.70		1.70	
Minimum Charge	Job		181		181	
Rebound						
Demolish	S.Y.		.19		.19	Includes material and labor to install
Install	S.Y.	3.11	1.80		4.91	rebound carpet pad.
Demolish and Install	S.Y.	3.11	1.99		5.10	
Reinstall	S.Y.		1.44		1.44	
Minimum Charge	Job		181		181	

Stair Components

Stair Components	Unit	Material	Labor	Equip.	Total	Specification
Carpeting						
Demolish	Ea.		2.01		2.01	Includes material and labor to install
Install	Riser	51	9.50		60.50	carpet and pad on stairs.
Demolish and Install	Riser	51	11.51		62.51	
Reinstall	Riser		7.61		7.61	
Clean	Ea.		4.68		4.68	
Minimum Charge	Job		181		181	

Tub/Shower

Stainless Steel Double Sink

Water Closet

Commode	Unit	Material	Labor	Equip.	Total	Specification
Demolish	Ea.		46		46	Includes material and labor to install a
Install	Ea.	264	157		421	toilet with valve, seat and cover.
Demolish and Install	Ea.	264	203		467	
Reinstall	Ea.		125.58		125.58	
Clean	Ea.	.52	14.95		15.47	
Minimum Charge	Job		231		231	
Wall w / Flush Valve						
Demolish	Ea.		46		46	Includes material and labor to install a
Install	Ea.	490	143		633	wall hung toilet with flush valve, seat
Demolish and Install	Ea.	490	189		679	and cover.
Reinstall	Ea.		114.76		114.76	
Clean	Ea.	.52	14.95		15.47	
Minimum Charge	Job		231		231	
Designer Floor Mount						
Demolish	Ea.		46		46	Includes material and labor to install a
Install	Ea.	1100	157		1257	toilet with valve, seat and cover.
Demolish and Install	Ea.	1100	203		1303	
Reinstall	Ea.		125.58		125.58	
Clean	Ea.	.52	14.95		15.47	
Minimum Charge	Job		231		231	
Urinal						
Demolish	Ea.		46		46	Includes material and labor to install a
Install	Ea.	320	277		597	wall hung urinal with flush valve.
Demolish and Install	Ea.	320	323		643	
Reinstall	Ea.		221.87		221.87	
Clean	Ea.	.52	14.95		15.47	
Minimum Charge	Job		231		231	
Bidet						
Vitreous China						
Demolish	Ea.		46		46	Includes material and labor to install a
Install	Ea.	750	166		916	vitreous china bidet complete with
Demolish and Install	Ea.	750	212		962	trim.
Reinstall	Ea.		133.12		133.12	
Clean	Ea.	.52	14.95		15.47	
Minimum Charge	Job		231		231	

Finish Mechanical

Commode		Unit	Material	Labor	Equip.	Total	Specification
Chrome Fittings							
	Install	Ea.	189	58		247	Includes labor and materials to install chrome fittings for a bidet.
Brass Fittings							
	Install	Ea.	208	58		266	Includes labor and materials to install brass fittings for a bidet.
Seat							
	Demolish	Ea.		19.25		19.25	Includes material and labor to install a toilet seat and cover.
	Install	Ea.	32	19.25		51.25	
	Demolish and Install	Ea.	32	38.50		70.50	
	Reinstall	Ea.		15.41		15.41	
	Clean	Ea.	.26	6.25		6.51	
	Minimum Charge	Job		231		231	
Rough-in							
	Install	Ea.	400	293		693	Includes labor and materials to install water supply pipe with valves and drain, waste and vent pipe with all couplings, hangers and fasteners necessary.

Sink (assembly)		Unit	Material	Labor	Equip.	Total	Specification
Single							
Porcelain							
	Demolish	Ea.		29		29	Includes material and labor to install a single bowl enamel finished cast iron kitchen sink with faucet and drain.
	Install	Ea.	550	149		699	
	Demolish and Install	Ea.	550	178		728	
	Reinstall	Ea.		118.86		118.86	
	Clean	Ea.	.34	10.70		11.04	
	Minimum Charge	Job		231		231	
Stainless Steel							
	Demolish	Ea.		29		29	Includes material and labor to install a single bowl stainless steel kitchen sink with faucet and drain.
	Install	Ea.	710	149		859	
	Demolish and Install	Ea.	710	178		888	
	Reinstall	Ea.		118.86		118.86	
	Clean	Ea.	.34	10.70		11.04	
	Minimum Charge	Job		231		231	
Double							
Porcelain							
	Demolish	Ea.		33		33	Includes material and labor to install a double bowl enamel finished cast iron kitchen sink with faucet and drain.
	Install	Ea.	1125	173		1298	
	Demolish and Install	Ea.	1125	206		1331	
	Reinstall	Ea.		138.67		138.67	
	Clean	Ea.	.52	14.95		15.47	
	Minimum Charge	Job		231		231	
Stainless Steel							
	Demolish	Ea.		33		33	Includes material and labor to install a double bowl stainless steel kitchen sink with faucet and drain.
	Install	Ea.	455	173		628	
	Demolish and Install	Ea.	455	206		661	
	Reinstall	Ea.		138.67		138.67	
	Clean	Ea.	.52	14.95		15.47	
	Minimum Charge	Job		231		231	
Bar							
	Demolish	Ea.		29		29	Includes material and labor to install a small single bowl stainless steel bar / vegetable / kitchen sink with faucet and drain.
	Install	Ea.	190	116		306	
	Demolish and Install	Ea.	190	145		335	
	Reinstall	Ea.		92.48		92.48	
	Clean	Ea.	.34	10.70		11.04	
	Minimum Charge	Job		231		231	

Finish Mechanical

Sink (assembly)

	Unit	Material	Labor	Equip.	Total	Specification
Floor						
Demolish	Ea.		92.50		92.50	Includes material and labor to install
Install	Ea.	930	189		1119	an enameled cast iron floor mounted
Demolish and Install	Ea.	930	281.50		1211.50	corner service sink with faucet and
Reinstall	Ea.		151.27		151.27	drain.
Clean	Ea.	.52	7.50		8.02	
Minimum Charge	Job		231		231	
Pedestal						
Demolish	Ea.		29		29	Includes material and labor to install a
Install	Ea.	435	130		565	vitreous china pedestal lavatory with
Demolish and Install	Ea.	435	159		594	faucet set and pop-up drain.
Reinstall	Ea.		104		104	
Clean	Ea.	.34	10.70		11.04	
Minimum Charge	Job		231		231	
Vanity Lavatory						
Demolish	Ea.		29		29	Includes material and labor to install a
Install	Ea.	294	154		448	vitreous china lavatory with faucet set
Demolish and Install	Ea.	294	183		477	and pop-up drain.
Reinstall	Ea.		123.26		123.26	
Clean	Ea.	.34	10.70		11.04	
Minimum Charge	Job		231		231	
Rough-in						
Install	Ea.	400	390		790	Includes labor and materials to install copper supply pipe with valves and drain, waste and vent pipe with all couplings, hangers and fasteners necessary.
Laundry						
Demolish	Ea.		30		30	Includes material and labor to install a
Install	Ea.	160	128		288	laundry sink (wall mounted or with
Demolish and Install	Ea.	160	158		318	legs) including faucet and pop up
Clean	Ea.	.34	10.70		11.04	drain.
Minimum Charge	Job		231		231	

Sink Only

	Unit	Material	Labor	Equip.	Total	Specification
Single						
Porcelain						
Demolish	Ea.		29		29	Includes material and labor to install a
Install	Ea.	475	165		640	single bowl enamel finished cast iron
Demolish and Install	Ea.	475	194		669	kitchen sink.
Reinstall	Ea.		132.11		132.11	
Clean	Ea.	.34	10.70		11.04	
Minimum Charge	Job		231		231	
Stainless Steel						
Demolish	Ea.		29		29	Includes material and labor to install a
Install	Ea.	625	116		741	single bowl stainless steel kitchen sink.
Demolish and Install	Ea.	625	145		770	
Reinstall	Ea.		92.48		92.48	
Clean	Ea.	.34	10.70		11.04	
Minimum Charge	Job		231		231	

Finish Mechanical

Sink Only		Unit	Material	Labor	Equip.	Total	Specification
Double							
Porcelain							Includes material and labor to install a double bowl enamel finished cast iron kitchen sink.
	Demolish	Ea.		33		33	
	Install	Ea.	210	193		403	
	Demolish and Install	Ea.	210	226		436	
	Reinstall	Ea.		154.13		154.13	
	Clean	Ea.	.52	14.95		15.47	
	Minimum Charge	Job		231		231	
Stainless Steel							Includes material and labor to install a double bowl stainless steel kitchen sink.
	Demolish	Ea.		33		33	
	Install	Ea.	935	149		1084	
	Demolish and Install	Ea.	935	182		1117	
	Reinstall	Ea.		119.33		119.33	
	Clean	Ea.	.52	14.95		15.47	
	Minimum Charge	Job		231		231	
Bar							Includes material and labor to install a small single bowl stainless steel bar / vegetable / kitchen sink.
	Demolish	Ea.		29		29	
	Install	Ea.	75.50	116		191.50	
	Demolish and Install	Ea.	75.50	145		220.50	
	Reinstall	Ea.		92.48		92.48	
	Clean	Ea.	.34	10.70		11.04	
	Minimum Charge	Job		231		231	
Floor							Includes material and labor to install an enameled cast iron floor mounted corner service sink.
	Demolish	Ea.		92.50		92.50	
	Install	Ea.	790	210		1000	
	Demolish and Install	Ea.	790	302.50		1092.50	
	Reinstall	Ea.		168.15		168.15	
	Clean	Ea.	.52	7.50		8.02	
	Minimum Charge	Job		231		231	
Pedestal							Includes material and labor to install a vitreous china pedestal lavatory.
	Demolish	Ea.		29		29	
	Install	Ea.	315	145		460	
	Demolish and Install	Ea.	315	174		489	
	Reinstall	Ea.		115.60		115.60	
	Clean	Ea.	.34	10.70		11.04	
	Minimum Charge	Job		231		231	
Vanity Lavatory							Includes material and labor to install a vitreous china lavatory.
	Demolish	Ea.		29		29	
	Install	Ea.	168	145		313	
	Demolish and Install	Ea.	168	174		342	
	Reinstall	Ea.		115.60		115.60	
	Clean	Ea.	.34	10.70		11.04	
	Minimum Charge	Job		231		231	
Rough-in							Includes labor and materials to install copper supply pipe with valves and drain, waste and vent pipe with all couplings, hangers and fasteners necessary.
	Install	Ea.	350	360		710	
Faucet Sink							
Good Grade							Includes material and labor to install a sink faucet and fittings.
	Demolish	Ea.		23		23	
	Install	Ea.	67.50	32		99.50	
	Demolish and Install	Ea.	67.50	55		122.50	
	Reinstall	Ea.		25.53		25.53	
	Clean	Ea.	.21	9.35		9.56	
	Minimum Charge	Job		231		231	

Finish Mechanical

Sink Only		Unit	Material	Labor	Equip.	Total	Specification
Better Grade							
	Demolish	Ea.		23		23	Includes material and labor to install a
	Install	Ea.	114	32		146	sink faucet and fittings.
	Demolish and Install	Ea.	114	55		169	
	Reinstall	Ea.		25.53		25.53	
	Clean	Ea.	.21	9.35		9.56	
	Minimum Charge	Job		231		231	
Premium Grade							
	Demolish	Ea.		23		23	Includes material and labor to install a
	Install	Ea.	222	40		262	sink faucet and fittings.
	Demolish and Install	Ea.	222	63		285	
	Reinstall	Ea.		31.83		31.83	
	Clean	Ea.	.21	9.35		9.56	
	Minimum Charge	Job		231		231	
Drain & Basket							
	Demolish	Ea.		14.45		14.45	Includes material and labor to install a
	Install	Ea.	13.35	29		42.35	sink drain and basket.
	Demolish and Install	Ea.	13.35	43.45		56.80	
	Reinstall	Ea.		23.12		23.12	
	Clean	Ea.	.21	9.35		9.56	
	Minimum Charge	Job		231		231	

Bathtub		Unit	Material	Labor	Equip.	Total	Specification
Enameled							
Steel							
	Demolish	Ea.		83		83	Includes labor and material to install a
	Install	Ea.	530	151		681	formed steel bath tub with spout,
	Demolish and Install	Ea.	530	234		764	mixing valve, shower head and
	Reinstall	Ea.		121.02		121.02	pop-up drain.
	Clean	Ea.	1.05	25		26.05	
	Minimum Charge	Job		231		231	
Cast Iron							
	Demolish	Ea.		83		83	Includes material and labor to install a
	Install	Ea.	1100	189		1289	cast iron bath tub with spout, mixing
	Demolish and Install	Ea.	1100	272		1372	valve, shower head and pop-up drain.
	Reinstall	Ea.		151.27		151.27	
	Clean	Ea.	1.05	25		26.05	
	Minimum Charge	Job		231		231	
Fiberglass							
	Demolish	Ea.		83		83	Includes material and labor to install
	Install	Ea.	1125	151		1276	an acrylic soaking tub with spout,
	Demolish and Install	Ea.	1125	234		1359	mixing valve, shower head and
	Reinstall	Ea.		121.02		121.02	pop-up drain.
	Clean	Ea.	1.05	25		26.05	
	Minimum Charge	Job		231		231	
Institutional							
	Demolish	Ea.		83		83	Includes material and labor to install a
	Install	Ea.	1275	277		1552	hospital / institutional type bathtub
	Demolish and Install	Ea.	1275	360		1635	with spout, mixing valve, shower head
	Reinstall	Ea.		221.87		221.87	and pop-up drain.
	Clean	Ea.	1.05	25		26.05	
	Minimum Charge	Job		231		231	

Finish Mechanical

Bathtub

	Unit	Material	Labor	Equip.	Total	Specification
Whirlpool (Acrylic)						
Demolish	Ea.		257		257	Includes material and labor to install a
Install	Ea.	3275	830		4105	molded fiberglass whirlpool tub.
Demolish and Install	Ea.	3275	1087		4362	
Reinstall	Ea.		665.60		665.60	
Clean	Ea.	1.05	25		26.05	
Minimum Charge	Job		231		231	
Pump / Motor						
Demolish	Ea.		64		64	Includes material and labor to install a
Install	Ea.	246	139		385	whirlpool tub pump / motor.
Demolish and Install	Ea.	246	203		449	
Reinstall	Ea.		111.09		111.09	
Clean	Ea.	.26	18.70		18.96	
Minimum Charge	Job		231		231	
Heater / Motor						
Demolish	Ea.		64		64	Includes material and labor to install a
Install	Ea.	350	206		556	whirlpool tub heater.
Demolish and Install	Ea.	350	270		620	
Reinstall	Ea.		164.41		164.41	
Clean	Ea.	.26	18.70		18.96	
Minimum Charge	Job		231		231	
Thermal Cover						
Demolish	Ea.		10.30		10.30	Includes material and labor to install a
Install	Ea.	228	29		257	whirlpool tub thermal cover.
Demolish and Install	Ea.	228	39.30		267.30	
Reinstall	Ea.		23.12		23.12	
Clean	Ea.	2.60	18.70		21.30	
Minimum Charge	Job		231		231	
Tub / Shower Combination						
Demolish	Ea.		73.50		73.50	Includes material and labor to install a
Install	Ea.	860	208		1068	fiberglass module tub with shower
Demolish and Install	Ea.	860	281.50		1141.50	surround with spout, mixing valve,
Reinstall	Ea.		166.40		166.40	shower head and pop-up drain.
Clean	Ea.	1.30	37.50		38.80	
Minimum Charge	Job		231		231	
Accessories						
Sliding Door						
Demolish	Ea.		21		21	Includes material and labor to install a
Install	Ea.	480	95		575	48" aluminum framed tempered glass
Demolish and Install	Ea.	480	116		596	shower door.
Reinstall	Ea.		75.92		75.92	
Clean	Ea.	2.17	12.45		14.62	
Minimum Charge	Job		231		231	
Shower Head						
Demolish	Ea.		5.80		5.80	Includes material and labor to install a
Install	Ea.	54.50	19.25		73.75	water saving shower head.
Demolish and Install	Ea.	54.50	25.05		79.55	
Reinstall	Ea.		15.41		15.41	
Clean	Ea.	.02	3.74		3.76	
Minimum Charge	Job		231		231	
Faucet Set						
Demolish	Ea.		29		29	Includes material and labor to install a
Install	Ea.	95	58		153	combination spout / diverter for a
Demolish and Install	Ea.	95	87		182	bathtub.
Reinstall	Ea.		46.24		46.24	
Clean	Ea.	.21	9.35		9.56	
Minimum Charge	Job		231		231	

Finish Mechanical

Bathtub

	Unit	Material	Labor	Equip.	Total	Specification
Shower Rod						Includes material and labor to install a chrome plated shower rod.
Demolish	Ea.		3.46		3.46	
Install	Ea.	27.50	31		58.50	
Demolish and Install	Ea.	27.50	34.46		61.96	
Reinstall	Ea.		24.84		24.84	
Clean	Ea.		3.74		3.74	
Minimum Charge	Job		231		231	
Rough-in						Includes labor and materials to install copper supply pipe with valves and drain, waste and vent pipe with all couplings, hangers and fasteners necessary.
Install	Ea.	435	400		835	

Shower

	Unit	Material	Labor	Equip.	Total	Specification
Fiberglass						
32" x 32"						Includes material and labor to install a fiberglass shower stall with door, mixing valve and shower head and drain fitting.
Demolish	Ea.		173		173	
Install	Ea.	600	151		751	
Demolish and Install	Ea.	600	324		924	
Reinstall	Ea.		121.02		121.02	
Clean	Ea.	1.05	25		26.05	
Minimum Charge	Job		231		231	
36" x 36"						Includes material and labor to install a fiberglass shower stall with door, mixing valve and shower head and drain fitting.
Demolish	Ea.		173		173	
Install	Ea.	610	151		761	
Demolish and Install	Ea.	610	324		934	
Reinstall	Ea.		121.02		121.02	
Clean	Ea.	1.05	25		26.05	
Minimum Charge	Job		231		231	
35" x 60"						Includes material and labor to install a handicap fiberglass shower stall with door & seat, mixing valve and shower head and drain fitting.
Demolish	Ea.		173		173	
Install	Ea.	825	208		1033	
Demolish and Install	Ea.	825	381		1206	
Reinstall	Ea.		166.40		166.40	
Clean	Ea.	1.05	25		26.05	
Minimum Charge	Job		231		231	
Accessories						
Single Door						Includes material and labor to install a shower door.
Demolish	Ea.		21		21	
Install	Ea.	145	50		195	
Demolish and Install	Ea.	145	71		216	
Reinstall	Ea.		40.07		40.07	
Clean	Ea.	2.17	12.45		14.62	
Minimum Charge	Job		231		231	
Shower Head						Includes material and labor to install a water saving shower head.
Demolish	Ea.		5.80		5.80	
Install	Ea.	54.50	19.25		73.75	
Demolish and Install	Ea.	54.50	25.05		79.55	
Reinstall	Ea.		15.41		15.41	
Clean	Ea.	.02	3.74		3.76	
Minimum Charge	Job		231		231	

Shower

	Unit	Material	Labor	Equip.	Total	Specification
Faucet Set						
Demolish	Ea.		29		29	Includes material and labor to install a
Install	Ea.	95	58		153	combination spout / diverter for a
Demolish and Install	Ea.	95	87		182	bathtub.
Reinstall	Ea.		46.24		46.24	
Clean	Ea.	.21	9.35		9.56	
Minimum Charge	Job		231		231	
Shower Pan						
Demolish	Ea.		21.50		21.50	Includes material and labor to install
Install	Ea.	118	58		176	the base portion of a fiberglass
Demolish and Install	Ea.	118	79.50		197.50	shower unit.
Reinstall	Ea.		46.24		46.24	
Clean	Ea.	1.05	25		26.05	
Minimum Charge	Job		231		231	
Rough-in						
Install	Ea.	535	405		940	Includes labor and materials to install copper supply pipe with valves and drain, waste and vent pipe with all couplings, hangers and fasteners necessary.

Ductwork

	Unit	Material	Labor	Equip.	Total	Specification
Return Grill						
Under 10" Wide						
Demolish	Ea.		10		10	Includes material and labor to install a
Install	Ea.	37	25		62	10" x 10" air return register.
Demolish and Install	Ea.	37	35		72	
Reinstall	Ea.		20.04		20.04	
Clean	Ea.	.26	8.30		8.56	
Minimum Charge	Job		225		225	
12" to 20" Wide						
Demolish	Ea.		10		10	Includes material and labor to install a
Install	Ea.	55.50	26.50		82	16" x 16" air return register.
Demolish and Install	Ea.	55.50	36.50		92	
Reinstall	Ea.		21.21		21.21	
Clean	Ea.	.26	8.30		8.56	
Minimum Charge	Job		225		225	
Over 20" Wide						
Demolish	Ea.		15.20		15.20	Includes material and labor to install a
Install	Ea.	101	41		142	24" x 24" air return register.
Demolish and Install	Ea.	101	56.20		157.20	
Reinstall	Ea.		32.79		32.79	
Clean	Ea.	.26	9.35		9.61	
Minimum Charge	Job		225		225	
Supply Grill						
Baseboard Type						
Demolish	Ea.		7.15		7.15	Includes material and labor to install a
Install	Ea.	20.50	22.50		43	14" x 6" baseboard air supply
Demolish and Install	Ea.	20.50	29.65		50.15	register.
Reinstall	Ea.		18.03		18.03	
Clean	Ea.	.26	8.30		8.56	
Minimum Charge	Job		225		225	

Ductwork

	Unit	Material	Labor	Equip.	Total	Specification
10" Wide						
Demolish	Ea.		8.35		8.35	Includes material and labor to install a
Install	Ea.	43	22.50		65.50	10" x 6" air supply register.
Demolish and Install	Ea.	43	30.85		73.85	
Reinstall	Ea.		18.03		18.03	
Clean	Ea.	.26	8.30		8.56	
Minimum Charge	Job		225		225	
12" to 15" Wide						
Demolish	Ea.		8.35		8.35	Includes material and labor to install a
Install	Ea.	59.50	26.50		86	14" x 8" air supply register.
Demolish and Install	Ea.	59.50	34.85		94.35	
Reinstall	Ea.		21.21		21.21	
Clean	Ea.	.26	8.30		8.56	
Minimum Charge	Job		225		225	
18" to 24" Wide						
Demolish	Ea.		10		10	Includes material and labor to install a
Install	Ea.	82	34.50		116.50	24" x 8" air supply register.
Demolish and Install	Ea.	82	44.50		126.50	
Reinstall	Ea.		27.74		27.74	
Clean	Ea.	.26	9.35		9.61	
Minimum Charge	Job		225		225	
30" to 36" Wide						
Demolish	Ea.		12.50		12.50	Includes material and labor to install a
Install	Ea.	107	32		139	30" x 8" air supply register.
Demolish and Install	Ea.	107	44.50		151.50	
Reinstall	Ea.		25.76		25.76	
Clean	Ea.	.26	18.70		18.96	
Minimum Charge	Job		225		225	

Diffuser

	Unit	Material	Labor	Equip.	Total	Specification
12" Louver						
Demolish	Ea.		10		10	Includes material and labor to install a
Install	Ea.	48	32		80	12" aluminum louvered diffuser.
Demolish and Install	Ea.	48	42		90	
Reinstall	Ea.		25.76		25.76	
Clean	Ea.	.26	8.30		8.56	
Minimum Charge	Job		225		225	
14" to 20" Louver						
Demolish	Ea.		10		10	Includes material and labor to install a
Install	Ea.	53.50	45		98.50	14" to 20" aluminum louvered diffuser.
Demolish and Install	Ea.	53.50	55		108.50	
Reinstall	Ea.		36.06		36.06	
Clean	Ea.	.26	9.35		9.61	
Minimum Charge	Job		225		225	
25" to 32" Louver						
Demolish	Ea.		15.20		15.20	Includes material and labor to install a
Install	Ea.	70	64.50		134.50	25" to 32" aluminum louvered diffuser.
Demolish and Install	Ea.	70	79.70		149.70	
Reinstall	Ea.		51.52		51.52	
Clean	Ea.	.26	12.45		12.71	
Minimum Charge	Job		225		225	
12" Round						
Demolish	Ea.		13.90		13.90	Includes material and labor to install a
Install	Ea.	45.50	37.50		83	12" diameter aluminum diffuser with a
Demolish and Install	Ea.	45.50	51.40		96.90	butterfly damper.
Reinstall	Ea.		30.05		30.05	
Clean	Ea.	.26	8.30		8.56	
Minimum Charge	Job		225		225	

Ductwork		Unit	Material	Labor	Equip.	Total	Specification
14″ to 20″ Round							
	Demolish	Ea.		18.55		18.55	Includes material and labor to install a
	Install	Ea.	155	50		205	20″ diameter aluminum diffuser with a
	Demolish and Install	Ea.	155	68.55		223.55	butterfly damper.
	Reinstall	Ea.		40.07		40.07	
	Clean	Ea.	.26	9.35		9.61	
	Minimum Charge	Job		225		225	
Flush-out / Sanitize							
	Install	L.F.	1.05	3.74		4.79	Includes labor and material costs to
	Minimum Charge	Job		225		225	clean ductwork.

Lighting Fixture   Duplex Receptacle

Electrical Per S.F.	Unit	Material	Labor	Equip.	Total	Specification
Residential						
Light Fixtures						
Install	S.F.	.26	.22		.48	Includes labor and material to replace house light fixtures. Apply S.F. cost to floor area including garages but not basements.

Circuits	Unit	Material	Labor	Equip.	Total	Specification
Outlet with Wiring						
Demolish	Ea.		24.50		24.50	Includes material and labor to install
Install	Ea.	10	30		40	general purpose outlet with cover, up
Demolish and Install	Ea.	10	54.50		64.50	to 20 feet of #12/2 wire.
Reinstall	Ea.		24.04		24.04	
Clean	Ea.		1.87		1.87	
Minimum Charge	Job		219		219	
GFCI Outlet w / Wiring						
Demolish	Ea.		24.50		24.50	Cost includes material and labor to
Install	Ea.	48	35.50		83.50	install 120V GFCI receptacle and wall
Demolish and Install	Ea.	48	60		108	plate, with up to 20 feet of #12/2
Reinstall	Ea.		28.41		28.41	wire.
Clean	Ea.		1.87		1.87	
Minimum Charge	Job		219		219	
Exterior Outlet w / Wiring						
Demolish	Ea.		24.50		24.50	Cost includes material and labor to
Install	Ea.	39.50	36.50		76	install 110V waterproof external
Demolish and Install	Ea.	39.50	61		100.50	receptacle and cover plate with up to
Reinstall	Ea.		29.15		29.15	20' of #12/2 wire.
Clean	Ea.		1.87		1.87	
Minimum Charge	Job		219		219	
240V Outlet w / Wiring						
Demolish	Ea.		24.50		24.50	Cost includes material and labor to
Install	Ea.	74.50	68		142.50	install 240V receptacle and cover
Demolish and Install	Ea.	74.50	92.50		167	plate with up to 20' of #12/2 wire.
Reinstall	Ea.		54.56		54.56	
Clean	Ea.		1.87		1.87	
Minimum Charge	Job		219		219	

Finish Electrical

Circuits

	Unit	Material	Labor	Equip.	Total	Specification
TV / Cable Jack w / Wiring						
Demolish	Ea.		24.50		24.50	Includes material and labor to install
Install	Ea.	21	27.50		48.50	TV/cable outlet box and cover plate
Demolish and Install	Ea.	21	52		73	including 20' of wiring.
Reinstall	Ea.		21.86		21.86	
Clean	Ea.		1.87		1.87	
Minimum Charge	Job		219		219	
Phone Jack with Wiring						
Demolish	Ea.		24.50		24.50	Includes material and labor to install
Install	Ea.	12.10	16.80		28.90	phone jack and cover plate including
Demolish and Install	Ea.	12.10	41.30		53.40	up to 20' of telephone cable.
Reinstall	Ea.		13.45		13.45	
Clean	Ea.		1.17		1.17	
Minimum Charge	Job		219		219	

Light Switch

	Unit	Material	Labor	Equip.	Total	Specification
Single						
Switch						
Demolish	Ea.		4.86		4.86	Includes material and labor to install
Install	Ea.	6.15	21		27.15	single switch and wall plate. Wiring is
Demolish and Install	Ea.	6.15	25.86		32.01	not included.
Reinstall	Ea.		16.66		16.66	
Clean	Ea.		1.87		1.87	
Minimum Charge	Job		219		219	
Plate						
Demolish	Ea.		2.43		2.43	Includes material and labor to install a
Install	Ea.	.43	5.45		5.88	one gang brown wall switch plate.
Demolish and Install	Ea.	.43	7.88		8.31	
Reinstall	Ea.		4.37		4.37	
Clean	Ea.	.10	.37		.47	
Minimum Charge	Job		219		219	
Double						
Switch						
Demolish	Ea.		9.70		9.70	Includes material and labor to install
Install	Ea.	9.25	31		40.25	double switch and wall plate. Wiring
Demolish and Install	Ea.	9.25	40.70		49.95	is not included.
Reinstall	Ea.		24.98		24.98	
Clean	Ea.	.10	6		6.10	
Minimum Charge	Job		219		219	
Plate						
Demolish	Ea.		2.43		2.43	Includes material and labor to install a
Install	Ea.	.91	8.25		9.16	two gang brown wall switch plate.
Demolish and Install	Ea.	.91	10.68		11.59	
Reinstall	Ea.		6.60		6.60	
Clean	Ea.	.10	.37		.47	
Minimum Charge	Job		219		219	
Triple						
Switch						
Demolish	Ea.		14.70		14.70	Includes material and labor to install
Install	Ea.	27	36.50		63.50	triple switch and wall plate. Wiring is
Demolish and Install	Ea.	27	51.20		78.20	not included.
Reinstall	Ea.		29.15		29.15	
Clean	Ea.	.10	9		9.10	
Minimum Charge	Job		219		219	

Finish Electrical

Light Switch

Light Switch	Unit	Material	Labor	Equip.	Total	Specification
Plate						
Demolish	Ea.		2.43		2.43	Includes material and labor to install a
Install	Ea.	1.36	13.65		15.01	three gang brown wall switch plate.
Demolish and Install	Ea.	1.36	16.08		17.44	
Reinstall	Ea.		10.93		10.93	
Clean	Ea.	.10	.37		.47	
Minimum Charge	Job		219		219	
Dimmer						
Switch						
Demolish	Ea.		4.86		4.86	Includes material and labor to install
Install	Ea.	23	25.50		48.50	dimmer switch. Wiring is not included.
Demolish and Install	Ea.	23	30.36		53.36	
Reinstall	Ea.		20.57		20.57	
Clean	Ea.		1.87		1.87	
Minimum Charge	Job		219		219	
Plate						
Demolish	Ea.		2.43		2.43	Includes material and labor to install a
Install	Ea.	.43	5.45		5.88	one gang brown wall switch plate.
Demolish and Install	Ea.	.43	7.88		8.31	
Reinstall	Ea.		4.37		4.37	
Clean	Ea.	.10	.37		.47	
Minimum Charge	Job		219		219	
With Wiring						
Single						
Demolish	Ea.		24.50		24.50	Includes material and labor to install
Install	Ea.	11.75	25.50		37.25	single switch and plate including up to
Demolish and Install	Ea.	11.75	50		61.75	20' of romex cable.
Reinstall	Ea.		20.45		20.45	
Clean	Ea.		1.87		1.87	
Minimum Charge	Job		219		219	
Double						
Demolish	Ea.		24.50		24.50	Includes material and labor to install
Install	Ea.	29	43.50		72.50	double switch and plate including up
Demolish and Install	Ea.	29	68		97	to 20' of romex cable.
Reinstall	Ea.		34.98		34.98	
Clean	Ea.	.10	6		6.10	
Minimum Charge	Job		219		219	
Triple						
Demolish	Ea.		36.50		36.50	Includes material and labor to install
Install	Ea.	35	49		84	triple switch and plate including up to
Demolish and Install	Ea.	35	85.50		120.50	20' of romex cable.
Reinstall	Ea.		39.34		39.34	
Clean	Ea.	.10	9		9.10	
Minimum Charge	Job		219		219	
Dimmer						
Demolish	Ea.		24.50		24.50	Includes material and labor to install
Install	Ea.	28.50	30		58.50	dimmer switch and cover plate
Demolish and Install	Ea.	28.50	54.50		83	including up to 20' of romex cable.
Reinstall	Ea.		24.04		24.04	
Clean	Ea.		1.87		1.87	
Minimum Charge	Job		219		219	

Finish Electrical

Cover for Outlet / Switch

	Unit	Material	Labor	Equip.	Total	Specification
High Grade						
Demolish	Ea.		2.43		2.43	Includes material and labor to install
Install	Ea.	2.75	5.45		8.20	wall plate, stainless steel, 1 gang.
Demolish and Install	Ea.	2.75	7.88		10.63	
Reinstall	Ea.		4.37		4.37	
Clean	Ea.	.10	.37		.47	
Minimum Charge	Job		219		219	
Deluxe Grade						
Demolish	Ea.		2.43		2.43	Includes material and labor to install
Install	Ea.	5.80	5.45		11.25	wall plate, brushed brass, 1 gang.
Demolish and Install	Ea.	5.80	7.88		13.68	
Reinstall	Ea.		4.37		4.37	
Clean	Ea.	.10	.37		.47	
Minimum Charge	Job		219		219	

Residential Light Fixture

	Unit	Material	Labor	Equip.	Total	Specification
Ceiling						
Good Quality						
Demolish	Ea.		10.10		10.10	Includes material and labor to install
Install	Ea.	38	10.95		48.95	standard quality incandescent ceiling
Demolish and Install	Ea.	38	21.05		59.05	light fixture. Wiring is not included.
Reinstall	Ea.		8.74		8.74	
Clean	Ea.	.13	25		25.13	
Minimum Charge	Job		219		219	
Better Quality						
Demolish	Ea.		10.10		10.10	Includes material and labor to install
Install	Ea.	94.50	23		117.50	custom quality incandescent ceiling
Demolish and Install	Ea.	94.50	33.10		127.60	light fixture. Wiring is not included.
Reinstall	Ea.		18.41		18.41	
Clean	Ea.	.13	25		25.13	
Minimum Charge	Job		219		219	
Premium Quality						
Demolish	Ea.		10.10		10.10	Includes material and labor to install
Install	Ea.	278	23		301	deluxe quality incandescent ceiling
Demolish and Install	Ea.	278	33.10		311.10	light fixture. Wiring is not included.
Reinstall	Ea.		18.41		18.41	
Clean	Ea.	.13	25		25.13	
Minimum Charge	Job		219		219	
Recessed Ceiling						
Demolish	Ea.		20		20	Includes material and labor to install
Install	Ea.	48	14.55		62.55	standard quality recessed eyeball
Demolish and Install	Ea.	48	34.55		82.55	spotlight with housing. Wiring is not
Reinstall	Ea.		11.66		11.66	included.
Clean	Ea.	.06	3.12		3.18	
Minimum Charge	Job		219		219	
Recessed Eyeball						
Demolish	Ea.		20		20	Includes material and labor to install
Install	Ea.	71	15.60		86.60	custom quality recessed eyeball
Demolish and Install	Ea.	71	35.60		106.60	spotlight with housing. Wiring is not
Reinstall	Ea.		12.49		12.49	included.
Clean	Ea.	.06	3.12		3.18	
Minimum Charge	Job		219		219	

Finish Electrical

Residential Light Fixture	Unit	Material	Labor	Equip.	Total	Specification
Recessed Shower Type						
Demolish	Ea.		20		20	Includes material and labor to install
Install	Ea.	59	14.55		73.55	deluxe quality recessed eyeball
Demolish and Install	Ea.	59	34.55		93.55	spotlight with housing. Wiring is not
Reinstall	Ea.		11.66		11.66	included.
Clean	Ea.	.06	3.12		3.18	
Minimum Charge	Job		219		219	
Run Wiring						
Install	Ea.	19.45	17.50		36.95	Includes labor and material to install a
Minimum Charge	Job		219		219	electric fixture utility box with
						non-metallic cable.
Fluorescent						
Good Quality						
Demolish	Ea.		22		22	Includes material and labor to install
Install	Ea.	49	62.50		111.50	standard quality 12" wide by 48" long
Demolish and Install	Ea.	49	84.50		133.50	decorative surface mounted fluorescent
Reinstall	Ea.		49.97		49.97	fixture w/acrylic diffuser.
Clean	Ea.	.06	3.12		3.18	
Minimum Charge	Job		219		219	
Better Quality						
Demolish	Ea.		22		22	Includes material and labor to install
Install	Ea.	100	70.50		170.50	an interior fluorescent lighting fixture.
Demolish and Install	Ea.	100	92.50		192.50	
Reinstall	Ea.		56.41		56.41	
Clean	Ea.	.06	3.12		3.18	
Minimum Charge	Job		219		219	
Premium Quality						
Demolish	Ea.		22		22	Includes material and labor to install
Install	Ea.	104	82.50		186.50	deluxe quality 24" wide by 48" long
Demolish and Install	Ea.	104	104.50		208.50	decorative surface mounted fluorescent
Reinstall	Ea.		65.99		65.99	fixture w/acrylic diffuser.
Clean	Ea.	.06	3.12		3.18	
Minimum Charge	Job		219		219	
Run Wiring						
Install	Ea.	19.45	17.50		36.95	Includes labor and material to install a
Minimum Charge	Job		219		219	electric fixture utility box with
						non-metallic cable.
Exterior						
Good Quality						
Demolish	Ea.		19.45		19.45	Includes material and labor to install
Install	Ea.	46	27.50		73.50	standard quality incandescent outdoor
Demolish and Install	Ea.	46	46.95		92.95	light fixture. Wiring is not included.
Reinstall	Ea.		21.86		21.86	
Clean	Ea.	.26	12.45		12.71	
Minimum Charge	Job		219		219	
Better Quality						
Demolish	Ea.		19.45		19.45	Includes material and labor to install
Install	Ea.	116	27.50		143.50	custom quality incandescent outdoor
Demolish and Install	Ea.	116	46.95		162.95	light fixture. Wiring is not included.
Reinstall	Ea.		21.86		21.86	
Clean	Ea.	.26	12.45		12.71	
Minimum Charge	Job		219		219	
Premium Quality						
Demolish	Ea.		19.45		19.45	Includes material and labor to install
Install	Ea.	175	109		284	deluxe quality incandescent outdoor
Demolish and Install	Ea.	175	128.45		303.45	light fixture. Wiring is not included.
Reinstall	Ea.		87.44		87.44	
Clean	Ea.	.26	12.45		12.71	
Minimum Charge	Job		219		219	

Finish Electrical

Residential Light Fixture	Unit	Material	Labor	Equip.	Total	Specification
Outdoor w / Pole						Includes material and labor to install
Demolish	Ea.		19.45		19.45	post lantern type incandescent outdoor
Install	Ea.	129	109		238	light fixture. Wiring is not included.
Demolish and Install	Ea.	129	128.45		257.45	
Reinstall	Ea.		87.44		87.44	
Clean	Ea.	.26	12.45		12.71	
Minimum Charge	Job		219		219	
Run Wiring						
Install	Ea.	19.45	17.50		36.95	Includes labor and material to install a
Minimum Charge	Job		219		219	electric fixture utility box with
						non-metallic cable.
Track Lighting						
Demolish	L.F.		6.75		6.75	Includes material and labor to install
Install	L.F.	17.55	18.20		35.75	track lighting.
Demolish and Install	L.F.	17.55	24.95		42.50	
Reinstall	L.F.		14.57		14.57	
Clean	L.F.	.26	6		6.26	
Minimum Charge	Job		219		219	

Commercial Light Fixture	Unit	Material	Labor	Equip.	Total	Specification
Fluorescent						
2 Bulb, 2'						
Demolish	Ea.		19.45		19.45	Includes material and labor to install a
Install	Ea.	38	54.50		92.50	2' long surface mounted fluorescent
Demolish and Install	Ea.	38	73.95		111.95	light fixture with two 40 watt bulbs.
Reinstall	Ea.		43.72		43.72	
Clean	Ea.	1.30	21.50		22.80	
Minimum Charge	Job		219		219	
2 Bulb, 4'						
Demolish	Ea.		19.45		19.45	Includes material and labor to install a
Install	Ea.	69	62.50		131.50	4' long surface mounted fluorescent
Demolish and Install	Ea.	69	81.95		150.95	light fixture with two 40 watt bulbs.
Reinstall	Ea.		49.97		49.97	
Clean	Ea.	1.30	21.50		22.80	
Minimum Charge	Job		219		219	
3 Bulb, 4'						
Demolish	Ea.		19.45		19.45	Includes material and labor to install a
Install	Ea.	103	62.50		165.50	4' long pendant mounted fluorescent
Demolish and Install	Ea.	103	81.95		184.95	light fixture with three 34 watt bulbs.
Reinstall	Ea.		49.97		49.97	
Clean	Ea.	1.30	21.50		22.80	
Minimum Charge	Job		219		219	
4 Bulb, 4'						
Demolish	Ea.		19.45		19.45	Includes material and labor to install a
Install	Ea.	94.50	67.50		162	4' long pendant mounted fluorescent
Demolish and Install	Ea.	94.50	86.95		181.45	light fixture with four 34 watt bulbs.
Reinstall	Ea.		53.81		53.81	
Clean	Ea.	1.30	21.50		22.80	
Minimum Charge	Job		219		219	
2 Bulb, 8'						
Demolish	Ea.		24.50		24.50	Includes material and labor to install a
Install	Ea.	106	82.50		188.50	8' long surface mounted fluorescent
Demolish and Install	Ea.	106	107		213	light fixture with two 110 watt bulbs.
Reinstall	Ea.		65.99		65.99	
Clean	Ea.	1.30	21.50		22.80	
Minimum Charge	Job		219		219	

Finish Electrical

Commercial Light Fixture		Unit	Material	Labor	Equip.	Total	Specification
Run Wiring							
	Install	Ea.	19.45	17.50		36.95	Includes labor and material to install a
	Minimum Charge	Job		219		219	electric fixture utility box with
							non-metallic cable.
Ceiling, Recessed							
Eyeball Type							
	Demolish	Ea.		20		20	Includes material and labor to install
	Install	Ea.	71	15.60		86.60	custom quality recessed eyeball
	Demolish and Install	Ea.	71	35.60		106.60	spotlight with housing. Wiring is not
	Reinstall	Ea.		12.49		12.49	included.
	Clean	Ea.	.06	3.12		3.18	
	Minimum Charge	Job		219		219	
Shower Type							
	Demolish	Ea.		20		20	Includes material and labor to install
	Install	Ea.	59	14.55		73.55	deluxe quality recessed eyeball
	Demolish and Install	Ea.	59	34.55		93.55	spotlight with housing. Wiring is not
	Reinstall	Ea.		11.66		11.66	included.
	Clean	Ea.	.06	3.12		3.18	
	Minimum Charge	Job		219		219	
Run Wiring							
	Install	Ea.	19.45	17.50		36.95	Includes labor and material to install a
	Minimum Charge	Job		219		219	electric fixture utility box with
							non-metallic cable.
Ceiling Grid Type							
2 Tube							
	Demolish	Ea.		28.50		28.50	Cost includes material and labor to
	Install	Ea.	64	82.50		146.50	install 2 lamp fluorescent light fixture
	Demolish and Install	Ea.	64	111		175	in 2' x 4' ceiling grid system including
	Reinstall	Ea.		65.99		65.99	lens and tubes.
	Clean	Ea.	1.30	21.50		22.80	
	Minimum Charge	Job		219		219	
4 Tube							
	Demolish	Ea.		32.50		32.50	Cost includes material and labor to
	Install	Ea.	73.50	93		166.50	install 4 lamp fluorescent light fixture
	Demolish and Install	Ea.	73.50	125.50		199	in 2' x 4' ceiling grid system including
	Reinstall	Ea.		74.42		74.42	lens and tubes.
	Clean	Ea.	1.30	21.50		22.80	
	Minimum Charge	Job		219		219	
Acrylic Diffuser							
	Demolish	Ea.		5.05		5.05	Includes material and labor to install
	Install	Ea.	53.50	13.25		66.75	fluorescent light fixture w/acrylic
	Demolish and Install	Ea.	53.50	18.30		71.80	diffuser.
	Reinstall	Ea.		10.60		10.60	
	Clean	Ea.	.84	3.74		4.58	
	Minimum Charge	Job		219		219	
Louver Diffuser							
	Demolish	Ea.		6.05		6.05	Includes material and labor to install
	Install	Ea.	60	13.25		73.25	fluorescent light fixture w/louver
	Demolish and Install	Ea.	60	19.30		79.30	diffuser.
	Reinstall	Ea.		10.60		10.60	
	Clean	Ea.	.84	3.74		4.58	
	Minimum Charge	Job		219		219	
Run Wiring							
	Install	Ea.	19.45	17.50		36.95	Includes labor and material to install a
	Minimum Charge	Job		219		219	electric fixture utility box with
							non-metallic cable.

Finish Electrical

Commercial Light Fixture

Commercial Light Fixture	Unit	Material	Labor	Equip.	Total	Specification
Track Lighting						
Demolish	L.F.		6.75		6.75	Includes material and labor to install
Install	L.F.	17.55	18.20		35.75	track lighting.
Demolish and Install	L.F.	17.55	24.95		42.50	
Reinstall	L.F.		14.57		14.57	
Clean	L.F.	.26	6		6.26	
Minimum Charge	Job		219		219	
Emergency						
Demolish	Ea.		34.50		34.50	Includes material and labor to install
Install	Ea.	151	109		260	battery-powered emergency lighting
Demolish and Install	Ea.	151	143.50		294.50	unit with two (2) lights, including
Reinstall	Ea.		87.44		87.44	wiring.
Clean	Ea.	.65	21.50		22.15	
Minimum Charge	Job		219		219	
Run Wiring						
Install	Ea.	19.45	17.50		36.95	Includes labor and material to install a
Minimum Charge	Job		219		219	electric fixture utility box with
						non-metallic cable.

Fan

Fan	Unit	Material	Labor	Equip.	Total	Specification
Ceiling Paddle						
Good Quality						
Demolish	Ea.		27		27	Includes material and labor to install
Install	Ea.	95	43.50		138.50	standard ceiling fan.
Demolish and Install	Ea.	95	70.50		165.50	
Reinstall	Ea.		34.98		34.98	
Clean	Ea.	.52	18.70		19.22	
Minimum Charge	Job		219		219	
Better Quality						
Demolish	Ea.		27		27	Includes material and labor to install
Install	Ea.	144	43.50		187.50	better ceiling fan.
Demolish and Install	Ea.	144	70.50		214.50	
Reinstall	Ea.		34.98		34.98	
Clean	Ea.	.52	18.70		19.22	
Minimum Charge	Job		219		219	
Premium Quality						
Demolish	Ea.		27		27	Includes material and labor to install
Install	Ea.	340	54.50		394.50	deluxe ceiling fan.
Demolish and Install	Ea.	340	81.50		421.50	
Reinstall	Ea.		43.72		43.72	
Clean	Ea.	.52	18.70		19.22	
Minimum Charge	Job		219		219	
Light Kit						
Install	Ea.	42.50	54.50		97	Includes labor and material to install a
Minimum Charge	Job		219		219	ceiling fan light kit.
Bathroom Exhaust						
Ceiling Mounted						
Demolish	Ea.		22.50		22.50	Cost includes material and labor to
Install	Ea.	55.50	43.50		99	install 60 CFM ceiling mounted
Demolish and Install	Ea.	55.50	66		121.50	bathroom exhaust fan, up to 10' of
Reinstall	Ea.		34.87		34.87	wiring with one wall switch.
Clean	Ea.	.26	7.50		7.76	
Minimum Charge	Job		219		219	

Finish Electrical

Fan

Fan	Unit	Material	Labor	Equip.	Total	Specification
Wall Mounted						
Demolish	Ea.		22.50		22.50	Cost includes material and labor to
Install	Ea.	70	43.50		113.50	install 110 CFM wall mounted
Demolish and Install	Ea.	70	66		136	bathroom exhaust fan, up to 10' of
Reinstall	Ea.		34.87		34.87	wiring with one wall switch.
Clean	Ea.	.26	7.50		7.76	
Minimum Charge	Job		219		219	
Lighted						
Demolish	Ea.		22.50		22.50	Cost includes material and labor to
Install	Ea.	51.50	43.50		95	install 50 CFM ceiling mounted lighted
Demolish and Install	Ea.	51.50	66		117.50	exhaust fan, up to 10' of wiring with
Reinstall	Ea.		34.87		34.87	one wall switch..
Clean	Ea.	.26	7.50		7.76	
Minimum Charge	Job		219		219	
Blower Heater w / Light						
Demolish	Ea.		22.50		22.50	Includes material and labor to install
Install	Ea.	104	72.50		176.50	ceiling blower type ventilator with
Demolish and Install	Ea.	104	95		199	switch, light and snap-on grill. Includes
Reinstall	Ea.		58.12		58.12	1300 watt/120 volt heater.
Clean	Ea.	.26	7.50		7.76	
Minimum Charge	Job		219		219	
Fan Heater w / Light						
Demolish	Ea.		22.50		22.50	Includes material and labor to install
Install	Ea.	142	72.50		214.50	circular ceiling fan heater unit, 1500
Demolish and Install	Ea.	142	95		237	watt, surface mounted.
Reinstall	Ea.		58.12		58.12	
Clean	Ea.	.26	7.50		7.76	
Minimum Charge	Job		219		219	
Whole House Exhaust						
36" Ceiling Mounted						
Install	Ea.	930	109		1039	Includes material and labor to install a
Clean	Ea.	.08	5.45		5.53	whole house exhaust fan.
Minimum Charge	Job		219		219	
Kitchen Exhaust						
Standard Model						
Install	Ea.	76.50	29		105.50	Includes labor and materials to install
Clean	Ea.	.08	5.45		5.53	a bathroom or kitchen vent fan.
Minimum Charge	Job		219		219	
Low Noise Model						
Install	Ea.	94.50	29		123.50	Includes labor and materials to install
Clean	Ea.	.08	5.45		5.53	a bathroom or kitchen vent fan, low
Minimum Charge	Job		219		219	noise model.

Low Voltage Systems

Low Voltage Systems	Unit	Material	Labor	Equip.	Total	Specification
Smoke Detector						
Pre-wired						
Demolish	Ea.		10.10		10.10	Includes material and labor to install
Install	Ea.	22	82		104	AC type smoke detector including
Demolish and Install	Ea.	22	92.10		114.10	wiring.
Reinstall	Ea.		65.62		65.62	
Clean	Ea.	.10	9.35		9.45	
Minimum Charge	Job		219		219	

Finish Electrical

Low Voltage Systems		Unit	Material	Labor	Equip.	Total	Specification
Run Wiring							
	Install	Ea.	19.45	17.50		36.95	Includes labor and material to install a
	Minimum Charge	Job		219		219	electric fixture utility box with
							non-metallic cable.
Door Bell / Chimes							
Good Quality							
	Demolish	Ea.		30.50		30.50	Includes material and labor to install
	Install	Ea.	63.50	109		172.50	surface mounted 2 note door bell.
	Demolish and Install	Ea.	63.50	139.50		203	Wiring is not included.
	Reinstall	Ea.		87.44		87.44	
	Clean	Ea.	.26	9.35		9.61	
	Minimum Charge	Job		219		219	
Better Quality							
	Demolish	Ea.		30.50		30.50	Includes material and labor to install
	Install	Ea.	88	109		197	standard quality surface mounted 2
	Demolish and Install	Ea.	88	139.50		227.50	note door bell. Wiring is not included.
	Reinstall	Ea.		87.44		87.44	
	Clean	Ea.	.26	9.35		9.61	
	Minimum Charge	Job		219		219	
Premium Quality							
	Demolish	Ea.		30.50		30.50	Includes material and labor to install
	Install	Ea.	99.50	109		208.50	deluxe quality surface mounted 2 note
	Demolish and Install	Ea.	99.50	139.50		239	door bell. Wiring is not included.
	Reinstall	Ea.		87.44		87.44	
	Clean	Ea.	.26	9.35		9.61	
	Minimum Charge	Job		219		219	
Run Wiring							
	Install	Ea.	19.45	17.50		36.95	Includes labor and material to install a
	Minimum Charge	Job		219		219	electric fixture utility box with
							non-metallic cable.
Intercom System							
Intercom (master)							
	Demolish	Ea.		81		81	Includes material and labor to install
	Install	Ea.	620	219		839	master intercom station with AM/FM
	Demolish and Install	Ea.	620	300		920	music and room monitoring. Wiring is
	Reinstall	Ea.		174.88		174.88	not included.
	Clean	Ea.	.26	25		25.26	
	Minimum Charge	Job		219		219	
Intercom (remote)							
	Demolish	Ea.		48.50		48.50	Includes material and labor to install
	Install	Ea.	56.50	54.50		111	remote station for master intercom
	Demolish and Install	Ea.	56.50	103		159.50	system. Wiring is not included.
	Reinstall	Ea.		43.72		43.72	
	Clean	Ea.	.26	9.35		9.61	
	Minimum Charge	Job		219		219	
Security System							
Alarm Panel							
	Demolish	Ea.		97		97	Includes material and labor to install a
	Install	Ea.	163	219		382	6 zone burglar alarm panel.
	Demolish and Install	Ea.	163	316		479	
	Reinstall	Ea.		174.88		174.88	
	Clean	Ea.	.26	9.35		9.61	
	Minimum Charge	Job		219		219	

Finish Electrical

Low Voltage Systems

	Unit	Material	Labor	Equip.	Total	Specification
Motion Detector						
Demolish	Ea.		69.50		69.50	Includes material and labor to install a
Install	Ea.	248	190		438	ultrasonic motion detector for a
Demolish and Install	Ea.	248	259.50		507.50	security system.
Reinstall	Ea.		152.07		152.07	
Clean	Ea.	.26	9.35		9.61	
Minimum Charge	Job		219		219	
Door Switch						
Demolish	Ea.		30.50		30.50	Includes material and labor to install a
Install	Ea.	150	82.50		232.50	door / window contact for a security
Demolish and Install	Ea.	150	113		263	system.
Reinstall	Ea.		65.99		65.99	
Clean	Ea.	.26	2.99		3.25	
Minimum Charge	Job		219		219	
Window Switch						
Demolish	Ea.		30.50		30.50	Includes material and labor to install a
Install	Ea.	150	82.50		232.50	door / window contact for a security
Demolish and Install	Ea.	150	113		263	system.
Reinstall	Ea.		65.99		65.99	
Clean	Ea.	.26	2.99		3.25	
Minimum Charge	Job		219		219	
Satellite System						
Dish						
Demolish	Ea.		135		135	Includes material, labor and
Install	Ea.	1275	365		1640	equipment to install 10' mesh dish.
Demolish and Install	Ea.	1275	500		1775	
Reinstall	Ea.		291.47		291.47	
Clean	Ea.	5.20	37.50		42.70	
Minimum Charge	Job		219		219	
Motor						
Demolish	Ea.		67.50		67.50	Includes material and labor to install a
Install	Ea.	395	182		577	television satellite dish motor unit.
Demolish and Install	Ea.	395	249.50		644.50	
Reinstall	Ea.		145.73		145.73	
Clean	Ea.	.26	9.35		9.61	
Minimum Charge	Job		219		219	
Television Antenna						
40' Pole						
Demolish	Ea.		76		76	Includes material and labor to install
Install	Ea.	27	137		164	stand-alone 1"-2" metal pole, 10' long.
Demolish and Install	Ea.	27	213		240	Cost does not include antenna.
Reinstall	Ea.		109.30		109.30	
Clean	Ea.	1.05	37.50		38.55	
Paint	Ea.	7.15	43.50		50.65	
Minimum Charge	Job		219		219	
Rotor Unit						
Demolish	Ea.		60.50		60.50	Includes material and labor to install a
Install	Ea.	98.50	54.50		153	television antenna rotor.
Demolish and Install	Ea.	98.50	115		213.50	
Reinstall	Ea.		43.72		43.72	
Clean	Ea.	1.05	37.50		38.55	
Minimum Charge	Job		219		219	
Single Booster						
Demolish	Ea.		60.50		60.50	Includes material and labor to install
Install	Ea.	44	54.50		98.50	standard grade VHF television signal
Demolish and Install	Ea.	44	115		159	booster unit and all hardware required
Reinstall	Ea.		43.72		43.72	for connection to TV cable.
Clean	Ea.	.06	4.68		4.74	
Minimum Charge	Job		219		219	

| Gazebo | Gutter | Shutter |

Window Treatment	Unit	Material	Labor	Equip.	Total	Specification
Drapery						
Good Grade						
Install	L.F.	44.50	6		50.50	Includes material and labor to install
Reinstall	L.F.		4.79		4.79	good quality drapery.
Clean	L.F.	2.66	.15		2.81	
Minimum Charge	Job		150		150	
Premium Grade						
Install	L.F.	78	6		84	Includes material and labor to install
Reinstall	L.F.		4.79		4.79	premium quality drapery.
Clean	L.F.	2.66	.17		2.83	
Minimum Charge	Job		150		150	
Lining						
Install	L.F.	19.35	6		25.35	Includes material and labor to install
Reinstall	L.F.		4.79		4.79	drapery lining.
Clean	L.F.	1.33	.09		1.42	
Minimum Charge	Job		150		150	
Valance Board						
Demolish	L.F.		1.66		1.66	Includes material and labor to install a
Install	L.F.	4.74	11.95		16.69	drapery valance board.
Demolish and Install	L.F.	4.74	13.61		18.35	
Reinstall	L.F.		9.57		9.57	
Clean	L.F.	1.33	.30		1.63	
Minimum Charge	Job		150		150	
Rod						
Demolish	L.F.		4.16		4.16	Includes material and labor to install
Install	L.F.	3.76	6.85		10.61	standard traverse drapery hardware.
Demolish and Install	L.F.	3.76	11.01		14.77	
Reinstall	L.F.		5.47		5.47	
Clean	L.F.	.10	.27		.37	
Paint	L.F.	.06	.67		.73	
Minimum Charge	Job		150		150	
Blinds						
Mini-type						
Demolish	S.F.		.88		.88	Includes material and labor to install
Install	S.F.	5.80	.68		6.48	horizontal 1" slat blinds.
Demolish and Install	S.F.	5.80	1.56		7.36	
Reinstall	S.F.		.55		.55	
Clean	S.F.	.51	.03		.54	
Minimum Charge	Job		150		150	

Window Treatment	Unit	Material	Labor	Equip.	Total	Specification
Vertical Type						
Demolish	S.F.		.88		.88	Includes material and labor to install
Install	S.F.	6.55	.88		7.43	vertical 3″ - 5″ cloth or PVC blinds.
Demolish and Install	S.F.	6.55	1.76		8.31	
Reinstall	S.F.		.70		.70	
Clean	S.F.	.26	.03		.29	
Minimum Charge	Job		150		150	
Vertical Type per L.F.						
Demolish	L.F.		1.39		1.39	Includes material and labor to install
Install	L.F.	39	3.99		42.99	vertical 3″ - 5″ cloth or PVC blinds x
Demolish and Install	L.F.	39	5.38		44.38	72″ long.
Reinstall	L.F.		3.19		3.19	
Clean	L.F.	1.88	.21		2.09	
Minimum Charge	Job		150		150	
Venetian Type						
Demolish	S.F.		.88		.88	Includes material and labor to install
Install	S.F.	8.90	.68		9.58	horizontal 2″ slat blinds.
Demolish and Install	S.F.	8.90	1.56		10.46	
Reinstall	S.F.		.55		.55	
Clean	S.F.	.26	.03		.29	
Minimum Charge	Job		150		150	

Wood Shutter

27″ x 36″, 4 Panel

	Unit	Material	Labor	Equip.	Total	Specification
Demolish	Ea.		28		28	Includes material and labor to install
Install	Pr.	92.50	23.50		116	moveable louver, up to 33″ x 36″, 4
Demolish and Install	Pr.	92.50	51.50		144	panel shutter.
Reinstall	Pr.		18.99		18.99	
Clean	Ea.	.10	9.10		9.20	
Paint	Ea.	1.14	24.50		25.64	
Minimum Charge	Job		202		202	

33″ x 36″, 4 Panel

	Unit	Material	Labor	Equip.	Total	Specification
Demolish	Ea.		28		28	Includes material and labor to install
Install	Pr.	92.50	23.50		116	moveable louver, up to 33″ x 36″, 4
Demolish and Install	Pr.	92.50	51.50		144	panel shutter.
Reinstall	Pr.		18.99		18.99	
Clean	Ea.	.10	9.10		9.20	
Paint	Ea.	1.19	26.50		27.69	
Minimum Charge	Job		202		202	

39″ x 36″, 4 Panel

	Unit	Material	Labor	Equip.	Total	Specification
Demolish	Ea.		28		28	Includes material and labor to install
Install	Pr.	99	23.50		122.50	moveable louver, up to 47″ x 36″, 4
Demolish and Install	Pr.	99	51.50		150.50	panel shutter.
Reinstall	Pr.		18.99		18.99	
Clean	Ea.	.10	9.10		9.20	
Paint	Ea.	1.19	26.50		27.69	
Minimum Charge	Job		202		202	

47″ x 36″, 4 Panel

	Unit	Material	Labor	Equip.	Total	Specification
Demolish	Ea.		28		28	Includes material and labor to install
Install	Pr.	99	23.50		122.50	moveable louver, up to 47″ x 36″, 4
Demolish and Install	Pr.	99	51.50		150.50	panel shutter.
Reinstall	Pr.		18.99		18.99	
Clean	Ea.	.10	9.10		9.20	
Paint	Ea.	1.24	29		30.24	
Minimum Charge	Job		202		202	

Improvements / Appliances / Treatments

Stairs

Stairs	Unit	Material	Labor	Equip.	Total	Specification
Concrete Steps						
Precast						
Demolish	Ea.		57	36	93	Includes material and labor to install
Install	Flight	440	139	42.50	621.50	precast concrete front entrance stairs,
Demolish and Install	Flight	440	196	78.50	714.50	4' wide, with 48" platform and 2
Clean	Ea.		4.16		4.16	risers.
Paint	Ea.	3.82	43.50		47.32	
Minimum Charge	Job		360		360	
Metal						
Concrete Filled						
Demolish	Ea.		16.60		16.60	Includes material and labor to install
Install	Riser	525	67	4	596	steel, cement filled metal pan stairs
Demolish and Install	Riser	525	83.60	4	612.60	with picket rail.
Clean	Ea.	.17	2.55		2.72	
Paint	Ea.	.62	2.57		3.19	
Minimum Charge	Job		248		248	
Landing						
Demolish	S.F.		4.16		4.16	Includes material and labor to install
Install	S.F.	108	7.90	.47	116.37	pre-erected conventional steel pan
Demolish and Install	S.F.	108	12.06	.47	120.53	landing.
Clean	S.F.	.17	.53		.70	
Paint	S.F.	.21	.74		.95	
Minimum Charge	Job		248		248	
Railing						
Demolish	L.F.		2.29		2.29	Includes material and labor to install
Install	L.F.	14.40	11.45	.68	26.53	primed steel pipe.
Demolish and Install	L.F.	14.40	13.74	.68	28.82	
Clean	L.F.	1.05	1.87		2.92	
Paint	L.F.	.68	5.75		6.43	
Minimum Charge	Job		248		248	

Elevator

Elevator	Unit	Material	Labor	Equip.	Total	Specification
2 Stop Residential						
Install	Ea.	12100	5875		17975	Includes labor, material and
Clean	Ea.	1.17	18.70		19.87	equipment to install 2 stop elevator for
Minimum Charge	Job		585		585	residential use.
2 Stop Commercial						
Install	Ea.	40300	11700		52000	Includes labor, material and
Clean	Ea.	1.17	18.70		19.87	equipment to install 2 stop elevator for
Minimum Charge	Job		585		585	apartment or commercial building with
						2,000 lb/13 passenger capacity.
3 Stop Commercial						
Install	Ea.	54500	18000		72500	Includes labor, material and
Clean	Ea.	1.17	18.70		19.87	equipment to install 3 stop elevator for
Minimum Charge	Job		585		585	apartment or commercial building with
						2,000 lb/13 passenger capacity.
4 Stop Commercial						
Install	Ea.	68000	24400		92400	Includes labor, material and
Clean	Ea.	1.17	18.70		19.87	equipment to install 4 stop elevator for
Minimum Charge	Job		585		585	apartment or commercial building with
						2,000 lb/13 passenger capacity.

Improvements / Appliances / Treatments

Elevator

	Unit	Material	Labor	Equip.	Total	Specification
5 Stop Commercial						Includes labor, material and
Install	Ea.	82500	30900		113400	equipment to install 5 stop elevator for
Clean	Ea.	1.17	18.70		19.87	apartment or commercial building with
Minimum Charge	Job		585		585	2,000 lb/13 passenger capacity.

Rangetop

	Unit	Material	Labor	Equip.	Total	Specification
4-burner						Cost includes material and labor to
Demolish	Ea.		30		30	install 4-burner electric surface unit.
Install	Ea.	310	73		383	
Demolish and Install	Ea.	310	103		413	
Reinstall	Ea.		58.29		58.29	
Clean	Ea.	.08	27.50		27.58	
Minimum Charge	Job		75		75	
6-burner						Includes material and labor to install a
Demolish	Ea.		30		30	6-burner cooktop unit.
Install	Ea.	2200	87.50		2287.50	
Demolish and Install	Ea.	2200	117.50		2317.50	
Reinstall	Ea.		69.95		69.95	
Clean	Ea.	.08	27.50		27.58	
Minimum Charge	Job		75		75	
Premium Brand w / Grill						Includes material and labor to install
Demolish	Ea.		30		30	electric downdraft cooktop with grill.
Install	Ea.	950	87.50		1037.50	
Demolish and Install	Ea.	950	117.50		1067.50	
Reinstall	Ea.		69.95		69.95	
Clean	Ea.	.08	27.50		27.58	
Minimum Charge	Job		75		75	

Rangehood

	Unit	Material	Labor	Equip.	Total	Specification
Vented						
30"						
Demolish	Ea.		27.50		27.50	Includes material and labor to install a
Install	Ea.	69	87.50		156.50	vented range hood.
Demolish and Install	Ea.	69	115		184	
Reinstall	Ea.		69.95		69.95	
Clean	Ea.	.08	7.80		7.88	
Minimum Charge	Job		75		75	
36"						
Demolish	Ea.		27.50		27.50	Includes material and labor to install a
Install	Ea.	154	87.50		241.50	vented range hood.
Demolish and Install	Ea.	154	115		269	
Reinstall	Ea.		69.95		69.95	
Clean	Ea.	.08	7.80		7.88	
Minimum Charge	Job		75		75	
42"						
Demolish	Ea.		27.50		27.50	Includes material and labor to install a
Install	Ea.	207	103		310	vented range hood.
Demolish and Install	Ea.	207	130.50		337.50	
Reinstall	Ea.		82.06		82.06	
Clean	Ea.	.08	7.80		7.88	
Minimum Charge	Job		75		75	

Improvements / Appliances / Treatments

Rangehood

	Unit	Material	Labor	Equip.	Total	Specification
Ventless						
30″						
Demolish	Ea.		27.50		27.50	Includes material and labor to install a
Install	Ea.	84.50	54.50		139	ventless range hood.
Demolish and Install	Ea.	84.50	82		166.50	
Reinstall	Ea.		43.72		43.72	
Clean	Ea.	.08	7.80		7.88	
Minimum Charge	Job		75		75	
36″						
Demolish	Ea.		27.50		27.50	Includes material and labor to install a
Install	Ea.	133	87.50		220.50	ventless range hood.
Demolish and Install	Ea.	133	115		248	
Reinstall	Ea.		69.95		69.95	
Clean	Ea.	.08	7.80		7.88	
Minimum Charge	Job		75		75	
42″						
Demolish	Ea.		27.50		27.50	Includes material and labor to install a
Install	Ea.	230	73		303	ventless range hood.
Demolish and Install	Ea.	230	100.50		330.50	
Reinstall	Ea.		58.29		58.29	
Clean	Ea.	.08	7.80		7.88	
Minimum Charge	Job		75		75	

Oven

	Unit	Material	Labor	Equip.	Total	Specification
Free Standing						
Demolish	Ea.		30		30	Cost includes material and labor to
Install	Ea.	560	60		620	install 30″ free standing electric range
Demolish and Install	Ea.	560	90		650	with self-cleaning oven.
Reinstall	Ea.		47.87		47.87	
Clean	Ea.	.08	27.50		27.58	
Minimum Charge	Job		75		75	
Single Wall Oven						
Demolish	Ea.		30		30	Includes material and labor to install a
Install	Ea.	565	109		674	built-in oven.
Demolish and Install	Ea.	565	139		704	
Reinstall	Ea.		87.44		87.44	
Clean	Ea.	.08	27.50		27.58	
Minimum Charge	Job		75		75	
Double Wall Oven						
Demolish	Ea.		30		30	Includes material and labor to install a
Install	Ea.	1475	202		1677	conventional double oven.
Demolish and Install	Ea.	1475	232		1707	
Reinstall	Ea.		161.44		161.44	
Clean	Ea.	.08	27.50		27.58	
Minimum Charge	Job		75		75	
Drop-in Type w / Range						
Demolish	Ea.		30		30	Includes material and labor to install a
Install	Ea.	665	73		738	built-in cooking range with oven.
Demolish and Install	Ea.	665	103		768	
Reinstall	Ea.		58.29		58.29	
Clean	Ea.	.08	27.50		27.58	
Minimum Charge	Job		75		75	

Improvements / Appliances / Treatments

Oven

Oven	Unit	Material	Labor	Equip.	Total	Specification
Hi/Lo w / Range, Microwave						Includes material and labor to install a double oven, one conventional, one microwave.
Demolish	Ea.		30		30	
Install	Ea.	1750	405		2155	
Demolish and Install	Ea.	1750	435		2185	
Reinstall	Ea.		322.88		322.88	
Clean	Ea.	.08	27.50		27.58	
Minimum Charge	Job		75		75	
Hi/Lo w/ Range / Double Oven						Includes material and labor to install a conventional double oven.
Demolish	Ea.		30		30	
Install	Ea.	1475	202		1677	
Demolish and Install	Ea.	1475	232		1707	
Reinstall	Ea.		161.44		161.44	
Clean	Ea.	.08	27.50		27.58	
Minimum Charge	Job		75		75	
Countertop Microwave						Includes material and labor to install a 1.0 cubic foot microwave oven.
Demolish	Ea.		10.40		10.40	
Install	Ea.	120	37.50		157.50	
Demolish and Install	Ea.	120	47.90		167.90	
Reinstall	Ea.		29.92		29.92	
Clean	Ea.	.08	13.65		13.73	
Minimum Charge	Job		75		75	
Cabinet / Wall Mounted Microwave						Includes material and labor to install a space saver microwave oven.
Demolish	Ea.		21		21	
Install	Ea.	735	109		844	
Demolish and Install	Ea.	735	130		865	
Reinstall	Ea.		87.44		87.44	
Clean	Ea.	.08	13.65		13.73	
Minimum Charge	Job		75		75	

Dryer

Dryer	Unit	Material	Labor	Equip.	Total	Specification
Basic Grade						Includes material and labor to install electric or gas dryer. Vent kit not included.
Demolish	Ea.		13.85		13.85	
Install	Ea.	375	234		609	
Demolish and Install	Ea.	375	247.85		622.85	
Reinstall	Ea.		187.52		187.52	
Clean	Ea.	.08	27.50		27.58	
Minimum Charge	Job		75		75	
Good Grade						Includes material and labor to install electric or gas dryer. Vent kit not included.
Demolish	Ea.		13.85		13.85	
Install	Ea.	470	234		704	
Demolish and Install	Ea.	470	247.85		717.85	
Reinstall	Ea.		187.52		187.52	
Clean	Ea.	.08	27.50		27.58	
Minimum Charge	Job		75		75	
Premium Grade						Includes material and labor to install electric or gas dryer. Vent kit not included.
Demolish	Ea.		13.85		13.85	
Install	Ea.	1600	350		1950	
Demolish and Install	Ea.	1600	363.85		1963.85	
Reinstall	Ea.		281.28		281.28	
Clean	Ea.	.08	27.50		27.58	
Minimum Charge	Job		75		75	

Improvements / Appliances / Treatments

Dryer

	Unit	Material	Labor	Equip.	Total	Specification
Washer / Dryer Combination Unit						
Demolish	Ea.		13.85		13.85	Includes material and labor to install
Install	Ea.	1050	60		1110	electric washer/dryer combination
Demolish and Install	Ea.	1050	73.85		1123.85	unit, 27" wide, stackable or unitized.
Reinstall	Ea.		47.87		47.87	
Clean	Ea.	.08	27.50		27.58	
Minimum Charge	Job		75		75	

Washer

	Unit	Material	Labor	Equip.	Total	Specification
Basic Grade						
Demolish	Ea.		13.85		13.85	Includes material and labor to install
Install	Ea.	440	154		594	washing machine. New hoses not
Demolish and Install	Ea.	440	167.85		607.85	included.
Reinstall	Ea.		123.31		123.31	
Clean	Ea.	.08	27.50		27.58	
Minimum Charge	Job		75		75	
Good Grade						
Demolish	Ea.		13.85		13.85	Includes material and labor to install
Install	Ea.	720	231		951	washing machine. New hoses not
Demolish and Install	Ea.	720	244.85		964.85	included.
Reinstall	Ea.		184.96		184.96	
Clean	Ea.	.08	27.50		27.58	
Minimum Charge	Job		75		75	
Premium Grade						
Demolish	Ea.		13.85		13.85	Includes material and labor to install
Install	Ea.	1425	460		1885	washing machine with digital
Demolish and Install	Ea.	1425	473.85		1898.85	computer readouts and large capacity.
Reinstall	Ea.		369.92		369.92	New hoses not included.
Clean	Ea.	.08	27.50		27.58	
Minimum Charge	Job		75		75	
Washer / Dryer Combination Unit						
Demolish	Ea.		13.85		13.85	Includes material and labor to install
Install	Ea.	1050	60		1110	electric washer/dryer combination
Demolish and Install	Ea.	1050	73.85		1123.85	unit, 27" wide, stackable or unitized.
Reinstall	Ea.		47.87		47.87	
Clean	Ea.	.08	27.50		27.58	
Minimum Charge	Job		75		75	

Refrigerator

	Unit	Material	Labor	Equip.	Total	Specification
12 Cubic Foot						
Demolish	Ea.		41.50		41.50	Includes material and labor to install a
Install	Ea.	455	60		515	refrigerator.
Demolish and Install	Ea.	455	101.50		556.50	
Reinstall	Ea.		47.87		47.87	
Clean	Ea.	.08	27.50		27.58	
Minimum Charge	Job		75		75	
16 Cubic Foot						
Demolish	Ea.		41.50		41.50	Includes material and labor to install a
Install	Ea.	530	66.50		596.50	refrigerator.
Demolish and Install	Ea.	530	108		638	
Reinstall	Ea.		53.19		53.19	
Clean	Ea.	.08	27.50		27.58	
Minimum Charge	Job		75		75	

Improvements / Appliances / Treatments

Refrigerator		Unit	Material	Labor	Equip.	Total	Specification
18 Cubic Foot							
	Demolish	Ea.		41.50		41.50	Includes material and labor to install a
	Install	Ea.	675	75		750	refrigerator.
	Demolish and Install	Ea.	675	116.50		791.50	
	Reinstall	Ea.		59.84		59.84	
	Clean	Ea.	.08	27.50		27.58	
	Minimum Charge	Job		75		75	
21 Cubic Foot							
	Demolish	Ea.		41.50		41.50	Includes material and labor to install a
	Install	Ea.	1050	85.50		1135.50	refrigerator.
	Demolish and Install	Ea.	1050	127		1177	
	Reinstall	Ea.		68.39		68.39	
	Clean	Ea.	.08	27.50		27.58	
	Minimum Charge	Job		75		75	
24 Cubic Foot							
	Demolish	Ea.		41.50		41.50	Includes material and labor to install a
	Install	Ea.	1400	85.50		1485.50	refrigerator.
	Demolish and Install	Ea.	1400	127		1527	
	Reinstall	Ea.		68.39		68.39	
	Clean	Ea.	.08	27.50		27.58	
	Minimum Charge	Job		75		75	
27 Cubic Foot							
	Demolish	Ea.		41.50		41.50	Includes material and labor to install a
	Install	Ea.	3125	60		3185	refrigerator.
	Demolish and Install	Ea.	3125	101.50		3226.50	
	Reinstall	Ea.		47.87		47.87	
	Clean	Ea.	.08	27.50		27.58	
	Minimum Charge	Job		75		75	
Ice Maker							
	Install	Ea.	67	58		125	Includes labor and material to install
	Minimum Charge	Job		75		75	an automatic ice maker in a
							refrigerator.

Freezer		Unit	Material	Labor	Equip.	Total	Specification
15 Cubic Foot							
	Demolish	Ea.		41.50		41.50	Cost includes material and labor to
	Install	Ea.	605	60		665	install 15 cubic foot freezer.
	Demolish and Install	Ea.	605	101.50		706.50	
	Reinstall	Ea.		47.87		47.87	
	Clean	Ea.	.08	27.50		27.58	
	Minimum Charge	Job		75		75	
18 Cubic Foot							
	Demolish	Ea.		41.50		41.50	Cost includes material and labor to
	Install	Ea.	805	60		865	install 18 cubic foot freezer.
	Demolish and Install	Ea.	805	101.50		906.50	
	Reinstall	Ea.		47.87		47.87	
	Clean	Ea.	.08	27.50		27.58	
	Minimum Charge	Job		75		75	
21 Cubic Foot							
	Demolish	Ea.		41.50		41.50	Includes material and labor to install a
	Install	Ea.	720	60		780	15 to 23 cubic foot deep freezer.
	Demolish and Install	Ea.	720	101.50		821.50	
	Reinstall	Ea.		47.87		47.87	
	Clean	Ea.	.08	27.50		27.58	
	Minimum Charge	Job		75		75	

Improvements / Appliances / Treatments

Freezer

	Unit	Material	Labor	Equip.	Total	Specification
24 Cubic Foot						
Demolish	Ea.		41.50		41.50	Includes material and labor to install a
Install	Ea.	805	120		925	24 cubic foot deep freezer.
Demolish and Install	Ea.	805	161.50		966.50	
Reinstall	Ea.		95.74		95.74	
Clean	Ea.	.08	27.50		27.58	
Minimum Charge	Job		75		75	
Chest-type						
Demolish	Ea.		41.50		41.50	Cost includes material and labor to
Install	Ea.	605	60		665	install 15 cubic foot freezer.
Demolish and Install	Ea.	605	101.50		706.50	
Clean	Ea.	.08	27.50		27.58	
Minimum Charge	Job		75		75	

Dishwasher

	Unit	Material	Labor	Equip.	Total	Specification
4 Cycle						
Demolish	Ea.		33		33	Includes material and labor to install
Install	Ea.	360	143		503	good grade automatic dishwasher.
Demolish and Install	Ea.	360	176		536	
Reinstall	Ea.		114.34		114.34	
Clean	Ea.	.08	27.50		27.58	
Minimum Charge	Job		75		75	

Garbage Disposal

	Unit	Material	Labor	Equip.	Total	Specification
In Sink Unit						
Demolish	Ea.		32		32	Cost includes material and labor to
Install	Ea.	156	57		213	install 1/2 HP custom disposal unit.
Demolish and Install	Ea.	156	89		245	
Reinstall	Ea.		45.74		45.74	
Clean	Ea.	.04	7.80		7.84	
Minimum Charge	Job		75		75	

Trash Compactor

	Unit	Material	Labor	Equip.	Total	Specification
4 to 1 Compaction						
Demolish	Ea.		30.50		30.50	Includes material and labor to install a
Install	Ea.	780	80.50		860.50	trash compactor.
Demolish and Install	Ea.	780	111		891	
Reinstall	Ea.		64.58		64.58	
Clean	Ea.	.08	18.70		18.78	
Minimum Charge	Job		75		75	

Kitchenette Unit

	Unit	Material	Labor	Equip.	Total	Specification
Range, Refrigerator and Sink						
Demolish	Ea.		121		121	Includes material and labor to install
Install	Ea.	4625	475		5100	range/refrigerator/sink unit, 72"
Demolish and Install	Ea.	4625	596		5221	wide, base unit only.
Reinstall	Ea.		381.13		381.13	
Clean	Ea.	1.30	13.65		14.95	
Minimum Charge	Job		75		75	

Improvements / Appliances / Treatments

Bath Accessories

		Unit	Material	Labor	Equip.	Total	Specification
Towel Bar							Includes material and labor to install
	Demolish	Ea.		6.95		6.95	towel bar up to 24" long.
	Install	Ea.	53.50	16.80		70.30	
	Demolish and Install	Ea.	53.50	23.75		77.25	
	Reinstall	Ea.		13.45		13.45	
	Clean	Ea.		3.74		3.74	
	Minimum Charge	Job		202		202	
Toothbrush Holder							Includes material and labor to install a
	Demolish	Ea.		6.95		6.95	surface mounted tumbler and
	Install	Ea.	14.60	20		34.60	toothbrush holder.
	Demolish and Install	Ea.	14.60	26.95		41.55	
	Reinstall	Ea.		16.14		16.14	
	Clean	Ea.		3.74		3.74	
	Minimum Charge	Job		202		202	
Grab Rail							Includes material and labor to install a
	Demolish	Ea.		10.40		10.40	24" long grab bar. Blocking is not
	Install	Ea.	32.50	17.55		50.05	included.
	Demolish and Install	Ea.	32.50	27.95		60.45	
	Reinstall	Ea.		14.04		14.04	
	Clean	Ea.	.52	6.25		6.77	
	Minimum Charge	Job		202		202	
Soap Dish							Includes material and labor to install a
	Demolish	Ea.		6.95		6.95	surface mounted soap dish.
	Install	Ea.	5.80	20		25.80	
	Demolish and Install	Ea.	5.80	26.95		32.75	
	Reinstall	Ea.		16.14		16.14	
	Clean	Ea.		3.74		3.74	
	Minimum Charge	Job		202		202	
Toilet Paper Roller							Includes material and labor to install a
	Demolish	Ea.		6.95		6.95	surface mounted toilet tissue dispenser.
	Install	Ea.	18.65	13.45		32.10	
	Demolish and Install	Ea.	18.65	20.40		39.05	
	Reinstall	Ea.		10.76		10.76	
	Clean	Ea.	.52	9.35		9.87	
	Minimum Charge	Job		202		202	
Dispenser							
Soap							Includes material and labor to install a
	Demolish	Ea.		9.25		9.25	surface mounted soap dispenser.
	Install	Ea.	46	20		66	
	Demolish and Install	Ea.	46	29.25		75.25	
	Reinstall	Ea.		16.14		16.14	
	Clean	Ea.	.52	9.35		9.87	
	Minimum Charge	Job		202		202	
Towel							Includes material and labor to install a
	Demolish	Ea.		10.40		10.40	surface mounted towel dispenser.
	Install	Ea.	37	25		62	
	Demolish and Install	Ea.	37	35.40		72.40	
	Reinstall	Ea.		20.18		20.18	
	Clean	Ea.	.52	12.45		12.97	
	Minimum Charge	Job		202		202	
Seat Cover							Includes material and labor to install a
	Demolish	Ea.		6.95		6.95	surface mounted toilet seat cover
	Install	Ea.	33	27		60	dispenser.
	Demolish and Install	Ea.	33	33.95		66.95	
	Reinstall	Ea.		21.53		21.53	
	Clean	Ea.	.52	9.35		9.87	
	Minimum Charge	Job		202		202	

Improvements / Appliances / Treatments

Bath Accessories

	Unit	Material	Labor	Equip.	Total	Specification
Sanitary Napkin						
Demolish	Ea.		17.50		17.50	Includes material and labor to install a
Install	Ea.	43.50	42.50		86	surface mounted sanitary napkin
Demolish and Install	Ea.	43.50	60		103.50	dispenser.
Reinstall	Ea.		33.99		33.99	
Clean	Ea.	.26	12.45		12.71	
Minimum Charge	Job		202		202	
Partition						
Urinal						
Demolish	Ea.		21		21	Includes material and labor to install a
Install	Ea.	268	101		369	urinal screen.
Demolish and Install	Ea.	268	122		390	
Reinstall	Ea.		80.72		80.72	
Clean	Ea.	.78	8.30		9.08	
Minimum Charge	Job		202		202	
Toilet						
Demolish	Ea.		61.50		61.50	Includes material and labor to install
Install	Ea.	650	161		811	baked enamel standard size partition,
Demolish and Install	Ea.	650	222.50		872.50	floor or ceiling mounted with one wall
Reinstall	Ea.		129.15		129.15	and one door.
Clean	Ea.	5.20	18.70		23.90	
Minimum Charge	Job		202		202	
Handicap						
Demolish	Ea.		61.50		61.50	Includes material and labor to install
Install	Ea.	965	161		1126	baked enamel handicap partition,
Demolish and Install	Ea.	965	222.50		1187.50	floor or ceiling mounted with one wall
Reinstall	Ea.		129.15		129.15	and one door.
Clean	Ea.	5.20	18.70		23.90	
Minimum Charge	Job		202		202	

Fire Prevention / Protection

	Unit	Material	Labor	Equip.	Total	Specification
Fire Extinguisher						
5# Carbon Dioxide						
Install	Ea.	146			146	Includes labor and material to install one wall mounted 5 lb. carbon dioxide factory charged unit, complete with hose, horn and wall mounting bracket.
10# Carbon Dioxide						
Install	Ea.	210			210	Includes labor and material to install one wall mounted 10 lb. carbon dioxide factory charged unit, complete with hose, horn and wall mounting bracket.
15# Carbon Dioxide						
Install	Ea.	275			275	Includes labor and material to install one wall mounted 15 lb. carbon dioxide factory charged unit, complete with hose, horn and wall mounting bracket.

Improvements / Appliances / Treatments

Fire Prevention / Protection		Unit	Material	Labor	Equip.	Total	Specification
5# Dry Chemical	Install	Ea.	48.50			48.50	Includes labor and material to install one wall mounted 5 lb. dry chemical factory charged unit, complete with hose, horn and wall mounting bracket.
20# Dry Chemical	Install	Ea.	124			124	Includes labor and material to install one wall mounted 20 lb. dry chemical factory charged unit, complete with hose, horn and wall mounting bracket.

Gutters		Unit	Material	Labor	Equip.	Total	Specification
Galvanized	Demolish	L.F.		1.39		1.39	Cost includes material and labor to install 5" galvanized steel gutter with enamel finish, fittings, hangers, and corners.
	Install	L.F.	1.66	3.76		5.42	
	Demolish and Install	L.F.	1.66	5.15		6.81	
	Reinstall	L.F.		3.01		3.01	
	Clean	L.F.		.40		.40	
	Paint	L.F.	.19	1.07		1.26	
	Minimum Charge	Job		225		225	
Aluminum	Demolish	L.F.		1.39		1.39	Cost includes material and labor to install 5" aluminum gutter with enamel finish, fittings, hangers, and corners.
	Install	L.F.	2.84	3.76		6.60	
	Demolish and Install	L.F.	2.84	5.15		7.99	
	Reinstall	L.F.		3.01		3.01	
	Clean	L.F.		.40		.40	
	Paint	L.F.	.19	1.07		1.26	
	Minimum Charge	Job		225		225	
Copper	Demolish	L.F.		1.39		1.39	Cost includes material and labor to install 5" half-round copper gutter with fittings, hangers, and corners.
	Install	L.F.	9.40	3.76		13.16	
	Demolish and Install	L.F.	9.40	5.15		14.55	
	Reinstall	L.F.		3.01		3.01	
	Clean	L.F.		.40		.40	
	Minimum Charge	Job		225		225	
Plastic	Demolish	L.F.		1.39		1.39	Cost includes material and labor to install 4" white vinyl gutter fittings, hangers, and corners.
	Install	L.F.	1.19	3.67		4.86	
	Demolish and Install	L.F.	1.19	5.06		6.25	
	Reinstall	L.F.		2.94		2.94	
	Clean	L.F.		.40		.40	
	Paint	L.F.	.19	1.07		1.26	
	Minimum Charge	Job		225		225	

Downspouts		Unit	Material	Labor	Equip.	Total	Specification
Galvanized	Demolish	L.F.		.95		.95	Cost includes material and labor to install 4" diameter downspout with enamel finish.
	Install	L.F.	2.59	3.11		5.70	
	Demolish and Install	L.F.	2.59	4.06		6.65	
	Reinstall	L.F.		2.49		2.49	
	Clean	L.F.		.40		.40	
	Paint	L.F.	.19	1.07		1.26	
	Minimum Charge	Job		225		225	

Improvements / Appliances / Treatments

Downspouts	Unit	Material	Labor	Equip.	Total	Specification
Aluminum						
Demolish	L.F.		.95		.95	Includes material and labor to install
Install	L.F.	3.03	3.22		6.25	aluminum enameled downspout.
Demolish and Install	L.F.	3.03	4.17		7.20	
Reinstall	L.F.		2.58		2.58	
Clean	L.F.		.40		.40	
Paint	L.F.	.19	1.07		1.26	
Minimum Charge	Job		225		225	
Copper						
Demolish	L.F.		.95		.95	Includes material and labor to install
Install	L.F.	7.60	2.37		9.97	round copper downspout.
Demolish and Install	L.F.	7.60	3.32		10.92	
Reinstall	L.F.		1.90		1.90	
Clean	L.F.		.40		.40	
Paint	L.F.	.19	1.07		1.26	
Minimum Charge	Job		225		225	
Plastic						
Demolish	L.F.		.95		.95	Cost includes material and labor to
Install	L.F.	2.13	2.15		4.28	install 2″ x 3″ vinyl rectangular
Demolish and Install	L.F.	2.13	3.10		5.23	downspouts.
Reinstall	L.F.		1.72		1.72	
Clean	L.F.		.40		.40	
Paint	L.F.	.19	1.07		1.26	
Minimum Charge	Job		225		225	

Shutters	Unit	Material	Labor	Equip.	Total	Specification
Exterior						
25″ High						
Demolish	Ea.		10.40		10.40	Includes material and labor to install
Install	Pr.	119	40.50		159.50	pair of exterior shutters 25″ x 16″,
Demolish and Install	Pr.	119	50.90		169.90	unpainted, installed as fixed shutters
Reinstall	Pr.		40.36		40.36	on concrete or wood frame.
Clean	Ea.	.10	9.10		9.20	
Paint	Ea.	1.52	18.60		20.12	
Minimum Charge	Job		202		202	
39″ High						
Demolish	Ea.		10.40		10.40	Includes material and labor to install
Install	Pr.	129	40.50		169.50	pair of shutters 39″ x 16″, unpainted,
Demolish and Install	Pr.	129	50.90		179.90	installed as fixed shutters on concrete
Reinstall	Pr.		40.36		40.36	or wood frame.
Clean	Ea.	.10	9.10		9.20	
Paint	Ea.	2.35	25		27.35	
Minimum Charge	Job		202		202	
51″ High						
Demolish	Ea.		10.40		10.40	Includes material and labor to install
Install	Pr.	143	40.50		183.50	pair of shutters 51″ x 16″, unpainted,
Demolish and Install	Pr.	143	50.90		193.90	installed as fixed shutters on concrete
Reinstall	Pr.		40.36		40.36	or wood frame.
Clean	Ea.	.10	9.10		9.20	
Paint	Ea.	3.06	26		29.06	
Minimum Charge	Job		202		202	

Improvements / Appliances / Treatments

Shutters

	Unit	Material	Labor	Equip.	Total	Specification
59″ High						Includes material and labor to install
Demolish	Ea.		10.40		10.40	pair of shutters 59″ x 16″, unpainted,
Install	Pr.	201	40.50		241.50	installed as fixed shutters on concrete
Demolish and Install	Pr.	201	50.90		251.90	or wood frame.
Reinstall	Pr.		40.36		40.36	
Clean	Ea.	.10	9.10		9.20	
Paint	Ea.	3.53	28.50		32.03	
Minimum Charge	Job		202		202	
67″ High						Includes material and labor to install
Demolish	Ea.		10.40		10.40	pair of shutters 67″ x 16″, unpainted,
Install	Pr.	202	45		247	installed as fixed shutters on concrete
Demolish and Install	Pr.	202	55.40		257.40	or wood frame.
Reinstall	Pr.		44.84		44.84	
Clean	Ea.	.10	9.10		9.20	
Paint	Ea.	4.04	32		36.04	
Minimum Charge	Job		202		202	

Interior Wood

	Unit	Material	Labor	Equip.	Total	Specification
23″ x 24″, 2 Panel						Cost includes material and labor to
Demolish	Ea.		10.40		10.40	install 23″ x 24″, 4 panel interior
Install	Ea.	70.50	23.50		94	moveable pine shutter, 1-1/4″ louver,
Demolish and Install	Ea.	70.50	33.90		104.40	knobs and hooks and hinges.
Reinstall	Ea.		18.99		18.99	
Clean	Ea.	.10	9.10		9.20	
Paint	Ea.	1.14	24.50		25.64	
Minimum Charge	Job		202		202	
27″ x 24″, 4 Panel						Cost includes material and labor to
Demolish	Ea.		10.40		10.40	install 27″ x 24″, 4 panel interior
Install	Ea.	77	23.50		100.50	moveable pine shutter, 1-1/4″ louver,
Demolish and Install	Ea.	77	33.90		110.90	knobs and hooks and hinges.
Reinstall	Ea.		18.99		18.99	
Clean	Ea.	.10	9.10		9.20	
Paint	Ea.	1.14	24.50		25.64	
Minimum Charge	Job		202		202	
31″ x 24″, 4 Panel						Cost includes material and labor to
Demolish	Ea.		10.40		10.40	install 31″ x 24″, 4 panel interior
Install	Ea.	88	23.50		111.50	moveable pine shutter, 1-1/4″ louver,
Demolish and Install	Ea.	88	33.90		121.90	knobs and hooks and hinges.
Reinstall	Ea.		18.99		18.99	
Clean	Ea.	.10	9.10		9.20	
Paint	Ea.	1.14	24.50		25.64	
Minimum Charge	Job		202		202	
35″ x 24″, 4 Panel						Cost includes material and labor to
Demolish	Ea.		10.40		10.40	install 35″ x 24″, 4 panel interior
Install	Ea.	94.50	23.50		118	moveable pine shutter, 1-1/4″ louver,
Demolish and Install	Ea.	94.50	33.90		128.40	knobs and hooks and hinges.
Reinstall	Ea.		18.99		18.99	
Clean	Ea.	.10	9.10		9.20	
Paint	Ea.	1.14	24.50		25.64	
Minimum Charge	Job		202		202	
39″ x 24″, 4 Panel						Cost includes material and labor to
Demolish	Ea.		10.40		10.40	install 39″ x 24″, 4 panel interior
Install	Ea.	103	23.50		126.50	moveable pine shutter, 1-1/4″ louver,
Demolish and Install	Ea.	103	33.90		136.90	knobs and hooks and hinges.
Reinstall	Ea.		18.99		18.99	
Clean	Ea.	.10	9.10		9.20	
Paint	Ea.	1.14	24.50		25.64	
Minimum Charge	Job		202		202	

Improvements / Appliances / Treatments

Shutters

	Unit	Material	Labor	Equip.	Total	Specification
47″ x 24″, 4 Panel						
Demolish	Ea.		10.40		10.40	Cost includes material and labor to
Install	Ea.	119	23.50		142.50	install 47″ x 24″, 4 panel interior
Demolish and Install	Ea.	119	33.90		152.90	moveable pine shutter, 1-1/4″ louver,
Reinstall	Ea.		18.99		18.99	knobs and hooks and hinges.
Clean	Ea.	.10	9.10		9.20	
Paint	Ea.	1.19	26.50		27.69	
Minimum Charge	Job		202		202	

Awning

	Unit	Material	Labor	Equip.	Total	Specification
Standard Aluminum						
36″ Wide x 30″ Deep						
Demolish	Ea.		10.40		10.40	Includes material and labor to install
Install	Ea.	206	33.50		239.50	one aluminum awning with
Demolish and Install	Ea.	206	43.90		249.90	weather-resistant finish.
Reinstall	Ea.		26.91		26.91	
Clean	Ea.		12.45		12.45	
Minimum Charge	Job		202		202	
48″ Wide x 30″ Deep						
Demolish	Ea.		10.40		10.40	Includes material and labor to install
Install	Ea.	237	40.50		277.50	one aluminum awning with
Demolish and Install	Ea.	237	50.90		287.90	weather-resistant finish.
Reinstall	Ea.		32.29		32.29	
Clean	Ea.		12.45		12.45	
Minimum Charge	Job		202		202	
60″ Wide x 30″ Deep						
Demolish	Ea.		21		21	Includes material and labor to install
Install	Ea.	270	45		315	one aluminum awning with
Demolish and Install	Ea.	270	66		336	weather-resistant finish.
Reinstall	Ea.		35.88		35.88	
Clean	Ea.		12.45		12.45	
Minimum Charge	Job		202		202	
72″ Wide x 30″ Deep						
Demolish	Ea.		21		21	Includes material and labor to install
Install	Ea.	305	50.50		355.50	one aluminum awning with
Demolish and Install	Ea.	305	71.50		376.50	weather-resistant finish.
Reinstall	Ea.		40.36		40.36	
Clean	Ea.		12.45		12.45	
Minimum Charge	Job		202		202	
Roll-up Type						
Demolish	S.F.		.75		.75	Includes material and labor to install
Install	S.F.	11.35	4.04		15.39	an aluminum roll-up awning.
Demolish and Install	S.F.	11.35	4.79		16.14	
Reinstall	S.F.		3.23		3.23	
Clean	S.F.	.06	.62		.68	
Minimum Charge	Job		202		202	
Canvas						
30″ Wide						
Demolish	Ea.		6.25		6.25	Includes material and labor to install a
Install	Ea.	202	33.50		235.50	canvas window awning.
Demolish and Install	Ea.	202	39.75		241.75	
Reinstall	Ea.		26.91		26.91	
Clean	Ea.		3.74		3.74	
Minimum Charge	Job		202		202	

Improvements / Appliances / Treatments

Awning

		Unit	Material	Labor	Equip.	Total	Specification
36" Wide							Includes material and labor to install a
	Demolish	Ea.		6.25		6.25	canvas window awning.
	Install	Ea.	221	40.50		261.50	
	Demolish and Install	Ea.	221	46.75		267.75	
	Reinstall	Ea.		32.29		32.29	
	Clean	Ea.		4.10		4.10	
	Minimum Charge	Job		202		202	
42" Wide							Includes material and labor to install a
	Demolish	Ea.		6.25		6.25	canvas window awning.
	Install	Ea.	233	50.50		283.50	
	Demolish and Install	Ea.	233	56.75		289.75	
	Reinstall	Ea.		40.36		40.36	
	Clean	Ea.		4.87		4.87	
	Minimum Charge	Job		202		202	
48" Wide							Includes material and labor to install a
	Demolish	Ea.		6.25		6.25	canvas window awning.
	Install	Ea.	246	57.50		303.50	
	Demolish and Install	Ea.	246	63.75		309.75	
	Reinstall	Ea.		46.13		46.13	
	Clean	Ea.		5.65		5.65	
	Minimum Charge	Job		202		202	

Cloth Canopy Cover

		Unit	Material	Labor	Equip.	Total	Specification
8' x 10'							Includes material and labor to install
	Demolish	Ea.		340		340	one 8' x 10' cloth canopy patio cover
	Install	Ea.	425	202		627	with front bar and tension support
	Demolish and Install	Ea.	425	542		967	rafters and 9" valance.
	Reinstall	Ea.		161.44		161.44	
	Clean	Ea.	4.16	50		54.16	
	Minimum Charge	Job		405		405	
8' x 15'							Includes material and labor to install
	Demolish	Ea.		340		340	one 8' x 15' cloth canopy patio cover
	Install	Ea.	580	202		782	with front bar and tension support
	Demolish and Install	Ea.	580	542		1122	rafters and 9" valance.
	Reinstall	Ea.		161.44		161.44	
	Clean	Ea.	4.16	75		79.16	
	Minimum Charge	Job		405		405	

Vent

		Unit	Material	Labor	Equip.	Total	Specification
Small Roof Turbine							Includes material and labor to install
	Demolish	Ea.		10.40		10.40	spinner ventilator, wind driven,
	Install	Ea.	55	40.50		95.50	galvanized, 4" neck diam, 180 CFM.
	Demolish and Install	Ea.	55	50.90		105.90	
	Reinstall	Ea.		32.47		32.47	
	Clean	Ea.		6.65		6.65	
	Minimum Charge	Job		231		231	
Large Roof Turbine							Includes material and labor to install
	Demolish	Ea.		8.30		8.30	spinner ventilator, wind driven,
	Install	Ea.	64	58		122	galvanized, 8" neck diam, 360 CFM.
	Demolish and Install	Ea.	64	66.30		130.30	
	Reinstall	Ea.		46.38		46.38	
	Clean	Ea.		7.50		7.50	
	Minimum Charge	Job		231		231	

Vent

	Unit	Material	Labor	Equip.	Total	Specification
Gable Louvered						
Demolish	Ea.		21		21	Includes material and labor to install a
Install	Ea.	40	13.45		53.45	vinyl gable end vent.
Demolish and Install	Ea.	40	34.45		74.45	
Reinstall	Ea.		10.76		10.76	
Clean	Ea.		3.99		3.99	
Paint	Ea.	.96	5.35		6.31	
Minimum Charge	Job		202		202	
Ridge Vent						
Demolish	L.F.		1.07		1.07	Includes material and labor to install a
Install	L.F.	3	2.91		5.91	mill finish aluminum ridge vent strip.
Demolish and Install	L.F.	3	3.98		6.98	
Minimum Charge	Job		202		202	
Foundation						
Demolish	Ea.		7.40		7.40	Includes material and labor to install
Install	Ea.	27	13.20		40.20	galvanized foundation block vent.
Demolish and Install	Ea.	27	20.60		47.60	
Reinstall	Ea.		10.57		10.57	
Clean	Ea.	.26	7.50		7.76	
Minimum Charge	Job		202		202	
Frieze						
Demolish	L.F.		.74		.74	Includes material and labor to install
Install	L.F.	1.17	.92		2.09	pine frieze board.
Demolish and Install	L.F.	1.17	1.66		2.83	
Reinstall	L.F.		.73		.73	
Clean	L.F.	.06	.25		.31	
Minimum Charge	Job		202		202	
Water Heater Cap						
Demolish	Ea.		16.05		16.05	Includes material and labor to install a
Install	Ea.	28.50	56.50		85	galvanized steel water heater cap.
Demolish and Install	Ea.	28.50	72.55		101.05	
Reinstall	Ea.		45.08		45.08	
Clean	Ea.	1.82	18.70		20.52	

Cupolas

	Unit	Material	Labor	Equip.	Total	Specification
22″ x 22″						
Demolish	Ea.		195		195	Includes material and labor to install a
Install	Ea.	315	101		416	cedar cupola with aluminum roof
Demolish and Install	Ea.	315	296		611	covering.
Reinstall	Ea.		80.72		80.72	
Minimum Charge	Job		202		202	
29″ x 29″						
Demolish	Ea.		195		195	Includes material and labor to install a
Install	Ea.	430	101		531	cedar cupola with aluminum roof
Demolish and Install	Ea.	430	296		726	covering.
Reinstall	Ea.		80.72		80.72	
Minimum Charge	Job		202		202	
35″ x 35″						
Demolish	Ea.		195		195	Includes material and labor to install a
Install	Ea.	725	135		860	cedar cupola with aluminum roof
Demolish and Install	Ea.	725	330		1055	covering.
Reinstall	Ea.		107.63		107.63	
Minimum Charge	Job		202		202	

Improvements / Appliances / Treatments

Cupolas

	Unit	Material	Labor	Equip.	Total	Specification
47" x 47"						
Demolish	Ea.		195		195	Includes material and labor to install a
Install	Ea.	1275	202		1477	cedar cupola with aluminum roof
Demolish and Install	Ea.	1275	397		1672	covering.
Reinstall	Ea.		161.44		161.44	
Minimum Charge	Job		202		202	
Weather Vane						
Install	Ea.	166	50.50		216.50	Includes minimum labor and
Minimum Charge	Job		202		202	equipment to install residential type weathervane.

Aluminum Carport

	Unit	Material	Labor	Equip.	Total	Specification
20' x 20' Complete						
Demolish	Ea.		208		208	Includes material, labor and
Install	Ea.	8475	670	119	9264	equipment to install an aluminum
Demolish and Install	Ea.	8475	878	119	9472	carport. Foundations are not included.
Reinstall	Ea.		535.01	95.52	630.53	
Clean	Ea.	.28	75		75.28	
Minimum Charge	Job		405		405	
24' x 24' Complete						
Demolish	Ea.		208		208	Includes material, labor and
Install	Ea.	11600	890	159	12649	equipment to install an aluminum
Demolish and Install	Ea.	11600	1098	159	12857	carport. Foundations are not included.
Reinstall	Ea.		713.34	127.36	840.70	
Clean	Ea.	.28	150		150.28	
Minimum Charge	Job		405		405	
Metal Support Posts						
Demolish	Ea.		2.77		2.77	Includes material and labor to install
Install	Ea.	18.80	50.50		69.30	metal support posts for a carport.
Demolish and Install	Ea.	18.80	53.27		72.07	
Reinstall	Ea.		40.36		40.36	
Clean	Ea.	.28	3.12		3.40	
Paint	Ea.	.18	6.95		7.13	
Minimum Charge	Job		405		405	

Storage Shed

	Unit	Material	Labor	Equip.	Total	Specification
Aluminum						
Pre-fab (8' x 10')						
Demolish	Ea.		60.50		60.50	Includes material and labor to install
Install	Ea.	1800	585		2385	an aluminum storage shed.
Demolish and Install	Ea.	1800	645.50		2445.50	
Clean	Ea.	1.74	37.50		39.24	
Minimum Charge	Ea.		495		495	
Pre-fab (10' x 12')						
Demolish	Ea.		113		113	Includes material and labor to install
Install	Ea.	2275	585		2860	an aluminum storage shed.
Demolish and Install	Ea.	2275	698		2973	
Clean	Ea.	1.74	41.50		43.24	
Minimum Charge	Ea.		495		495	

Improvements / Appliances / Treatments

Storage Shed

	Unit	Material	Labor	Equip.	Total	Specification
Wood						
Pre-fab (8' x 10')						
Demolish	Ea.		60.50		60.50	Includes material and labor to install a
Install	Ea.	1675	585		2260	pre-fabricated wood storage shed.
Demolish and Install	Ea.	1675	645.50		2320.50	
Clean	Ea.	1.74	37.50		39.24	
Minimum Charge	Ea.		495		495	
Pre-fab (10' x 12')						
Demolish	Ea.		113		113	Includes material and labor to install a
Install	Ea.	2175	585		2760	pre-fabricated wood storage shed.
Demolish and Install	Ea.	2175	698		2873	
Clean	Ea.	1.74	41.50		43.24	
Minimum Charge	Ea.		495		495	

Gazebo

	Unit	Material	Labor	Equip.	Total	Specification
Good Grade						
Demolish	S.F.		3.32		3.32	Includes material and labor to install a
Install	S.F.	50.50	30.50		81	gazebo.
Demolish and Install	S.F.	50.50	33.82		84.32	
Reinstall	S.F.		24.22		24.22	
Clean	S.F.	.21	1.99		2.20	
Minimum Charge	Job		202		202	
Custom Grade						
Demolish	S.F.		3.32		3.32	Includes material and labor to install a
Install	S.F.	73	30.50		103.50	gazebo.
Demolish and Install	S.F.	73	33.82		106.82	
Reinstall	S.F.		24.22		24.22	
Clean	S.F.	.21	1.99		2.20	
Minimum Charge	Job		202		202	
Bench Seating						
Demolish	L.F.		5.55		5.55	Includes material and labor to install
Install	L.F.	1.75	20		21.75	pressure treated bench seating.
Demolish and Install	L.F.	1.75	25.55		27.30	
Reinstall	L.F.		16.14		16.14	
Clean	L.F.	.21	1.50		1.71	
Paint	L.F.	.64	2.77		3.41	
Minimum Charge	Job		202		202	
Re-screen						
Install	S.F.	1.67	1.61		3.28	Includes labor and material to
Minimum Charge	Job		202		202	re-screen wood frame.

Pool

	Unit	Material	Labor	Equip.	Total	Specification
Screen Enclosure						
Re-screen						
Install	SF Wall		4.96		4.96	Includes material and labor to install a
Minimum Charge	Job		202		202	screen enclosure for a pool.
Screen Door						
Demolish	Ea.		8		8	Includes material and labor to install
Install	Ea.	246	67.50		313.50	wood screen door with aluminum cloth
Demolish and Install	Ea.	246	75.50		321.50	screen. Frame and hardware not
Reinstall	Ea.		53.81		53.81	included.
Clean	Ea.	.20	10.90		11.10	
Paint	Ea.	4.20	13.85		18.05	
Minimum Charge	Job		202		202	

Improvements / Appliances / Treatments

Pool	Unit	Material	Labor	Equip.	Total	Specification
Heater / Motor						Includes material and labor to install
Demolish	Ea.		40.50		40.50	swimming pool heater, not incl. base
Install	Ea.	2425	510		2935	or pad, elec., 12 kW, 4,800 gal
Demolish and Install	Ea.	2425	550.50		2975.50	pool, incl. pump.
Reinstall	Ea.		408.42		408.42	
Clean	Ea.	5.20	37.50		42.70	
Minimum Charge	Job		233		233	
Filter System						Includes material, labor and
Demolish	Ea.		66.50		66.50	equipment to install sand filter system
Install	Total	1650	370		2020	tank including hook-up to existing
Demolish and Install	Total	1650	436.50		2086.50	equipment. Pump and motor not
Reinstall	Total		295.94		295.94	included.
Minimum Charge	Job		231		231	
Pump / Motor						Includes material and labor to install a
Demolish	Ea.		40.50		40.50	22 GPM pump.
Install	Ea.	560	92.50		652.50	
Demolish and Install	Ea.	560	133		693	
Reinstall	Ea.		73.98		73.98	
Clean	Ea.	5.20	37.50		42.70	
Minimum Charge	Job		233		233	
Pump Water						Includes labor and equipment to pump
Install	Day		410	85.50	495.50	water from a swimming pool.
Minimum Charge	Job		183		183	
Replaster						Includes labor and material to
Install	SF Surf	1.32	9.60		10.92	replaster gunite pool with a surface
Minimum Charge	Job		183		183	area of 500 to 600 S.F.
Solar Panels						Includes material and labor to install
Demolish	S.F.		1.71		1.71	solar panel.
Install	S.F.	32.50	3.04		35.54	
Demolish and Install	S.F.	32.50	4.75		37.25	
Reinstall	S.F.		2.43		2.43	
Minimum Charge	Ea.		495		495	

Construction Clean-up	Unit	Material	Labor	Equip.	Total	Specification
Final						
Clean	S.F.		.26		.26	Includes labor for final site/job
Minimum Charge	Job		150		150	clean-up including detail cleaning.

Location Factors

Costs shown in *RSMeans Residential Cost Data* are based on national averages for materials and installation. To adjust these costs to a specific location, simply multiply the base cost by the factor for that city. The data is arranged alphabetically by state and postal zip code numbers. For a city not listed, use the factor for a nearby city with similar economic characteristics.

STATE	CITY	Residential
ALABAMA		
350-352	Birmingham	.87
354	Tuscaloosa	.77
355	Jasper	.73
356	Decatur	.77
357-358	Huntsville	.83
359	Gadsden	.74
360-361	Montgomery	.76
362	Anniston	.77
363	Dothan	.75
364	Evergreen	.73
365-366	Mobile	.82
367	Selma	.73
368	Phenix City	.73
369	Butler	.73
ALASKA		
995-996	Anchorage	1.25
997	Fairbanks	1.26
998	Juneau	1.23
999	Ketchikan	1.28
ARIZONA		
850,853	Phoenix	.86
851,852	Mesa/Tempe	.85
855	Globe	.76
856-857	Tucson	.84
859	Show Low	.78
860	Flagstaff	.86
863	Prescott	.77
864	Kingman	.84
865	Chambers	.77
ARKANSAS		
716	Pine Bluff	.78
717	Camden	.69
718	Texarkana	.73
719	Hot Springs	.69
720-722	Little Rock	.82
723	West Memphis	.78
724	Jonesboro	.76
725	Batesville	.74
726	Harrison	.74
727	Fayetteville	.70
728	Russellville	.76
729	Fort Smith	.81
CALIFORNIA		
900-902	Los Angeles	1.07
903-905	Inglewood	1.05
906-908	Long Beach	1.04
910-912	Pasadena	1.04
913-916	Van Nuys	1.07
917-918	Alhambra	1.08
919-921	San Diego	1.03
922	Palm Springs	1.04
923-924	San Bernardino	1.05
925	Riverside	1.07
926-927	Santa Ana	1.06
928	Anaheim	1.07
930	Oxnard	1.08
931	Santa Barbara	1.07
932-933	Bakersfield	1.06
934	San Luis Obispo	1.08
935	Mojave	1.05
936-938	Fresno	1.11
939	Salinas	1.14
940-941	San Francisco	1.26
942,956-958	Sacramento	1.13
943	Palo Alto	1.18
944	San Mateo	1.23
945	Vallejo	1.18
946	Oakland	1.24
947	Berkeley	1.26
948	Richmond	1.25
949	San Rafael	1.23
950	Santa Cruz	1.17
951	San Jose	1.22
952	Stockton	1.11
953	Modesto	1.10

STATE	CITY	Residential
CALIFORNIA (CONT'D)		
954	Santa Rosa	1.20
955	Eureka	1.12
959	Marysville	1.11
960	Redding	1.11
961	Susanville	1.11
COLORADO		
800-802	Denver	.92
803	Boulder	.92
804	Golden	.90
805	Fort Collins	.88
806	Greeley	.85
807	Fort Morgan	.92
808-809	Colorado Springs	.89
810	Pueblo	.90
811	Alamosa	.86
812	Salida	.89
813	Durango	.88
814	Montrose	.86
815	Grand Junction	.92
816	Glenwood Springs	.88
CONNECTICUT		
060	New Britain	1.10
061	Hartford	1.09
062	Willimantic	1.09
063	New London	1.09
064	Meriden	1.09
065	New Haven	1.09
066	Bridgeport	1.09
067	Waterbury	1.10
068	Norwalk	1.09
069	Stamford	1.10
D.C.		
200-205	Washington	.94
DELAWARE		
197	Newark	1.02
198	Wilmington	1.03
199	Dover	1.02
FLORIDA		
320,322	Jacksonville	.83
321	Daytona Beach	.88
323	Tallahassee	.79
324	Panama City	.77
325	Pensacola	.83
326,344	Gainesville	.82
327-328,347	Orlando	.89
329	Melbourne	.89
330-332,340	Miami	.88
333	Fort Lauderdale	.88
334,349	West Palm Beach	.88
335-336,346	Tampa	.92
337	St. Petersburg	.81
338	Lakeland	.89
339,341	Fort Myers	.87
342	Sarasota	.90
GEORGIA		
300-303,399	Atlanta	.87
304	Statesboro	.70
305	Gainesville	.77
306	Athens	.75
307	Dalton	.75
308-309	Augusta	.81
310-312	Macon	.80
313-314	Savannah	.81
315	Waycross	.80
316	Valdosta	.75
317,398	Albany	.77
318-319	Columbus	.81
HAWAII		
967	Hilo	1.18
968	Honolulu	1.20

291

Location Factors

STATE	CITY	Residential
STATES & POSS.		
969	Guam	.95
IDAHO		
832	Pocatello	.85
833	Twin Falls	.70
834	Idaho Falls	.73
835	Lewiston	.93
836-837	Boise	.85
838	Coeur d'Alene	.91
ILLINOIS		
600-603	North Suburban	1.18
604	Joliet	1.21
605	South Suburban	1.18
606-608	Chicago	1.21
609	Kankakee	1.10
610-611	Rockford	1.11
612	Rock Island	.97
613	La Salle	1.09
614	Galesburg	1.02
615-616	Peoria	1.05
617	Bloomington	1.03
618-619	Champaign	1.05
620-622	East St. Louis	1.01
623	Quincy	1.01
624	Effingham	1.02
625	Decatur	1.03
626-627	Springfield	1.03
628	Centralia	1.02
629	Carbondale	.99
INDIANA		
460	Anderson	.91
461-462	Indianapolis	.94
463-464	Gary	1.05
465-466	South Bend	.91
467-468	Fort Wayne	.90
469	Kokomo	.91
470	Lawrenceburg	.87
471	New Albany	.87
472	Columbus	.92
473	Muncie	.92
474	Bloomington	.94
475	Washington	.91
476-477	Evansville	.91
478	Terre Haute	.91
479	Lafayette	.93
IOWA		
500-503,509	Des Moines	.92
504	Mason City	.78
505	Fort Dodge	.77
506-507	Waterloo	.84
508	Creston	.86
510-511	Sioux City	.86
512	Sibley	.75
513	Spencer	.76
514	Carroll	.81
515	Council Bluffs	.87
516	Shenandoah	.82
520	Dubuque	.87
521	Decorah	.79
522-524	Cedar Rapids	.94
525	Ottumwa	.84
526	Burlington	.89
527-528	Davenport	.96
KANSAS		
660-662	Kansas City	.98
664-666	Topeka	.77
667	Fort Scott	.89
668	Emporia	.83
669	Belleville	.81
670-672	Wichita	.78
673	Independence	.88
674	Salina	.80
675	Hutchinson	.79
676	Hays	.81
677	Colby	.83
678	Dodge City	.81
679	Liberal	.80
KENTUCKY		
400-402	Louisville	.91
403-405	Lexington	.87

STATE	CITY	Residential
KENTUCKY (CONT'D)		
406	Frankfort	.83
407-409	Corbin	.74
410	Covington	.96
411-412	Ashland	.94
413-414	Campton	.75
415-416	Pikeville	.84
417-418	Hazard	.71
420	Paducah	.89
421-422	Bowling Green	.89
423	Owensboro	.85
424	Henderson	.90
425-426	Somerset	.74
427	Elizabethtown	.87
LOUISIANA		
700-701	New Orleans	.85
703	Thibodaux	.82
704	Hammond	.75
705	Lafayette	.81
706	Lake Charles	.83
707-708	Baton Rouge	.83
710-711	Shreveport	.76
712	Monroe	.72
713-714	Alexandria	.72
MAINE		
039	Kittery	.90
040-041	Portland	.90
042	Lewiston	.89
043	Augusta	.92
044	Bangor	.88
045	Bath	.90
046	Machias	.90
047	Houlton	.91
048	Rockland	.91
049	Waterville	.90
MARYLAND		
206	Waldorf	.82
207-208	College Park	.88
209	Silver Spring	.83
210-212	Baltimore	.90
214	Annapolis	.84
215	Cumberland	.87
216	Easton	.66
217	Hagerstown	.86
218	Salisbury	.73
219	Elkton	.84
MASSACHUSETTS		
010-011	Springfield	1.06
012	Pittsfield	1.05
013	Greenfield	1.04
014	Fitchburg	1.11
015-016	Worcester	1.13
017	Framingham	1.15
018	Lowell	1.16
019	Lawrence	1.16
020-022, 024	Boston	1.21
023	Brockton	1.15
025	Buzzards Bay	1.13
026	Hyannis	1.13
027	New Bedford	1.15
MICHIGAN		
480,483	Royal Oak	1.00
481	Ann Arbor	1.02
482	Detroit	1.05
484-485	Flint	.97
486	Saginaw	.93
487	Bay City	.94
488-489	Lansing	.95
490	Battle Creek	.94
491	Kalamazoo	.93
492	Jackson	.94
493,495	Grand Rapids	.86
494	Muskegon	.90
496	Traverse City	.84
497	Gaylord	.82
498-499	Iron mountain	.91
MINNESOTA		
550-551	Saint Paul	1.14
553-555	Minneapolis	1.16
556-558	Duluth	1.09

Location Factors

STATE	CITY	Residential
MINNESOTA (CONT'd)		
559	Rochester	1.07
560	Mankato	1.02
561	Windom	.95
562	Willmar	1.00
563	St. Cloud	1.09
564	Brainerd	1.00
565	Detroit Lakes	.98
566	Bemidji	.96
567	Thief River Falls	.96
MISSISSIPPI		
386	Clarksdale	.76
387	Greenville	.83
388	Tupelo	.77
389	Greenwood	.79
390-392	Jackson	.82
393	Meridian	.81
394	Laurel	.78
395	Biloxi	.80
396	Mccomb	.75
397	Columbus	.77
MISSOURI		
630-631	St. Louis	1.02
633	Bowling Green	.96
634	Hannibal	.92
635	Kirksville	.89
636	Flat River	.96
637	Cape Girardeau	.89
638	Sikeston	.87
639	Poplar Bluff	.86
640-641	Kansas City	1.03
644-645	St. Joseph	.95
646	Chillicothe	.87
647	Harrisonville	.99
648	Joplin	.85
650-651	Jefferson City	.93
652	Columbia	.92
653	Sedalia	.93
654-655	Rolla	.95
656-658	Springfield	.87
MONTANA		
590-591	Billings	.88
592	Wolf Point	.82
593	Miles City	.85
594	Great Falls	.89
595	Havre	.82
596	Helena	.87
597	Butte	.86
598	Missoula	.85
599	Kalispell	.82
NEBRASKA		
680-681	Omaha	.91
683-685	Lincoln	.84
686	Columbus	.84
687	Norfolk	.89
688	Grand Island	.89
689	Hastings	.91
690	Mccook	.82
691	North Platte	.89
692	Valentine	.83
693	Alliance	.82
NEVADA		
889-891	Las Vegas	1.05
893	Ely	1.00
894-895	Reno	.91
897	Carson City	.91
898	Elko	.92
NEW HAMPSHIRE		
030	Nashua	.94
031	Manchester	.94
032-033	Concord	.93
034	Keene	.73
035	Littleton	.79
036	Charleston	.72
037	Claremont	.72
038	Portsmouth	.94

STATE	CITY	Residential
NEW JERSEY		
070-071	Newark	1.14
072	Elizabeth	1.16
073	Jersey City	1.13
074-075	Paterson	1.14
076	Hackensack	1.13
077	Long Branch	1.13
078	Dover	1.13
079	Summit	1.14
080,083	Vineland	1.10
081	Camden	1.12
082,084	Atlantic City	1.14
085-086	Trenton	1.10
087	Point Pleasant	1.11
088-089	New Brunswick	1.14
NEW MEXICO		
870-872	Albuquerque	.83
873	Gallup	.83
874	Farmington	.83
875	Santa Fe	.84
877	Las Vegas	.83
878	Socorro	.83
879	Truth/Consequences	.83
880	Las Cruces	.82
881	Clovis	.83
882	Roswell	.83
883	Carrizozo	.83
884	Tucumcari	.84
NEW YORK		
100-102	New York	1.38
103	Staten Island	1.30
104	Bronx	1.31
105	Mount Vernon	1.15
106	White Plains	1.18
107	Yonkers	1.19
108	New Rochelle	1.19
109	Suffern	1.13
110	Queens	1.31
111	Long Island City	1.33
112	Brooklyn	1.35
113	Flushing	1.33
114	Jamaica	1.32
115,117,118	Hicksville	1.20
116	Far Rockaway	1.32
119	Riverhead	1.22
120-122	Albany	.97
123	Schenectady	.98
124	Kingston	1.05
125-126	Poughkeepsie	1.19
127	Monticello	1.07
128	Glens Falls	.91
129	Plattsburgh	.94
130-132	Syracuse	.97
133-135	Utica	.93
136	Watertown	.93
137-139	Binghamton	.95
140-142	Buffalo	1.05
143	Niagara Falls	1.00
144-146	Rochester	.98
147	Jamestown	.89
148-149	Elmira	.92
NORTH CAROLINA		
270,272-274	Greensboro	.80
271	Winston-Salem	.80
275-276	Raleigh	.81
277	Durham	.81
278	Rocky Mount	.72
279	Elizabeth City	.73
280	Gastonia	.81
281-282	Charlotte	.82
283	Fayetteville	.80
284	Wilmington	.78
285	Kinston	.71
286	Hickory	.76
287-288	Asheville	.79
289	Murphy	.70
NORTH DAKOTA		
580-581	Fargo	.78
582	Grand Forks	.73
583	Devils Lake	.75
584	Jamestown	.71
585	Bismarck	.76

293

Location Factors

STATE	CITY	Residential
NORTH DAKOTA (CONT'D)		
586	Dickinson	.74
587	Minot	.81
588	Williston	.74
OHIO		
430-432	Columbus	.96
433	Marion	.88
434-436	Toledo	.99
437-438	Zanesville	.88
439	Steubenville	.94
440	Lorain	.97
441	Cleveland	1.01
442-443	Akron	.98
444-445	Youngstown	.94
446-447	Canton	.93
448-449	Mansfield	.93
450	Hamilton	.92
451-452	Cincinnati	.92
453-454	Dayton	.92
455	Springfield	.93
456	Chillicothe	.95
457	Athens	.89
458	Lima	.91
OKLAHOMA		
730-731	Oklahoma City	.77
734	Ardmore	.76
735	Lawton	.79
736	Clinton	.75
737	Enid	.75
738	Woodward	.75
739	Guymon	.65
740-741	Tulsa	.75
743	Miami	.85
744	Muskogee	.69
745	Mcalester	.72
746	Ponca City	.75
747	Durant	.75
748	Shawnee	.74
749	Poteau	.76
OREGON		
970-972	Portland	.98
973	Salem	.96
974	Eugene	.97
975	Medford	.96
976	Klamath Falls	.97
977	Bend	.98
978	Pendleton	.96
979	Vale	.95
PENNSYLVANIA		
150-152	Pittsburgh	1.00
153	Washington	.95
154	Uniontown	.93
155	Bedford	.90
156	Greensburg	.96
157	Indiana	.93
158	Dubois	.91
159	Johnstown	.91
160	Butler	.93
161	New Castle	.92
162	Kittanning	.94
163	Oil City	.90
164-165	Erie	.94
166	Altoona	.88
167	Bradford	.90
168	State College	.91
169	Wellsboro	.91
170-171	Harrisburg	.94
172	Chambersburg	.89
173-174	York	.92
175-176	Lancaster	.92
177	Williamsport	.84
178	Sunbury	.93
179	Pottsville	.92
180	Lehigh Valley	1.03
181	Allentown	1.04
182	Hazleton	.92
183	Stroudsburg	.92
184-185	Scranton	.97
186-187	Wilkes-Barre	.94
188	Montrose	.91
189	Doylestown	1.08

STATE	CITY	Residential
PENNSYLVANIA (CONT'D)		
190-191	Philadelphia	1.17
193	Westchester	1.12
194	Norristown	1.12
195-196	Reading	.97
PUERTO RICO		
009	San Juan	.73
RHODE ISLAND		
028	Newport	1.07
029	Providence	1.07
SOUTH CAROLINA		
290-292	Columbia	.81
293	Spartanburg	.81
294	Charleston	.84
295	Florence	.77
296	Greenville	.80
297	Rock Hill	.79
298	Aiken	.99
299	Beaufort	.79
SOUTH DAKOTA		
570-571	Sioux Falls	.77
572	Watertown	.74
573	Mitchell	.74
574	Aberdeen	.75
575	Pierre	.74
576	Mobridge	.73
577	Rapid City	.76
TENNESSEE		
370-372	Nashville	.84
373-374	Chattanooga	.83
375,380-381	Memphis	.82
376	Johnson City	.72
377-379	Knoxville	.75
382	Mckenzie	.74
383	Jackson	.78
384	Columbia	.77
385	Cookeville	.71
TEXAS		
750	Mckinney	.73
751	Waxahackie	.79
752-753	Dallas	.84
754	Greenville	.70
755	Texarkana	.73
756	Longview	.68
757	Tyler	.74
758	Palestine	.76
759	Lufkin	.79
760-761	Fort Worth	.83
762	Denton	.74
763	Wichita Falls	.77
764	Eastland	.75
765	Temple	.74
766-767	Waco	.77
768	Brownwood	.71
769	San Angelo	.72
770-772	Houston	.84
773	Huntsville	.77
774	Wharton	.73
775	Galveston	.82
776-777	Beaumont	.81
778	Bryan	.73
779	Victoria	.72
780	Laredo	.72
781-782	San Antonio	.79
783-784	Corpus Christi	.76
785	Mc Allen	.74
786-787	Austin	.77
788	Del Rio	.71
789	Giddings	.77
790-791	Amarillo	.79
792	Childress	.79
793-794	Lubbock	.79
795-796	Abilene	.75
797	Midland	.76
798-799,885	El Paso	.74
UTAH		
840-841	Salt Lake City	.81
842,844	Ogden	.80
843	Logan	.80

Location Factors

STATE	CITY	Residential
UTAH (CONT'D)		
845	Price	.78
846-847	Provo	.80
VERMONT		
050	White River Jct.	.74
051	Bellows Falls	.81
052	Bennington	.80
053	Brattleboro	.80
054	Burlington	.79
056	Montpelier	.80
057	Rutland	.79
058	St. Johnsbury	.76
059	Guildhall	.76
VIRGINIA		
220-221	Fairfax	1.02
222	Arlington	1.03
223	Alexandria	1.07
224-225	Fredericksburg	.91
226	Winchester	.88
227	Culpeper	.97
228	Harrisonburg	.87
229	Charlottesville	.88
230-232	Richmond	.95
233-235	Norfolk	.97
236	Newport News	.96
237	Portsmouth	.90
238	Petersburg	.93
239	Farmville	.85
240-241	Roanoke	.94
242	Bristol	.82
243	Pulaski	.80
244	Staunton	.87
245	Lynchburg	.92
246	Grundy	.80
WASHINGTON		
980-981,987	Seattle	1.03
982	Everett	1.04
983-984	Tacoma	1.01
985	Olympia	1.00
986	Vancouver	.96
988	Wenatchee	.93
989	Yakima	.98
990-992	Spokane	.97
993	Richland	.97
994	Clarkston	.93
WEST VIRGINIA		
247-248	Bluefield	.89
249	Lewisburg	.90
250-253	Charleston	.96
254	Martinsburg	.86
255-257	Huntington	.97
258-259	Beckley	.90
260	Wheeling	.92
261	Parkersburg	.92
262	Buckhannon	.92
263-264	Clarksburg	.91
265	Morgantown	.92
266	Gassaway	.92
267	Romney	.90
268	Petersburg	.90
WISCONSIN		
530,532	Milwaukee	1.07
531	Kenosha	1.03
534	Racine	1.02
535	Beloit	.99
537	Madison	.99
538	Lancaster	.97
539	Portage	.97
540	New Richmond	1.00
541-543	Green Bay	1.01
544	Wausau	.96
545	Rhinelander	.96
546	La Crosse	.96
547	Eau Claire	.99
548	Superior	.98
549	Oshkosh	.91
WYOMING		
820	Cheyenne	.80
821	Yellowstone Nat. Pk.	.74
822	Wheatland	.74

STATE	CITY	Residential
WYOMING (CONT'D)		
823	Rawlins	.74
824	Worland	.73
825	Riverton	.73
826	Casper	.74
827	Newcastle	.73
828	Sheridan	.78
829-831	Rock Springs	.78
CANADIAN FACTORS (reflect Canadian currency)		
ALBERTA		
	Calgary	1.17
	Edmonton	1.16
	Fort McMurray	1.17
	Lethbridge	1.14
	Lloydminster	1.09
	Medicine Hat	1.09
	Red Deer	1.09
BRITISH COLUMBIA		
	Kamloops	1.08
	Prince George	1.07
	Vancouver	1.10
	Victoria	1.05
MANITOBA		
	Brandon	1.04
	Portage la Prairie	1.04
	Winnipeg	1.04
NEW BRUNSWICK		
	Bathurst	.96
	Dalhousie	.97
	Fredericton	1.04
	Moncton	.97
	Newcastle	.97
	St. John	1.03
NEWFOUNDLAND		
	Corner Brook	.98
	St Johns	1.02
NORTHWEST TERRITORIES		
	Yellowknife	1.10
NOVA SCOTIA		
	Bridgewater	1.00
	Dartmouth	1.00
	Halifax	1.02
	New Glasgow	.99
	Sydney	.98
	Truro	.99
	Yarmouth	.99
ONTARIO		
	Barrie	1.16
	Brantford	1.18
	Cornwall	1.16
	Hamilton	1.16
	Kingston	1.16
	Kitchener	1.09
	London	1.13
	North Bay	1.14
	Oshawa	1.16
	Ottawa	1.15
	Owen Sound	1.15
	Peterborough	1.15
	Sarnia	1.18
	Sault Ste Marie	1.09
	St. Catharines	1.10
	Sudbury	1.08
	Thunder Bay	1.12
	Timmins	1.14
	Toronto	1.18
	Windsor	1.12
PRINCE EDWARD ISLAND		
	Charlottetown	.94
	Summerside	.93
QUEBEC		
	Cap-de-la-Madeleine	1.16
	Charlesbourg	1.16
	Chicoutimi	1.15
	Gatineau	1.15
	Granby	1.15

Location Factors

STATE	CITY	Residential
QUEBEC (CONT'D)		
	Hull	1.15
	Joliette	1.16
	Laval	1.15
	Montreal	1.18
	Quebec	1.17
	Rimouski	1.15
	Rouyn-Noranda	1.15
	Saint Hyacinthe	1.15
	Sherbrooke	1.15
	Sorel	1.16
	St Jerome	1.15
	Trois Rivieres	1.16
SASKATCHEWAN		
	Moose Jaw	.96
	Prince Albert	.95
	Regina	1.07
	Saskatoon	1.06
YUKON		
	Whitehorse	.95

Abbreviations

A	Area
ASTM	American Society for Testing and Materials
B.F.	Board feet
Carp.	Carpenter
C.F.	Cubic feet
CWJ	Composite wood joist
C.Y.	Cubic yard
Ea.	Each
Equip.	Equipment
Exp.	Exposure
Ext.	Exterior
F	Fahrenheit
Ft.	Foot, feet
Gal.	Gallon
Hr.	Hour
in.	Inch, inches
Inst.	Installation
Int.	Interior
Lb.	Pound
L.F.	Linear feet
LVL	Laminated veneer lumber
Mat.	Material
Max.	Maximum
MBF	Thousand board feet
MBM	Thousand feet board measure
MSF	Thousand square feet
Min.	Minimum
O.C.	On center
O&P	Overhead and profit
OWJ	Open web wood joist
Oz.	Ounce
Pr.	Pair
Quan.	Quantity
S.F.	Square foot
Sq.	Square, 100 square feet
S.Y.	Square yard
V.L.F.	Vertical linear feet
'	Foot, feet
"	Inch, inches
°	Degrees

Index

Index

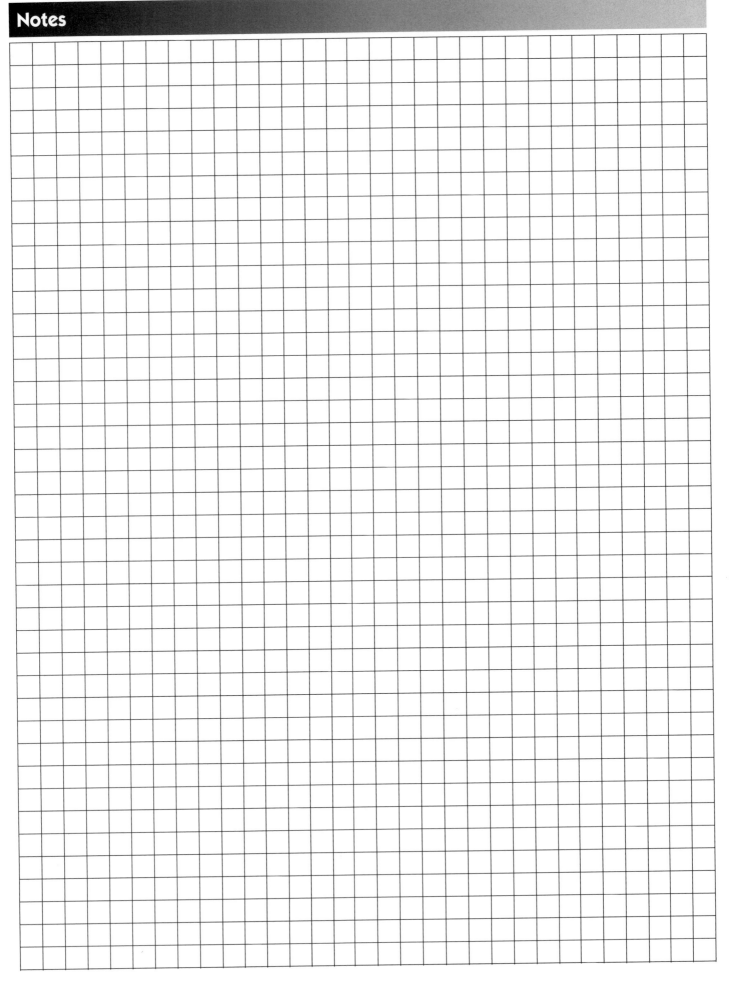

Annual Cost Guides

For more information
visit the RSMeans website
at www.rsmeans.com

RSMeans Building Construction Cost Data 2011

Offers you unchallenged unit price reliability in an easy-to-use format. Whether used for verifying complete, finished estimates or for periodic checks, it supplies more cost facts better and faster than any comparable source. Over 21,000 unit prices have been updated for 2011. The City Cost Indexes and Location Factors cover over 930 areas, for indexing to any project location in North America. Order and get *RSMeans Quarterly Update Service* FREE. You'll have year-long access to the RSMeans Estimating **HOTLINE** FREE with your subscription. Expert assistance when using RSMeans data is just a phone call away.

$174.95 per copy
Available Sept. 2010
Catalog no. 60011

Unit prices organized according to the latest MasterFormat!

RSMeans Green Building Cost Data 2011

Estimate, plan, and budget the costs of green building for both new commercial construction and renovation work with this first edition of RSMeans Green Building Cost Data. More than 9,000 unit costs for a wide array of green building products plus assemblies costs. Easily identified cross references to LEED and Green Globes building rating systems criteria.

$144.95 per copy
Available Nov. 2010
Catalog no. 60551

RSMeans Mechanical Cost Data 2011

• **HVAC**

• **Controls**

Total unit and systems price guidance for mechanical construction. . . materials, parts, fittings, and complete labor cost information. Includes prices for piping, heating, air conditioning, ventilation, and all related construction.

Plus new 2011 unit costs for:

• Thousands of installed HVAC/controls assemblies components

• "On-site" Location Factors for over 930 cities and towns in the U.S. and Canada

• Crews, labor, and equipment

$174.95 per copy
Available Oct. 2010
Catalog no. 60021

Unit prices organized according to the latest MasterFormat!

RSMeans Facilities Construction Cost Data 2011

For the maintenance and construction of commercial, industrial, municipal, and institutional properties. Costs are shown for new and remodeling construction and are broken down into materials, labor, equipment, and overhead and profit. Special emphasis is given to sections on mechanical, electrical, furnishings, site work, building maintenance, finish work, and demolition.

More than 45,000 unit costs, plus assemblies costs and a comprehensive Reference Section are included.

$439.95 per copy
Available Nov. 2010
Catalog no. 60201

For more information
visit the RSMeans website
at www.rsmeans.com

Annual Cost Guides

RSMeans Square Foot Costs 2011

Accurate and Easy To Use!

- **Updated price information** based on nationwide figures from suppliers, estimators, labor experts, and contractors

- "How-to-Use" sections, with **clear examples** of commercial, residential, industrial, and institutional structures

- Realistic graphics, offering true-to-life illustrations of building projects

- Extensive information on using square foot cost data, including sample estimates and alternate pricing methods

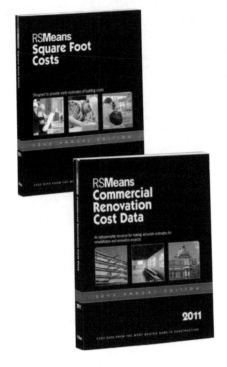

$184.95 per copy
Available Oct. 2010
Catalog no. 60051

RSMeans Commercial Renovation Cost Data 2011
Commercial/Multifamily Residential

Use this valuable tool to estimate commercial and multifamily residential renovation and remodeling.

Includes: New costs for hundreds of unique methods, materials, and conditions that only come up in repair and remodeling, PLUS:

- Unit costs for more than 15,000 construction components
- Installed costs for more than 90 assemblies
- More than 930 "on-site" localization factors for the U.S. and Canada

Unit prices organized according to the latest MasterFormat!

$144.95 per copy
Available Oct. 2010
Catalog no. 60041

RSMeans Electrical Cost Data 2011

Pricing information for every part of electrical cost planning. More than 13,000 unit and systems costs with design tables; clear specifications and drawings; engineering guides; illustrated estimating procedures; complete labor-hour and materials costs for better scheduling and procurement; and the latest electrical products and construction methods.

- A variety of special electrical systems including cathodic protection

- Costs for maintenance, demolition, HVAC/mechanical, specialties, equipment, and more

$174.95 per copy
Available Oct. 2010
Catalog no. 60031

Unit prices organized according to the latest MasterFormat!

RSMeans Electrical Change Order Cost Data 2011

RSMeans Electrical Change Order Cost Data provides you with electrical unit prices exclusively for pricing change orders—based on the recent, direct experience of contractors and suppliers. Analyze and check your own change order estimates against the experience others have had doing the same work. It also covers productivity analysis and change order cost justifications. With useful information for calculating the effects of change orders and dealing with their administration.

$169.95 per copy
Available Dec. 2010
Catalog no. 60231

Annual Cost Guides

For more information
visit the RSMeans website
at www.rsmeans.com

RSMeans Assemblies Cost Data 2011

RSMeans Assemblies Cost Data takes the guesswork out of preliminary or conceptual estimates. Now you don't have to try to calculate the assembled cost by working up individual component costs. We've done all the work for you.

Presents detailed illustrations, descriptions, specifications, and costs for every conceivable building assembly—240 types in all—arranged in the easy-to-use UNIFORMAT II system. Each illustrated "assembled" cost includes a complete grouping of materials and associated installation costs, including the installing contractor's overhead and profit.

$285.95 per copy
Available Sept. 2010
Catalog no. 60061

RSMeans Open Shop Building Construction Cost Data 2011

The latest costs for accurate budgeting and estimating of new commercial and residential construction. . . renovation work. . . change orders. . . cost engineering.

RSMeans Open Shop "BCCD" will assist you to:

• Develop benchmark prices for change orders
• Plug gaps in preliminary estimates and budgets
• Estimate complex projects
• Substantiate invoices on contracts
• Price ADA-related renovations

Unit prices organized according to the latest MasterFormat!

$134.95 per copy
Available Dec. 2010
Catalog no. 60151

RSMeans Residential Cost Data 2011

Contains square foot costs for 30 basic home models with the look of today, plus hundreds of custom additions and modifications you can quote right off the page. With costs for the 100 residential systems you're most likely to use in the year ahead. Complete with blank estimating forms, sample estimates, and step-by-step instructions.

Now contains line items for cultured stone and brick, PVC trim lumber, and TPO roofing.

$109.95 per copy
Available Oct. 2010
Catalog no. 60171

Unit prices organized according to the latest MasterFormat!

RSMeans Site Work & Landscape Cost Data 2011

Includes unit and assemblies costs for earthwork, sewerage, piped utilities, site improvements, drainage, paving, trees & shrubs, street openings/repairs, underground tanks, and more. Contains 57 tables of assemblies costs for accurate conceptual estimates.

Includes:

• Estimating for infrastructure improvements
• Environmentally-oriented construction
• ADA-mandated handicapped access
• Hazardous waste line items

$169.95 per copy
Available Dec. 2010
Catalog no. 60281

RSMeans Facilities Maintenance & Repair Cost Data 2011

RSMeans Facilities Maintenance & Repair Cost Data gives you a complete system to manage and plan your facility repair and maintenance costs and budget efficiently. Guidelines for auditing a facility and developing an annual maintenance plan. Budgeting is included, along with reference tables on cost and management, and information on frequency and productivity of maintenance operations.

The only nationally recognized source of maintenance and repair costs. Developed in cooperation with the Civil Engineering Research Laboratory (CERL) of the Army Corps of Engineers.

$389.95 per copy
Available Nov. 2010
Catalog no. 60301

RSMeans Light Commercial Cost Data 2011

Specifically addresses the light commercial market, which is a specialized niche in the construction industry. Aids you, the owner/designer/contractor, in preparing all types of estimates—from budgets to detailed bids. Includes new advances in methods and materials.

Assemblies Section allows you to evaluate alternatives in the early stages of design/planning.

Over 11,000 unit costs ensure that you have the prices you need. . . when you need them.

Unit prices organized according to the latest MasterFormat !

$119.95 per copy
Available Nov. 2010
Catalog no. 60181

For more information
visit the RSMeans website
at www.rsmeans.com

Annual Cost Guides

RSMeans Concrete & Masonry Cost Data 2011

Provides you with cost facts for virtually all concrete/masonry estimating needs, from complicated formwork to various sizes and face finishes of brick and block—all in great detail. The comprehensive Unit Price Section contains more than 8,000 selected entries. Also contains an Assemblies [Cost] Section, and a detailed Reference Section that supplements the cost data.

Unit prices organized according to the latest MasterFormat !

$159.95 per copy
Available Dec. 2010
Catalog no. 60111

RSMeans Labor Rates for the Construction Industry 2011

Complete information for estimating labor costs, making comparisons, and negotiating wage rates by trade for more than 300 U.S. and Canadian cities. With 46 construction trades listed by local union number in each city, and historical wage rates included for comparison. Each city chart lists the county and is alphabetically arranged with handy visual flip tabs for quick reference.

$389.95 per copy
Available Dec. 2010
Catalog no. 60121

RSMeans Construction Cost Indexes 2011

What materials and labor costs will change unexpectedly this year? By how much?

• Breakdowns for 318 major cities
• National averages for 30 key cities
• Expanded five major city indexes
• Historical construction cost indexes

$362.00 per year (subscription)
Catalog no. 50141

$90.50 individual quarters
Catalog no. 60141 A,B,C,D

RSMeans Interior Cost Data 2011

Provides you with prices and guidance needed to make accurate interior work estimates. Contains costs on materials, equipment, hardware, custom installations, furnishings, and labor costs. . . for new and remodel commercial and industrial interior construction, including updated information on office furnishings, and reference information.

Unit prices organized according to the latest MasterFormat !

$179.95 per copy
Available Nov. 2010
Catalog no. 60091

RSMeans Heavy Construction Cost Data 2011

A comprehensive guide to heavy construction costs. Includes costs for highly specialized projects such as tunnels, dams, highways, airports, and waterways. Information on labor rates, equipment, and materials costs is included. Features unit price costs, systems costs, and numerous reference tables for costs and design.

$174.95 per copy
Available Dec. 2010
Catalog no. 60161

Unit prices organized according to the latest MasterFormat!

RSMeans Plumbing Cost Data 2011

Comprehensive unit prices and assemblies for plumbing, irrigation systems, commercial and residential fire protection, point-of-use water heaters, and the latest approved materials. This publication and its companion, *RSMeans Mechanical Cost Data*, provide full-range cost estimating coverage for all the mechanical trades.

Now contains updated costs for potable water and radiant heat systems and high efficiency fixtures.

$174.95 per copy
Available Oct. 2010
Catalog no. 60211

Reference Books

**For more information
visit the RSMeans website
at www.rsmeans.com**

Value Engineering: Practical Applications

For Design, Construction, Maintenance & Operations

by Alphonse Dell'Isola, PE

A tool for immediate application—for engineers, architects, facility managers, owners, and contractors. Includes making the case for VE—the management briefing; integrating VE into planning, budgeting, and design; conducting life cycle costing; using VE methodology in design review and consultant selection; case studies; VE workbook; and a life cycle costing program on disk.

$79.95 per copy
**Over 450 pages, illustrated, softcover
Catalog no. 67319A**

Facilities Operations & Engineering Reference

by the Association for Facilities Engineering and RSMeans

An all-in-one technical reference for planning and managing facility projects and solving day-to-day operations problems. Selected as the official certified plant engineer reference, this handbook covers financial analysis, maintenance, HVAC and energy efficiency, and more.

$54.98 per copy
**Over 700 pages, illustrated, hardcover
Catalog no. 67318**

The Building Professional's Guide to Contract Documents

3rd Edition

by Waller S. Poage, AIA, CSI, CVS

A comprehensive reference for owners, design professionals, contractors, and students

- Structure your documents for maximum efficiency.
- Effectively communicate construction requirements.
- Understand the roles and responsibilities of construction professionals.
- Improve methods of project delivery.

$32.48 per copy, 400 pages
**Diagrams and construction forms, hardcover
Catalog no. 67261A**

Complete Book of Framing

by Scot Simpson

This straightforward, easy-to-learn method will help framers, carpenters, and handy homeowners build their skills in rough carpentry and framing. Shows how to frame all the parts of a house: floors, walls, roofs, door & window openings, and stairs—with hundreds of color photographs and drawings that show every detail.

The book gives beginners all the basics they need to go from zero framing knowledge to a journeyman level.

$29.95 per copy
**352 pages, softcover
Catalog no. 67353**

Cost Planning & Estimating for Facilities Maintenance

In this unique book, a team of facilities management authorities shares their expertise on:

- Evaluating and budgeting maintenance operations
- Maintaining and repairing key building components
- Applying *RSMeans Facilities Maintenance & Repair Cost Data* to your estimating

Covers special maintenance requirements of the ten major building types.

$89.95 per copy
**Over 475 pages, hardcover
Catalog no. 67314**

Life Cycle Costing for Facilities

by Alphonse Dell'Isola and Dr. Steven Kirk

Guidance for achieving higher quality design and construction projects at lower costs! Cost-cutting efforts often sacrifice quality to yield the cheapest product. Life cycle costing enables building designers and owners to achieve both. The authors of this book show how LCC can work for a variety of projects — from roads to HVAC upgrades to different types of buildings.

$99.95 per copy
**450 pages, hardcover
Catalog no. 67341**

For more information
visit the RSMeans website
at www.rsmeans.com

Reference Books

Interior Home Improvement Costs 9th Edition

Updated estimates for the most popular remodeling and repair projects—from small, do-it-yourself jobs to major renovations and new construction. Includes: kitchens & baths; new living space from your attic, basement, or garage; new floors, paint, and wallpaper; tearing out or building new walls; closets, stairs, and fireplaces; new energy-saving improvements, home theaters, and more!

$24.95 per copy
250 pages, illustrated, softcover
Catalog no. 67308E

Exterior Home Improvement Costs 9th Edition

Updated estimates for the most popular remodeling and repair projects—from small, do-it-yourself jobs, to major renovations and new construction. Includes: curb appeal projects—landscaping, patios, porches, driveways, and walkways; new windows and doors; decks, greenhouses, and sunrooms; room additions and garages; roofing, siding, and painting; "green" improvements to save energy & water.

$24.95 per copy
Over 275 pages, illustrated, softcover
Catalog no. 67309E

Builder's Essentials: Plan Reading & Material Takeoff

For Residential and Light Commercial Construction

by Wayne J. DelPico

A valuable tool for understanding plans and specs, and accurately calculating material quantities. Step-by-step instructions and takeoff procedures based on a full set of working drawings.

$35.95 per copy
Over 420 pages, softcover
Catalog no. 67307

Means Unit Price Estimating Methods

New 4th Edition

This new edition includes up-to-date cost data and estimating examples, updated to reflect changes to the CSI numbering system and new features of RSMeans cost data. It describes the most productive, universally accepted ways to estimate, and uses checklists and forms to illustrate shortcuts and timesavers. A model estimate demonstrates procedures. A new chapter explores computer estimating alternatives.

$59.95 per copy
Over 350 pages, illustrated, softcover
Catalog no. 67303B

Concrete Repair and Maintenance Illustrated

by Peter Emmons

Hundreds of illustrations show users how to analyze, repair, clean, and maintain concrete structures for optimal performance and cost effectiveness. From parking garages to roads and bridges to structural concrete, this comprehensive book describes the causes, effects, and remedies for concrete wear and failure. Invaluable for planning jobs, selecting materials, and training employees, this book is a must-have for concrete specialists, general contractors, facility managers, civil and structural engineers, and architects.

$34.98 per copy
300 pages, illustrated, softcover
Catalog no. 67146

Total Productive Facilities Management

by Richard W. Sievert, Jr.

Today, facilities are viewed as strategic resources. . . elevating the facility manager to the role of asset manager supporting the organization's overall business goals. Now, Richard Sievert Jr., in this well-articulated guidebook, sets forth a new operational standard for the facility manager's emerging role. . . a comprehensive program for managing facilities as a true profit center.

$29.98 per copy
275 pages, softcover
Catalog no. 67321

Reference Books

**For more information
visit the RSMeans website
at www.rsmeans.com**

Means Illustrated Construction Dictionary Condensed, 2nd Edition

The best portable dictionary for office or field use—an essential tool for contractors, architects, insurance and real estate personnel, facility managers, homeowners, and anyone who needs quick, clear definitions for construction terms. The second edition has been further enhanced with updates and hundreds of new terms and illustrations . . . in keeping with the most recent developments in the construction industry.

Now with a quick-reference Spanish section. Includes tools and equipment, materials, tasks, and more!

$59.95 per copy
Over 500 pages, softcover
Catalog no. 67282A

Repair & Remodeling Estimating 4th Edition
By Edward B. Wetherill and RSMeans

This important reference focuses on the unique problems of estimating renovations of existing structures, and helps you determine the true costs of remodeling through careful evaluation of architectural details and a site visit.

New section on disaster restoration costs.

$69.95 per copy
Over 450 pages, illustrated, hardcover
Catalog no. 67265B

Facilities Planning & Relocation
by David D. Owen

A complete system for planning space needs and managing relocations. Includes step-by-step manual, over 50 forms, and extensive reference section on materials and furnishings.

New lower price and user-friendly format.

$49.98 per copy
Over 450 pages, softcover
Catalog no. 67301

Square Foot & UNIFORMAT Assemblies Estimating Methods 3rd Edition

Develop realistic square foot and assemblies costs for budgeting and construction funding. The new edition features updated guidance on square foot and assemblies estimating using UNIFORMAT II. An essential reference for anyone who performs conceptual estimates.

$69.95 per copy
Over 300 pages, illustrated, softcover
Catalog no. 67145B

Electrical Estimating Methods 3rd Edition

Expanded edition includes sample estimates and cost information in keeping with the latest version of the CSI MasterFormat and UNIFORMAT II. Complete coverage of fiber optic and uninterruptible power supply electrical systems, broken down by components, and explained in detail. Includes a new chapter on computerized estimating methods. A practical companion to *RSMeans Electrical Cost Data*.

$64.95 per copy
Over 325 pages, hardcover
Catalog no. 67230B

Mechanical Estimating Methods 4th Edition

Completely updated, this guide assists you in making a review of plans, specs, and bid packages, with suggestions for takeoff procedures, listings, substitutions, and pre-bid scheduling for all components of HVAC. Includes suggestions for budgeting labor and equipment usage. Compares materials and construction methods to allow you to select the best option.

$64.95 per copy
Over 350 pages, illustrated, softcover
Catalog no. 67294B

Construction Business Management
by Nick Ganaway

Only 43% of construction firms stay in business after four years. Make sure your company thrives with valuable guidance from a pro with 25 years of success as a commercial contractor. Find out what it takes to build all aspects of a business that is profitable, enjoyable, and enduring. With a bonus chapter on retail construction.

$49.95 per copy
200 pages, softcover
Catalog no. 67352

Project Scheduling & Management for Construction
3rd Edition
by David R. Pierce, Jr.

A comprehensive yet easy-to-follow guide to construction project scheduling and control—from vital project management principles through the latest scheduling, tracking, and controlling techniques. The author is a leading authority on scheduling, with years of field and teaching experience at leading academic institutions. Spend a few hours with this book and come away with a solid understanding of this essential management topic.

$64.95 per copy
Over 300 pages, illustrated, hardcover
Catalog no. 67247B

For more information
visit the RSMeans website
at www.rsmeans.com

Reference Books

The Practice of Cost Segregation Analysis

by Bruce A. Desrosiers and Wayne J. DelPico

This expert guide walks you through the practice of cost segregation analysis, which enables property owners to defer taxes and benefit from "accelerated cost recovery" through depreciation deductions on assets that are properly identified and classified.

With a glossary of terms, sample cost segregation estimates for various building types, key information resources, and updates via a dedicated website, this book is a critical resource for anyone involved in cost segregation analysis.

$99.95 per copy
Over 225 pages
Catalog no. 67345

Preventive Maintenance for Multi-Family Housing

by John C. Maciha

Prepared by one of the nation's leading experts on multi-family housing.

This complete PM system for apartment and condominium communities features expert guidance, checklists for buildings and grounds maintenance tasks and their frequencies, a reusable wall chart to track maintenance, and a dedicated website featuring customizable electronic forms. A must-have for anyone involved with multi-family housing maintenance and upkeep.

$89.95 per copy
225 pages
Catalog no. 67346

How to Estimate with Means Data & CostWorks

New 3rd Edition

by RSMeans and Saleh A. Mubarak, Ph.D.

New 3rd Edition—fully updated with new chapters, plus new CD with updated *CostWorks* cost data and MasterFormat organization. Includes all major construction items—with more than 300 exercises and two sets of plans that show how to estimate for a broad range of construction items and systems—including general conditions and equipment costs.

$59.95 per copy
272 pages, softcover
Includes CostWorks CD
Catalog no. 67324B

Job Order Contracting

Expediting Construction Project Delivery

by Allen Henderson

Expert guidance to help you implement JOC—fast becoming the preferred project delivery method for repair and renovation, minor new construction, and maintenance projects in the public sector and in many states and municipalities. The author, a leading JOC expert and practitioner, shows how to:

• Establish a JOC program

• Evaluate proposals and award contracts

• Handle general requirements and estimating

• Partner for maximum benefits

$89.95 per copy
192 pages, illustrated, hardcover
Catalog no. 67348

Estimating Building Costs

For the Residential & Light Commercial Contractor

by Wayne J. DelPico

Step-by-step estimating methods for residential and light commercial contractors. Includes a detailed look at every construction specialty—explaining all the components, takeoff units, and labor needed for well-organized, complete estimates. Covers correctly interpreting plans and specifications, and developing accurate and complete labor and material costs.

$29.95 per copy
Over 400 pages, illustrated, softcover
Catalog no. 67343

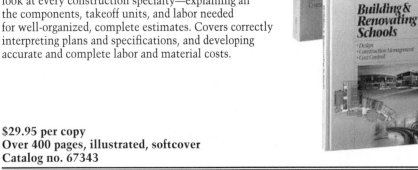

Building & Renovating Schools

This all-inclusive guide covers every step of the school construction process—from initial planning, needs assessment, and design, right through moving into the new facility. A must-have resource for anyone concerned with new school construction or renovation. With square foot cost models for elementary, middle, and high school facilities, and real-life case studies of recently completed school projects.

The contributors to this book—architects, construction project managers, contractors, and estimators who specialize in school construction—provide start-to-finish, expert guidance on the process.

$69.98 per copy
Over 425 pages, hardcover
Catalog no. 67342

Reference Books

For more information
visit the RSMeans website
at www.rsmeans.com

The Homeowner's Guide to Mold By Michael Pugliese

Expert guidance to protect your health and your home.

Mold, whether caused by leaks, humidity or flooding, is a real health and financial issue—for homeowners and contractors. This full-color book explains:
- Construction and maintenance practices to prevent mold
- How to inspect for and remove mold
- Mold remediation procedures and costs
- What to do after a flood
- How to deal with insurance companies

$21.95 per copy
144 pages, softcover
Catalog no. 67344

Universal Design Ideas for Style, Comfort & Safety
by RSMeans and Lexicon Consulting, Inc.

Incorporating universal design when building or remodeling helps people of any age and physical ability more fully and safely enjoy their living spaces. This book shows how universal design can be artfully blended into the most attractive homes. It discusses specialized products like adjustable countertops and chair lifts, as well as simple ways to enhance a home's safety and comfort. With color photos and expert guidance, every area of the home is covered. Includes budget estimates that give an idea how much projects will cost.

$21.95
160 pages, illustrated, softcover
Catalog no. 67354

Landscape Estimating Methods
5th Edition

Answers questions about preparing competitive landscape construction estimates, with up-to-date cost estimates and the new MasterFormat classification system. Expanded and revised to address the latest materials and methods, including new coverage on approaches to green building. Includes:
- Step-by-step explanation of the estimating process
- Sample forms and worksheets that save time and prevent errors

$64.95 per copy
Over 350 pages, softcover
Catalog no. 67295C

Plumbing Estimating Methods 3rd Edition
by Joseph Galeno and Sheldon Greene

Updated and revised! This practical guide walks you through a plumbing estimate, from basic materials and installation methods through change order analysis. *Plumbing Estimating Methods* covers residential, commercial, industrial, and medical systems, and features sample takeoff and estimate forms and detailed illustrations of systems and components.

$29.98 per copy
330+ pages, softcover
Catalog no. 67283B

Understanding & Negotiating Construction Contracts
by Kit Werremeyer

Take advantage of the author's 30 years' experience in small-to-large (including international) construction projects. Learn how to identify, understand, and evaluate high risk terms and conditions typically found in all construction contracts—then negotiate to lower or eliminate the risk, improve terms of payment, and reduce exposure to claims and disputes. The author avoids "legalese" and gives real-life examples from actual projects.

$69.95 per copy
300 pages, softcover
Catalog no. 67350

Spanish/English Construction Dictionary 2nd Edition
by RSMeans and the International Code Council

This expanded edition features thousands of the most common words and useful phrases in the construction industry with easy-to-follow pronunciations in both Spanish and English. Over 800 new terms, phrases, and illustrations have been added. It also features a new stand-alone "Safety & Emergencies" section, with colored pages for quick access.

Unique to this dictionary are the systems illustrations showing the relationship of components in the most common building systems for all major trades.

$23.95 per copy
Over 400 pages
Catalog no. 67327A

How Your House Works
by Charlie Wing

A must-have reference for every homeowner, handyman, and contractor—for repair, remodeling, and new construction. This book uncovers the mysteries behind just about every major appliance and building element in your house—from electrical, heating and AC, to plumbing, framing, foundations and appliances. Clear, "exploded" drawings show exactly how things should be put together and how they function—what to check if they don't work, and what you can do that might save you having to call in a professional.

$21.95 per copy
160 pages, softcover
Catalog no. 67351

For more information
visit the RSMeans website
at www.rsmeans.com

Professional Development

Means CostWorks® CD Training

This one-day course helps users become more familiar with the functionality of *Means CostWorks* program. Each menu, icon, screen, and function found in the program is explained in depth. Time is devoted to hands-on estimating exercises.

Some of what you'll learn:
- Searching the database utilizing all navigation methods
- Exporting RSMeans Data to your preferred spreadsheet format
- Viewing crews, assembly components, and much more!
- Automatically regionalizing the database

You are required to bring your own laptop computer for this course.

When you register for this course you will receive an outline for your laptop requirements.

Also offering web training for CostWorks CD!

Unit Price Estimating

This interactive *two-day* seminar teaches attendees how to interpret project information and process it into final, detailed estimates with the greatest accuracy level.

The most important credential an estimator can take to the job is the ability to visualize construction, and estimate accurately.

Some of what you'll learn:
- Interpreting the design in terms of cost
- The most detailed, time-tested methodology for accurate pricing
- Key cost drivers—material, labor, equipment, staging, and subcontracts
- Understanding direct and indirect costs for accurate job cost accounting and change order management

Who should attend: Corporate and government estimators and purchasers, architects, engineers… and others needing to produce accurate project estimates.

Square Foot & Assemblies Estimating

This *two-day* course teaches attendees how to quickly deliver accurate square foot estimates using limited budget and design information.

Some of what you'll learn:
- How square foot costing gets the estimate done faster
- Taking advantage of a "systems" or "assemblies" format
- The RSMeans "building assemblies/square foot cost approach"
- How to create a reliable preliminary systems estimate using bare-bones design information

Who should attend: Facilities managers, facilities engineers, estimators, planners, developers, construction finance professionals… and others needing to make quick, accurate construction cost estimates at commercial, government, educational, and medical facilities.

Facilities Maintenance & Repair Estimating

This *two-day* course teaches attendees how to plan, budget, and estimate the cost of ongoing and preventive maintenance and repair for existing buildings and grounds.

Some of what you'll learn:
- The most financially favorable maintenance, repair, and replacement scheduling and estimating
- Auditing and value engineering facilities
- Preventive planning and facilities upgrading
- Determining both in-house and contract-out service costs
- Annual, asset-protecting M&R plan

Who should attend: Facility managers, maintenance supervisors, buildings and grounds superintendents, plant managers, planners, estimators… and others involved in facilities planning and budgeting.

Mechanical & Electrical Estimating

This *two-day* course teaches attendees how to prepare more accurate and complete mechanical/electrical estimates, avoiding the pitfalls of omission and double-counting, while understanding the composition and rationale within the RSMeans Mechanical/Electrical database.

Some of what you'll learn:
- The unique way mechanical and electrical systems are interrelated
- M&E estimates–conceptual, planning, budgeting, and bidding stages
- Order of magnitude, square foot, assemblies, and unit price estimating
- Comparative cost analysis of equipment and design alternatives

Who should attend: Architects, engineers, facilities managers, mechanical and electrical contractors… and others needing a highly reliable method for developing, understanding, and evaluating mechanical and electrical contracts.

Green Building: Planning & Construction

In this *two-day* course, learn about tailoring a building and its placement on the site to the local climate, site conditions, culture, and community. Includes information to reduce resource consumption and augment resource supply.

Some of what you'll learn:
- Green technologies, materials, systems, and standards
- Modeling tools and how to use them
- Cost vs. value of green products over their life cycle
- Low-cost green strategies, and economic incentives and funding
- Health, comfort, and productivity

Who should attend: Contractors, project managers, building owners, building officials, healthcare and insurance professionals.

Practical Project Management for Construction Professionals

In this *two-day* course, acquire the essential knowledge and develop the skills to effectively and efficiently execute the day-to-day responsibilities of the construction project manager.

Covers:
- General conditions of the construction contract
- Contract modifications: change orders and construction change directives
- Negotiations with subcontractors and vendors
- Effective writing: notification and communications
- Dispute resolution: claims and liens

Who should attend: Architects, engineers, owner's representatives, project managers.

Facilities Construction Estimating

In this *two-day* course, professionals working in facilities management can get help with their daily challenges to establish budgets for all phase of a project

Some of what you'll learn:
- Determine the full scope of a project
- Identify the scope of risks & opportunities
- Creative solutions to estimating issues
- Organizing estimates for presentation & discussion
- Special techniques for repair/remodel and maintenance projects
- Negotiating project change orders

Who should attend: Facility managers, engineers, contractors, facility trades-people, planners & project managers.

Professional Development

For more information
visit the RSMeans website
at www.rsmeans.com

Assessing Scope of Work for Facility Construction Estimating

This *two-day* practical training program addresses the vital importance of understanding the SCOPE of projects in order to produce accurate cost estimates for facility repair and remodeling.

Some of what you'll learn:
- Discussions of site visits, plans/specs, record drawings of facilities, and site-specific lists
- Review of CSI divisions, including means, methods, materials, and the challenges of scoping each topic
- Exercises in SCOPE identification and SCOPE writing for accurate estimating of projects
- Hands-on exercises that require SCOPE, take-off, and pricing

Who should attend: Corporate and government estimators, planners, facility managers, and others who need to produce accurate project estimates.

Site Work & Heavy Construction Estimating

This *two-day* course teaches attendees how to estimate earthwork, site utilities, foundations, and site improvements, using the assemblies and the unit price methods.

Some of what you'll learn:
- Basic site work and heavy construction estimating skills
- Estimating foundations, utilities, earthwork, and site improvements
- Correct equipment usage, quality control, and site investigation for estimating purposes

Who should attend: Project managers, design engineers, estimators, and contractors doing site work and heavy construction.

2011 RSMeans Seminar Schedule

Note: call for exact dates and details.

Location	Dates
Las Vegas, NV	March
Washington, DC	April
Denver, CO	May
San Francisco, CA	June
Washington, DC	September
Dallas, TX	September
Las Vegas, NV	October
Atlantic City, NJ	October
Orlando, FL	November
San Diego, CA	December

2011 Regional Seminar Schedule

Location	Dates	Location	Dates
Seattle, WA	January and August	St. Louis, MO	August
Dallas/Ft. Worth, TX	January	Houston, TX	October
Austin, TX	February	Colorado Springs, CO	October
Anchorage, AK	March and September	Baltimore, MD	November
Oklahoma City, OK	March	Sacramento, CA	November
Phoenix, AZ	March	San Antonio, TX	December
Aiea, HI	May	Raleigh, NC	December
Kansas City, MO	May		
Bethesda, MD	June		
Columbus, GA	June		
El Segundo, CA	August		

1-800-334-3509, ext. 5115

For more information
visit the RSMeans website
at www.rsmeans.com

Registration Information

Register early... Save up to $100! Register 30 days before the start date of a seminar and save $100 off your total fee. *Note: This discount can be applied only once per order. It cannot be applied to team discount registrations or any other special offer.*

How to register Register by phone today! The RSMeans toll-free number for making reservations is **1-800-334-3509, ext. 5115.**

Individual seminar registration fee - $935. *Means CostWorks®* **training registration fee - $375.** To register by mail, complete the registration form and return, with your full fee, to: RSMeans Seminars, 700 Longwater Drive, Norwell, MA 02061.

Government pricing All federal government employees save off the regular seminar price. Other promotional discounts cannot be combined with the government discount.

Team discount program for two to four seminar registrations. Call for pricing: 1-800-334-3509, ext. 5115

Multiple course discounts When signing up for two or more courses, call for pricing.

Refund policy Cancellations will be accepted up to ten business days prior to the seminar start. There are no refunds for cancellations received later than ten working days prior to the first day of the seminar. A $150 processing fee will be applied for all cancellations. Written notice of cancellation is required. Substitutions can be made at any time before the session starts. **No-shows are subject to the full seminar fee.**

AACE approved courses Many seminars described and offered here have been approved for 14 hours (1.4 recertification credits) of credit by the AACE

International Certification Board toward meeting the continuing education requirements for recertification as a Certified Cost Engineer/Certified Cost Consultant.

AIA Continuing Education We are registered with the AIA Continuing Education System (AIA/CES) and are committed to developing quality learning activities in accordance with the CES criteria. Many seminars meet the AIA/CES criteria for Quality Level 2. AIA members may receive (14) learning units (LUs) for each two-day RSMeans course.

Daily course schedule The first day of each seminar session begins at 8:30 a.m. and ends at 4:30 p.m. The second day begins at 8:00 a.m. and ends at 4:00 p.m. Participants are urged to bring a hand-held calculator, since many actual problems will be worked out in each session.

Continental breakfast Your registration includes the cost of a continental breakfast, and a morning and afternoon refreshment break. These informal segments allow you to discuss topics of mutual interest with other seminar attendees. (You are free to make your own lunch and dinner arrangements.)

Hotel/transportation arrangements RSMeans arranges to hold a block of rooms at most host hotels. To take advantage of special group rates when making your reservation, be sure to mention that you are attending the RSMeans seminar. You are, of course, free to stay at the lodging place of your choice. **(Hotel reservations and transportation arrangements should be made directly by seminar attendees.)**

Important Class sizes are limited, so please register as soon as possible.

Note: Pricing subject to change.

Registration Form

ADDS-1000

Call 1-800-334-3509, ext. 5115 to register or FAX this form 1-800-632-6732. Visit our website: www.rsmeans.com

Please register the following people for the RSMeans construction seminars as shown here. We understand that we must make our own hotel reservations if overnight stays are necessary.

☐ Full payment of $_____ enclosed.

☐ Bill me

Please print name of registrant(s)

(To appear on certificate of completion)

_____

_____

_____

_____

P.O. #: _____
GOVERNMENT AGENCIES MUST SUPPLY PURCHASE ORDER NUMBER OR TRAINING FORM.

Firm name_____

Address_____

City/State/Zip_____

Telephone no._____ Fax no._____

E-mail address_____

Charge registration(s) to: ☐ MasterCard ☐ VISA ☐ American Express

Account no._____ Exp. date_____

Cardholder's signature_____

Seminar name_____

Seminar City _____

Please mail check to: RSMeans Seminars, 700 Longwater Drive, Norwell, MA 02061 USA

For more information
visit the RSMeans website
at www.rsmeans.com

New Titles

The Gypsum Construction Handbook by USG

An invaluable reference of construction procedures for gypsum drywall, cement board, veneer plaster, and conventional plaster. This new edition includes the newest product developments, installation methods, fire- and sound-rated construction information, illustrated framing-to-finish application instructions, estimating and planning information, and more. Great for architects and engineers; contractors, builders, and dealers; apprentices and training programs; building inspectors and code officials; and anyone interested in gypsum construction. Features information on tools and safety practices, a glossary of construction terms, and a list of important agencies and associations. Also available in Spanish.

$29.95
Over 575 pages, illustrated, softcover
Catalog no. 67357A

RSMeans Estimating Handbook 3rd Edition

Widely used in the industry for tasks ranging from routine estimates to special cost analysis projects, this handbook has been completely updated and reorganized with new and expanded technical information.

RSMeans Estimating Handbook will help construction professionals:

• Evaluate architectural plans and specifications
• Prepare accurate quantity takeoffs
• Compare design alternatives and costs
• Perform value engineering
• Double-check estimates and quotes
• Estimate change orders

$99.95 per copy
Over 900 pages, hardcover
Catalog No. 67276B

Means Illustrated Construction Dictionary

Unabridged 4th Edition, with CD-ROM

Long regarded as the industry's finest, *Means Illustrated Construction Dictionary* is now even better. With nearly 20,000 terms and more than 1,400 illustrations and photos, it is the clear choice for the most comprehensive and current information. The companion CD-ROM that comes with this new edition adds extra features such as: larger graphics and expanded definitions.

Green Building: Project Planning & Cost Estimating 3rd Edition

Since the widely read first edition of this book, green building has gone from a growing trend to a major force in design and construction.

This new edition has been updated with the latest in green building technologies, design concepts, standards, and costs. Full-color with all new case studies—plus a new chapter on commercial real estate.

$99.95 per copy
Over 790 pages, illustrated, hardcover
Catalog no. 67292B

$99.95 per copy
Over 450 pages, softcover
Catalog no. 67338B

Green Home Improvement
by Daniel D. Chiras, PhD

With energy costs rising and environmental awareness increasing, many people are looking to make their homes greener. This book makes it easy, with 65 projects and actual costs and projected savings that will help homeowners prioritize their green improvements.

Projects range from simple water savers that cost only a few dollars, to bigger-ticket items such as efficient appliances and HVAC systems, green roofing, flooring, landscaping, and much more. With color photos and cost estimates, each project compares options and describes the work involved, the benefits, and the savings.

$24.95
320 pages, illustrated, softcover
Catalog no. 67355

Residential & Light Commercial Construction Standards 3rd Edition, Updated
by RSMeans and contributing authors

This book provides authoritative requirements and recommendations compiled from leading professional associations, industry publications, and building code organizations. This all-in-one reference helps establish a standard for workmanship, quickly resolve disputes, and avoid defect claims. Updated third edition includes new coverage of green building, seismic, hurricane, and mold-resistant construction.

$59.95
Over 550 pages, illustrated, softcover
Catalog no. 67322B

Qty.	Book no.	COST ESTIMATING BOOKS	Unit Price	Total
	60061	Assemblies Cost Data 2011	$285.95	
	60011	Building Construction Cost Data 2011	174.95	
	60111	Concrete & Masonry Cost Data 2011	154.95	
	50141	Construction Cost Indexes 2011 (subscription)	362.00	
	60141A	Construction Cost Index–January 2011	90.50	
	60141B	Construction Cost Index–April 2011	90.50	
	60141C	Construction Cost Index–July 2011	90.50	
	60141D	Construction Cost Index–October 2011	90.50	
	60341	Contr. Pricing Guide: Resid. R & R Costs 2011	39.95	
	60231	Electrical Change Order Cost Data 2011	169.95	
	60031	Electrical Cost Data 2011	174.95	
	60201	Facilities Construction Cost Data 2011	439.95	
	60301	Facilities Maintenance & Repair Cost Data 2011	389.95	
	60551	Green Building Cost Data 2011	144.95	
	60161	Heavy Construction Cost Data 2011	174.95	
	60091	Interior Cost Data 2011	179.95	
	60121	Labor Rates for the Const. Industry 2011	389.95	
	60181	Light Commercial Cost Data 2011	119.95	
	60021	Mechanical Cost Data 2011	174.95	
	60151	Open Shop Building Const. Cost Data 2011	134.95	
	60211	Plumbing Cost Data 2011	174.95	
	60041	Commercial Renovation Cost Data 2011	144.95	
	60171	Residential Cost Data 2011	109.95	
	60281	Site Work & Landscape Cost Data 2011	169.95	
	60051	Square Foot Costs 2011	184.95	
	62010	Yardsticks for Costing (2010)	174.95	
	62011	Yardsticks for Costing (2011)	174.95	
		REFERENCE BOOKS		
	67329	Bldrs Essentials: Best Bus. Practices for Bldrs	29.95	
	67298A	Bldrs Essentials: Framing/Carpentry 2nd Ed.	15.98	
	67298AS	Bldrs Essentials: Framing/Carpentry Spanish	15.98	
	67307	Bldrs Essentials: Plan Reading & Takeoff	35.95	
	67342	Building & Renovating Schools	69.98	
	67339	Building Security: Strategies & Costs	44.98	
	67353	Complete Book of Framing	29.95	
	67146	Concrete Repair & Maintenance Illustrated	34.98	
	67352	Construction Business Management	49.95	
	67314	Cost Planning & Est. for Facil. Maint.	89.95	
	67328A	Designing & Building with the IBC, 2nd Ed.	99.95	
	67230B	Electrical Estimating Methods, 3rd Ed.	64.95	
	64777A	Environmental Remediation Est. Methods, 2nd Ed.	49.98	
	67343	Estimating Bldg. Costs for Resi. & Lt. Comm.	29.95	
	67276B	Estimating Handbook, 3rd Ed.	$99.95	
	67318	Facilities Operations & Engineering Reference	54.98	
	67301	Facilities Planning & Relocation	49.98	
	67338B	Green Building: Proj. Planning & Cost Est., 3rd Ed.	99.95	
	67355	Green Home Improvement	24.95	
	67357A	The Gypsum Construction Handbook	29.95	
	67357S	The Gypsum Construction Handbook (Spanish)	29.95	
	67323	Historic Preservation: Proj. Planning & Est.	49.98	
	67308E	Home Improvement Costs–Int. Projects, 9th Ed.	24.95	

Qty.	Book no.	REFERENCE BOOKS (Cont.)	Unit Price	Total
	67309E	Home Improvement Costs–Ext. Projects, 9th Ed.	24.95	
	67344	Homeowner's Guide to Mold	21.95	
	67324B	How to Est.w/Means Data & CostWorks, 3rd Ed.	59.95	
	67351	How Your House Works	21.95	
	67282A	Illustrated Const. Dictionary, Condensed, 2nd Ed.	59.95	
	67292B	Illustrated Const. Dictionary, w/CD-ROM, 4th Ed.	99.95	
	67348	Job Order Contracting	89.95	
	67295C	Landscape Estimating Methods, 5th Ed.	64.95	
	67341	Life Cycle Costing for Facilities	99.95	
	67294B	Mechanical Estimating Methods, 4th Ed.	64.95	
	67283B	Plumbing Estimating Methods, 3rd Ed.	29.98	
	67345	Practice of Cost Segregation Analysis	99.95	
	67337	Preventive Maint. for Higher Education Facilities	149.95	
	67346	Preventive Maint. for Multi-Family Housing	89.95	
	67326	Preventive Maint. Guidelines for School Facil.	149.95	
	67247B	Project Scheduling & Management for Constr. 3rd Ed.	64.95	
	67265B	Repair & Remodeling Estimating Methods, 4th Ed.	69.95	
	67322B	Resi. & Light Commercial Const. Stds., 3rd Ed.	59.95	
	67327A	Spanish/English Construction Dictionary, 2nd Ed.	23.95	
	67145B	Sq. Ft. & Assem. Estimating Methods, 3rd Ed.	69.95	
	67321	Total Productive Facilities Management	29.98	
	67350	Understanding and Negotiating Const. Contracts	69.95	
	67303B	Unit Price Estimating Methods, 4th Ed.	59.95	
	67354	Universal Design	21.95	
	67319A	Value Engineering: Practical Applications	79.95	

MA residents add 6.25% state sales tax	
Shipping & Handling**	
Total (U.S. Funds)*	

Prices are subject to change and are for U.S. delivery only. *Canadian customers may call for current prices. **Shipping & handling charges: Add 7% of total order for check and credit card payments. Add 9% of total order for invoiced orders.

Send order to: **ADDV-1000**

Name (please print) _____

Company _____

☐ **Company**

☐ **Home   Address** _____

_____

City/State/Zip _____

Phone # _____ P.O. # _____

(Must accompany all orders being billed)

Mail to: RSMeans, 700 Longwater Drive, Norwell, MA 02061